An Introduction to Music Technology

An Introduction to Music Technology provides a clear overview of the essential elements of music technology for today's musician. It is designed to provide music students with the background necessary to apply technology in their creating, teaching, and performing.

This book focuses on five topics that underlie the hardware and software in use today: Sound, Audio, MIDI, Synthesis and Sampling, and Computer Notation and Computer-Assisted Instruction. In addition, there is an appendix that covers necessary computer hardware and software concepts.

Features:

- Thorough explanations of key topics in music technology
- Content applicable to all software and hardware, not linked to just one piece of software or gear
- In-depth discussion of digital audio topics, such as sampling rates, resolutions, and file formats
- Explanations of standard audio plug-ins including dynamics processors, EQs, and delay-based effects
- Coverage of synthesis and sampling in software instruments
- Pedagogical features, including:
  - Further Reading sections that allow the student to delve deeper into topics of interest
  - Suggested Activities that can be carried out with a variety of different programs
  - Key Terms at the end of each chapter
  - *What do I need?* Chapters covering the types of hardware and software needed in order to put together Audio and MIDI systems
  - The companion website contains links to audio examples that demonstrate various concepts, step-by-step tutorials, relevant hardware, software, and additional audio and video resources.

Dan Hosken is Professor of Music at California State University, Northridge, where he teaches courses in music technology, electronic music, composition, and theory. As an educator, he is an active member of the Association for Technology in Music Instruction (ATMI). As a composer, he specializes in interactive electronic music involving dancers and musicians using live motion sensing and audio processing.

Visit the companion website **www.routledge.com/textbooks/9780415997294**

An Introduction to Music Technology

Dan Hosken

California State University, Northridge

NEW YORK AND LONDON

First published 2011
by Routledge
711 Third Avenue, New York, NY 10017

Simultaneously published in the UK
by Routledge
2 Park Square, Milton Park, Abingdon, Oxon OX14 4RN

Routledge is an imprint of the Taylor & Francis Group, an informa business

Typeset in Bembo and Helvetica Neue by
Florence Production Ltd, Stoodleigh, Devon

Library of Congress Cataloging in Publication Data
Hosken, Daniel W. (Daniel William)
An introduction to music technology/Dan Hosken.—1st ed.
p. cm.
Includes bibliographical references.
1. Music—Data processing. 2. Sound—Recording and reproducing—Digital techniques. I. Title.
ML74.H67 2010
780.285—dc22 2009051982

ISBN13: 978–0–415–87827–2 (hbk)
ISBN13: 978–0–415–99729–4 (pbk)
ISBN13: 978–0–203–84951–4 (ebk)

Contents

Illustrations

FIGURES

TABLES

Preface

My motivation for writing this book is to provide a clear overview of the *essential* elements of music technology in order to improve students' understanding and use of technology in their music performing, creating, and teaching. This textbook is designed to accompany a one- or two-semester undergraduate course in music technology, depending on the extent of the practical exercises and projects that accompany the course and the amount of further reading and research required.

There are five sections in the book: Sound, Audio, MIDI, Synthesis and Sampling, and Computer Notation and Computer-assisted Instruction. There are a number of suggested activities, ranging from informational, such as taking stock of available audio equipment, to active, such as taking a melody/chords/bass MIDI sequence and expanding it to ten tracks.

ABOUT THIS BOOK

In addition to the five main sections of this book, referenced above—Sound, Audio, MIDI, Synthesis and Sampling, and Computer Notation and Computer-assisted Instruction—there is an appendix containing chapters on Computer Hardware and Computer Software. Each section begins with an overview of the material covered in its chapters and concludes with suggested activities that can be carried out using various software and hardware, as well as recommendations for further reading (in Section V, these features appear at the end of each chapter). There is also a Review of Key Terms (which are bold in the text) at the end of each chapter.

Sound consists of a chapter discussing the basics of sound as created by some vibrating source and received by the ears and brain, a chapter discussing the properties of sound as seen through the waveform representation, and a chapter discussing the properties of sound as seen through the spectrum representation. Along the way, I touch on a variety of topics, such as the difference between the physical properties of sounds and their perception by our ears and brain, the issue of loudness and hearing loss, and the distinctions between equal temperament and tuning systems derived from the overtone series.

Audio consists of a chapter on audio hardware, including microphones, mixers, audio interfaces, and speakers; a chapter on digital audio data, including digital specifications, audio file types, and audio file compression; a chapter on audio recording and editing software, including recording levels, editing techniques, and audio effects; and a chapter on what hardware and software you would need in order to put together audio systems of varying degrees of complexity. I also touch on such topics as analog signal levels and connector types, perceptual issues relating to higher sampling rates and resolutions, and latency in monitoring.

MIDI consists of a chapter on MIDI hardware, including controllers, modules, and synthesizers; a chapter on MIDI data, including note, program, and expressive messages; a chapter on MIDI sequencing software, including recording and editing techniques; and a chapter on the hardware and software you would need in order to put together MIDI and audio systems of varying degrees of complexity. I also discuss aspects of synthesizer history that impacted the development of MIDI, alternate MIDI controllers and MIDI-controllable devices, the details of the most-used MIDI messages, and MIDI software that goes beyond the sequencing paradigm.

Synthesis and Sampling consists of a chapter on electronic sound production, including hardware synths, software synths, and a basic synthesis model; a chapter on synthesis methods, including additive, subtractive, FM, physical modeling, and granular synthesis; and a chapter on sampling techniques, including keymapping, multisampling, and velocity switching. I also discuss low frequency oscillators (LFOs) and envelopes, plug-in types and ReWire, talk boxes and vocoders, non-commercial software synths, and sample libraries. The hardware and software needs for synthesis and sampling are related to those of the "Audio" and "MIDI" sections and are covered in the section overview.

Computer Notation and Computer-assisted Instruction consists of a chapter on computer notation, including various note entry methods and editing techniques; and a chapter on computer-assisted instruction (CAI) software, including programs for musicianship and theory, programs for form and analysis, programs for history, terminology, and instruments, programs for performance skills, and programs for creative skills. The hardware and software needs for computer notation and CAI are related to those of the "Audio" and "MIDI" sections and are covered in the individual chapters.

The **Computer Hardware** chapter in the appendix covers input and output devices, processing components, storage devices, and network connections. **Computer Software** in the appendix covers operating systems, applications software, malware, software licenses, copy protection, and network software and data issues, including client-server relationships, peer-to-peer relationships, Web 2.0, and Internet2. The appendix includes suggestions for further reading and suggested activities for computer hardware and software.

The **website** for this book, which can be found at **www.routledge.com/textbooks/9780415997294**, contains many audio examples to help explain various concepts.

I believe these examples provide an important link between what the students read and their aural musical experiences. In addition, there are a variety of links for each section, including links to relevant software and hardware and links to additional audio and video resources.

The suggested activities in each section that involve software can be carried out in a variety of different programs. If music technology is being presented in a course, the class may have practical assignments to carry out using software available in the school's computer lab. If you are studying this material on your own, you can use software that you already have, or use widely available inexpensive software or even freeware. The book's website contains a list of widely available programs, both commercial and freeware, that would be suitable for these suggested activities.

Because there are so many programs available for carrying out the activities, and these programs change so quickly, this book doesn't contain instructions for specific pieces of software (except for a few activities that utilize the freeware audio editor Audacity). Fortunately, the documentation for most commercial programs and many freeware programs is quite good and doing some of their tutorials and reading parts of the manual (often available electronically from within the program itself) can get one up to speed on a particular program. In addition, there are specific instructions for some of the suggested activities for a few programs available on the book's website.

TO THE INSTRUCTOR

Writing this book posed a number of challenges both in choosing appropriate content and in selecting the most useful organization for that content. In making such decisions, I was greatly helped by a number of anonymous reviewers, but in the end I had to decide on a structure that made the most pedagogical sense to me, based on my years of experience teaching music technology. For example:

- **The subject of MIDI**—MIDI has long been a staple of an introductory music technology course. However, with the migration of sound generation from hardware to software and the increasing dominance of direct USB (universal serial bus) connections for controllers, current students are often unaware that they are using MIDI at all when they're recording notes to be played back by sample libraries or displayed in a music notation program. In fact, for them MIDI is synonymous with "cheesy" sound, despite the fact that MIDI doesn't inherently "sound" like anything! As a result, while MIDI is still an essential topic, it is no longer first and foremost.

  While writing, I have moved the MIDI section to almost every position in the book, finally settling on its current position after the section on audio, so that both recording and loops are introduced as creative resources before delving into MIDI. In addition, I have tried to emphasize in the book that, while MIDI cables are fast disappearing, notes played on a controller are still encoded as MIDI, and MIDI messages, with all their utility and their limitations, are still the elements that are manipulated when creating non-loop-based synthesized or sampled parts.

- **The topics of computer hardware and software**—These posed another organizational dilemma. When I began teaching in the 1990s, only some students had their own computers, few had an email account aside from the one given by the university, and those who had Internet access at home were using sub-56K dialup. In that environment, understanding the basics of computing was the first essential topic of a music technology course. The current generation of students has grown up with their own laptops, email, and broadband Internet connections, so the basics of computing, while still relevant, are no longer the necessary first step for every student. As a result, I placed the chapters on computer hardware and computer software in the appendix so that the book starts right off dealing with sound. However, that material might be valuable for students who haven't had a great deal of computer experience or for a course in which computer hardware and software are covered in some depth.
- **Amount and depth of coverage**—In each of the sections, I have had to limit the depth of coverage and give short shrift to some of the more complex issues to keep the presentation of the material suitable for an introductory class, while at the same time not simplifying away important concepts. I have tried to be thorough with each of the topics, if not fully comprehensive. For example, in the chapter on electronic sound production (Chapter 12), I introduce a basic synthesis model consisting of an oscillator, a filter, and an amplifier, and I touch on such topics as envelopes and LFOs and their roles in creating dynamic synthesized sound. However, I felt it necessary to avoid such complexities as oscillator sync, chorusing, and intricate modulation routings to avoid overloading students who are new to the subject. A second book is currently in production entitled *Music technology and the project studio* and this will take up and expand some of these concepts for the more advanced student.
- **Course organization**—A one-semester basic course for all music majors might cover each of the chapters in the book, with the possible exceptions of the chapters in the appendix, and include one or two projects for each section. A one-semester course that was more focused on preparing students for further study in audio recording might skip the section on "Computer Notation and Computer-assisted Instruction" and include more projects in the "Audio" section. A one-semester course for future music educators might skip the more detailed chapters in the "Synthesis and Sampling" section (Chapters 13 and 14) and spend more time on projects in the "Computer Notation and Computer-assisted Instruction" section. A two-semester course might cover each of the chapters in the book, perhaps including the chapters in the appendix, include several projects for each section, and include reading and writing projects utilizing the material suggested in the "Further Reading" recommendations for each section.
- **Choice of software**—I have consciously avoided connecting this book to a specific piece of hardware or software. While we all have our favorite digital audio workstation (DAW) or notation software, there are several different programs that could serve those functions equally well. However, I have tried to identify the features

that are common to most programs and illustrate how different programs implement those features. As a result, the tasks in the "Suggested Activities" for each section are presented with generic instructions that will have to be translated into instructions specific to the software you choose to use.

One possible solution to this is to have the students do the translating themselves: they can utilize the user guides and tutorials for the given software to figure out which buttons to push and which menu items to choose to accomplish the suggested activities. This would, I believe, set the students solidly along the path to technological independence and prepare them for their encounters with new software in the future. However, this can be a time-consuming process for students and can be frustrating for those who have had relatively little experience in learning new software.

Another possible solution would be for you as the instructor to provide the students with some variety of step-by-step instructions specific to your software of choice. I've done this for my classes for years, and it has the advantage of getting the students up and running quickly with the software. As the semester progresses, the instructions can become more general, providing students with the motivation to utilize user guides and tutorials that will set them on that path toward technological independence.

The website for the book contains step-by-step tutorials for some of the projects for a few pieces of software. This repository is necessarily incomplete in both the software and the projects covered. Nevertheless, I hope it can be directly useful for some of you and provide a template for others to create their own step-by-step instructions.

I welcome feedback and criticism from my fellow music technology instructors in order to improve future versions of this book. Please send such feedback to **dan.hosken@csun.edu**.

TO THE STUDENT

This is a book written for *you*, as an aspiring musician, about the principles that underlie modern music technology, and how these principles appear in common music hardware and software. It goes deeper than the books that teach you which button to push or which menu item to choose in a specific piece of software, but it does not go so deep that you must be an electrical engineer or computer scientist to follow it. My goal in writing this book is to give you the background to apply technology as you perform, compose, teach, analyze, or engage in any other musical activities.

While eventually you must choose a specific piece of software or hardware for a task and learn which buttons to push to make it do what you want, I firmly believe that understanding common principles behind music software and hardware will enable you to learn to use it more quickly and powerfully as well as adapt to new software and hardware that has yet to be developed. This capacity to adapt to new technologies will be critical during your career. In my own professional lifetime, music technology has changed dramatically and will undoubtedly continue to do so. Understanding what lies behind the technology has helped me negotiate these changes and utilize new technologies in my own performing, composing, and teaching, and I believe that it will help you as well.

A book about anything having to do with music is necessarily incomplete—music is experienced through our ears. To remedy this, the website for this book contains audio examples for many of the topics discussed in the book, as well as links to additional material that can be found on the Internet. This is an important resource and I strongly recommend that you listen to the audio examples as you read the book.

Though this book is primarily concerned with the principles underlying music technology, it is important to do practical work with hardware and software as you delve into these principles. The suggested activities in each section of the book were designed for just this purpose.

I've used the term "musician" to describe you, and while this book was written with the college music major in mind, technology has opened up music-making to many students who are not part of traditional university music programs and don't have a great deal of experience with written music. Fortunately for those of you who fall into this latter category, this book largely avoids extensive use of notated examples and discussions that require substantial knowledge of music theory. I don't avoid talking about musical issues and I use note names and music notation where it clarifies the topic, but the book should be readable by all types of musicians. The exceptions are the chapters on music notation programs and computer-assisted instruction, which necessarily rely on an understanding of common music notation.

ACKNOWLEDGEMENTS

Though only my name appears on the cover of this book, it was far from a solo effort. I want to thank Constance Ditzel, my editor at Routledge, for supporting this project through its various transformations and helping me to shape it into this final form. I also want to thank Denny Tek, Nicole Solano, Mhairi Baxter, and the rest of the team at Routledge/Taylor & Francis for their invaluable assistance. Thanks also to Fiona Isaac of Florence Production Ltd and Sue Edwards for excellent copy-editing and many useful suggestions.

This book has benefited at several stages of its development from a number of anonymous reviewers who read proposals and chapters and delivered candid opinions that helped me to greatly improve everything from the content to the order of presentation to the prose. These reviews reminded me what an excellent set of musical and technological minds populate the diverse field of music technology. My thanks also to my colleague at California State University, Northridge, Phil Calvert, who read several chapters and gave me excellent, detailed notes. Any errors, naturally, are mine.

I've had many excellent teachers over the years who have influenced my path in composition and music technology, including Tod Machover and Barry Vercoe at MIT, Robert Ceely at New England Conservatory, and Stephen Dembski, John Wm Schaffer, and Todd Welbourne at the University of Wisconsin–Madison. Each of them generously offered me their knowledge, experience, and inspiration.

I am also indebted to many people at California State University, Northridge. This book comes directly out of my decade-plus of teaching future performers, composers, educators, and music industry professionals. Their dedication to learning has fueled my dedication to teaching and my desire to give them the very best that I have to give. CSUN and the Mike Curb College of Arts, Media, and Communication have also supported the writing of this book with a sabbatical when I was just beginning to develop the proposal for it and some release time from teaching when I desperately needed the time to complete it.

Last, but certainly not least, this book would not have been possible without the support of my family. My parents, Ann and Bill Hosken, have supported me unfailingly throughout my life, and managed to maintain that support even when their son, the physics major, told them that he'd really rather make strange sounds with computers. My wonderful children, Graham and Olivia, finally have the answer to their question: "When is Daddy done with his book?" As with all things in my life, this book would never have been started or finished without the constant support and love of my lovely wife, Rebekka.

Introduction

Music technology is a broad term encompassing everything from microphones to saxophones. In fact, it's difficult to find a musical activity that isn't impacted by technology. In some circumstances, the technology is obvious, such as a synthesizer performance by a pop musician or the use of microphones, mixers, and computers in the recording studio. However, even "acoustic" musicians use technology everyday. They might use music notation software to compose or arrange a work, a portable recorder to capture a rehearsal for later analysis, or audio and video editing software to create demos in order to get gigs. Even a vocalist who doesn't use a microphone sings in a concert hall, itself an exquisite (we hope!) piece of technology.

It would be impossible in a single book to cover instrument building, architectural acoustics, recording, computer-assisted instruction, interactive sound installations, and all of the other ways that technology and music intersect. Instead, this book focuses on five topics that underlie the many different activities in music technology. The five topics are: (1) the physical aspects of sound and sound representation; (2) audio hardware, digital audio data, and computer-based recording, editing, processing, and mixing; (3) MIDI hardware, MIDI messages, and MIDI sequencing; (4) electronic sound production using sampling and synthesis; and (5) computer notation and computer-assisted instruction. In addition, there is an appendix that covers the computer hardware and software concepts necessary for music technology.

Clearly there are dozens of other topics in music technology that are also important and interesting, but these five topics provide the basis for further exploration. Music technology is not a subject that is learned and mastered by taking one course or reading one book; rather, it is something to be actively engaged with throughout your professional career. As you work with music technology over a span of years, it becomes a partner in your music making, improving your creating, teaching, and performing, and opening up new musical vistas to explore.

WHY DO YOU NEED TO UNDERSTAND MUSIC TECHNOLOGY?

For most of you, technology has surrounded you all of your life: YouTube, Craigslist, Facebook, Wikipedia, emailing, IM'ing, texting, Googling, Skyping . . . it's all second nature. Technology is neither your friend nor your enemy: it just *is*. In one writer's term, you are "digital natives" (Prensky, 2001)—*using* technology is not going to be a problem for you.

For some technologies, it's OK to just use them. You don't have to know *how* Facebook or Google work; there are buttons to click and places to type and everything just works. However, for technologies that you are going to use professionally, you must go beneath the surface to find the underlying concepts in order to use them *effectively*.

To take an example from another field, you don't have to know how a movie camera works or how CGI effects are done in order to *watch* a movie. But if you wanted to *make* movies, you would. Many DVD commentaries and extras featuring movie directors are full of technical details about camera lenses and green screen techniques. The same principle holds true for music technology: if you want to create, perform, or educate using music technology, you have to understand how it works in order to use it effectively.

If using music technology effectively were just a matter of learning a piece of gear or a piece of software, the video tutorials that you can probably find on YouTube would do the job. However, to really use technology to its fullest, to grasp the software and hardware concepts when they appear in different contexts, to evaluate the impact and value of new technologies, it is necessary to discover the ideas and concepts that connect different music technologies together. When you are in command of the underlying ideas in music technology, you are in command of the technology itself.

This book is dedicated to the proposition that a greater understanding of music technology can enrich your professional life and give you the tools to expand beyond your current experiences. Whether you find it intimidating, exhilarating, or just an ordinary part of the fabric of everyday life, music technology provides critical tools for the modern musician.

With the exception of a relatively small number of famous opera stars, high-profile conductors, and top-selling bands, most musicians make their living in a variety of ways, including performing, teaching, composing, and arranging—often engaging in all of these tasks in a single day. For this vast majority of musicians, ignorance of music technology is not an option. Sure, you can always hire someone to computer-notate your music, develop your teaching materials, and create your demos, but that's money coming out of *your* pocket. In addition, in the early stages of your music career, *you* could be the one who gets paid by another musician to perform these tasks, *if* you have the skills!

Some musicians are concerned that making music with technology becomes about the technology rather than about the music. Strange as it sounds, the solution to this is a *greater* engagement with technology. We interact with the basic functions of hardware and software through an interface of some sort, whether the physical knobs and sliders of hardware or their virtual counterparts in software. Each of these interface controls represents an underlying process. Some represent simple processes, such as a knob that increases volume. Other interface controls represent more involved concepts, such as beat detection, or downright complicated ideas, such as the excitation model in a physical modeling softsynth. In order to make the computer do what *you* want, you have to master the concepts that lie beneath the interface.

The interfaces of music software and hardware—the real and virtual knobs and sliders—often encourage an intuitive and experiential approach, and you should always be willing to experiment with settings and functions to figure out what they do and how they might be useful. However, once your intuition and experimentation has led you somewhere, it is important to take stock of just how you got there and whether this is the place you want to be. In order to evaluate this, you have to understand the data and the processes that were affected by those intuitive actions, so that you can repeat those actions if you like the result, modify them intelligently if the result is close to what you want, or avoid them forever if the result is unpleasant. Again, fundamental knowledge of music technology forms the basis for these analytical abilities. In this way, mastering the technology allows you to make it "all about the music."

SECTION I

Sound

OVERVIEW

Though it's not exactly a "technology," the end result of music-making is sound, and in the end all of the other technologies in the book are fundamentally related to sound. Audio recording is concerned with capturing sound, MIDI sequencing is concerned with controlling sound, sampling and synthesis are concerned with creating sound, computer notation is concerned with encoding performance information that will be turned into sound, and computer-assisted instruction is concerned with teaching us to relate sound to various musical concepts, such as intervals, scales, and melodies.

This section includes a chapter on the physical aspects of sound generation and perception, a chapter on understanding sound properties through the waveform view, and a chapter on understanding sound properties through the spectrum view. Both the waveform and the spectrum views are essential ways of visualizing sound and are used extensively in recording and synthesis programs.

WHAT'S IN THIS SECTION?

Chapter 1: What is Sound?

This chapter covers:

- sound generation and propagation, including the formation of a series of compressions and rarefactions by a vibrating source;
- sound generation by musical instruments, including strings, reeds, flutes, brass, and voices;
- the impact of instrument bodies on pitch and timbre through resonance;
- the need for a medium through which sound can pass and its essential properties;
- the basics of hearing including the anatomy of the outer, middle, and inner ear and the function of the inner ear.

Chapter 2: Sound Properties and the Waveform View

This chapter covers:

- the relationship between perceptual and physical properties of sound;
- pitch and frequency, including the range of human hearing and Shephard tones;
- loudness and amplitude, including the range of human hearing for loudness expressed in decibels and the relationship between loudness and hearing damage;
- timbre and waveform, including basic waveforms such as sine, triangle, square, sawtooth, and noise;
- articulation and amplitude envelopes, including bowed/blown envelopes vs. struck/plucked envelopes;
- rhythm and amplitude transients, including their use in beat detection.

Chapter 3: The Overtone Series and the Spectrum View

This chapter covers:

- the overtone series, including the relationship between the partial numbers and frequency and between frequencies ratios and tuning;
- the spectrum representation of the overtone series and the spectrogram view;
- the spectra of the basic waveforms and Fourier's theorem;
- harmonic, inharmonic, and noise spectra;
- equalization and the modification of timbre.

At the end of the section, there are suggestions for "Further Reading" and a list of "Suggested Activities" related to the material in this section.

CHAPTER 1

What is Sound?

If a tree falls in a forest and no one is there to hear it, does it make a sound? In order to answer this classic philosophical question, you must first ask: what is sound? The too-short answer to this simple question is that sound is caused by vibrations in the air. A fuller definition of sound involves three components: generation, propagation, and reception.

GENERATION AND PROPAGATION

The air around and in your ears is made up of molecules of various types: oxygen, nitrogen, carbon dioxide, carbon monoxide, and others that we probably don't want to think about. Between the molecules in the air is . . . nothing. This means that the air molecules can be pushed together, or compressed, into a smaller space. A property of air known as elasticity causes the molecules that have been compressed together to spring apart again.

You can see this property at work when you blow up and then pop a balloon. When you force air into a balloon with your lungs, the air inside the balloon becomes compressed. When you pop that balloon, thereby removing the material that was keeping the air compressed, the elasticity of the air causes it to quickly expand again.

Sound waves are generated when air molecules are pushed together, allowed to spring apart, and then pushed together again in a repeating pattern. This pattern of "push together, spring apart" is what allows sound to move through the air.

If you think of air molecules as a bunch of pool balls randomly distributed on a pool table with some space between them, and you hit the cue ball into one of the balls, those two balls will be compressed together. They will then spring apart and the energy you imparted to the cue ball will be transferred to the other ball. That ball in turn will hit another ball, which will hit another ball, which will hit another, and so on. In other words, hitting one pool ball causes a chain reaction in the other pool balls, which takes the form of a moving pattern of compressed-together pool balls across the table. The cue ball soon stops, but the *energy* imparted to the cue ball moves across the table through this chain reaction process. Another useful analogy is a crowded party.

If you are in a crowded party and you push the person in front of you, that person will, in addition to spilling their beverage, bump into the person in front of them who will bump into the person in front of them, and so on. You stay put, but the "bump" moves across the room, just as the collision of pool balls moves across the table, even though the balls themselves don't necessarily move very far.

To generate sound, then, you need a device that can cause molecules in the air to compress together and then allow them to spring apart again. Fortunately, every musical instrument, blown soda bottle, and human voice fits this description. Take a plucked guitar string as an example.

To pluck a string, you must first pull it out of its resting position. When you release the string, the tension pulls it forward toward its resting position and its momentum carries it beyond that resting point. In this way, it's a little like letting go of a pendulum. As the string moves forward, the molecules in front of the string are pushed together, temporarily compressing them. This region of air where the molecules have been compressed together is sensibly referred to as a **compression** (see Figure 1.1).

These compressed air molecules then spring apart and cause a compression further on. The molecules in that compression also spring apart and the cycle continues. The energy that was imparted to the molecules by the string thus moves, or **propagates**, through the air.

While this compression is propagating through the air, the guitar string continues to move. After it has reached its furthest forward point, the tension in the string pulls it back toward its resting point and its momentum again carries it beyond that point. By now, however, the forward motion of the string has "cleared out" many of the molecules in front of the string, leaving an area in front of the string in which there

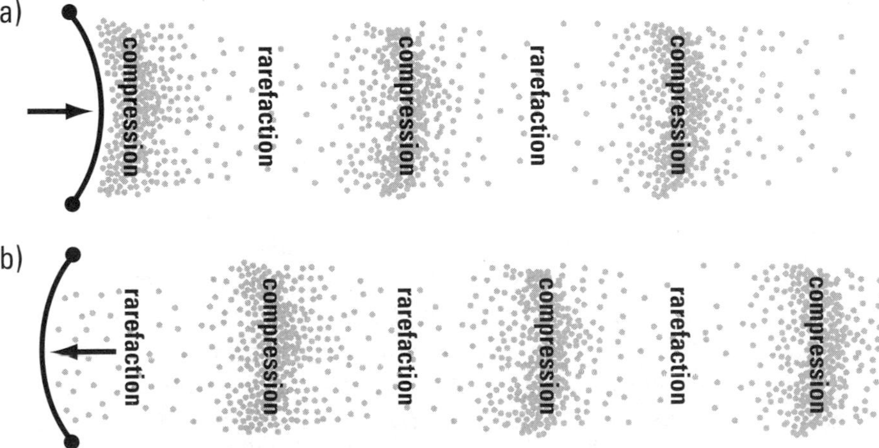

Figure 1.1 (a) A string moving forward causing a compression; and (b) a string moving backward causing a rarefaction.

are fewer air molecules than before. This is the opposite of a compression and would logically be called something like a de-compression, but the official term for it is **rarefaction**. As the tension in the string again pulls the string forward, the cycle begins again. The string's motion will eventually subside due to forces such as friction.

As the string moves forward and backward it creates a series of compressions and rarefactions that propagate through the air. This type of wave, in which the disturbance of the medium is in the same direction as the wave propagates, is referred to as a **compression wave** or a longitudinal wave. In ocean waves, however, the disturbance of the medium is up and down while the wave propagates horizontally—this type of wave is called a **transverse wave**. The compression waves created by the string or some other vibrating body are the "vibrations in the air" that are usually described as sound.

Sound Generation by Musical Instruments

While this discussion has used a guitar string as an example of sound wave generation, all vibrating bodies that make sound necessarily create chain reactions of compressions and rarefactions. Instruments such as plucked strings, drums, and cymbals all affect air in a similar manner by physically moving back and forth. For bowed strings, such as a violin, the bow uses its "stickiness" to first pull the string out of normal position, at which point the bow slips and the string snaps back. This fast stick-slip cycle creates the back and forth motion necessary to create compressions and rarefactions.

A reed on an instrument such as a clarinet or saxophone creates compressions and rarefactions by moving up and down (see Figure 1.2). When air passes over the reed, it rises in the same way that an airplane wing lifts when air passes over it. While the reed is lifting up, the performer's air stream is causing the air molecules within the instrument to compress together. When the raised reed causes the opening to the mouthpiece to narrow, little air flows into the instrument. Since the compression has begun to move, or propagate, via chain reaction through the instrument, the absence of airflow allows a rarefaction to form. Also, due to the reduced airflow over the reed, there is no more lift on the reed and the reed opens back up, allowing the air to flow freely into the instrument again. The open-close-open cycle causes the performer's steady air stream to become a series of very fast puffs of air in the instrument creating compressions and rarefactions. A double-reed instrument such as an oboe works similarly, except that there are two reeds that close together due to the airflow.

An instrument like a flute also creates compressions and rarefactions by interrupting the performer's air stream. In the case of a flute, air blown across the blowhole is split by the edge of the blowhole and some of the air enters the flute, causing a compression (see Figure 1.3). This build-up of pressure then deflects the entering air out of the blowhole. The compression moves down the inside of the flute and, with no air entering the mouthpiece, a rarefaction forms. With the backpressure thus relieved, the performer's blown air again enters the flute mouthpiece and creates another compression. As with the reed instruments, a steady stream of air from the performer is converted by the mouthpiece of the instrument into very fast puffs—compressions and rarefactions.

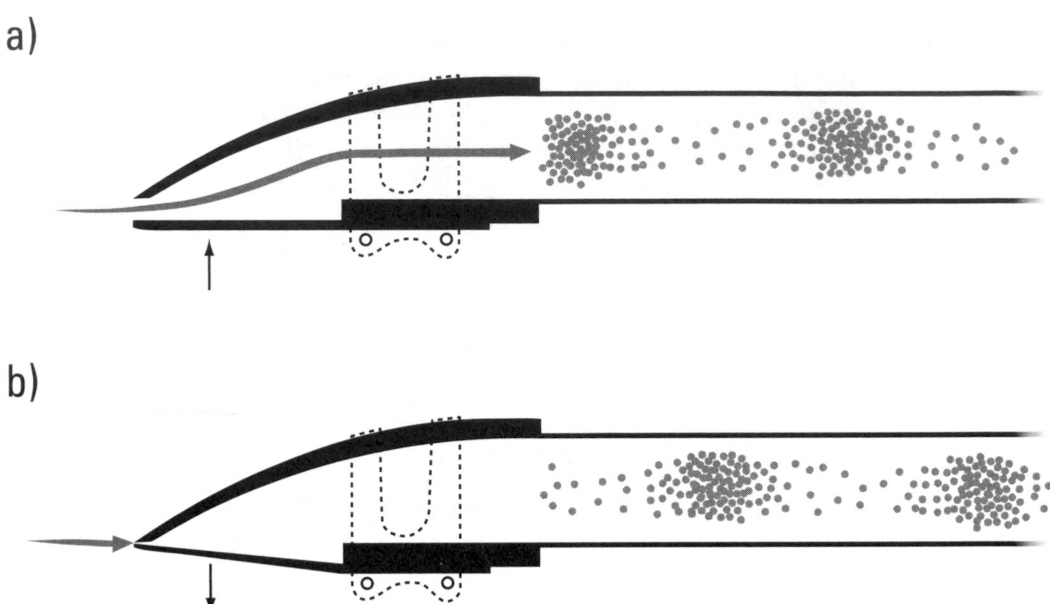

Figure 1.2 (a) Air entering a clarinet mouthpiece causes a compression in the barrel. The air over the reed causes the reed to rise and reduce the airflow. (b) With the reed closing off the air stream, a rarefaction forms in the wake of the compression. The reduced airflow over the reed causes the reed to open back up and the cycle starts again.

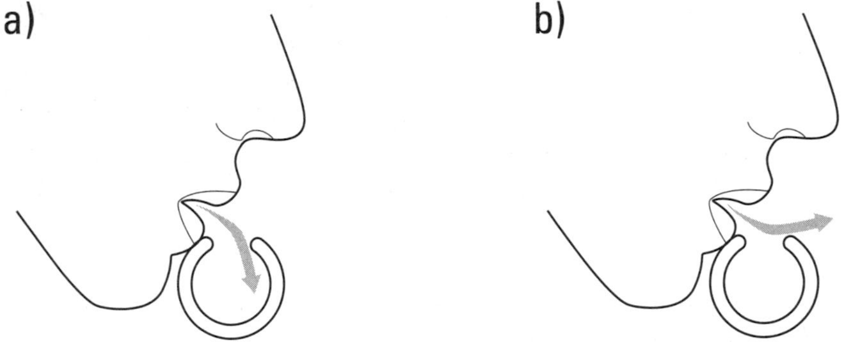

Figure 1.3 (a) Side cutaway view of a flute blowhole. Air is blown across the blowhole of the flute and is deflected into the flute, creating a compression. (b) Pressure from the compression deflects air out of the flute. A rarefaction forms as the compression propagates down the pipe.

Flutes that you blow directly into, such as toy flutes, whistles, ocarinas, and recorders, work similarly in that when you blow into them the air is split by the edge of the vent. The air that goes into the instrument creates a compression. This pressure build-up causes the air to be redirected out of the vent thereby creating a rarefaction. With the backpressure relieved, the air split by the edge of the vent again enters the pipe. The pipe organ, the "King of Instruments," works in a similar way to a toy flute, except that the lungs do not provide the air. In addition to "flue" pipes, which are flute-like, pipe organs also have reed pipes in which the air pumped into the pipe passes over a reed to generate the pitch.

In brass instruments, such as trumpets, trombones, French horns, and tubas, lip buzzing creates compressions and rarefactions. The performer starts with closed lips and no air flowing into the instrument (see Figure 1.4). When the performer blows, the pressure forces the lips open and air flows into the instrument creating a compression. The tension of the performer's lips and the high flow of air through them cause the lips to close again thereby cutting off the airflow and creating a rarefaction. The pressure again builds up behind the performer's closed lips, the lips are forced open again, and air flow resumes.

Vocal production is similar in many ways to the production of sound in brass instruments. The vocal folds (also known as "vocal cords") located in the larynx start off closed and are forced open by air pressure from the lungs, just as a brass player's lips start off closed and are forced open. Once air is flowing past the vocal folds, the pressure decreases, causing the folds to close together, just as the air stream through a brass player's lips causes the lips to close. This repeated opening and closing creates the compressions and rarefactions necessary for sound. As with each of these physical descriptions, vocal production is actually somewhat more complex. Nevertheless, the description here gives you a sense of what's going on.

The vocal folds can vibrate, while at the same time that stream of air is also used to buzz a brass mouthpiece, vibrate a reed, or excite the air column in a flute. Since the pitch of the singing voice is determined by the tension of the vocal folds, and the pitch of the instrument is determined by the vibration of the reed/mouthpiece coupled with the body of the instrument, it is possible to sing one pitch while playing another. Singing-while-playing is a common contemporary classical performance technique used in music from the twentieth century to today. It's worth noting that there are other elements to vocal production that produce the unvoiced consonants and the noisy portions of voiced consonants.

Much of the music we listen to comes out of loudspeakers and headphones. Although this music may have originally been created in a variety of ways by the

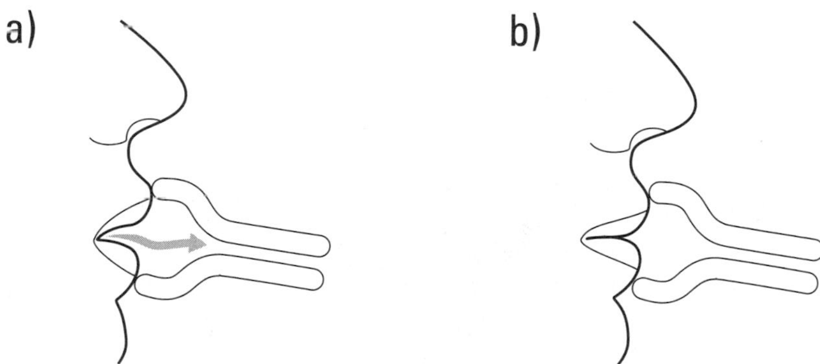

Figure 1.4 (a) Side cutaway view of the mouthpiece of a brass instrument. Air pressure from the lungs forces open the lips and causes a compression in the instrument's air column, which then propagates through the instrument. (b) The moving air and the tension of the lips close off the air stream and a rarefaction forms. This repeated cycle creates the "buzzing" of the mouthpiece.

instruments discussed above, their combined compressions and rarefactions are re-created by the moving elements in speakers. The simplest kind of speaker has a cone that moves back and forth in response to an analog electrical signal from an electric guitar, stereo, or iPod (see Figure 1.5). An electromagnet attached to the speaker converts this electrical signal into the physical movement of the cone. When the cone moves forward, a compression forms and when it moves backward a rarefaction forms.

Resonance

In the description above of sound generation by musical instruments, the discussion stopped once the mouthpiece, vocal cords, or string had produced a series of compressions and rarefactions. However, there is a reason that these instruments all have bodies, barrels, or pipes: **resonance**. Once the initial vibration is started, the sound wave passes into the body of the instrument, which can determine pitch and overall timbre.

The pitch of stringed instruments, percussive instruments, and voices is determined by the vibrating elements of strings, membranes or bars, and vocal cords. The resonators for those instruments—the body of a violin, the shell of a drum, and the throat, mouth, and nasal cavities of a human—are responsible for shaping the timbre of the sound. This should not be thought of as a trivial task. For example, in order to speak, we must shape our resonators continuously to produce different vowels. To make a violin sound beautiful, the sound wave created by the bow and strings must be modified by the materials and overall shape of the body of the instrument. A bowed string without a resonator can sound quite thin and unimpressive.

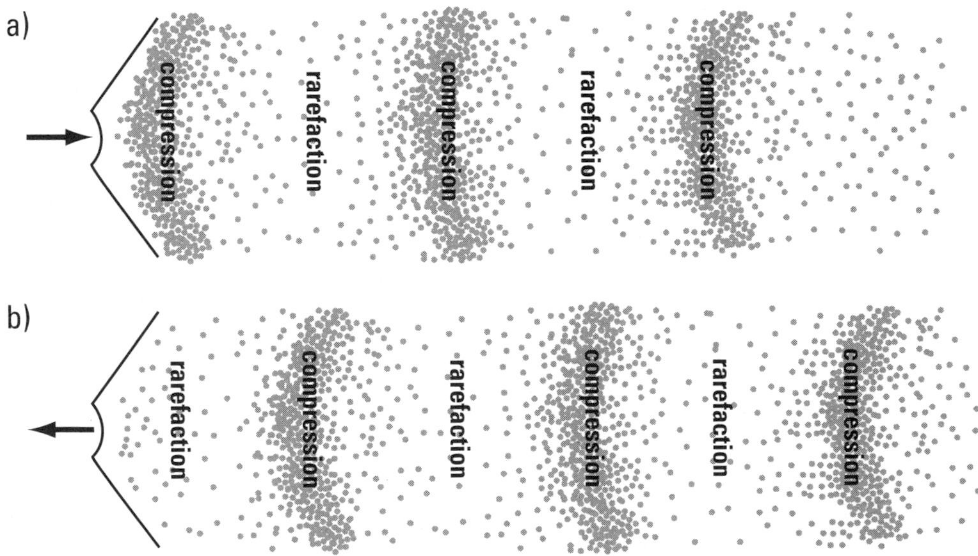

Figure 1.5 (a) Side cutaway view of a speaker cone. The forward motion of the speaker cone causes a compression. (b) The backward motion of the speaker cone causes a rarefaction.

The pitch of brass and woodwind instruments is determined by a combination of the mouthpiece and the resonator. These instruments have key or valve systems or other methods of changing the length of the resonator that determine which pitches can be "activated" by the sound wave generated by the mouthpiece. For brass instruments, the pitch is determined by the length of the air column and the pitch of the buzzing from the mouthpiece. For woodwinds, the pitch is almost entirely determined by the length of the air column as controlled by the keys. In addition to strongly influencing the pitch of brass and woodwind instruments, the resonator also shapes the timbre as it does with strings, percussion, and voice.

The Medium

Thus far, it has been assumed that the forward and backward activity of a vibrating object is taking place in air. However, if you've ever dived into a pool you know that you can hear sound underwater as well. For sound to propagate, it requires an elastic medium, and the molecules in water fulfill this requirement. However, there are places where sound cannot travel either because the medium is not elastic or because the molecules aren't close enough together to create a chain reaction. The classic example of the latter is the vacuum of space. Technically, "space" contains a great many molecules—actually, *all* of them—in the form of asteroids, comets, planets, and suns. However, the density of the molecules in between these celestial bodies is not high enough to allow the chain reaction of compressions and rarefactions to form. In the words of the advertising campaign for the classic 1979 movie *Alien*: "In space, no one can hear you scream."

RECEPTION: THE BETTER TO HEAR YOU WITH

So far, we've discussed the generation of sound waves by a voice or instrument and the propagation of those waves through a medium such as air. The next step is for someone, or something, to receive this series of compressions and rarefactions and interpret them. In other words, we need ears with which to hear. The ear can be divided into three basic parts: the outer ear, the middle ear, and the inner ear (see Figure 1.6).

The outer ear consists of the fleshy part on the outside of your head and a canal that funnels sound waves into your head. The flesh of the ear, or **pinna**, helps us locate the sound source, because it changes the incoming sound subtly (filters it) depending on what direction the sound is coming from. The two ears working together also provide directional cues through the time difference between when sound reaches one ear and the other and through an intensity difference if sound arriving at one ear is partially blocked by the head.

The shape and length of the **ear canal** influences the frequency balance of the sound waves that pass through it by emphasizing frequencies between about 2,000 and 5,000 Hz, just as speaking into a tube changes the quality of your voice by emphasizing certain frequencies. As a result, our hearing is most acute around those frequencies.

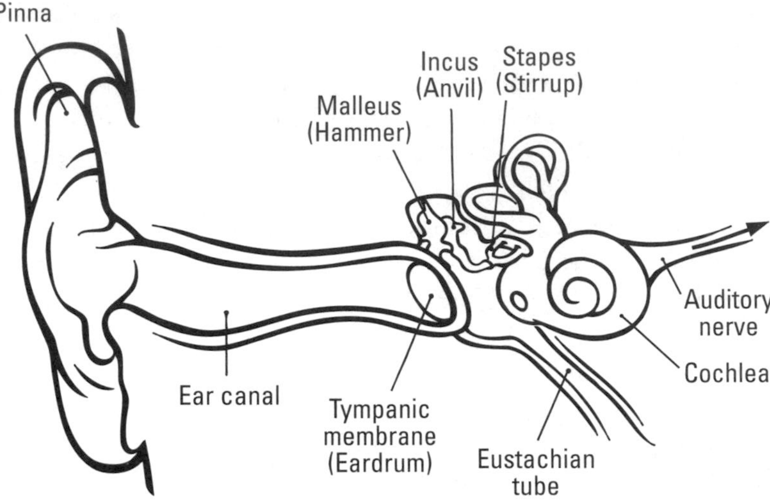

Figure 1.6 Basic anatomy of the human ear. (Based on a drawing in Chittka, L. and A. Brockmann. 2005. *Perception Space—The Final Frontier.* PLoS Biol 3(4): e137.)

The middle ear consists of the tympanic membrane, or **eardrum**, and a series of three bones, collectively referred to as the **ossicles**, which connect the eardrum to the inner ear. When a sound wave reaches the eardrum, it vibrates in sympathy. To get a sense of how this works, try pointing a trumpet, or some other loud instrument, at the head of a timpani drum and playing loudly. The drumhead will vibrate madly without ever being struck. Similarly, you can also sing into a piano while holding the damper pedal down and hear the strings vibrate in sympathy with your voice. With your eardrum moving back and forth, the energy that a voice or instrument originally imparted to the air has now been turned into a vibration in your body. The vibration of the eardrum is next passed to the ossicles.

The individual ossicles are called the malleus, the incus, and the stapes, and are known colloquially as the hammer, the anvil, and the stirrup due to their respective shapes. These three bones work together to amplify mechanically the relatively small movement of the eardrum; this is one of the reasons why our hearing is so sensitive. The middle ear also connects to your **Eustachian tubes**, which connect at the other end to your throat and allow your body to keep the air pressure in the middle ear matched with the air pressure outside of your head. It's the pressure imbalance between the inner and outer ear that makes your ears pop when going up or down in a plane or going up or down in the elevator of a tall building. The last of the three ossicles connects to the **oval window** of an organ called the cochlea, which makes up your inner ear.

The **cochlea** is a fluid-filled tube that is coiled up like a snail. When the ossicles move back and forth in response to the movement of the eardrum, the stapes transfers that vibration to the fluid inside the cochlea through the movement of a membrane called the oval window. So far all of the changes in energy have been mechanical: vibrating string to vibrating air to vibrating eardrum to vibrating ossicles to vibrating fluid. It's the cochlea that finally does the job of translating this mechanical energy into neural impulses that are then transferred to the brain through the auditory nerve.

The vibrating fluid in the cochlea causes various parts of the **basilar membrane**, which runs down the middle of the cochlea, to vibrate as well (see Figure 1.7). On this membrane are thousands of tiny hair cells and corresponding nerve receptors that are part of the **organ of Corti**. As different parts of the basilar membrane are set in motion by the vibrating fluid, the moving hair cells cause nerves to fire, sending signals down the auditory nerve to the brain.

The movement of the basilar membrane is dependent on the frequencies present in the incoming sound wave, which causes different hair cells to fire for different frequencies. As a result, different parts of the basilar membrane are sensitive to different frequencies: high frequencies nearest to the oval window, low frequencies toward the center of the spiral. In this way, the basilar membrane separates the incoming sound wave into its component frequencies. This is one reason that we can identify multiple simultaneous pitches in music: each pitch causes the most movement in a different part of the basilar membrane, and the nerves that fire at each location are sent separately to the brain. In Chapter 3, we'll see that most pitches are made up of more than one frequency, but only one of those frequencies is heard as the "pitch."

As we age, the part of the cochlea responsible for transmitting high frequencies to our brains gradually becomes less responsive and we hear less of the high frequency content of sound. If you expose your ear to damagingly loud sounds, you may cause more severe degradation to your cochlea's high frequency response, which can lead to profound hearing loss. Since the consonants in your speech that help you determine what words are being said often contain relatively high frequencies ("s," "t," "k," etc.),

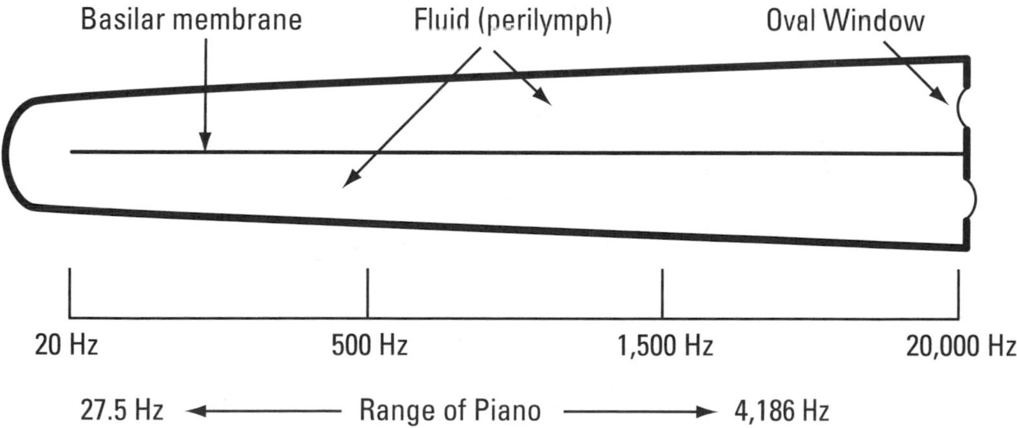

Figure 1.7 A simplified view of an "unrolled" cochlea, showing the positions on the basilar membrane that are responsible for detecting various frequencies. The frequency range of the piano is given for reference.

severe loss of high frequencies results in difficulty distinguishing between words that contain the same vowel sounds but different consonants. Your cochlea is a powerful, but sensitive, organ, and damage to it is irreversible. Hearing loss will be discussed in the next chapter, where the amplitude of sounds is considered.

Once the cochlea has done its job, the nerve signals are sent to the brain. It's in the brain itself that we decode these impulses, remember them (or forget them), analyze them, and act on them. It is our brain that decides that a sound represents squealing tires and we'd better move quickly or that a sound represents music that we can analyze and appreciate.

The study of our auditory system and the way the brain decodes and analyzes the resultant nerve impulses is referred to as **music perception**, or **psychoacoustics**. Some aspects of this field of study will be taken up in future chapters as they relate to sound, audio, sampling, and synthesis. The study of mental processes and mental representation in music is referred to as **music cognition**. Naturally, there can be a great degree of overlap between the study of music perception and the study of music cognition.

Fundamentally, sound "happens" in the brain. So if a tree falls in the forest and no one is there to hear it, the tree still causes a pattern of compressions and rarefactions that propagate through the air, but with no ears to receive the disturbances and no brain to process the signals, there is no sound. Do squirrels count?

REVIEW OF KEY TERMS

compression 8
propagation 8
rarefaction 9
compression wave 9
transverse wave 9
resonance 12
pinna 13
ear canal 13
eardrum 14
ossicles 14
Eustachian tubes 14
oval window 14
cochlea 14
basilar membrane 15
organ of Corti 15
music perception/psychoacoustics 16
music cognition 16

CHAPTER 2

Sound Properties and the Waveform View

SOUND PROPERTIES

As you saw in the previous chapter, a sound wave is generated by some vibrating source, propagates through a medium as a series of compressions and rarefactions, and is finally received by our ears and brain (see Figure 2.1).

This is helpful in understanding the mechanics of sound production, but it doesn't provide much information about the sound itself. If this is a musical sound, there are a variety of questions that you might have about it. What is its pitch? How loud is it? What does it actually sound like? How is it articulated? What is its rhythm? These questions can be boiled down to a list of musical sound properties that are of interest: pitch, loudness, timbre, articulation, and rhythm.

This list focuses on "musical" sounds, but many of these properties can also be found in non-musical sounds such as speech, ocean waves, and car crashes. However, while these properties are present in some way in all sounds, they are not as well defined for non-musical sounds as they are for musical ones. Care must be taken, of course, when declaring one sound or another to be "not musical;" the twentieth-century composer, Edgard Varèse, famously defined music itself as "organized sound."

In order to determine the properties for a given sound, it is useful to use the **waveform view** of sound. The waveform view is a graph of the change in air pressure

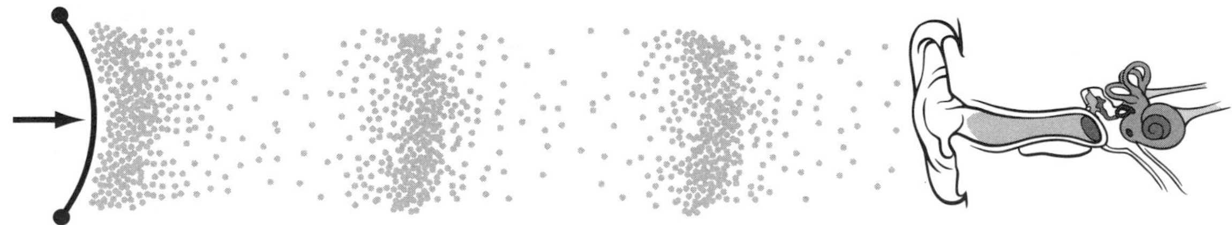

Figure 2.1 A vibrating string produces a series of compressions and rarefactions that are received by the ear, coded as neural impulses, and sent to the brain.

at a particular location over time due to a compression wave. If you were measuring the air pressure right in front of a vibrating string, the pressure would change as shown in Table 2.1.

This change in air pressure over time can be graphed on a simple *x*-*y* graph with time being the *x* and the air pressure being the *y*. This gives us the waveform view of sound (see Figure 2.2). Each of steps in Table 2.1 is marked in Figure 2.2 along with the location of the compression and rarefaction in that cycle.

PITCH

Pitch is a measurement of sound made by your brain. Pitch can therefore be described as a *perceptual* property of sound. The waveform view shows what is happening to air molecules when they are disturbed by something that vibrates, *not* what is happening in your brain. The waveform view, then, is a *physical* representation, not a perceptual

Table 2.1 **Motion of string and corresponding air pressure in front of string**

	Motion of string	*Air pressure*
1.	Not moving; in regular position	Normal
2.	Moving "forward" to furthest displacement	Higher than normal
3.	Moving "backward" to center position	Normal
4.	Moving "backward" to furthest displacement	Less than normal
5.	Moving "forward" to center position	Normal
. . .	. . . cycle repeats . . .	. . . cycle repeats . . .

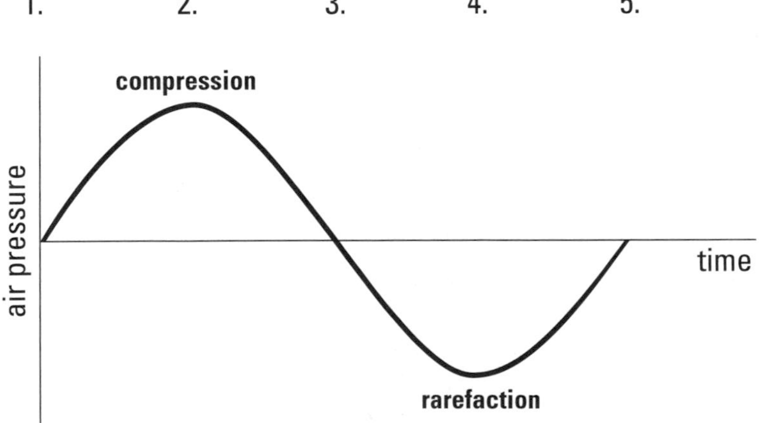

Figure 2.2 Waveform view of sound. The numbers above the graph correspond to the numbered string motions in Table 2.1.

representation. Each of the sound properties mentioned above—pitch, loudness, timbre, articulation, and rhythm—is a perceptual property. In order to use the physical waveform view to understand something about these perceptual properties, we need to identify physical properties that are related to them.

At first, this may seem like a meaningless distinction. However, in the act of perception, our ears change the physical properties of sound in various ways, such as emphasizing certain frequencies, and our brain analyzes the perceived sound properties in relation to perceptions it has encountered before, such as identifying a sound as the harmonic interval of a perfect fifth played on a piano. In addition, the ear can be fooled. There are a variety of aural illusions in which the brain's perception of a sound differs from the sound's actual physical properties.

The physical property that is related to pitch is **frequency**. In the string example, frequency is the rate at which a string moves through a full cycle of motions from center, to forward, to center, to backward, to center and then repeats. These cycles of motion in turn create compression and rarefaction cycles in the air that repeat at the same rate (frequency). As discussed in the previous chapter, various musical instruments and other sound sources have different physical motions, but they all produce the necessary compression and rarefaction cycles at a rate related to the rate of their physical motions.

Frequency, then, is measured by the number of cycles of compression/rarefaction that occur per second. The cycles per second, or cps, measurement is also referred to as **hertz**, or **Hz**, after the German physicist, Heinrich Hertz. This rate can be determined from the waveform view by measuring the amount of time the sound wave takes to go through a compression-rarefaction cycle. This measurement is called the **period** of the waveform and is measured in seconds per cycle. The letter "T" will stand for the period (see Figures 2.3a and 2.3b).

Since the period gives us the number of seconds per cycle, we can obtain the number of cycles per second by inverting the period. The frequency, *f*, is equal to the reciprocal of the period, T.

$$f = 1 \div T = 1/T$$

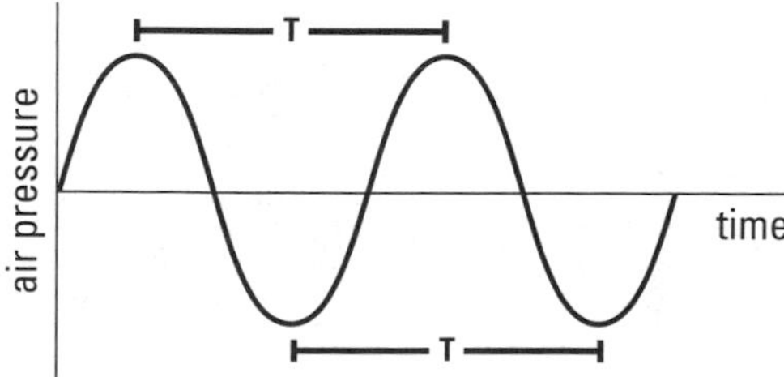

Figure 2.3a Waveform view showing the period of the waveform measured from two different starting points.

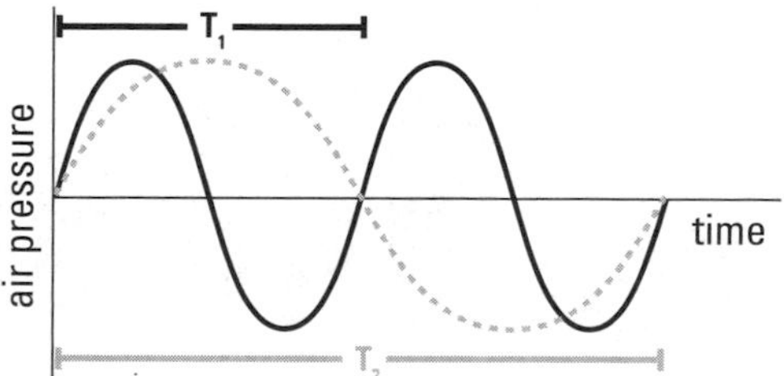

Figure 2.3b Two waves with the same amplitude but different frequencies graphed on the same axis. Period T_2 is twice as long as Period T_1, resulting in half the frequency.

As the period gets smaller, the frequency gets larger, and as the period gets larger, the frequency gets smaller. If you think about the vibrating string, this makes sense. The longer it takes the string to move back and forth, the slower the string is moving and the lower the frequency. If the string takes less time to move back and forth, the string must be moving faster and the frequency will be higher. Table 2.2 gives some examples of period–frequency relationships. The frequencies for the notes on a piano keyboard are given in Figure 2.4.

There are a wide range of frequencies that occur in the world, but we are only sensitive to a certain range. The frequency range of human hearing is about 20 Hz to 20,000 Hz (20 kHz). This forms one of the distinctions between frequency and pitch. Any back and forth motion of an object in a medium creates a compression wave at some frequency, but only those compression waves whose frequencies fall in the 20 Hz to 20 kHz range are really "sound waves." It is important to note that this range is only approximate and will vary from person to person and even vary in the same person from year to year.

As we age, our sensitivity to high frequencies gradually diminishes. One company has put this fact to interesting use by marketing an anti-loitering device that emits a relatively loud high frequency tone of approximately 17 kHz. Theoretically, this tone is only hearable by people under the age of about 25. As a result, the device has been referred to as a "teen repellent."

Other animals are more sensitive to different frequency ranges than we are. A dog whistle is a classic example of this phenomenon. A dog whistle is theoretically too high for humans to hear, but well within the hearing range of dogs (at least of small dogs). Frequencies like this above our hearing range are referred to as **ultrasonic**. Elephants,

Table 2.2 **Some period–frequency relationships**

Period	*Frequency*
2 seconds	1 ÷ 2 = 0.5 Hz
1 second	1 ÷ 1 = 1 Hz
1/2 second	1 ÷ ½ = 2 Hz
0.00227 seconds (2.27 milliseconds)	1 ÷ 0.00227 = 440 Hz (the tuning A)

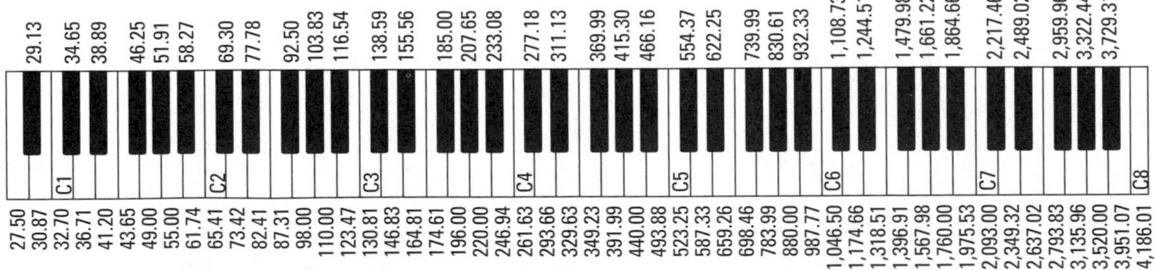

Figure 2.4 The frequencies associated with piano keys. C4 is middle C.

on the other hand, can communicate at frequencies below our hearing range, or **infrasonic** frequencies. Some organ pipes also produce infrasonic frequencies that are felt rather than heard.

It is possible to fool the ear in various ways with regard to the relationship between frequency and pitch. For example, the cognitive psychologist, Roger Shepard, developed an illusion in which a series of tones appears to rise endlessly, but never leaves a relatively narrow range of frequencies. In his honor, these are referred to as **Shepard tones**. The tones in this illusion are made up a number of frequencies in octaves. As all the frequencies rise, the higher frequencies gradually fade out and frequencies below them gradually fade in. As the loudness relationships between the octaves change, our ears shift smoothly from the octaves that are fading out to the octaves that are fading in without us being consciously aware of it. This illusion has been likened to the visual illusions of M.C. Escher, particularly his *Ascending and Descending*, which was inspired by a design by Lionel and Roger Penrose. (See the book's website for an audio example of Shepard tones and a link to the Escher and Penrose images.)

LOUDNESS

The perceptual property of **loudness** is related to the physical property of **amplitude**. Amplitude is determined by how much the air pressure in a compression or rarefaction deviates from the normal air pressure. In the case of a stringed instrument, the harder the string is plucked or bowed, the farther from the normal position the string moves and the greater the deviation in air pressure from the norm is in a compression or rarefaction. Struck instruments such as percussion generate greater amplitude in the same way. For instruments driven by breath, the greater the airflow, the more the air molecules get packed together before the reed, lips, or vocal cords close, and the greater the amplitude of the resultant sound wave.

On the waveform view, amplitude is measured from the x-axis to the peak (or the trough) so that it represents the deviation of air pressure from normal (see Figures 2.5a and 2.5b). The vertical axis of the waveform view will hereafter be re-labeled as "amplitude," and the letter "A" will stand for the amplitude.

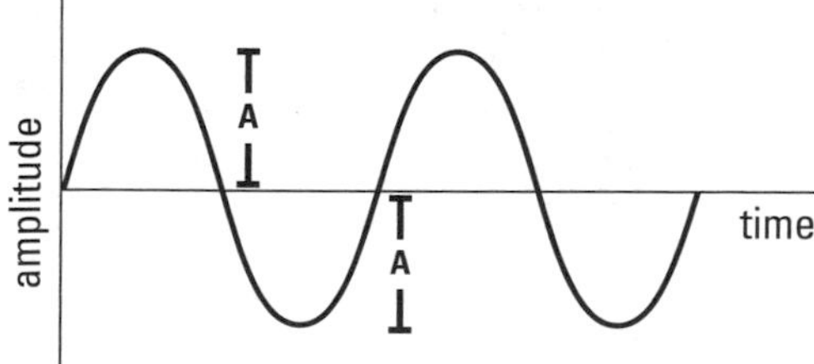

Figure 2.5a Waveform view showing the amplitude of the waveform measured in two different ways.

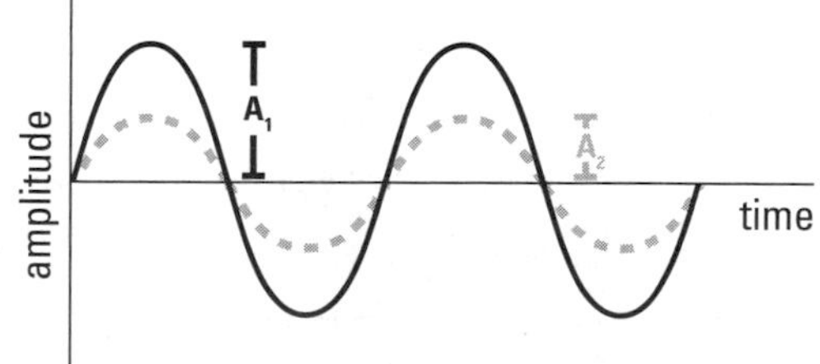

Figure 2.5b Two waves with the same frequency but different amplitudes graphed on the same axis.

Thus far, we've been talking about amplitude in terms of the deviation in air pressure from the norm in a compression or rarefaction. This amplitude measurement is usually given in relation to a reference value, resulting in a sound pressure level. This level is expressed in units known as decibels (dB), or specifically **decibels of sound pressure level (dB SPL)**. There are many different kinds of decibel measurements in music technology, so it is important to remember the "SPL" part of dB SPL.

As with frequency, the range of human hearing for loudness is limited to just a part of the full range of possible sound pressure levels. The quietest sound we can possibly hear is given as 0 dB SPL and is referred to as the **threshold of hearing**. The "0" does not mean that there is no pressure in the sound wave, just that the sound pressure of the compression wave we're measuring is the same as the sound pressure of a compression wave that was experimentally determined to be the quietest that humans can hear. Any compression wave with a lower pressure or intensity would be measured in negative dB SPL and would not be perceivable by humans.

The loudest sound that we can bear is approximately 120 dB SPL and is referred to as the **threshold of pain**. Anything above this is both physically painful and damaging to our hearing. However, it is important to note that prolonged exposure to sound pressure levels significantly lower than this can still cause hearing damage. Table 2.3 lists several sound sources and their average dB SPL.

Table 2.3 **Sound sources and related sound pressure levels**

Sound source	*Sound pressure level*
Rock music peak	150 dB
Jet engine at 30 meters away	140 dB
Threshold of pain	120 dB
Symphonic music peak	120–137 dB
Amplified rock music at 1–2 meters	105–120 dB
Subway train at 60 meters away	95 dB
Piano played loudly	92–95 dB
Train whistle at 150 meters away	90 dB
Telephone dial tone	80 dB
Chamber music in small auditorium	75–85 dB
Piano played at moderate levels	60–70 dB
Normal conversation at arm's length	45–55 dB
Whisper	30 dB
Threshold of hearing	0 dB

Source: Data from Sallows (2001) and ASHA website.

Loudness and Hearing Damage

Hearing is both a wondrous and fragile sense. As we get older, our hearing naturally gets worse, with the higher frequencies slowly falling away. However, our modern noisy lifestyle can cause our hearing to deteriorate faster.

Many people have had the experience of leaving a rock concert and noticing that their hearing is dull or muted. This sensation, referred to as **temporary threshold shift**, often goes away after a few hours (or days!), but just because the dullness has left doesn't mean that there are no lasting effects. Every time you subject your ears to extremely loud sounds, or even merely loud sound over a period of time, you contribute to the hastening deterioration of your hearing. The dullness comes from over-exciting the hair cells in the cochlea that are responsible for high frequency sounds. If the sonic abuse is severe enough, the dull sensation may be a *permanent* threshold shift instead of a temporary one; in other words: permanent hearing damage.

Persistent "ringing" in the ear, called tinnitus, is another possible outcome of hearing damage. The ringing sound in the ear can be temporary, like the post-concert muffled sensation discussed above, but it can also eventually become permanent.

There are mechanical devices that help reduce the effects of such hearing loss, ranging from hearing aids to cochlear implants, but there is currently no mechanical device that hears with the sensitivity of your natural hearing system. The best solution to hearing loss is to prevent it in the first place.

The first and best way to prevent loudness-induced hearing loss is to avoid loud sounds. It may not be necessary to have your car stereo so loud that the entire neighborhood can hear it. Perhaps that rock concert isn't a "must-see" after all. Maybe there's a better party than the one with the rafter-shaking stereo.

Table 2.4 gives maximum exposure times for a variety of sound pressure levels. The 85 dB mark is often used in workplace settings to determine whether hearing protection is required. If you compare these sound pressure levels to those in Table 2.3, you'll see

Table 2.4 **Maximum exposure time at various sound pressure levels**

Sound pressure level	*Max. exposure time*
82 dB	16 hours
85 dB	8 hours
88 dB	4 hours
91 dB	2 hours
94 dB	1 hour
97 dB	30 minutes
100 dB	15 minutes
103 dB	7.5 minutes

Source: Data from SHAPE (2005).

that there are a number of musical situations that require monitoring to make sure your ears aren't overexposed.

There has also been some concern that personal listening devices (PLDs), such as iPods, can contribute to hearing loss, and guidelines have been published that suggest volume limitations and a time limit on PLD listening per day. Rough guidelines are listed in Table 2.5. You should note that the numbers are dependent on the volume output by the specific PLD and each individual's ears. The greater number of dB SPL that a PLD outputs at a given percentage of maximum volume, the lower the exposure limit would be at that volume.

When loud sounds can't be avoided, earplugs can help to protect your ears (see Figure 2.6). For situations involving everyday noise, such as noise from a bus, subway, lawnmower, or chainsaw, inexpensive earplugs can reduce the loudness of these sounds before they reach your hearing system. However, inexpensive earplugs tend to change the balance of frequencies, and hence the timbre, of sounds that reach your middle and inner ears by reducing higher frequencies more than lower ones. This is problematic for music. In musical situations, more expensive earplugs that are molded specifically to fit your ears can reduce the loudness of sounds evenly across all frequency ranges. These custom-molded earplugs are naturally more expensive than the cheap earplugs; you can consider it an investment in the longevity of your career. You may feel like the most uncool audience member at a rock concert because of your earplugs, but you'll thank yourself later when you still have a musical career.

Amplitude and Loudness Perception

Decibels are used when expressing sound pressure levels because they reduce a wide range of numbers down to a manageable range. Our hearing is very sensitive, resulting in a ratio of the intensity of a sound at the threshold of pain to the intensity of a sound at the threshold of hearing of about 1,000,000,000,000 (one trillion) to 1. Small changes in decibel values, then, can reflect rather large changes in the actual intensity of a sound. A change of 3 dB SPL indicates a *doubling* of the physical measurement of intensity.

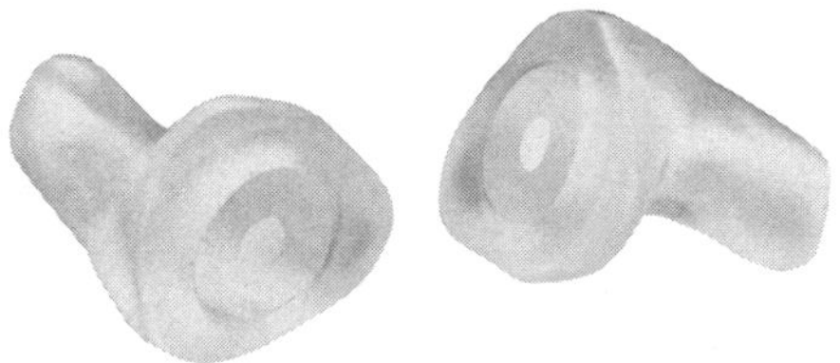

Figure 2.6 Custom-molded earplugs designed especially for music. Different filters can be inserted to reduce sound by 9 dB, 15 dB, or 25 dB. (Copyright © Etymotic Research Inc. Used with permission)

Table 2.5 **Recommended exposure limits for personal listening devices**

% of PLD max. volume	*Exposure limits*
10–50	No limit
60	18 hours
70	4.6 hours
80	1.2 hours
90	18 minutes
100	5 minutes

Source: Portnuff and Fligor (2006).

However, in terms of our perception of dB SPL, an increase of 10 dB sounds about twice as loud.

Another discrepancy between physical measurements and perception is the difference in perceived loudness levels for sounds at different frequencies. We are more sensitive to frequencies between about 1 kHz and 5 kHz, so those sounds require less intensity, and hence fewer dB SPL, to sound as loud as lower frequency sounds. Our sensitivity to this frequency range makes some sense given that a number of consonants in our language have significant energy in that range.

TIMBRE

The perceptual property of **timbre** is related to the physical property of the shape of the wave, or the **waveform**. Timbre is also related to the physical property of the sound's spectrum, which will be covered in the next chapter. Thus far in the discussion of sound, it has been assumed that the vibrating object is moving in the simplest possible way. The shape produced by that simple back and forth motion is called a **sine wave** after the mathematical function that produces such a shape. Figures 2.2, 2.3, and 2.5 are all sine waves.

A real-world vibrating object seldom moves in such a simple fashion. Typically, the back and forth motion will be more complicated, resulting in an equally complicated graph of the changing amplitude over time. Figure 2.7 shows the waveform of a trumpet.

It's difficult to make many generalizations about the waveforms of actual instruments, so the waveform view is a bit limited in what it can tell us about timbre. In addition, timbre is a complicated phenomenon and can be influenced by the other sound properties (pitch, loudness, articulation) and the overall sonic context (what other instruments are playing, whether it is noisy, etc.). The discussion of the spectrum in the next chapter will provide us with more tools for analyzing timbre. However, there is a collection of largely artificial waveforms that can be used as a sort of rudimentary timbral vocabulary.

The simplest is the sine wave mentioned above. The other standard waveforms are the **triangle wave**, the **sawtooth wave**, the **square wave**, and a version of the square wave called a **pulse wave**. A single cycle of each of these waveforms is shown in Figure 2.8. These waveforms are primarily relevant because they formed the basis for early analog synthesizer sounds. This may appear to be historical trivia, but many current software synthesizers and some hardware synths use analog-modeling techniques to create sound. There are even some actual analog hardware synthesizers that are still being made. The term "analog-modeling" is used to describe digital synthesis methods that are designed to mimic original analog synthesis techniques, usually with some modern digital twists.

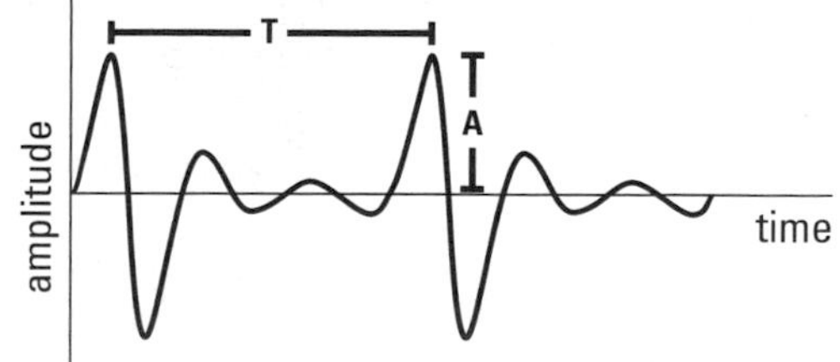

Figure 2.7 Two cycles of a trumpet waveform. Period and amplitude are indicated.

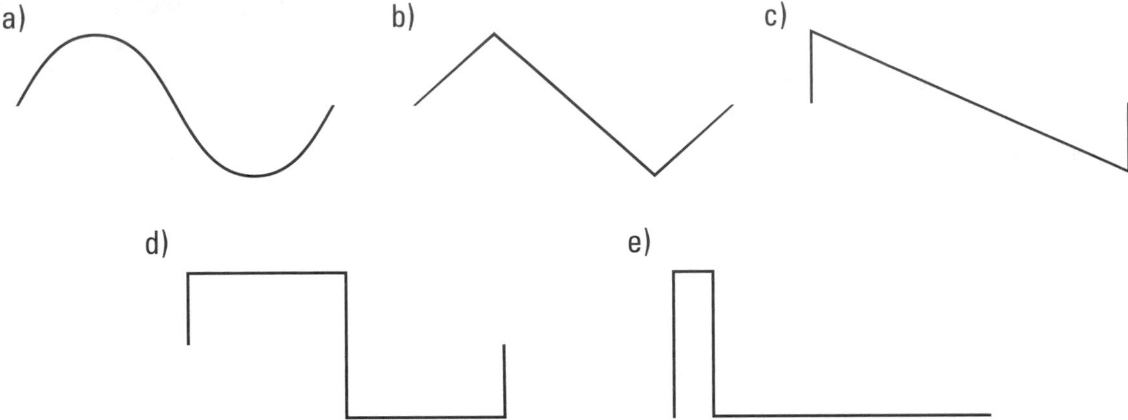

Figure 2.8 Basic waveforms: (a) sine, (b) triangle, (c) sawtooth, (d) square, and (e) pulse.

Another standard waveform is one that has no regular pattern at all: **noise**. Noise is, of course, all around us in the form of traffic sound, jackhammers, and ocean waves, but it is also very much present in musical sounds. Noise is an important sound component during the attack phase of almost all instruments, such as flutes, guitars, and violins, and is a prominent component in most percussion sounds, such as cymbals and snare drums.

Noise was also an important sound source in analog synthesizers and is used today in analog and analog-modeling synthesis. Noise can have a variety of qualities that are usually described using colors, such as **white noise** (very harsh and grating) and **pink noise** (still noisy, but more pleasant). Representative waveforms for white noise and pink noise are given in Figure 2.9. These are only representative, because noise does not have a predictable amplitude pattern.

ARTICULATION

The perceptual property **articulation** refers to how the loudness of the sound changes over time. For example, the loudness of an accented note rises more quickly from silence and to a higher maximum loudness than a note that is not accented. A note that is staccato will have a quick rise and a quick fall off at the end.

Articulation is not just limited to musical notes: the loudness of the non-musical sounds around us also changes over time. A thunderclap has a sudden jump in loudness

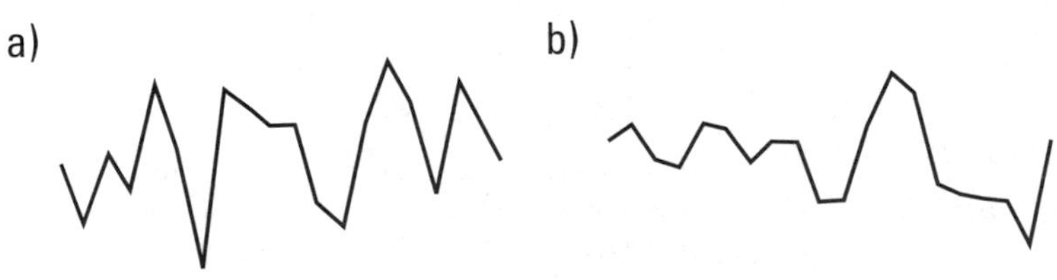

Figure 2.9 Amplitude plots of noise: (a) white noise, and (b) pink noise. The duration for each is about the same as the period of a 440 Hz periodic waveform.

followed by a long fall away. A motorcycle roaring toward you has a long, slow increase in loudness followed by a long slow decrease as it passes you and roars on. Each of these sounds has its own articulation.

When loudness was discussed above, it was related to the amplitude of the individual cycle of a waveform, whose duration is quite short: the period of A 440 (the tuning A) is just over 0.002 seconds (2 milliseconds) in length. The changes in loudness referred to as articulation are taking place over much larger spans of time. An eighth note at quarter equals 120 is 0.25 seconds long, over 100 times as long as the period of the individual waveform at A 440. In other words, you could fit over 100 cycles of a waveform whose frequency is 440 Hz into that eighth note. Even at the lowest frequency that humans can hear, 20 Hz, the period is 0.05 seconds; you could fit five of those cycles into that eighth note.

The physical property that is related to articulation is referred to as an **amplitude envelope** because it contains or envelops many repetitions of the waveform (see Figure 2.10). To represent the amplitude envelope, we will continue to use the waveform view (amplitude vs. time), but now we "zoom out" to look at changes in amplitude at the timescale of the note.

"Bowed or Blown" Envelopes

As with waveforms, every instrument's amplitude envelope is a little bit different and it changes depending on how the notes are articulated. However, we can make the distinction between instruments that are "bowed or blown" and instruments that are "struck or plucked." Instruments that are bowed, such as a violin, or blown, such as a trumpet, can be modeled by an **attack-decay-sustain-release envelope**, or **ADSR** (see Figure 2.11). This envelope also has its roots in analog synthesis and is widely found in various forms on hardware and software synthesizers.

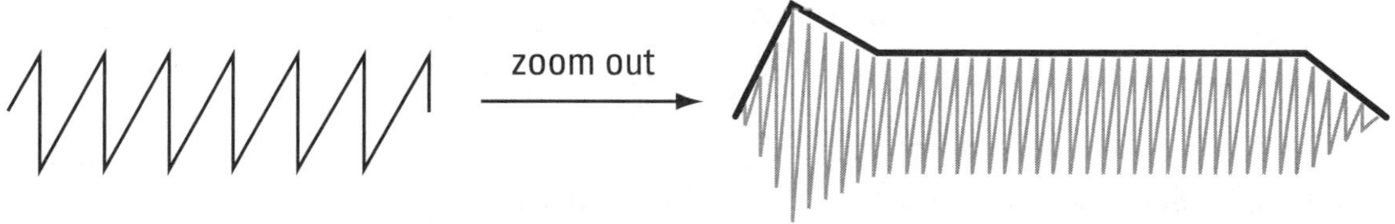

Figure 2.10 A "zoom out" from individual cycles of a waveform to see the amplitude envelope. Only the top of the envelope is usually shown because many waveforms are the same on the top and on the bottom. The frequency is extremely low—20 Hz—so you can still see the individual waveforms within the envelope.

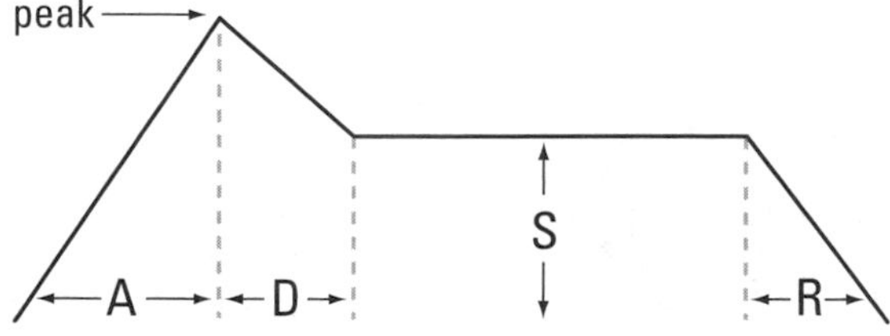

Figure 2.11 An attack-decay-sustain-release (ADSR) amplitude envelope characteristic of bowed or blown instruments.

The attack-decay segments roughly model the beginning of an instrument's note, where the amplitude rises from silence to an initial peak and then falls somewhat to a sustained level. The difference in amplitude between the peak and the sustain levels reflects the degree of initial accent on the note. A strong accent will have a greater peak and a greater fall off from the peak to the sustain level, whereas a note that is attacked more gently will have a lower peak and a smaller difference between those two levels.

The sustain segment is the most characteristic segment for this envelope model. Only instruments in which the performer continuously supplies energy to the instrument by blowing, bowing, or some other means, will have such a sustain segment. These instruments include flutes, clarinets, trumpets, trombones, violins, cellos, and organs. The release portion of the envelope reflects how the sound falls away from the sustain level to silence. In the envelope for a staccato note, this transition will happen very quickly (very small release time), but if a note is allowed to "ring into the hall," the transition will take longer (longer release time).

"Struck or Plucked" Envelopes

Instruments that are struck, such as a drum, or plucked, such as a guitar, can be modeled by an **attack-release envelope**, or **AR** (see Figure 2.12). With a struck or plucked instrument, the performer initially imparts energy to the instrument and then allows the vibrations to damp down naturally. Examples of this type of instrument include drums, cymbals, vibraphones, guitars, and pizzicato violins.

The duration of the attack segment reflects the force with the instrument is activated—how hard the string is plucked or the drum is hit. It can also reflect the materials that impart the initial impulse. A drum hit with a big fuzzy mallet will likely have a somewhat longer attack than one hit with a hard mallet, and a guitar string plucked with the flesh of the finger will have a somewhat longer attack than one plucked by a pick. The duration of the release portion of the envelope is related to how hard the instrument was struck or plucked: the harder the strike, the longer the release. The size and material of the vibrating object also impact the release: a longer string or larger drumhead is likely to vibrate longer than short strings and small drumheads.

Of course, these envelope models are not necessarily mutually exclusive. A brass or woodwind instrument can be played with a "bell-like tone" and individual notes in a rapid succession of plucked or struck tones will not seem to be significantly different in articulation from individual notes in a rapid succession of bowed or blown tones.

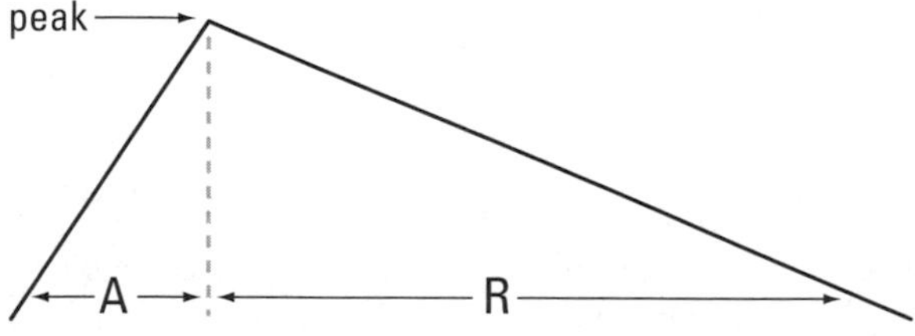

Figure 2.12 An attack-release (AR) amplitude envelope characteristic of struck or plucked instruments.

One significant difference is that struck or plucked tones cannot truly be "slurred" and will always have an attack of some kind, whereas the pitch of blown or bowed notes can be changed while the energy is still being imparted to the instrument, allowing the new note to "take over" the envelope of the previous note. In struck or plucked notes, the release of one note can overlap the attack of the next, but the envelope will still be articulated for each note. A good example of this is a pianist's legato technique.

Many hardware and software synthesizers do not have separate controls for these two envelope types. However, the AR envelope can be simulated with an ADSR envelope in which the sustain level is set to zero. The "release" of the AR will then either be determined by the ADSR's decay or a combination of the ADSR's decay and release lengths, depending on the length of the decay segment and how long the note is held down. Many synths also allow for more complex envelopes with more segments (multiple attacks, multiple decays) and/or different line shapes for the segments. Exponential line segments are common in many synths. Envelopes will be discussed later in the text in the section on "Sampling and Synthesis."

RHYTHM

Rhythm is a perceptual property whose physical counterpart is complex, because rhythm is really a meta-property consisting of multiple notes or sounds. In this, rhythm is similar to melody, which also consists of multiple notes. In addition, rhythm is often perceived in a hierarchical fashion with individual events combining to form beats and beats combining to form meter. There are also different levels of rhythm from a single sound that has its own internal rhythm, such as a "bubbling" synthetic sound, to a group of notes forming a rhythmic pattern, to a group of rhythmic patterns forming a phrase, and so on.

At the level of a group of notes, aspects of rhythm can be seen in the waveform view by identifying patterns in the attacks of the notes, referred to as **transient patterns**. The term transient is used because the attack-decay portions of an envelope form a short-term transition from no sound to the sustain or release of a sound. Some sound types, such as drums, form patterns that have strong transients and no sustain, whereas other sounds, such as slurred woodwinds, brass, or strings, form patterns in which the transient can be difficult to see. Viewing transients in the waveform view involves even more zooming out than with amplitude envelopes (see Figure 2.13).

The analysis of transients as a pattern of beats and bars is a standard feature in many recording programs and is generally referred to as **beat detection** (see Figure 2.14). This process allows you to manipulate audio as separate logical chunks, the same way you can manipulate notes. These audio beats can be "snapped" to bar and beats, thereby allowing the tempo of the audio to change in a naturally musical way. Many recording programs can extract "groove" information—variations in transient timing and amplitude—and then apply it to other audio files and to MIDI messages.

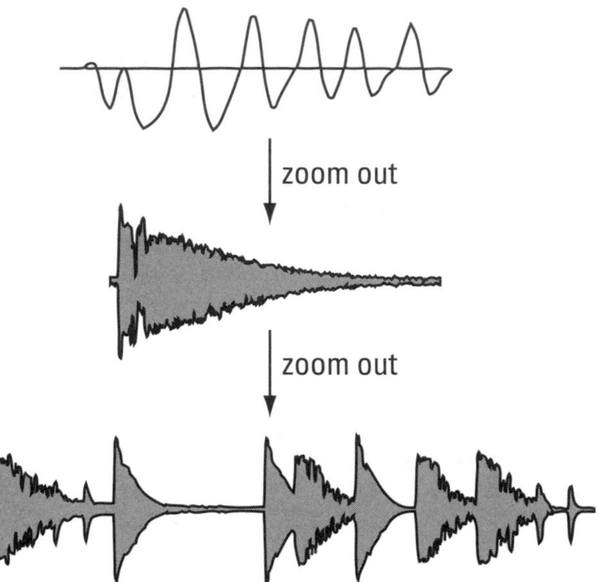

Figure 2.13 A "zoom out" from individual cycles of the waveform of a percussive sound to the amplitude envelope of that single event (AR envelope) to a pattern of percussive transients.

Figure 2.14 The results of transient analysis. The vertical lines indicate identified beats. (Courtesy of Digidesign, Inc.)

Sound that consists of clearly defined transients in a regular pattern is easier for humans and for software to parse into beats and bars. Legato passages in strings, winds, and brass where the notes are not re-attacked, and hence have fewer transients, are more difficult for software that relies solely on transient detection to parse. However, our perceptual system is more successful here because, in addition to transient detection, we can also bring pitch detection and other techniques to bear on the problem. Software that also utilizes such a multi-faceted approach will be similarly more successful.

SOUND PROPERTY SUMMARY

Table 2.6 summarizes the perceptual sound properties and their physical counterparts. This table will be further refined in the following chapter.

Table 2.6 **Perceptual and physical properties of sound**

Perceptual properties	*Physical properties*
Pitch	Frequency
Loudness	Amplitude
Timbre	Waveform
Articulation	Amplitude envelope
Rhythm	Transient patterns

REVIEW OF KEY TERMS

waveform view 17
pitch 18
frequency 19
hertz (Hz) 19
period 19
ultrasonic 20
infrasonic 21
Shepard tones 21
loudness 21
amplitude 21
decibels of sound pressure level (dB SPL) 22
threshold of hearing 22
threshold of pain 22
temporary threshold shift 23
timbre 25
waveform 25
sine wave 25
triangle wave 25
sawtooth wave 25
square wave 25
pulse wave 25
noise 26
white noise 26
pink noise 26
articulation 26
amplitude envelope 27
attack-decay-sustain-release envelope (ADSR) 27
attack-release envelope (AR) 28
rhythm 29
transient patterns 29
beat detection 29

CHAPTER 3

The Overtone Series and the Spectrum View

In the last chapter, we investigated a variety of sound properties using the waveform view of sound. That representation is useful in many instances, but it falls short with regard to timbre. The physical property related to timbre found in the waveform view is the waveform itself. However, the small collection of standard waveforms (sine, triangle, sawtooth, square, pulse) is of limited use when discussing real-world timbres. A better representation of sound for investigating timbre is the spectrum view. To understand the spectrum view it is useful first to consider the more familiar **overtone series**.

OVERTONE SERIES

Any note whose timbre is more complex than a sine wave contains the frequency that is heard as the pitch of the note—the **fundamental frequency**—*plus* some frequencies above that that are heard not as pitch but as the "color" or timbre of the sound. The overtone series represents the frequencies that are present in a single note, including the fundamental, and is usually shown using traditional music notation (see Figure 3.1; the fundamental is A).

This traditional notation is somewhat misleading, because it implies that every note is really a chord and that all the frequencies are distinct pitches. There is really just *one* pitch associated with an overtone series—the pitch related to the fundamental frequency. However, there are some useful features about the frequencies in the overtone series that can be seen with traditional notation. For example, for brass players, the fundamental frequencies of the pitches available at each valve fingering or slide position are found in the overtone series that is built on the lowest note at that fingering or position.

As implied by the name "overtone" series, the frequencies above the fundamental are often referred to as **overtones**. However, the terms **harmonics** and **partials** are also used. The distinction between these terms is subtle. The term overtone implies that those frequencies are over the fundamental, so the overtone series would consist of the

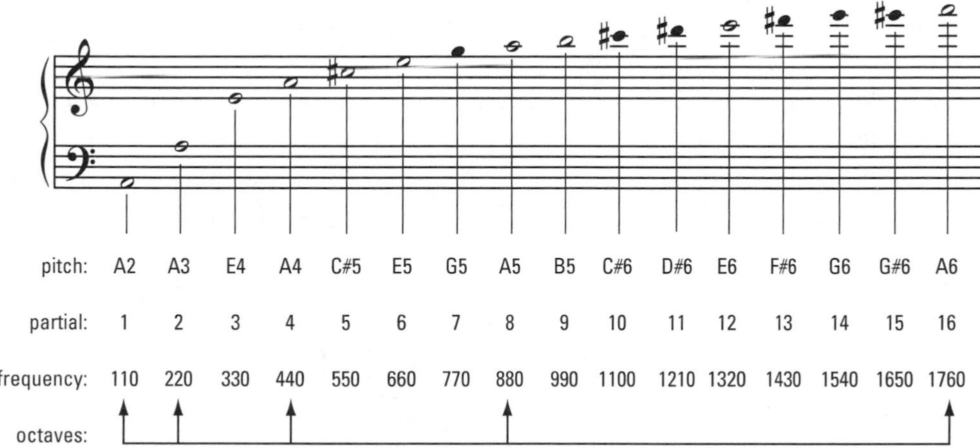

Figure 3.1 The first 16 partials of the overtone series built on A2. (From Holmes, 2008)

fundamental frequency plus the first overtone, the second overtone, etc. The term harmonic is somewhat ambiguous. It could refer to the frequencies above the fundamental: the fundamental, the first harmonic, the second harmonic, etc. However, it could include the fundamental as the first harmonic, so the series would be: first harmonic (fundamental), second harmonic, third harmonic, etc.

The term partial implies that all of the frequencies in a sound are all just parts of the sound: first partial (fundamental), second partial, third partial, etc. This term has some distinct advantages in that not every sound has frequencies that follow the overtone series, so the term partial could also be applied to frequencies of those sounds as well, whereas the terms overtone and harmonic only apply to sounds that follow the overtone series. Sounds whose frequencies follow the overtone series are referred to as "harmonic," and sounds whose frequencies do not follow the overtone series are referred to as "inharmonic"—not "enharmonic" as in G♯ and A♭, but "inharmonic" as in not harmonic. Most of the sounds in the world are inharmonic, but many of the sounds that we are concerned about in music, such as sounds made by many musical instruments, are harmonic. Inharmonic sounds will be discussed later in the chapter. This text will primarily use the term partial to describe frequencies in a spectrum and number them accordingly with the fundamental being the first partial (see Figure 3.1).

To see what the relationships are between the frequencies in the overtone series, we need to find some point of reference in this notational representation. Since this overtone series is based on A, it includes the familiar tuning A as the fourth partial, which has a frequency of 440 Hz. The only other fact we need to know is that octaves have a frequency relationship of 2 to 1. Armed with that information, we can see that the second partial, which is an octave below the fourth partial, would have a frequency of $\frac{1}{2} \times 440 = 220$. Similarly, the first partial is an octave below the second, giving it a frequency of 110, and the eighth partial is an octave above the fourth partial, giving it a frequency of 2 × 440 = 880. Table 3.1 shows the relationships derived so far (note that for the pitch-octave notation, middle C is C4).

From Table 3.1, you can see that each partial's frequency is the *partial number multiplied by the fundamental frequency*. Applying this principle to the other partials in this overtone series, you get the frequencies given in Table 3.2. If the fundamental is more generically given as some frequency *f*, then the partial frequencies are 2*f*, 3*f*, 4*f*, 5*f*, 6*f*, 7*f*, 8*f*, and so on.

Table 3.2 shows an additional drawback to representing the overtones series in traditional notation. The "G5" (remember it's a frequency, not a note) in the table has a frequency of 770 Hz. If you were to play G5 on a piano, the frequency would be 783.99 Hz (see Figure 3.4 on page 40). This needn't be seen as too troubling a discrepancy, because the G5 played on the piano is a note in its own right with its own overtone series, and the "G5" that is part of the overtone series built on the fundamental A2 is part of the timbre of that sound. Nevertheless, the frequency relationships found in the overtone series have inspired many different approaches to tuning.

Table 3.1 **Frequency relationships for overtone series on A (incomplete)**

Partial #	*"Note"*	*Frequency*
1 (fundamental)	A2	110
2	A3	220
4	A4	440
8	A5	880

Table 3.2 **Frequency relationships for overtone series on A**

Partial #	*"Note"*	*Frequency*
1 (fundamental)	A2	110
2	A3	220
3	E4	330
4	A4	440
5	C♯5	550
6	E5	660
7	G5	770
8	A5	880
9	B5	990
10	C♯6	1100
11	D♯6	1210
12	E6	1320
13	F♯6	1430
14	G6	1540
15	D♯6	1650
16	A6	1760
. . .	. . .	. . .

Tuning and Temperament

To derive the relationships between partial number and frequency above, we started with the fact that the ratio of two frequencies an octave apart is 2 to 1, often notated as 2:1. If we continue to look at the overtone series in traditional notation, it is possible to derive ideal ratios for other intervals as well. A perfect fifth is present in the overtone series as the relationship of partial 3 to partial 2, giving a 3:2 ratio. A perfect fourth is found between partial 4 and partial 3, giving a 4:3 ratio. A major third is found between partial 5 and partial 4, giving a 5:4 ratio, and a minor third is found between partial number 6 and partial number 5, giving a 6:5 ratio. It is important to note that these are *ideal* relationships. In practice they can present some difficulties.

One such difficulty is that it is possible to leap to the same note by different intervals and end up with contradictory frequencies. As a classic example of this, if you start with one note and go up repeatedly by a perfect fifth (proceeding through the circle of fifths) until you reach the beginning note several octaves higher, and then do the same by octaves, you reach different frequencies. Starting on C1, the lowest C on the piano (with C4 being middle C), you can get back to the pitch C by going up twelve fifths, and to that same C by going up seven octaves. This is C8, the highest C on the piano.

Using the interval ratio derived from the overtone series for a fifth of 3:2, the frequency for each successive fifth is generated by multiplying the frequency of the previous note by 3/2. The results of this are shown in Table 3.3, where the frequency of C1 is given as f. Using the interval ratios for an octave of 2:1, multiplying by 2 generates the frequency for each successive octave. The results of this are shown in Table 3.4.

You might expect, because both series of intervals arrive on the same note, that $(3/2)^{12}f$ and 2^7f would be the same. However:

$$(3/2)^{12}f = 129.75f$$

and

$$2^7f = 128f$$

Table 3.3 **Going up from C1 to C8 by fifths**

C1	*G1*	*D2*	*A2*	*E3*	*B3*	*F♯4*	*C♯5*	*G♯5*	*D♯6*	*A♯6*	*F7*	*C8*
f	$3/2f$	$(3/2)^2f$	$(3/2)^3f$	$(3/2)^4f$	$(3/2)^5f$	$(3/2)^6f$	$(3/2)^7f$	$(3/2)^8f$	$(3/2)^9f$	$(3/2)^{10}f$	$(3/2)^{11}f$	$(3/2)^{12}f$

Table 3.4 **Going up from C1 to C8 by octaves**

C1	*C2*	*C3*	*C4*	*C5*	*C6*	*C7*	*C8*
f	$2f$	2^2f	2^3f	2^4f	2^5f	2^6f	2^7f

The frequency of C1 is 32.7, so these two formulas give the frequency of C8 as:

129.75 × 32.70 = 4,243.24 Hz (going up by fifths)

and

128 × 32.70 = 4,186.01 Hz (going up by octaves)

If you look at Figure 2.4 in the previous chapter (page 20), you can see that going up by octaves gives you the frequency for C8 on the piano. Going up by fifths causes you to "overshoot" that frequency. The difference between going up by fifths and going up by octaves generates what's known as the **Pythagorean comma**.

There are a number of other discrepancies to be found by going from one note to another by different intervals, and overtone series built on different fundamentals can generate different frequencies for what is nominally the same note. What these and other discrepancies point to is that the ideal interval relationships derived from the overtone series by themselves don't form a solid basis for a musical system. However, in isolation, intervals formed from the ideal ratios are said to sound more pure than any of the compromise tuning systems that have been developed. A variety of such compromise systems have been proposed and used over the centuries, including Pythagorean tuning, meantone intonation, just intonation, and **equal temperament**.

In equal temperament, the ratio between every semitone is exactly the same, so each interval, regardless of the starting note, is also exactly the same. Essentially, all intervals, with the exception of the octave, are slightly "wrong" in equal temperament, but it allows music using this tuning system to modulate to any key and still have intervals the same size as the original key. Johann Sebastian Bach's famous *The Well-Tempered Clavier*, which includes preludes and fugues in all 24 major and minor keys, shows the advantage of such a tuning system, though well-tempered and equal-tempered tunings are slightly different. Table 3.5 shows some ideal interval ratios and the approximate equal-tempered ratios.

Table 3.5 **Equal-tempered and ideal interval ratios**

Interval	*Ideal ratio*	*Equal-tempered ratio*	*Equal-tempered "error"*
Major second	9:8 = 1.125:1	1.122:1	Flat
Minor third	6:5 = 1.2:1	1.189:1	Flat
Major third	5:4 = 1.25:1	1.26:1	Sharp
Fourth	4:3 = 1.333:1	1.335:1	Slightly sharp
Fifth	3:2 = 1.5:1	1.498:1	Slightly flat
Minor sixth	8:5 = 1.6:1	1.587:1	Flat
Major sixth	5:3 = 1.667:1	1.681:1	Sharp
Major seventh	15:8 = 1.875:1	1.888:1	Sharp
Octave	2:1	2:1	None

The last column in Table 3.5 shows the general error for each interval in equal-tempered tuning relative to the ideal ratios. In performance, many performers and conductors will adjust their tuning of chords to partially compensate for this error. For example, a performer holding the major third of a chord will often play it slightly flat relative to equal-tempered tuning to more closely approximate the pure intervals generated by the ideal ratios.

This brief discussion has really only scratched the surface of tuning issues, both historical and contemporary. There are many books and websites devoted to various tuning systems, particularly just intonation, and a number of contemporary composers have utilized various systems in their works. In addition, many hardware and software synthesizers contain resources for variable tuning.

THE SPECTRUM

The timbre of a note is determined in part by *which* frequencies are present in a sound and *how much* of them are present (their relative amplitudes). The notation representation of the overtone series has no way to show amplitude information, and shows frequency information inadequately given that the partial frequencies often don't match the equal-tempered pitches shown. To discuss timbre more generally, it is necessary to abandon traditional music notation altogether and use the **spectrum view** of sound.

The spectrum view represents sound as a graph of frequency vs. amplitude, as opposed to the waveform view that is a graph of time vs. amplitude. The spectrum view for the overtone series starting on A2 is given in Figure 3.2. The amplitudes of the frequency components are from a spectrum analysis of a trombone note.

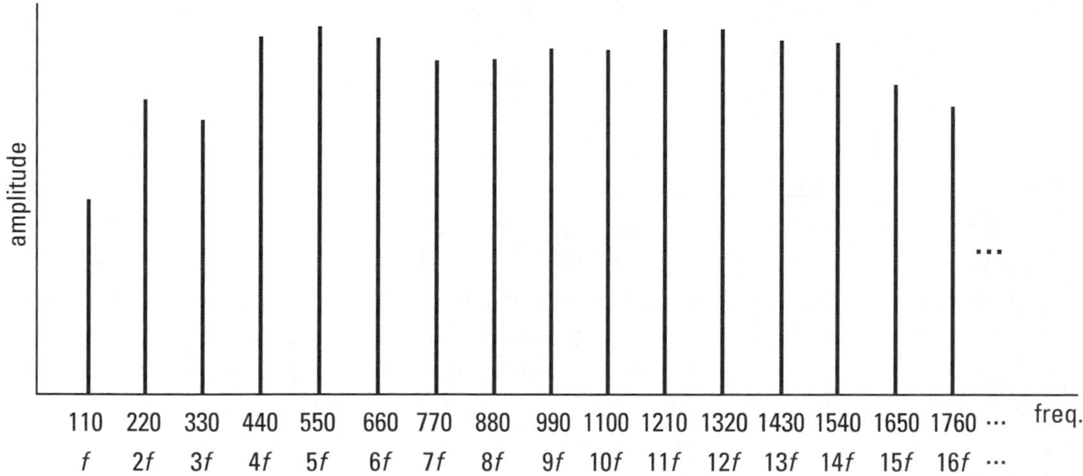

Figure 3.2 The spectrum view of sound with frequency on the *x*-axis and amplitude on the *y*-axis. The fundamental is A2 (110 Hz) and 16 total partials are shown, with the ellipses indicating that the partials continue. The relative amplitudes of the partials are based on a recording of a trombone. The frequency data is the same as in Figure 3.1 and Table 3.2.

There exist a number of standalone programs and plug-ins for sequencer/DAWs that perform frequency analysis of live audio or of an audio file. The amplitude axis of this view differs from the amplitude axis of the waveform view in that the amplitudes in the spectrum view show the amplitude of each individual partial, whereas the amplitude in the waveform view is the overall amplitude of the sound. The overall amplitude in the spectrum view comes from a complex interaction between the amplitudes of each individual partial—it's not as simple as just adding them up.

It's also important to note that, in this spectrum view, there is no time axis as there is in the waveform view. To see how a spectrum changes over the course of a note or sound event—and it can change quite a bit—you would have to look at successive spectrum views that would provide a time-lapse view of the spectrum. There are variations on the spectrum view that allow three dimensions to be shown at once: frequency, amplitude, and time. One is the **spectrogram view**, which gives time vs. frequency and then shows the amplitude by the intensity of the color (see Figure 3.3).

Another of these spectrum view variations is the **waterfall spectrum**, which typically shows frequency vs. amplitude with time coming out of or into the screen in a simulated 3-D effect. There is a downward visual component to this time axis that gives it the name "waterfall."

Spectra of Basic Waveforms and Fourier's Theorem

In the previous chapter, you were introduced to a collection of basic waveforms that are largely derived from analog synthesis. To understand these basic waveforms in some more detail, we can look at their spectra. (See the book's website for audio of these examples.)

The **sine wave** is the simplest possible waveform, having only one partial: the fundamental (see Figure 3.4a). By itself, the sine wave has a pure, pale timbre that can be spooky in the right situation. The **triangle wave** contains only the odd partials (1, 3, 5, 7, etc.) but at very low amplitudes after the fundamental, so it is a little bit brighter than the sine wave and more suitable as the basis of a synthetic timbre (see Figure 3.4b). The amplitudes of the partials in a triangle wave are inversely proportional to the square of the partial number, so the third partial has a relative amplitude of 1/9, the fifth partial an amplitude of 1/25, and so on.

The **square wave** also contains only the odd partials, but in greater proportion than the triangle wave, so it sounds brighter than the triangle wave (see Figure 3.4c). The amplitudes of the partials in a square wave are inversely proportional to the partial number, so the third partial has an amplitude of 1/3, the fifth partial an amplitude of 1/5, and so on. In the octave below middle C it can sound quite a bit like a clarinet, which also has very little energy in the even partials in that register. A guitar can also produce a tone like this by plucking an open string at the twelfth fret. Timbres built from a square wave can be quite penetrating.

The **sawtooth wave** contains both even and odd partials (see Figure 3.4d). The amplitudes of the partials in a sawtooth wave are inversely proportional to the partial number, so the second partial has an amplitude of 1/2, the third partial an amplitude

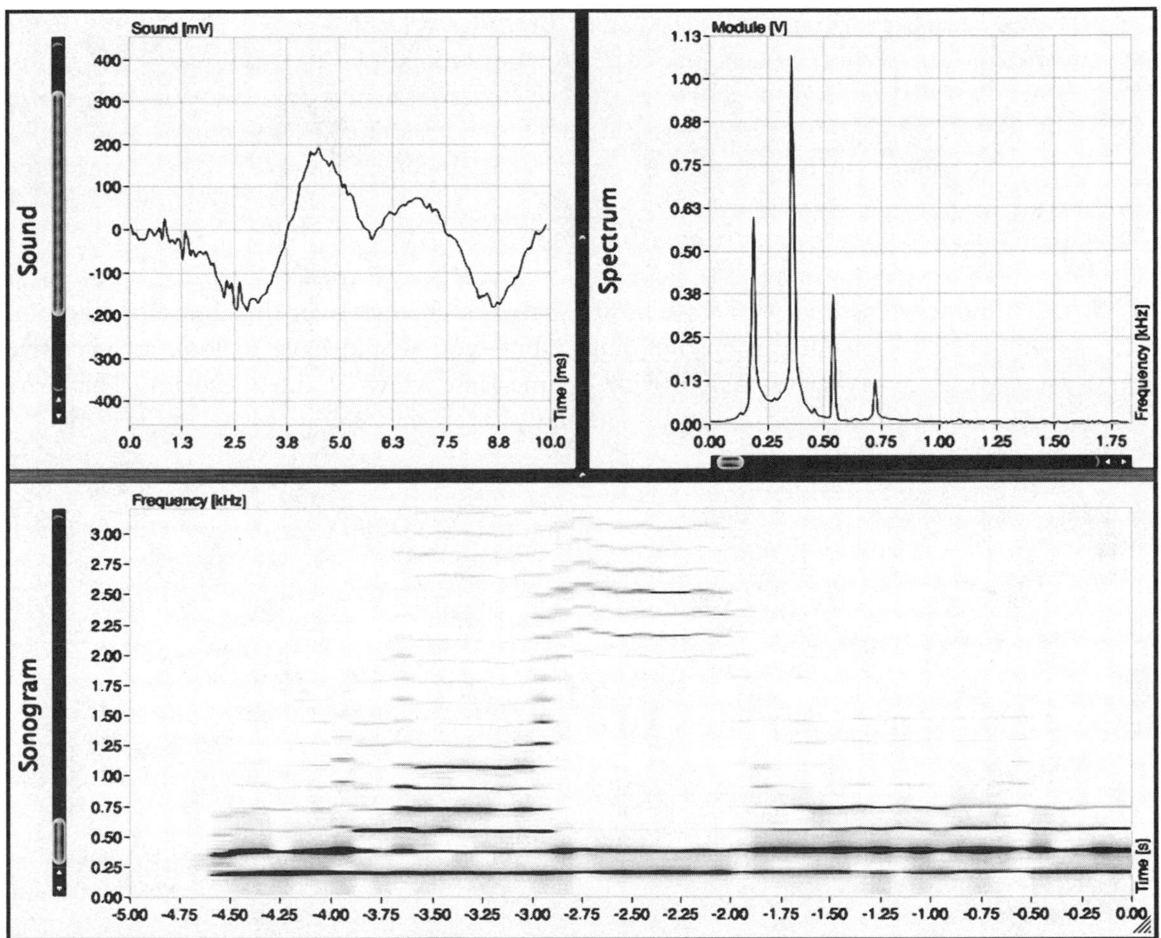

Figure 3.3 Three different views of a voice saying "oo-ah-ee-oh" on the same pitch. Upper left: waveform view frozen on "oh." Upper right: spectrum view frozen on "oh." Bottom: spectrogram view (also called the sonogram view) with time shown horizontally, frequency shown vertically, and amplitude shown by the intensity of the line. All four vowels are shown left to right. The different amplitudes of the partials for each vowel are shown clearly.

of 1/3, the fourth an amplitude of 1/4, and so on. As a result, the sawtooth wave is bright and nasal, which allows it to penetrate well when combined with other timbres. The sawtooth is one of the most common waveforms used for electronic timbres, particularly those meant to mimic analog synthesizer timbres.

Since the spectrum of a sine wave has only one partial, its fundamental, it is the most basic of the waveforms. In fact, each partial in the spectra of the other basic waveforms can be thought of as a separate sine wave. This implies that each of these spectra can be thought of as a sum of sine waves whose frequencies match the partial frequencies and whose amplitudes match the partial amplitudes. Figure 3.5 shows several sine waves adding together to form the beginnings of a sawtooth waveform. Many more partials would need to be added to create the sawtooth's characteristic shape.

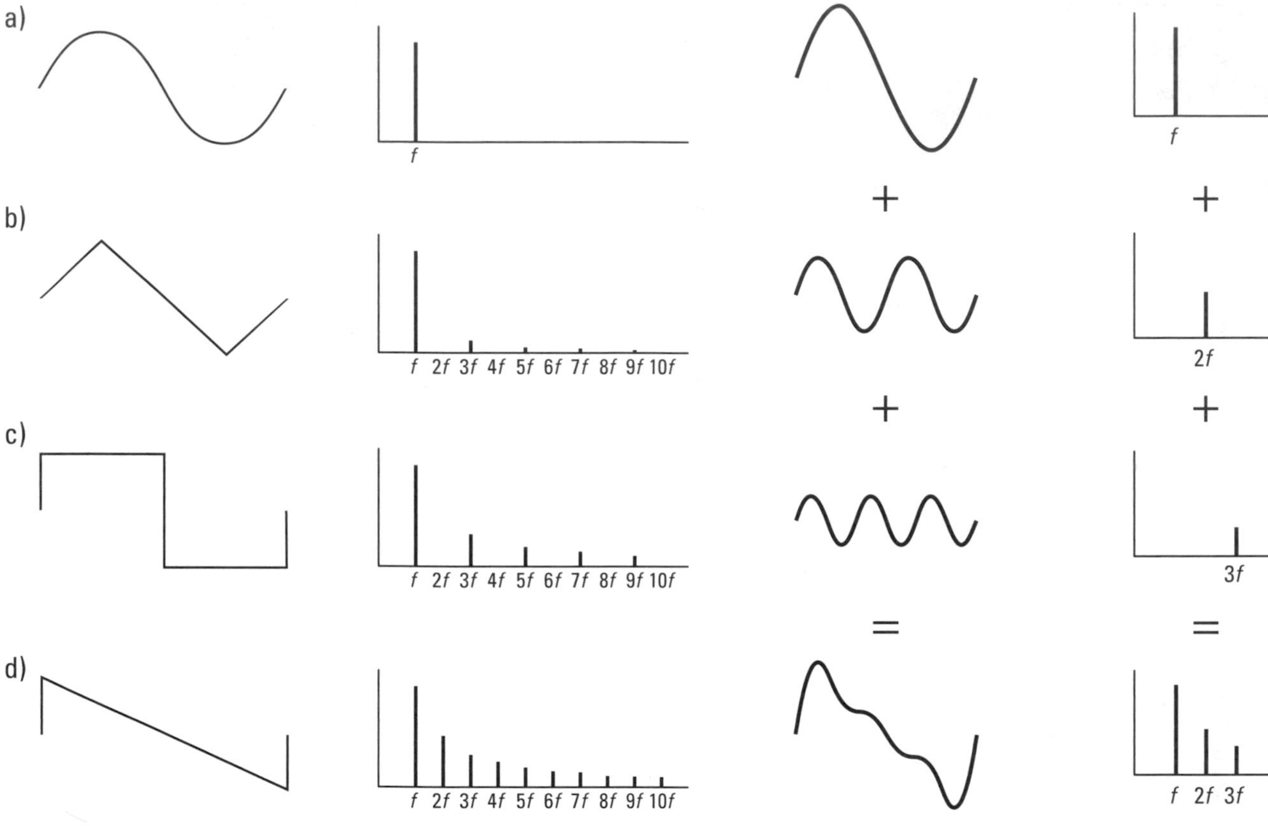

Figure 3.4 Basic waveforms and their spectra: (a) sine wave, (b) triangle wave, (c) square wave, and (d) sawtooth wave.

Figure 3.5 Waveform and spectrum view of three sine waves adding together to form a more complex waveform. If enough partials are added like this, a sawtooth wave will be formed.

The idea that a complex spectrum can be expressed as a sum of sine waves of various frequencies and amplitudes lies at the heart of **Fourier's theorem**. Fourier's theorem says that any periodic waveform can be expressed as a sum of sine waves. Periodic waveforms follow the overtone series, which means that most "musical" sounds made by winds, brass, strings, pianos, voices, and some percussion instruments all have spectra that can be thought of as sums of sine waves. Fourier's theorem is not only useful in the analysis of instrument spectra, but can also be used to synthesize new sounds through a technique known as additive synthesis, which is also referred to as Fourier synthesis. This method of synthesis along with a variety of others will be discussed later in the text in the chapter on synthesis methods.

Harmonic and Inharmonic Spectra

Thus far, we've been assuming that all sounds have partials that follow the overtone series. The spectra for those sounds are termed **harmonic spectra**. Despite the fact that sounds with harmonic spectra are only a small subset of all the possible sounds, it just so happens that many of the musical sounds we care about are part of this subset, including those made by brass, woodwinds, strings, pianos, voices, and certain percussion instruments.

The rest of the sounds in the world have partials that do *not* follow the overtone series and thus have **inharmonic spectra**. These sounds include everyday sounds such as ocean waves, car engines, and jackhammers, but there are also a number of musical instruments that have inharmonic spectra, such as bells and some kinds of percussion.

It is worth noting that even sounds whose spectra are essentially harmonic have partials that deviate from the precise ratios. The deviations in the piano spectrum that result in "stretched" octaves are perhaps the most famous example of this. In general real pipes, strings, and reeds have subtle physical characteristics that cause the resultant spectrum to deviate slightly from the pure overtone series. This deviation is sometimes termed **inharmonicity**. Nevertheless, they are still heard as being largely harmonic and belong in a different category from distinctly inharmonic sounds.

Figure 3.6 shows the spectrum of a bell sound. Notice that, while there are distinct partials, they do not form an overtone series of *f*, 2*f*, 3*f*, 4*f*, 5*f*, and so on. As a result, this spectrum is deemed inharmonic.

Noise Spectra

Noise does not have a harmonic spectrum, nor does it have distinct partials. Instead, the spectra of various kinds of noise are better conceived as a distribution of energy among bands of frequencies. **White noise**, for example, has a spectrum whose energy is distributed evenly among all the frequencies. This can be described as *equal energy in equal frequency bands*, so white noise will have the same amount of energy between 100 Hz and 200 Hz as between 200 Hz and 300 Hz, or 1,000 Hz and 1,100 Hz.

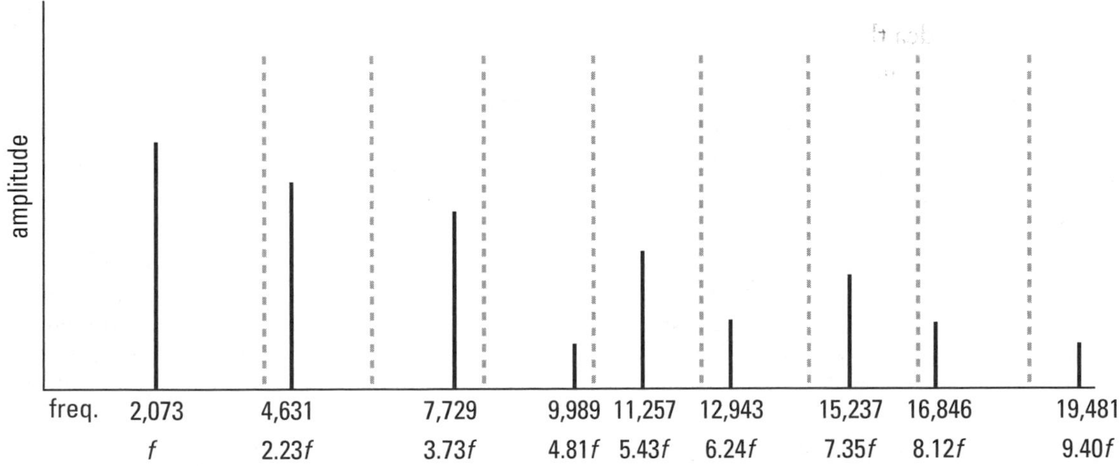

Figure 3.6 Inharmonic spectrum of a small bell. Note that the partials are not whole number multiples of the fundamental. Dashed lines indicate the positions of whole number multiples of the fundamental.

Pink noise, on the other hand, has *equal energy in each octave*, so there will be the same amount of energy between 100 Hz and 200 Hz as between 200 Hz and 400 Hz, or between 1,000 Hz and 2,000 Hz. Since we perceive these frequency bands as being of equal musical size (octaves), pink noise seems more evenly distributed and somewhat more pleasant to our ears. We perceive white noise as being louder at higher frequencies because the absolute size in hertz of musical intervals (thirds, fifths, octaves, etc.) gets larger as they go up in frequency. As a result, the white noise distribution contains more energy in higher octaves than in lower octaves. Figure 3.7 shows the frequency distributions of white noise (3.7a) and pink noise (3.7b).

MODIFYING TIMBRE

At first, the spectrum view may seem a bit esoteric, particularly because the waveform view of sound is so pervasive in audio recording programs. However, we actually have quite a bit of experience in manipulating timbre through the tone or **equalization** (**EQ**) controls of our home and car stereos.

Often stereos will have bass and treble controls, or bass, midrange, and treble controls. For each of these frequency bands, you can **cut** them (reduce the amplitude), leave them alone (flat), or **boost** them (increase the amplitude). Definitions of these ranges vary widely from device to device, but bass is roughly 20 to 200 Hz, midrange is roughly 200 to 5,000 Hz, and treble range is roughly 5,000 to 20,000 Hz. Many EQs have more than three bands and will often split the midrange up into two or three parts. Many manufacturers have their own definitions of these frequency bands.

Many stereos, other sound playback devices, and pieces of sound software have **graphic equalizers** that can adjust more than just two or three frequency bands. In consumer products graphic equalizers usually have presets that allow you to choose an appropriate setting for boosting and cutting the various frequency bands based on the type of music you're listening to. Figure 3.8 shows various settings for the graphic EQ in Apple's iTunes software. The "Hip-Hop" setting (3.8a) fittingly emphasizes the bass while the "Spoken Word" setting (3.8b) emphasizes the upper midrange, which improves the intelligibility of speech, particularly in a noisy setting.

More detailed discussions of EQ and timbre modification in general will be carried out later in the text in Chapter 6, "Digital Audio Software," and in the section on "Synthesis and Sampling."

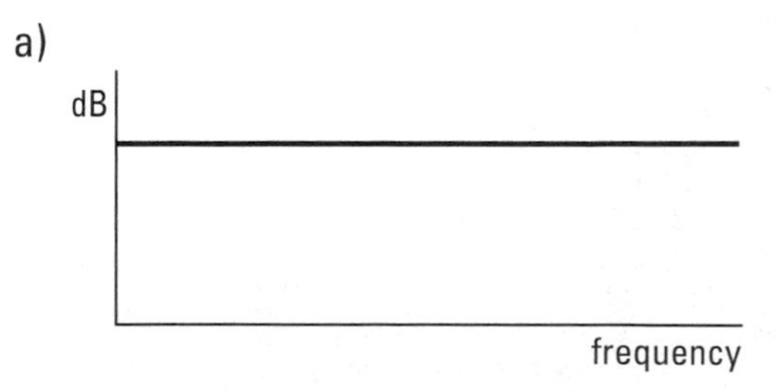

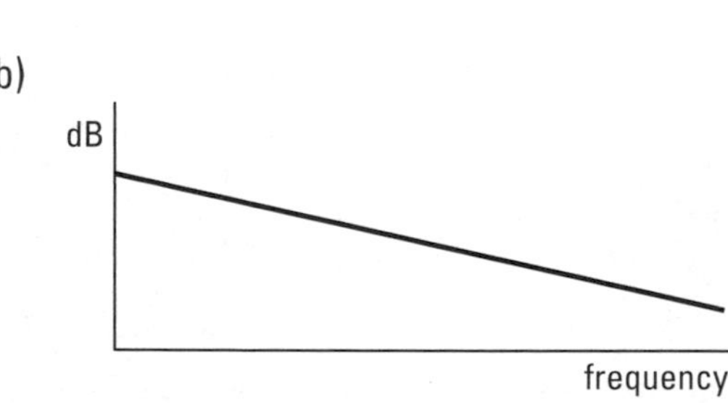

Figure 3.7 Two noise spectra shown as distributions of energy across the audible frequency range: (a) white noise, and (b) pink noise.

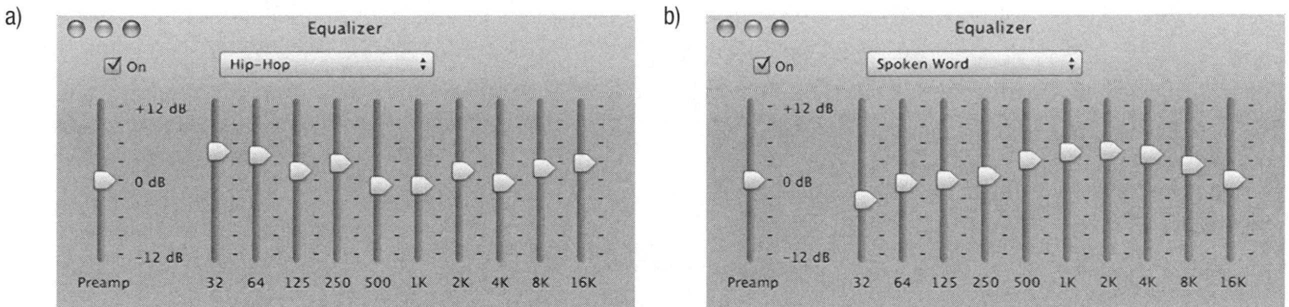

Figure 3.8 (a) The Hip-Hop setting of the graphic equalizer from Apple's iTunes; and (b) the Spoken Word setting of the graphic equalizer from Apple's iTunes. (Screenshots reprinted with permission from Apple Inc.)

REVISED SOUND PROPERTY SUMMARY

Table 3.6 is a slight revision of Table 2.6 from the previous chapter, and reflects the information presented in this chapter.

Table 3.6 **Revised perceptual and physical properties of sound**

Perceptual properties	*Physical properties*
Pitch	Fundamental frequency
Loudness	Amplitude
Timbre	Waveform *and* spectrum
Articulation	Amplitude envelope
Rhythm	Transient patterns

REVIEW OF KEY TERMS

- overtone series 32
- fundamental frequency 32
- overtones 32
- harmonics 32
- partials 32
- Pythagorean comma 36
- equal temperament 36
- spectrum view 37
- spectrogram view 38
- waterfall spectrum 38
- sine wave 38
- triangle wave 38
- square wave 38
- sawtooth wave 38
- Fourier's theorem 40
- harmonic spectra 40
- inharmonic spectra 41
- inharmonicity 41
- white noise 41
- pink noise 42
- equalization (EQ) 42
- cut 42
- boost 42
- graphic equalizers 42

Section I
Further Reading

An excellent introduction to sound is J.R. Pierce's *The science of musical sound* (1992). As a director at Bell Labs in the 1950s, Pierce championed the early computer music research there. This book is thorough and enjoyable, with just enough math to get the point across, but not so much that it is intimidating. It's out of print now, but widely available in libraries and used book websites. Ian Johnston's *Measured tones: The interplay of physics and music* (3rd ed., 2009) is written by a physicist, but for a lay audience. *Measured tones* weaves together physics, music, and the history of music into an engaging and informative narrative. A number of "interludes" detail the physical mechanisms of various instruments and the voice.

Another book for a non-specialized audience is Stuart Isacoff's *Temperament: The idea that solved music's greatest riddle* (2001). Isacoff's book explores tuning and temperament in a historical context. For those looking for a bit more math, Gareth Loy's *Musimathics: The mathematical foundations of music* (2006) explores the math behind a variety of topics, including the physical properties of sound, tuning and temperament, acoustics, and psychoacoustics. Despite the potentially daunting title, the material is carefully presented without much higher math.

In the realm of what your ears and your brain do with sound—perception and cognition, Perry Cook's *Music, cognition, and computerized sound* (1999) delves into issues ranging from pitch perception to consonance to musical memory. Daniel Levitin's *This is your brain on music: The science of a human obsession* (2006) is a book for non-specialists that explores a variety of concepts in music cognition in an engaging fashion. *An introduction to the psychology of hearing* by Brian C.J. Moore (5th ed., 2003) is a textbook in psychoacoustics that explores perception in depth and includes a section on the psychoacoustics of hi-fi sound reproduction and concert hall acoustics.

Section I
Suggested Activities

This chapter provides some suggested activities relating to sound. These activities utilize the free audio editor Audacity, which can be found at: **http://audacity.sourceforge.net/**.

Audacity is available for Windows, Mac OS, and Linux/Unix. The version referred to here is version 1.37beta, though these features will probably be available in the current version as well.

You will have to learn the basics of Audacity to complete these activities. The documentation is available on the website given above. Fortunately, Audacity is a relatively straightforward program. In the activities below, menu items will be listed as: menu title→menu item→submenu item, etc. For example, to create a new Audacity project, you would choose File→New, meaning you should click on the "File" menu and choose the "New" menu item.

You can use your own recording program for these activities, though most of the activities rely on Audacity's sound generation features and spectrum analysis option. You can substitute sound generated by softsynths for the generated waveforms described here.

1. EXPLORE BASIC WAVEFORMS

(a) Launch Audacity and choose File→New. Save this project to your disk so you can use it for later activities below.

(b) Generate 2 seconds of a sine wave, a square wave, and a sawtooth wave on separate tracks. The process is as follows:

- Create a new audio track (Tracks→Add New→Audio Track).
- Choose Generate→Tone . . ., and select "sine wave" from the pop-up menu.
- In the dialog box, choose a desired frequency (for example, 440 Hz), amplitude (1.0 is maximum, choose something like 0.5), and duration.
- Repeat these steps for square wave and sawtooth wave.

(c) Adjust the volume on your computer so it is not very loud; you can always turn it up later. Listen to each of them in turn by clicking on the "solo" button for the track you want to hear.
(d) Click on the zoom tool and zoom in until you can see the actual waveforms. What is their approximate period? Does it match the expected period given the frequency you entered above? (remember: $f = 1/T$ and $T = 1/f$).

2. EXPLORE NOISE

(a) Choose File→New to create a new Audacity project. Save this project to your disk so you can use it for later activities below.
(b) Generate 2 seconds of various kinds of noise on separate tracks in the same manner as above.
(c) Adjust the volume of your computer so it is not very loud; you can always turn it up later. Listen to each of them in turn by clicking on the "solo" button for the track you want to hear.
(d) Click on the zoom tool and zoom in until you can see the "waveform." How do these differ from the waveforms in step 1(d)? How do they differ from each other?

3. EXPLORE PLUCK AND DRUM WAVEFORMS

(a) Choose File→New to create a new Audacity project. Save this project to your disk so you can use it for later activities below.
(b) Generate 4 seconds of the "pluck" (set fade out to "gradual") and "Risset drum" sounds on separate tracks in the same manner as before.
(c) Adjust the volume of your computer so it is not very loud; you can always turn it up later. Listen to each of them in turn by clicking on the "solo" button for the track you want to hear.
(d) Click on the zoom tool and zoom in until you can see the waveform. How do these differ from the waveforms in steps 1(d) and 2(d)? How do they differ from each other?
(e) Scroll to the beginning and look at the waveforms and then scroll later in the tone and look at them again. In what two ways are they different?
(f) To make it easier to compare beginning and ending waveforms, you can take a screenshot at the beginning and a screenshot at the end of the tone. In Mac OS X, use shift-command-4 and then drag around the area. In Windows Vista, use the Snipping Tool program.
(g) Zoom out and notice the shape of the amplitude envelopes for pluck and drum. Are they ADSR or AR?

4. EXPLORE YOUR OWN RECORDED AUDIO

(a) Choose File→New to create a new Audacity project. Save this project to your disk so you can use it for later activities below.
(b) Hit the record button and record yourself playing or singing some notes using the built-in mic on your computer (or another mic if you have one). Try to use different articulations and different tone qualities (timbres) when you sing or play.
(c) Click on the zoom tool and zoom in until you can see the waveform for one of the notes. How does this differ from the waveforms from steps 1(d), 2(d), and 3(d)? How do the waveforms for the recorded notes differ from each other?
(d) Scroll to various parts of the notes. How do the waveforms differ at different points in each note?
(e) To make it easier to compare waveforms for various tone qualities and articulations, you can take a screenshot at the beginning and a screenshot at the end. In Mac OS X, use shift-command-4 and then drag around the area. In Windows Vista, use the Snipping Tool program.
(f) Zoom out and notice the shape of the amplitude envelopes for the different articulations. Are they ADSR or AR? How do the envelopes differ from the ideal ADSR or AR envelopes described on pages 27–29?

5. EXPLORE SPECTRA

(a) Choose project 1 (basic waveforms) above, select part of one of the tracks with the selection tool, and choose Analyze→Plot Spectrum. You may need to adjust some of the settings such as the size (512 or 1024 should do) to make the partials clear.
(b) Hold your mouse over the peaks to see the frequencies. Do they follow the overtone series?
(c) Listen to each waveform by using the "solo" button for that track while looking at its spectrum to "see" the differences you are hearing.
(d) Repeat this for project 2 (noise) above. Notice the broad distribution of energy for each of the types of noise and how they differ from each other at the higher frequencies.
(e) Repeat this for project 3 (pluck and drum) above. Look at the spectrum for different parts of each note (closer to the attack and closer to the tail). Use screenshots to compare if necessary. How are they different?
(f) Repeat this for project 4 (your own audio) above. How is the spectrum different for each tone quality? How does the spectrum change for different parts of a note? Use screenshots to compare if necessary.

6. EXPLORE EQUALIZATION

(a) Choose project 4 (your own audio), select audio on a track or an entire track and choose Edit→Duplicate. This will create a new track with the same audio as the source track.
(b) Select a note in the duplicated track and choose Effect→Equalization.
(c) In the dialog box, select "Graphic EQ" and then change the sliders to emphasize or de-emphasize parts of the spectrum. Click OK to apply the EQ.
(d) Select part of the modified audio and select Analyze→Plot Spectrum. Do the same for the unmodified audio. How do the two spectra now differ? Use screenshots to compare if necessary.

7. EXPLORE TEMPERED TUNING

(a) Choose File→New to create a new Audacity project. Save this project to your disk.
(b) Create a track and use Generate→Tone. . . to create 10 seconds of a sawtooth wave with a frequency of 440 Hz and an amplitude of 0.3.
(c) Create another track and use Generate→Tone. . . to create 5 seconds of a sawtooth wave with a frequency of 660 Hz and an amplitude of 0.3.
(d) Play these two tracks to hear a perfect fifth with an ideal 3:2 frequency ratio.
(e) Click in the second track at the end of the 660 Hz tone, and use Generate→Tone . . . to create 5 seconds of a sawtooth wave with a frequency of 659.255 Hz and an amplitude of 0.3. This is the frequency of an equal-tempered fifth.
(f) Play these two tracks to hear an ideal perfect fifth for 5 seconds and then an equal-tempered perfect fifth for 5 seconds. How do they sound different?
(g) Create a third track and use Generate→Tone. . . to create 5 seconds of a sawtooth wave with a frequency of 550 Hz. This is the ideal 5:4 ratio major third.
(h) Click at the end of that 5 seconds of 550 Hz and use Generate→Tone. . . to create 5 seconds of a sawtooth wave with a frequency of 554.365 Hz. This is the equal-tempered major third.
(i) Mute the second track and play the first and third tracks back to hear an ideal major third for 5 seconds followed by an equal-tempered major third for 5 seconds. How do they sound different?
(j) Un-mute the second track and play all three to hear 5 seconds of a triad tuned to ideal ratios and 5 seconds of an equal-tempered triad. If the tone of the sawtooth is too strident, you can select all of the audio and use the equalizer discussed in project 6 to reduce some of the high frequencies.

Audio

OVERVIEW

Audio is the electronic representation of sound as analog or digital signals. Though we live in the digital age, analog and digital audio are intertwined and it is impossible to consider one without the other. The audio we record, edit, and mix might come from live voices or instruments (analog), from hardware synthesizers (digital or analog), from software synthesizers and samplers (digital), from sample or loop libraries (digital), or all of the above. This section is designed to acquaint you with the basics of audio hardware, digital audio, and digital audio software.

Though the material in this section makes regular reference to audio recording, which is a specific application of audio technology, the concepts involved here are integral to the remaining sections of this text. MIDI, the subject of Section III, is a protocol designed to control the electronic generation of digital audio, whether through sampling or synthesis. Section IV describes various sampling and synthesis methods for generating this digital audio. Notation software and computer-assisted instruction software, the subjects of Section V, utilize digital audio extensively for playback, whether from audio files or generated from sampling and synthesis. In addition, even the simplest music technology hardware setup includes various types of audio connections and the use of speaker technology. More complex systems might also incorporate microphones, preamplifiers, mixers, and audio interfaces.

WHAT'S IN THIS SECTION?

Chapter 4: Audio Hardware

This chapter covers:

- the audio recording path from analog acoustic vibrations to digital audio and back;
- microphones and preamps, including microphone types and pickup (polar) patterns;
- signal levels, including mic, instrument, and line levels; balanced versus unbalanced connections; and various connector types;

- mixers, including a look at the specifications for a simple mixer;
- control surfaces for manipulating parameters in audio software;
- digital audio interfaces, including a look at the specifications for a basic interface;
- portable recorders and their basic specifications;
- amplifiers and speakers, including power amps, passive monitors, and active monitors.

Chapter 5: Digital Audio Data

This chapter covers:

- the sampling rate and its impact on the frequency content of digitized audio;
- the sample resolution and its impact on noise in digitized audio;
- "hi-def" digital audio specifications;
- digital audio file formats, including uncompressed, losslessly compressed, and lossy compressed formats;
- loop formats for electronic composition.

Chapter 6: Digital Audio Software—The Digital Audio Workstation

This chapter covers:

- common DAW interface elements, including the transport, clock, tracks, edit view, and mix view;
- recording concepts, including recording levels, monitoring, and latency;
- editing concepts, including non-destructive editing, fades and crossfades, and pitch and time shifting;
- mixing concepts, including volume and pan automation, basic dynamics processing, equalization, and time-based effects, such as chorus, flange, and reverb;
- bouncing down a project to an audio file.

Chapter 7: Audio—What Do I Need?

This chapter describes the hardware and software components for several recording setups:

- Audio System 0: recording, editing, and mixing with no additional hardware or purchased software beyond a computer;
- Audio System 1: recording, editing, and mixing with relatively inexpensive input and output devices;
- Audio System 2: recording, editing, and mixing with a simple audio interface and a couple of microphones;
- Audio System 3: recording, editing, and mixing with a variety of microphones, a more complex audio interface, a control surface, and higher-quality components.

At the end of the section, there are suggestions for "Further Reading" and a list of "Suggested Activities" related to the material in this section.

CHAPTER 4

Audio Hardware

ANALOG AND DIGITAL

Despite the fact that we live in a "digital world," some of the most important elements in modern audio recording are analog, because sound is inherently analog. Sound waves are generated by the continuous changes in the physical positions of strings, reeds, lips, vocal cords, and membranes that in turn generate continuous changes in air pressure. In order to be recorded, these continuous changes in air pressure must be converted into continuous changes in an electrical signal. While this electrical signal will eventually be converted into a non-continuous digital signal, the analog equipment used in the steps leading up to this analog-to-digital conversion are very important to the overall quality of digital audio.

Similarly, when the non-continuous digital signal is converted back into a continuous electrical signal and then to continuous changes in air pressure, analog equipment takes center stage again. Until a way is found to pipe digital signals directly into our brains, all sound will remain analog. Modern audio recording is inherently a mix of analog and digital technologies.

THE AUDIO RECORDING PATH

Audio recording involves capturing the patterns of vibrations in the air produced by an instrument or voice and converting them first to an analog electrical signal and then to a digital electrical signal. It is still possible to record to an analog medium such as reel-to-reel tape, but, even with the current resurgence of interest in all things analog, that would be unusual. Once converted to a digital signal, the audio can be edited, processed, mixed, mastered, and distributed. When someone purchases the product as an MP3 file, AAC file, CD, or DVD and presses "play," the path is reversed. The digital electrical signal is converted to an analog electrical signal, which is in turn converted into vibrations in the air that eventually reach your ears and brain. Let's look at this process in a little more detail.

Once an instrument or voice has produced vibrations in the air, a **transducer** carries out the conversion of these acoustic vibrations into an analog electrical signal. The term transducer refers to a device that converts energy from one form to another, such as a solar panel, which converts solar energy into electrical energy, or an electric motor, which converts electrical energy into physical energy. The transducer that converts acoustic energy into analog electrical energy is a **microphone**.

The electrical energy generated by a microphone is carried down a cable and, because the amount of energy produced by a microphone is usually quite small, it is then connected to a **preamplifier**, or **preamp**. A preamplifier's job is to take the small analog electrical signal and turn it into a larger analog electrical signal that can then be digitized. Preamps are often built into audio interfaces and mixing boards, but can also be separate standalone devices (see "Microphones and Preamps" below).

The device that converts an analog electrical signal into a digital electrical signal is an **analog to digital converter**, or **ADC** (see Figure 4.1). An ADC may sound like a fancy device, but every digital device that you can speak into has an ADC, such as your cell phone, your computer, or some children's toys. In the context of digital audio recording, ADCs are built into the audio inputs of your computer or into a specialized **audio interface**. Some microphones connect directly to your computer via USB and therefore have both preamps and ADCs built into them.

At this point, the signal has become a string of binary numbers expressed as an electrical signal (digital audio) that can be stored on some digital storage medium, such as a hard drive, flash drive, digital tape, or CD. Once the audio has entered the **digital domain**, the possibilities for editing, processing, and mixing are nearly endless. Some of these possibilities will be discussed in Chapter 6, "Digital Audio Software."

When digital audio is played back, the signal is first sent through a **digital to analog converter**, or **DAC** (see Figure 4.2). A DAC is also a very common device: almost any device that makes sound nowadays starts as digital audio and thus must be converted to analog audio to be played back over headphones or loudspeakers. In the context of digital audio playback, the DAC is built into the audio output of your computer or into an audio interface. Some computer speakers connect directly to your computer via USB and therefore have DACs built into them.

The analog electrical signal output from a DAC is sent to an **amplifier** to make the small electrical signal larger, and then to a transducer—a **speaker** in this case—to convert the electrical energy back into acoustic energy. **Powered speakers**, also

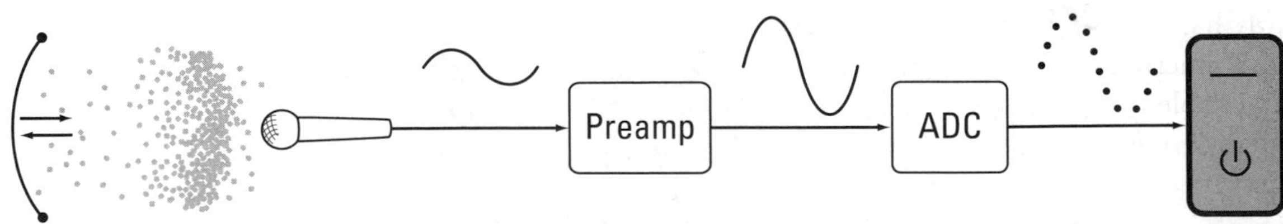

Figure 4.1 Audio recording path from acoustic vibrations to a digital signal recorded on a computer.

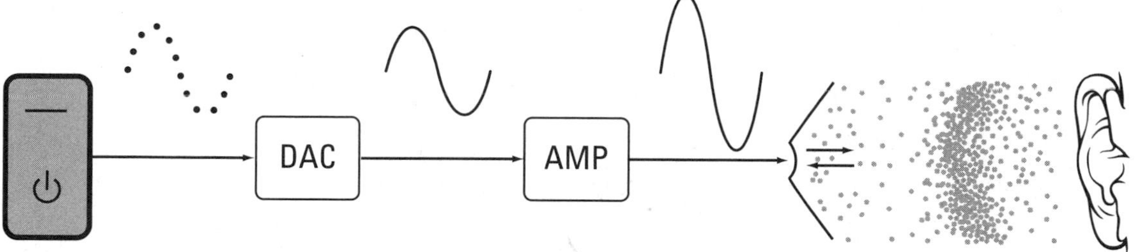

Figure 4.2 Audio playback path from digital signal to acoustic vibrations to your ears.

referred to as **active monitors**, combine the amplifier and speaker into one unit. A final conversion of sound by the cochlea (another transducer!) into neural energy completes the path.

Audio Recording Path Summary

The audio recording path can be summarized as follows:

1. Vibrations in the air are converted to an analog electrical signal by a microphone.
2. The microphone signal is increased by a preamplifier.
3. The preamplifier signal is converted to a digital signal by an ADC.
4. The digital signal is stored, edited, processed, mixed, and mastered in software (more on this stage in Chapter 6, "Digital Audio Software").
5. The digital signal is played back and converted to an analog electrical signal by a DAC.
6. The analog electrical signal is made larger by an amplifier.
7. The output of the amplifier is converted into vibrations in the air by a loudspeaker.

MICROPHONES AND PREAMPS

Some of the most important pieces of equipment in a recording or project studio are microphones. The conversion of acoustic energy into electrical energy must be done well; if it's not, no amount of digital magic can fix it. As a result, pound-for-pound, microphones are among the most expensive pieces of equipment in a studio. While truly high-quality microphones run into the thousands of dollars, it is possible to record with microphones that are merely a few hundred dollars, or even less, to create acceptable demos, podcasts, and other such projects. There are many different kinds of microphones, but there are two primary types that are widely used in audio recording: dynamic mics and condenser mics.

One common type of **dynamic microphone** uses a diaphragm attached to a coil that is suspended near a magnet (see Figures 4.3a and 4.4). The coil consists of some fine wire wrapped in a cylindrical fashion. The diaphragm, coil, and magnet make up the microphone's **capsule**. You can change the capsule in some microphones to achieve different frequency responses or pickup patterns (see "Microphone Polar Patterns" on pages 56–57).

In this moving-coil design, the diaphragm acts like an eardrum, moving back and forth when hit with sound waves. The back and forth motion of the diaphragm results in a back and forth motion of the attached coil near the magnet. When this coil moves within the field of the magnet, a small electrical signal is generated in the coil that ideally has the same frequency and waveform as the incoming sound wave, as well as an amplitude that is proportional to the sound wave's amplitude. In practice, the properties of the electrical signal produced by a microphone will always differ somewhat from those of the sound wave. The size of the diaphragm impacts the resultant sound, so moving-coil dynamic mics are often classed as **small diaphragm** or **large diaphragm** mics.

Moving-coil dynamic mics tend to be sturdy and many are not terribly expensive, making them ideal for sound reinforcement in live performance. Moving-coil dynamic mics are also used in a studio setting for applications such as miking guitar amps, drums, and vocals.

Another, less common, form of dynamic microphone is the **ribbon microphone**, which consists of a thin piece of corrugated, conductive metal—the ribbon—placed between two magnets (see Figure 4.3b). When sound waves hit the ribbon, it moves within the magnetic field, creating a small electrical current in the ribbon. In this way, the ribbon acts as both the diaphragm and the "coil." Because the ribbon is lighter than a diaphragm/coil, it can respond more quickly and represent transient signals better than other dynamic mics. Ribbon mics are also reputed to exhibit a "warm" low-end frequency response.

Another result of the lightness of the ribbon is that ribbon mics can be more delicate than other dynamic mics and have been largely used as studio mics. Early ribbon mics were easily destroyed by a sudden puff of air or by dropping the microphone (not a

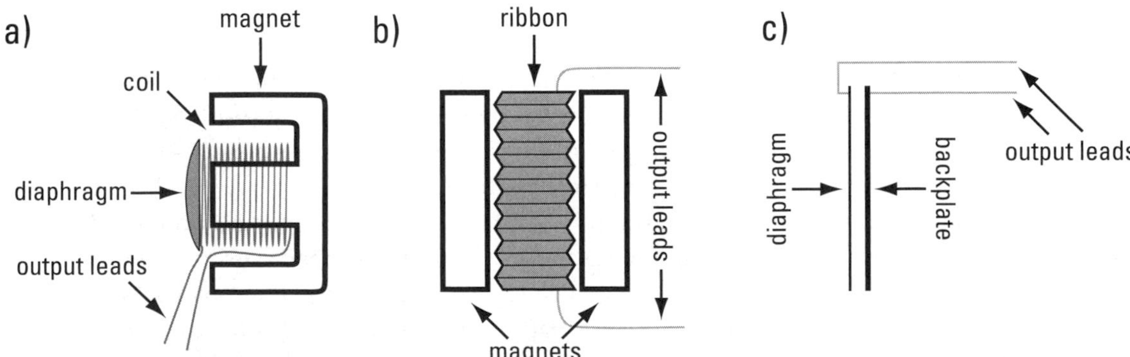

Figure 4.3 Simplified drawings of microphone capsules: (a) moving-coil dynamic (cutaway view from the side), (b) ribbon mic (view from the front), and (c) condenser mic (cutaway view from the side).

good idea with any mic!). More recent ribbon mic designs are more robust and ribbon mics are used in a wider variety of situations now.

Condenser microphones also use a diaphragm that vibrates back and forth when sound waves hit it. However, in this case, the diaphragm is metal-coated and suspended in proximity to another metal plate (see Figures 4.3c and 4.5). When a charge is applied across the plates they form a capacitor, which is an electronic element once called a condenser (these mics are also referred to as **capacitor microphones**). The capacitor (diaphragm and backplate) and its associated electronics make up the capsule for a condenser microphone.

The charge across the plates in a condenser mic's capsule is typically supplied by a signal from the preamp, called **phantom power**, which flows along the same cable as the microphone signal. This is sometimes labeled "+48 V" on audio interfaces and mixers. Less often, this power is supplied by a battery in the microphone itself.

As the diaphragm moves back and forth, the distance between the two plates changes periodically, causing a periodic change in the voltage across the plates and producing an electrical signal in wires attached to the diaphragm and backplate. Ideally, this electrical current has the same frequency and waveform as the sound wave with an amplitude that is proportional to the sound wave's amplitude. As with dynamic mics, the properties of the electrical current will differ somewhat from the properties of the sound wave. As with moving-coil dynamic mics, the size of the diaphragm impacts the resultant sound, so these mics are also classed according to their diaphragm size.

Condenser microphones are used frequently in studio settings and for recording live performances. They are more sensitive than dynamic mics and tend to reproduce the total frequency range more fully, due in part to the fact that the moving element, the diaphragm, is lighter than the diaphragm-coil unit of a moving-coil dynamic mic. Many condenser mics are more delicate and more expensive than moving-coil dynamic mics, though there are a number of robust, inexpensive condenser microphones available now.

A form of condenser mic called an **electret microphone** is commonly found in camcorder mics, computer mics, and lapel mics. Electret mics are condenser mics that have a permanent charge between the plates, instead of using phantom power or a battery to create the charge. Electret mics do need power for the rest of their electronics, which can be supplied by a battery or phantom power. While electret mics used in consumer-quality applications such as camcorders tend to be of mediocre quality, there are also some electret mics that are high-quality studio microphones.

Many microphones connect to a preamp, or audio interface with a built-in preamp, using a cable with XLR connectors (see Figure 4.12a and b on page 61). However, there are a number of **USB microphones** available that connect directly to your computer via a USB cable (see Figure 4.6). These microphones have a built-in preamp and ADC. In addition, there are a variety of **wireless microphones** ranging from lapel mics to regular hand-held or stand-mounted microphones used for live performance (see Figure 4.7).

Figure 4.4 Shure SM-58 end-address, small-diaphragm dynamic microphone. (Copyright Shure Incorporated. Used with permission)

Figure 4.5 AT4050 side-address, large-diaphragm condenser microphone. Omni, cardioid, and bidirectional polar patterns. (Photo courtesy of Audio-Technica)

Figure 4.6 Snowball USB microphone. Omni and cardioid polar patterns. (Courtesy of Blue Microphones, www.bluemic.com)

Figure 4.7 ATW-2120 wireless microphone/transmitter and receiver. (Photo courtesy of Audio-Technica)

Microphone Polar Patterns

An important characteristic of a microphone is its pickup pattern, or **polar pattern**. These patterns are typically indicated by a standard name and a diagram that shows the sensitivity of the microphone to sound waves coming from various directions. Some microphones have a fixed pattern, some can switch between patterns, and some can change patterns only if the capsule is changed.

In the standard polar pattern diagrams, the directional response is given in degrees, with zero degrees (the top of the diagram) representing sound coming directly at the mic's diaphragm and 180 degrees representing sound coming from the opposite direction. For **end-address microphones**, zero degrees is straight into the end of the mic (see Figure 4.4). For **side-address microphones**, zero degrees is directly into the side of the mic (see Figure 4.5). Both types often have a grill centered over the diaphragm.

One basic polar pattern is the **omnidirectional pattern**. Omnidirectional microphones accept sound from all directions more or less equally (see Figure 4.8a). These are useful when you're trying to capture the overall ambience of a performance in a good-sounding space or in an array with other microphones. A **bidirectional** (or **figure-8) pattern** microphone accepts sound largely without change from the front and back of the capsule—zero degrees and 180 degrees—but reduces sound from the sides—90 degrees and 270 degrees (see Figure 4.8b). A bidirectional mic could be used for an interview situation, for recording two vocal or instrumental parts at once, or in an array with other microphones.

A **cardioid pattern** accepts sound largely without change from the front, but reduces it from the back and somewhat from the sides (see Figure 4.8c). This pattern is best used when isolation of a particular instrument is desirable, as it often is when recording a group. A **hypercardioid pattern** rejects sound better from the sides than the cardioid, but picks up some sound directly from the back of the microphone (see Figure 4.8d). Hypercardioid pattern mics are used for film and TV, where it is important to be able to pick out a specific sound, such as a voice, but not the other ambient sounds, such as camera noise. There are a variety of other specialized patterns for use in certain circumstances. It is important to note that the pickup patterns of a mic can change somewhat depending on the frequency of the sound source.

Preamps

Microphones output a relatively small electrical signal. In order for this signal to be useful, it first needs to be amplified. The component that takes care of this is called a preamplifier, or preamp (see also page 52). Preamps can be standalone devices or built in to a mixer or audio interface.

Just as microphone quality is a critical factor in the proper conversion of acoustic energy into electrical energy, so is preamp quality an important factor in the boosting of this electrical signal without changing its properties. A poor preamp will introduce an unwanted "color" to the sound. Consequently, good standalone preamps and mixers

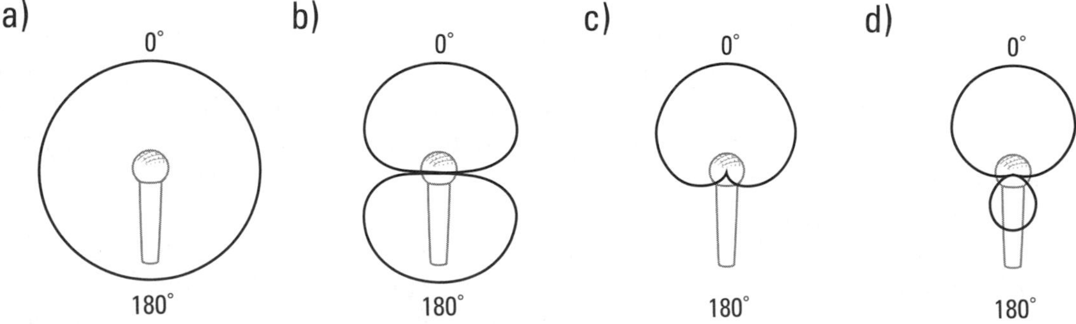

Figure 4.8 Microphone polar (directional) patterns with the diaphragm of microphone pointing toward the top: (a) omnidirectional, (b) bidirectional (figure-8), (c) cardioid, and (d) hypercardioid.

Figure 4.9 Grace Design M201 two-channel microphone preamp. (Photo courtesy of Grace Design, used by permission)

with good preamps are expensive. Fortunately, the preamps built into moderately priced audio interfaces and mixers are adequate for many circumstances.

While microphones output small electrical signals, the size of those signals varies from mic to mic. As a result, mic preamps will typically have a **trim/gain knob** that allows you to boost the signal by a variable amount to accommodate different microphone levels (see below) and different material being recorded. A mic preamp may also have a **pad**, which is a switch that reduces the decibel level of the incoming signal by some amount. Very loud inputs from, for example, a kick drum, could require use of a pad on the mic preamp. In addition to amplifying a microphone's small signal, a preamp also typically supplies phantom power to condenser mics. Phantom power is turned on or off using a button or switch on the standalone preamp, mixer, or audio interface (see Figure 4.9).

SIGNAL LEVELS

In addition to microphones, there are a variety of other sources that can be part of the recording path including guitars, synthesizers, and effects processors. The electrical signals to and from these devices are transmitted at various **signal levels** and may require different cables and connectors to integrate them into the recording path. In addition, some sound sources output digital signals that can be connected to digital inputs on an audio interface or digital mixing board.

Mic Level

We've encountered one electrical signal level already: the **mic level**. In general, microphones produce a small electrical signal that is sent out as a **balanced signal** down a cable that has **XLR connectors** (also called Canon connectors). This cable is then connected to a preamp. See Figure 4.12a for the XLR connector that plugs into a microphone and 4.12b for the XLR connector that plugs into a standalone preamp, mixer, or audio interface.

A **balanced cable** has three conductors, two signal conductors and one shield that wraps around them. This configuration allows equipment at the "receiving" end of the signal to eliminate any noise picked up by the cable over a long cable run. As you'll see below, cables with XLR connectors are useful for other signals in addition to mic signals.

Line Level

Devices such as synthesizers, audio processing gear, and mic preamps output **line level** signals, which are higher than mic level signals. Line level signals can be plugged directly into the line level inputs of an audio interface or mixing board. There are two different line level standards: *professional* line level, also referred to as +4 dBu, and *semipro* line level, also referred to variously as –10 dBV, "consumer" line level, or "pro-sumer" line level.

Professional line level signals (+4 dBu) are typically balanced signals carried on cables with XLR connectors or ¼-inch **TRS (tip-ring-sleeve) connectors** (see Figure 4.12c). Because these are balanced signals, cable runs can be fairly long without the signal acquiring additional noise.

Semipro line level signals (–10 dBV) are typically **unbalanced signals** carried on cables with ¼-inch **TS (tip-sleeve) connectors**, 3.5mm TS mini plugs, or **RCA connectors** (also called phono connectors) (see Figure 4.12d, f, and g). **Unbalanced cables** have one main conductor and shield. Unlike balanced cables, unbalanced cable runs need to be kept short to avoid added noise.

Instrument Level

Another common electrical signal level is the **instrument level**, which is associated most often with the output level of a guitar or bass guitar. The output of a guitar or bass guitar is an unbalanced signal carried on a cable with ¼-inch TS connectors (see Figure 4.12d). As noted above, unbalanced signals are more susceptible to interference than balanced signals, so the cables should be kept relatively short.

A guitar cable is, of course, most often plugged into a guitar amplifier. During recording, a microphone is usually positioned in front of the guitar amp to capture the characteristic amplified sound of the electric guitar. However, it is also sometimes desirable to capture the output of the guitar directly in order to mix it with the miked amp signal or to process it separately after recording. The output of a bass guitar is often captured directly during recording, but the bass amp can also be miked.

If a guitar or bass guitar is plugged directly into a regular line level input on a mixer or audio interface, its sound will be weak and of poor quality. The reason for this is that the output signal of a guitar or bass guitar has a **high impedance** (also referred to as **High-Z**). To capture the output of a guitar or bass guitar directly, it needs to be connected to a High-Z, or "Instrument," input on a preamp, mixer, or audio interface, or converted to a Low-Z signal by using a **direct injection box**, also referred to as a DI box or direct box. A DI box converts an instrument level signal into a mic level signal that is carried on a mic cable and connected to a preamp on a standalone preamp, audio interface, or mixing board. Impedance is a bit of an involved topic, but for our purposes it is sufficient to understand that direct guitar and bass guitar signals require a High-Z/Instrument input or a DI box.

Figure 4.10 shows a DI box with a ¼-inch unbalanced input for the guitar or bass guitar cable and a ¼-inch unbalanced "thru" output so the signal can also be sent to a

Figure 4.10 ART Z-direct passive direct box. (Courtesy of ART Pro Audio, Inc.)

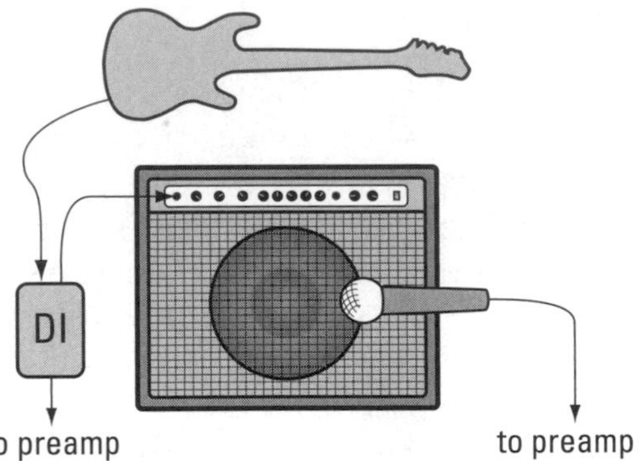

Figure 4.11 A typical configuration for capturing a guitar signal directly and through a microphone on the amp. The output of the guitar goes to a DI box where it is split. The original signal is sent through to the guitar amp and the Low-Z, balanced, mic level signal goes to a preamp. The guitar amp is also miked to capture the characteristic electric guitar sound.

guitar or bass amp. The other side of the DI box (not shown) has an XLR output to be connected by a mic cable to a preamp on a standalone preamp, mixer, or audio interface. Figure 4.11 illustrates a typical connection between a guitar/bass guitar, DI box, amplifier, and microphone.

Speaker Level

The output of a power amplifier that is sent to a passive speaker (see "Amplifiers and Speakers" on pages 69–70) is referred to as **speaker level**, and is higher than any of the other levels discussed in both voltage and power. Typically, speaker level signals don't interact with the other signals in the recording chain—they are designed only to be sent to speakers—and plugging them into other equipment can cause damage. Speaker cables often use bare, relatively heavy gauge stranded wires that connect to screw terminals or clamps. Speaker wires may also use **banana plug connectors** (see Figure 4.12h).

Digital Audio Signals

The data structures for digital audio will be discussed in some detail in the next chapter, but a brief summary of digital audio cables and connectors belongs here with the discussion of other source signals for recording.

The usual semipro standard for transmitting stereo digital data is the Sony/Philips Digital Interface, or **S/PDIF**. There are two standard cable/connector types: **coaxial cable** with RCA connectors (see Figure 4.12g) or plastic **fiber-optic cable** with **TOSLINK connectors** (see Figure 4.12i). It is important to note that the S/PDIF cables with RCA connectors are *not* the same as the cables with RCA connectors associated with home stereos. S/PDIF cables are coaxial cables with a specific impedance.

The usual professional level standard for transmitting stereo digital data is **AES/EBU** (also known as **AES3**). These signals are typically carried on balanced cables with XLR connectors. It is important to note that these are *not* microphone cables; AES/EBU cables have a specific impedance that is different from standard mic cables.

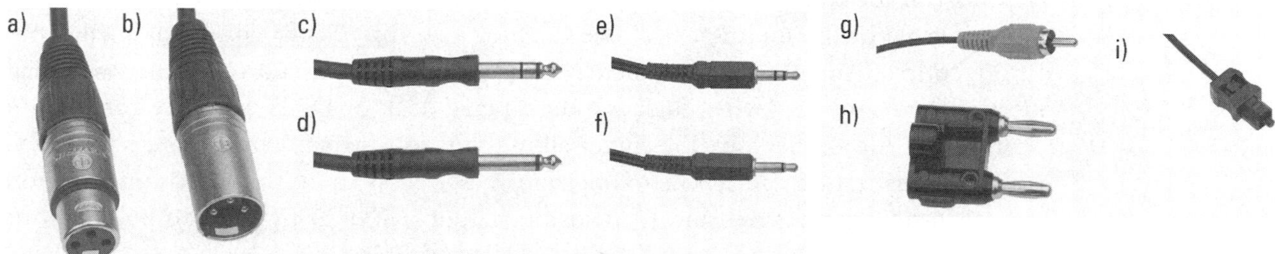

Figure 4.12 Connectors: (a) XLR female, (b) XLR male, (c) ¼-inch TRS, (d) ¼-inch TS, (e) 3.5mm (⅛-inch) TRS, (f) 3.5mm (⅛-inch) TS, (g) RCA, (h) banana plug, and (i) TOSLINK.

Table 4.1 **Recording sources and their cables/connectors. This table represents the most typical situations; there are applications that deviate from this**

Recording source	*Output type*	*Connector/cable*	*Notes*
Microphone	Mic level	Balanced XLR	Low-Z output; route to mic preamp (standalone, on audio interface, or on mixing board); some mics may be different
Microphone preamp	Pro line level	Balanced XLR or balanced TRS	Route to mixer line-in or audio interface line-in
Guitar or bass	Instrument level	Unbalanced TS	High-Z output; route to DI box or "Instrument/High-Z" input on audio interface; guitar amps are often miked
DI box	Mic level	Balanced XLR	Low-Z output; route to mic preamp (standalone, on audio interface, or on mixing board); active or passive
Pro equipment	Pro line level	Balanced XLR or balanced TRS	Recording decks, processors, etc.; route to mixer line-in or audio interface line-in
Semipro (or consumer) equipment	Semipro (or consumer) line level	All unbalanced. Mono: ¼-inch TS, 3.5mm TS, RCA; stereo: ¼-inch TRS, 3.5mm TRS	Synthesizers, home stereos, standard computer output, etc.; route to mixer line-in or audio interface line-in if short run and inputs accept unbalanced signal; route to DI box otherwise
Amplifiers	Speaker level	Unbalanced	Not fed back into recording chain; route to passive speakers
Semipro (or consumer) digital inputs/outputs	S/PDIF	Unbalanced 75 Ohm coax with RCA, fiber-optic with TOSLINK	Route to digital input on interface; most common for lower to mid-level audio interfaces; 2 channels
Pro digital inputs/outputs	AES/EBU	Balanced 110 Ohm cable with XLR	Route to digital input on interface; found on more upscale audio interfaces; 2 channels

S/PDIF and AES/EBU support the transmission of two channels of digital audio. There are other standards for multi-channel digital audio, including TDIF, Lightpipe, and MADI.

MIXERS

The heart of the traditional recording studio has long been the **mixer**, also referred to as the console or the mixing desk. The function of a mixer is to combine signals from various sources, such as microphones, synths, and processors, and route the combined output to a recording device, such as a digital tape deck or DAW software running on a computer. Along the way, the mixer allows you to independently change the level, pan, and equalization of each incoming signal, as well as route the signal, or a portion of it, to processing devices and then to the output. Modern mixers can be digital or analog, with digital mixers incorporating ADCs and DACs.

While mixers are still central to medium and large recording studios, they're less critical in a project studio setting where each input is recorded to a separate virtual track in DAW software, and the mixing, processing, and routing all take place within the software. A mixer in a project studio is more likely to be a relatively small mixer or a mixer combined with an audio interface. With the mixing taking place in software, a mixer-like device, referred to as a control surface (see page 64), which controls the software's virtual faders and knobs, is increasingly common.

A Simple Mixer

Mixers come in many shapes and sizes, from those that have only a few inputs to those that have hundreds (see Figures 4.13 and 4.14). In this section, we will look at common features of a simple analog mixer that might be found in a small project studio. Each mixer has its unique set of features, so just the most common features will be discussed here.

Input Channel Strips

Each input to this type of mixer has its own vertical strip with controls that determine how that input is processed and routed. Here are the common channel strip elements:

- *Input jacks/controls*. The channel strips will be a mix of two types: those that accept a single microphone or line level input and those that accept two line level inputs as a stereo pair.
  - A channel strip with a mic input will have an XLR jack for the microphone, a TRS or TS ¼-inch jack for a line level input, and a trim/gain knob. Phantom power for condenser mics is activated for all mic inputs by a switch or button.

Figure 4.13 Mackie 802-VLZ3 eight-input small analog mixer. (Courtesy of Mackie)

Figure 4.14 Yamaha MG82CX eight-input small analog mixer. (Courtesy of the Yamaha Corporation)

- A channel strip with stereo line inputs will have two TRS/TS jacks or two RCA jacks.

- *Auxiliary send knobs*. One or two aux send knobs to determine how much of the signal is sent to the auxiliary outputs for such purposes as external processing, creating a headphone mix for performers, or feeding an onstage monitor for performers.
- *Three-band equalizer* for boosting or cutting the high, middle, and low frequencies. EQ will be discussed more fully in Chapter 6, "Digital Audio Software."
- *Pan knob* for mono tracks and *balance knob* for stereo tracks for determining the position of that input in the stereo field.
- *Mute button* to stop the signal from being sent to the output.
- *Solo button* to allow only "soloed" tracks to be heard. Not all mixers at this level incorporate this feature.
- *Gain knob/fader* to determine how much of the input signal is sent to the main outputs. More complex mixers may allow a channel to be routed to a submix bus instead of the main outputs.

Output and Monitor Section

After each input signal has gone through its channel strip they are added together and sent to the output and monitor section of the mixer:

- *Aux master send knobs*, one for each aux send. The aux sends from the channel strips are combined and this knob controls the overall aux send output level to the external processor, headphone mix, or stage monitor. If there is more than one aux send, each is handled independently.

- *Aux send jacks*, one for each aux send. A TS unbalanced or TRS balanced ¼-inch jack.
- *Aux return jacks*, a stereo return (two jacks) for each mono aux send. Signals to an external processor, such as a reverb unit, are often sent mono and returned from the processor as stereo. TS unbalanced or TRS balanced ¼-inch jacks.
- *Aux return knobs*, one for each stereo return. This knob controls the amount of the return signal that is added to the mix.
- *Control room output knob*. This output from the mixing board allows you to send an appropriate level for recording to the main outputs and a comfortable listening level to the speakers in the control room. The *headphone output knob* similarly allows you to listen at an appropriate level in headphones.
- *Control room output jacks*. Two TS unbalanced or TRS balanced ¼-inch jacks. Headphone output jack is one TRS ¼-inch jack.
- *Main output knob/fader*. The main output fader controls how much of the mixed input signal is sent to the recording device or to main stage speakers.
- *Main ouput jacks*. Two TS unbalanced or TRS balanced ¼-inch jacks or two XLR jacks (balanced).

Control Surfaces

Mixing in a small project studio is often handled entirely within the software itself. However, it is difficult to control the many aspects of a mix with just a computer keyboard and a mouse. One solution to this problem is a **control surface** (see Figure 4.15).

A control surface has a variety of faders and knobs, but, instead of actively routing and processing audio, a control surface just sends MIDI messages to the software. The actual routing and processing of audio then takes place within the software. This allows you the convenient touch of multiple faders and knobs, but allows you to work entirely in software.

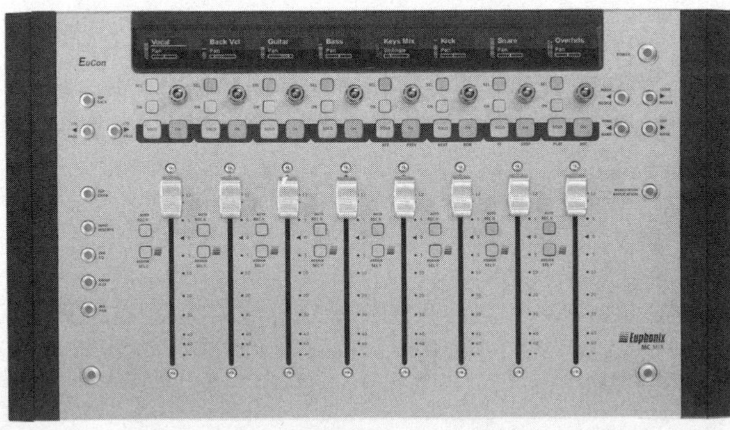

Figure 4.15 Euphonix MC Mix control surface. (Courtesy of Euphonix)

Control surfaces can also be combined with an audio interface so that the same faders you use to control the level of the audio inputs when recording can later be used to control the virtual faders in the software when mixing. We'll look at audio interfaces next.

DIGITAL AUDIO INTERFACES

As we saw in the "Audio Recording Path" section (see pages 51–53), once the vibrations in the air have been converted into a continuous electrical signal by a microphone and then run through a preamplifier, the next stage is conversion to a non-continuous digital signal by an ADC (see Figure 4.1 on page 52). To then play back the stored, edited, and processed digital audio, it must be converted to an analog signal by a DAC (see Figure 4.2 on page 53). For audio recording and playback, the ADC and DAC form the core of the **digital audio interface**.

Most computers are already equipped with at least a basic stereo audio output (DAC) using a 3.5mm jack for headphones or computer speakers. In addition, many computers have a built-in microphone (ADC) and a built-in stereo input (ADC) that uses a 3.5mm jack. These connections provide all the basic audio inputs for activities such as audio- or video-chatting and recording voice-overs for presentations or home movies, and the basic audio outputs necessary for activities such as playing songs, movies, and Internet audio and video. However, for semi-professional and professional audio recording, the quality of these inputs and outputs is generally insufficient, and an external digital audio interface is required.

Just having an audio interface is no guarantee of audio quality—a cheap interface may not be much better than the built-in inputs and outputs on a computer. Price is often some sort of indicator of quality, though it is as uneven an indicator for audio as it is for cars or refrigerators. The best gauge of quality will likely come from reviews in the independent technology media, knowledgeable peers, and your own experiences. Not all interfaces work equally well with every computer or piece of software. Again, reviews and other users' experiences are useful here. Documentation for audio recording software often includes a discussion of compatible hardware.

Deciding the appropriate interface usually involves the best match of desired features (including quality) and available budget. Audio interfaces come in a variety of forms, including external boxes that connect to a computer via USB or FireWire, PCI cards for desktops with external "breakout" boxes for connections, and PC cards for laptops. Audio interfaces also have a variety of features that range from simple stereo input and output to dozens of inputs and outputs with microphone preamps, digital audio ins and outs, audio and video synchronization, and MIDI ins and outs. Accordingly, audio interfaces can run from a few hundred dollars for a simple interface to about $1,000 for a midrange interface to over $10,000 for a high-end professional studio system.

To explore the various features of audio interfaces, we will look at the common components of relatively simple audio interfaces and some of the additional features found in more complex interfaces.

A Basic Audio Interface

A basic audio interface typically has two inputs of various types and two line level outputs, and connects to the computer via USB or FireWire (see Figures 4.16, 4.17 and 4.18). Each audio interface has its own unique set of features, but here we'll look at the features that are most common to this level of interface.

Analog Inputs

- *Two inputs* that can accommodate microphone level, instrument level, and line level using XLR and ¼-inch jacks or "combo" jacks that can accept either type of connector. RCA jacks may be used for line level signals, particularly for interfaces targeted at the DJ market.
- *Trim knob*, also called a gain knob, for each input, which accommodates varying microphone levels.
- *Phantom power switch*, which supplies power to condenser microphones.
- *Pad switch* for each input, which reduces the input level by some number of dB. This is useful for very loud sources, such as kick drums or guitar amps, where the signal might distort even if the trim/gain knob is all the way down.

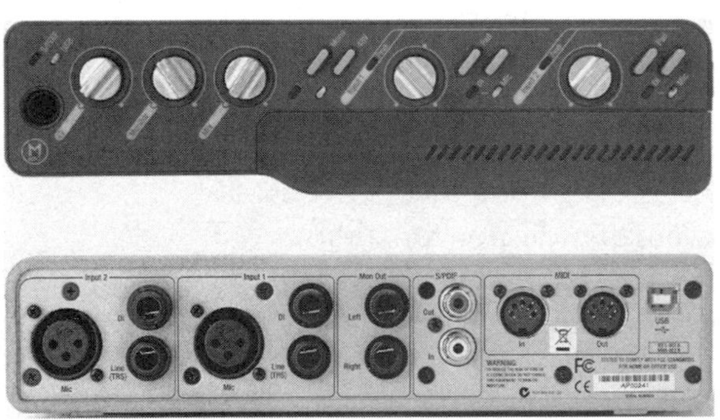

Figure 4.16 Front and back of Mbox 2 USB audio interface. (Courtesy of Digidesign)

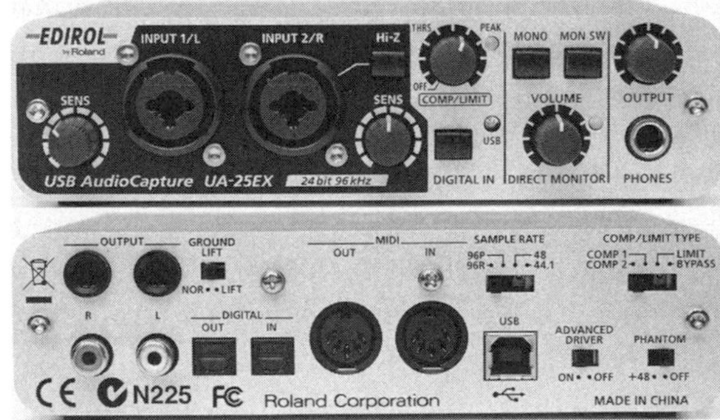

Figure 4.17 Front and back of Edirol UA-25EX USB audio interface. (Special thanks to Roland Corporation)

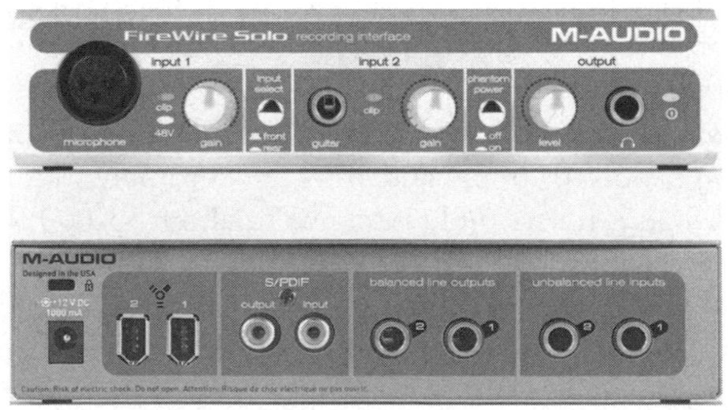

Figure 4.18 Front and back of M-Audio FireWire Solo audio interface. (Courtesy of M-Audio)

- *Note*: the limited number of inputs means that most tracks of a multi-track audio recording will be recorded separately with this interface. As a result, these interfaces are typical of small composing or hobby studios, not true recording studios.

Analog Outputs

- *Two main outputs* that are either ¼-inch TRS balanced jacks, ¼-inch TS unbalanced jacks, or RCA unbalanced jacks. The output level is controlled by a single knob. The choice of an interface with balanced or unbalanced outputs determines how long the cable run can be to a mixer or speakers without acquiring additional noise. Unbalanced RCA outputs are useful for DJ-style equipment, which tends to use RCA connectors.
- *Headphone output* with a separate volume control.

Digital Input/Output

- *S/PDIF digital input* (2 channels) and *output* (2 channels) using RCA jacks or TOSLINK jacks.
- *Note*: On some interfaces, the two digital inputs and outputs are independent of the two analog inputs and outputs resulting in a possible four simultaneous inputs and outputs.

MIDI Input/Output

- *One MIDI input* and *one MIDI output*. MIDI ins and outs are useful in that they eliminate the need for a separate MIDI interface for MIDI devices that connect using MIDI cables. Many MIDI controllers connect directly to the computer via USB and thus don't need these traditional MIDI jacks (see Section III, "MIDI").

Computer Connection and Power Source

- Connect via *USB* or *FireWire*. USB connectors are common on both PCs and Macs. Macs commonly have FireWire connectors and adapter cards are available for PC laptops and desktops.
- Interface is *bus-powered*, meaning that the USB or FireWire connection provides power to the interface from the computer. Many interfaces can utilize a power adapter as an alternative to bus power. The ability to draw power from the USB or FireWire bus allows for more flexibility in mobile recording with a laptop.

Supported Sampling Rates and Resolutions

- Most interfaces can operate at sampling rates of *44.1 kHz* and *48 kHz*. Some interfaces support higher sampling rates such as 88.2 kHz or 96 kHz. Sampling rates are discussed in Chapter 5, "Digital Audio Data."

- Most interfaces can operate at sample resolutions of *16-bit* and *24-bit*. Again, sample resolutions are discussed in Chapter 5.

More Complex Audio Interfaces

Though in-depth coverage of more complex audio interfaces is beyond the scope of this text, it is worth noting briefly what distinguishes a more complex audio interface from a basic one. More complex audio interfaces may have:

- more analog inputs and outputs; these are more likely to be balanced ins and outs except for ins and outs designed to interface with DJ equipment;
- more microphone preamps; at the higher price points, interfaces usually specialize in either more line ins/outs or more mic preamps;
- a mixer interface with faders and knobs, making it a combination of a mixer, an audio interface, and a control surface;
- support for professional digital input/output (AES/EBU) and support for multi-channel digital input/output such as Lightpipe, TDIF, or MADI. Also support for digital audio synchronization such as word clock.

The differences in costs among more complex audio interfaces often result from a combination of additional features and higher-quality components.

PORTABLE RECORDERS

So far, we have been assuming that audio is being recorded using DAW software and is stored on a computer hard drive. This is, of course, very common, but non-computer-based hardware recorders are still used in many settings. A discussion of hardware recorders in general is beyond the scope of this text, but portable recorders (see Figure 4.19) are in wide use in educational settings and in field recording, so we'll look briefly at the common features for this type of recorder.

- *Microphones*. Most include built-in stereo electret microphones and have an input for an external mic. Often this external mic input is a 3.5mm stereo jack for a stereo microphone, but some have XLR inputs with phantom power.
- *Supported sampling rates*. These include 44.1 kHz and 48 kHz, and supported sample resolutions include 16- or 24-bit. Some recorders feature sampling rates up to 96 kHz. Sample resolutions are discussed in Chapter 5, "Digital Audio Data."
- *Recording medium*. Portable recorders have utilized many different types of media over the years, including digital audio tape (DAT), minidisk, and CD, but most of current crop of portable recorders use some form of flash media, whether SD cards, compact flash, or memory stick. Recordings are stored as digital audio files, such as WAVE files, on the flash media. Some recorders support MP3s or other compressed file formats as well.

- *Output*. Headphone output via 3.5mm stereo jack. Some have more standard audio outputs, such as ¼-inch jacks, and some have small built-in speakers.
- *Computer connection via USB*. These recorders mount like other flash drives and allow the digital audio files to be copied to the computer and then imported into an audio editing program.
- *Powered* by batteries or a power adapter.
- *Special features*. Each device has its own special features that differentiate it from its competitors. Such features might include High-Z guitar inputs, line level inputs, and onboard effects.

Figure 4.19 Edirol R-09HR flash-based portable recorder with built-in stereo microphone. (Special thanks to Roland Corporation)

AMPLIFIERS AND SPEAKERS

In the audio recording path discussed at the beginning of this chapter (see Figure 4.2 on page 53), once the digital audio has been converted into an analog electrical signal, the next steps before hearing it are to amplify the electrical signal and then convert it into a series of vibrations in the air. In many ways, these steps are as important as the steps involving microphones and preamplifiers. If your mics and preamps are great, but your amplifier and speakers are poor, you won't be able to make good recording, editing, processing, or mixing decisions.

One common speaker design is closely related to the design of a moving-coil dynamic microphone, but in reverse. In a moving-coil dynamic mic, vibrations in the air cause a diaphragm to move back and forth. That diaphragm is attached to a coil, which moves back and forth near a magnet. This motion creates an alternating electrical signal in the coil that is the output of the microphone. In a speaker, an alternating electrical signal is fed into a coil that is attached to a "diaphragm" called a **speaker cone**. This assembly is suspended near a magnet. The alternating electrical signal in the coil near the magnet causes the coil/cone assembly to move back and forth causing compressions and rarefactions in the air. The combination of the magnet, coil, and cone is referred to as a **driver**.

In addition to the moving-coil driver, there are also electrostatic drivers, which operate like condenser microphones in reverse, and ribbon drivers, which operate like ribbon microphones in reverse. In each case, the analog electrical signal is converted into physical motions, which result in a series of compressions and rarefactions in the air.

Different-sized drivers are suitable for different frequency ranges—larger drivers for low frequencies and smaller drivers for high frequencies. There are usually two or three drivers in a full-range speaker. A three-way speaker contains a **woofer** (low), **midrange** (mid), and **tweeter** (high), and a two-way speaker contains a woofer and tweeter. When needed, a separate speaker, a **subwoofer**, handles the very low end.

In general, there are two types of amplifier/speaker systems in use: passive speakers driven by a separate power amplifier, and active speakers with a built-in amplifier.

Power Amplifiers and Passive Monitors

A power amplifier (see Figure 4.20) is made up of one or more channels that take in line level signals and convert them to speaker level signals with relatively high power (most signals in the audio recording path do not have much overall power). The inputs may be balanced on XLR or ¼-inch TRS jacks or unbalanced on ¼-inch TS jacks. The outputs to the speakers will likely be either terminals that connect to bare leads from speaker wire or a connector like a banana plug jack. The primary control on most amplifiers is a knob for each channel to control the overall output level.

The ratings for power amps are given as Watts of power driving a passive monitor with some number of Ohms of impedance, usually 4 or 8 Ohms. The Watts into Ohms rating of the amplifier must be appropriate for the impedance and power ratings of the speakers to avoid poor performance or distortion.

Active Monitors

Active monitors (see Figure 4.21) have their own amplifiers built into the speaker cabinet and take in balanced line level signals on ¼-inch TRS or XLR jacks, or unbalanced line level signals on ¼-inch TS, 3.5mm TS, or RCA jacks. Because the amplifier and speaker are designed together, their ratings are matched by design. As a result of their compactness and their quality, active monitors are a popular choice for home and project studios as well as larger studios.

Figure 4.20 Crown XLS 202 two-channel power amplifier. (Courtesy of Harman International)

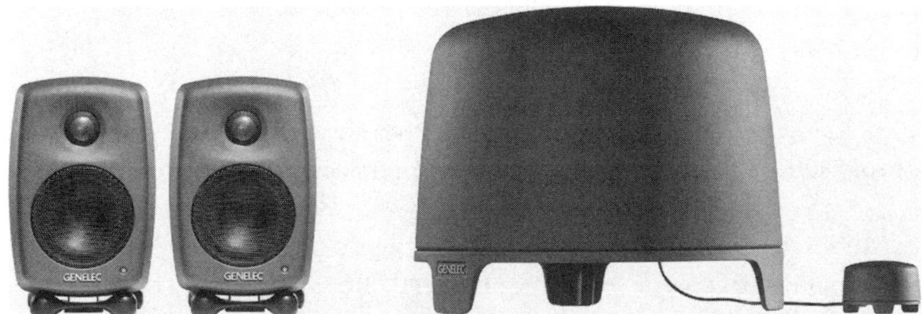

Figure 4.21 Genelec 6010A bi-amped nearfield active monitors and Genelec 5040A subwoofer with volume control. (Copyrighted property of Genelec Oy)

REVIEW OF KEY TERMS

transducer 52
microphone 52
preamplifier (preamp) 52
analog to digital converter (ADC) 52
audio interface 52
digital domain 52
digital to analog converter (DAC) 52
amplifier 52
speaker 52
powered speakers/active monitors 52–53
dynamic microphone 53
capsule 54
small/large diaphragm 54
ribbon microphone 54
condenser/capacitor microphone 55
phantom power 55
electret microphone 55
USB microphone 55
wireless microphone 55
polar pattern 56
end-address/side-address microphone 56
omnidirectional pattern 57
bidirectional (figure-8) pattern 57
cardioid/hypercardioid patterns 57
trim/gain knob 58
pad 58
signal levels 58
mic level 58
balanced signal 58
XLR connectors 58
balanced cable 58
line level 59
TRS (tip-ring-sleeve) connectors 59
unbalanced signals/cables 59
TS (tip-sleeve) connectors 59
RCA connectors 59
instrument level 59
high impedance (High-Z) 59
direct injection (DI) box 59
speaker level 60
banana plug connectors 60
S/PDIF 60
coaxial/fiber-optic cables 60
TOSLINK connectors 60
AES/EBU (AES3) 61
mixer 62
control surface 64
digital audio interface 65
speaker cone 69
driver 69
woofer/subwoofer 69
midrange 69
tweeter 69

CHAPTER 5

Digital Audio Data

In the last chapter, you were introduced to the ADC (analog to digital converter) and the DAC (digital to analog converter) as the entry-point and the exit-point of the digital domain. The ADC is responsible for converting an analog electrical signal into a digital electrical signal and the DAC is responsible for converting a digital electrical signal back into an analog electrical signal. To understand the difference between analog and digital representations it is useful to consider the analogy of a dimmer light switch vs a regular light switch (see Figure 5.1).

A light controlled by a dimmer switch changes continuously from one brightness level to another ranging from total darkness to fully on. This is fundamentally analog: theoretically, a dimmer has an infinite number of states. A light controlled by a regular switch, on the other hand, has two states—on and off—and nothing in between. This is fundamentally digital. To understand what happens when an analog audio signal is converted into a digital signal, we must look at what the ADC in a recording system does.

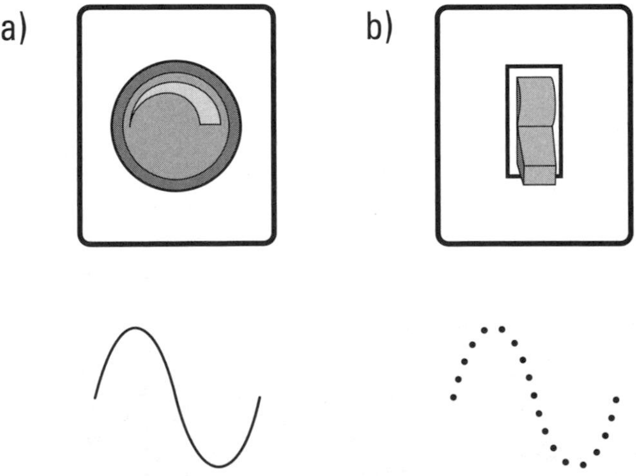

Figure 5.1 Analog and digital representations: (a) a dimmer switch and an analog waveform; (b) a lightswitch and a digitized waveform.

SAMPLING AND QUANTIZING

In order to convert a continuous analog signal into a series of numbers, the ADC has to **sample** the incoming analog waveform. To do this, the ADC measures the amplitude of the incoming waveform some number of times every second and assigns a numerical value to the amplitude. The number of samples taken per second is a frequency and is given in hertz (Hz), just as the number of cycles per second of a waveform is given in Hz. This frequency is called the **sampling rate**. The act of assigning an amplitude value to the sample is called quantizing and the number of amplitude values available to the ADC is called the **sample resolution**.

It is worth noting that the term "sampling" has at least three distinct meanings in music technology, each at a different timescale. The first meaning, given above, is the periodic measuring of an analog waveform's amplitude. In this sense, an individual sample represents an imperceptibly small amount of time. The second meaning is the act of recording single notes of musical instruments to be triggered later by MIDI messages. These are the samples forming sample libraries that are commonly used by composers to mimic the timbres of real instruments (see Chapter 14, "Sampling Methods"). The third meaning is drawn from hip-hop, in which a recognizable portion of an existing recording, such as several measures of music or a characteristic vocal sound, is used in the creation of a new song.

Throughout this discussion, the term "CD-quality" will be used as shorthand for the digital audio specifications associated with the audio CD medium. "CD-quality" is really a misnomer. The actual *quality* of the audio varies greatly depending on the microphones, preamps, and ADCs used to record it and the DACs, amps, and speakers used to listen to it.

The Sampling Rate

The **sampling rate** of CD-quality digital audio is 44,100 Hz (44.1 kHz), meaning that the ADC measures the amplitude of the incoming analog waveform 44,100 times per second for each channel of audio (two channels in the case of stereo audio). Another way of saying it is that the ADC measures the amplitude, waits a short period of time, takes another measurement, waits a short period of time, takes another measurement, and so on (see Figure 5.2).

You may remember from geometry that between any two points on a continuous line there are an infinite number of other points. This means that, while the ADC is waiting between samples, an infinite number of points are ignored. If the ADC actually tried

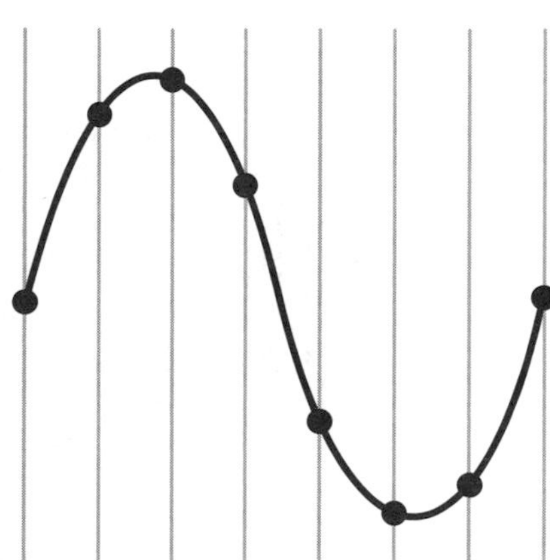

Figure 5.2 Waveform sampled in time. The distance between the vertical grid lines is determined by the sampling rate. The higher the rate, the closer the grid lines are together.

to sample *every* point, storing the data would use up all of the hard drives, flash drives, and CDs in the world before digitizing even a millisecond of the analog audio. The fact that an infinite number of points are thrown away when the ADC digitizes an analog signal has consequences in the resultant digital signal.

The Nyquist Frequency

The consequence of capturing only a finite (rather than infinite) number of samples is that the digital audio can contain no frequency that is higher than one-half of the sampling rate. This maximum frequency is called the **Nyquist frequency** after the physicist and engineer, Harry Nyquist, who contributed to what is known as the **sampling theorem**. For CD-quality digital audio:

Nyquist frequency = ½ × Sampling rate

Nyquist frequency = ½ × 44,100 Hz = 22,050 Hz = 22.05 kHz

What this means is that the maximum frequency that can be present on a CD, including fundamentals *and* all partials, is 22,050 Hz. As a result, every recording system first gets rid of any frequencies above the Nyquist frequency, using a filter, before digitizing the signal (see Figure 5.3). (There is more on filters in Chapter 6, "Digital Audio Software," and in the "Synthesis and Sampling" section.)

The infinite number of samples that the ADC threw away during digitization were necessary to represent all of the frequencies above the Nyquist frequency. Is the loss of all of the frequencies above 22,050 Hz, the Nyquist frequency, an acceptable compromise?

If you remember the discussion of the range of human hearing, we can hear frequencies (fundamentals and partials) up to about 20,000 Hz when we're young. Since 20,000 Hz < 22,050 Hz, digital audio sampled at the CD-quality sampling rate contains all of the frequencies that we can hear, and thus the compromise works.

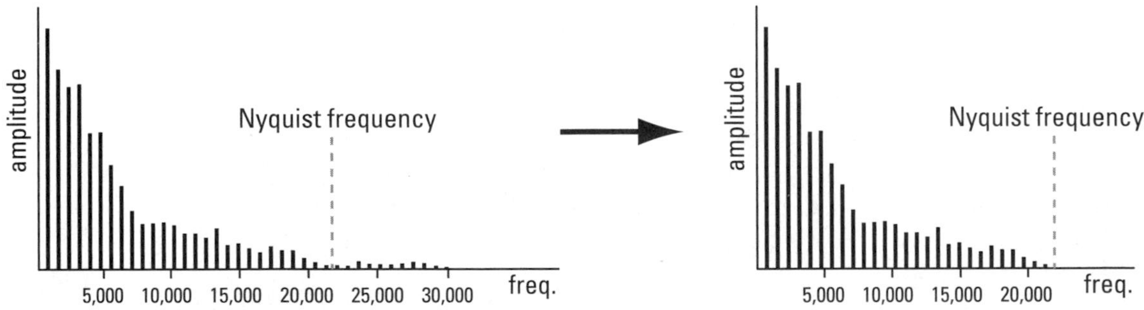

Figure 5.3 A hypothetical spectrum and the results after filtering out frequencies above the Nyquist frequency so that the sound can be digitized.

Higher Sampling Rates

Despite the fact that the CD-quality sampling rate properly represents all of the frequencies that we can hear, higher sampling rates are frequently used during recording, even when the result is eventually reduced to the CD-quality sampling rate or to a compressed format for distribution.

One common sampling rate is 48 kHz, which is only marginally higher than the CD-quality sampling rate. This sampling rate is the standard for audio that accompanies video; a video file ripped from a DVD will most often have audio at 48 kHz. Fortunately, even the built-in audio outputs of a computer can usually handle 48 kHz, so you don't have to do anything special to play it back.

There are two higher than CD-quality sampling rates often used in recording: 96 kHz and 192 kHz. The Nyquist frequencies for these two sampling rates are 48 kHz and 96 kHz respectively, both of which are far above human hearing. In addition, some audio interfaces support 88.2 kHz.

There are various arguments used to justify high sampling rates. There are the sound-quality justifications, including being able to perform the initial filtering far out of the range of human hearing, being able to capture ultrasonic frequencies that may combine in performance to produce audible components within the range of human hearing, or that the sound has more "sparkle." These arguments have been hotly debated with no clear resolution. There are also cultural justifications, including "everyone else is doing it" and "I can use these numbers to convince my clients that my studio is state-of-the-art."

Regardless of the reason, recording practice routinely includes 96 kHz and sometimes 192 kHz, even when the final product is distributed at 44.1 kHz or as a compressed audio file (more on that later).

Quantization and the Sample Resolution

The ADC measures the incoming analog electrical waveform 44,100 times per second, or more for higher sampling rates. Each time the ADC performs this measurement, it must assign a numerical value to that sample's amplitude. This assignment of a specific value to the measured amplitude is referred to as **quantizing** (see Figure 5.4). It is worth noting that this is *not* the same as the quantizing function found in MIDI sequencing. The sample resolution refers to how many numbers are available for that amplitude measurement. This is also called the **sample width** and the **bit depth**. However, this is *not* the "bitrate," which will be discussed later. Because there is only a specific number of values for a given sample resolution, the ADC will have to round the true amplitude measurement to one of those values.

If there were ten amplitude values available—0, 1, 2, 3, 4, 5, 6, 7, 8, and 9—then the ADC would assign a value of nine to the highest voltage part of the waveform, a value of 0 to the lowest, and other values for in-between voltages. This amplitude measurement would require storage space of one decimal digit since all of the amplitude

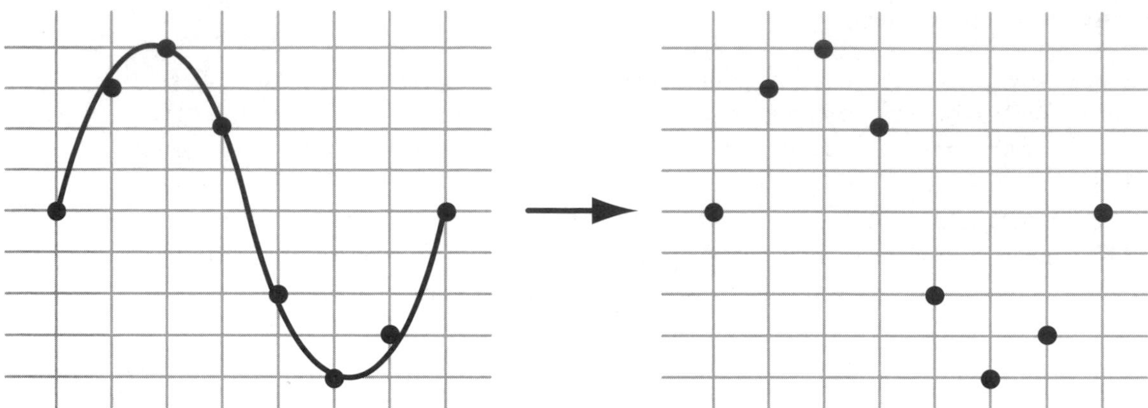

Figure 5.4 Waveform sampled in time *and* quantized in amplitude. The distance between the horizontal grid lines is determined by the sample resolution, which is expressed in bits. The actual amplitude of the waveform and the number assigned by the ADC may be slightly different, as shown in the figure.

values are single digits. If 100 amplitude values were available to the ADC—0, 1, 2, 3, . . . , 97, 98, 99—then the highest measured amplitude would be assigned a value of 99 and the lowest a value of 0. This number of amplitude values would require two decimal digits to store each amplitude measurement.

Computers don't use decimal digits (base 10 numbering system), but rather binary digits, or **bits** (base 2 numbering system), so the number of amplitude values available for the ADC would be given in bits rather than in decimal digits as it was in the examples above. If an ADC was given only one bit to store each of the amplitude measurements, the measured amplitude would have only two values: 0 and 1. If an ADC was given two bits for each amplitude value, there would be four possible values: 00, 01, 10, and 11. The relationship between the number of bits and corresponding number of possible values is shown in Table 5.1.

CD-quality digital audio uses 16 bits for each amplitude measurement with numbers ranging from 0 (binary 0000000000000000) to 65,535 (binary 1111111111111111). In practice, amplitude values are coded in a somewhat more complex way in binary, such that the lowest voltage is not given the value 0 and the highest voltage is not given the value 65,535. However, the simpler coding will be used here for convenience—it doesn't change any of the concepts discussed.

Despite the fact that 65,535 is a pretty large number, there will still be samples whose amplitudes fall in between two values, say, part way between 210 and 211. In that case, the ADC has to choose either 210 or 211—here the term "quantizing" really comes into play. The value 210.6 can't be used because the extra numbers after the decimal point would require additional storage space beyond 16 bits. As a result, the exact amplitude information of the incoming waveform is lost and only the approximation, 210 or 211, remains in the digital signal. As with the infinite number of time points in between samples discussed above, there is an infinite number of amplitude

Table 5.1 **Number of bits in the sample resolution and the corresponding number of values**

# of bits	*values*	*# of values*	*Power of 2*
1	0 1	2	2^1
2	00 10 01 11	4	2^2
3	000 100 001 101 010 110 011 111	8	2^3
...	...	...	...
8	too many to list	256	2^8
...	...	...	...
16	too many to list	65,536	2^{16}
...	...	...	...
24	too many to list	16,777,216	2^{24}

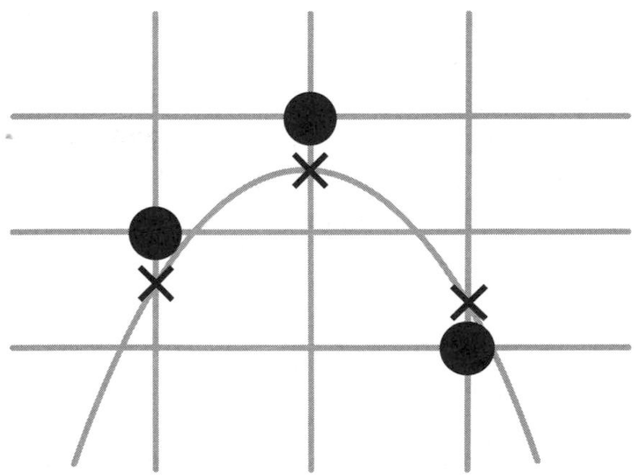

Figure 5.5 Zoomed-in view of the sampled and quantized waveform. The "X"s represent the actual amplitude for a sample and the dots represent the quantized amplitude. The difference between them is the quantization error and results in a small amount of noise in the digitized signal.

values in between the allowable values that are thrown away. Throwing away an infinite number of amplitude values must have some consequence in the resultant digital signal (see Figure 5.5).

Signal-to-Error Ratio and Dynamic Range

The consequence of having only a finite number of available amplitude values is that this results in a consistent average error in the amplitude measurement, which is heard as a small amount of noise in the system. One of the requirements of the sample resolution in a digital audio system is that it be high enough so that the noise due to the measurement error is very small compared to the signal itself. The ratio of the overall signal to the sampling error is referred to as the signal-to-error ratio, which can also be said to be the dynamic range of the system when the signal is at maximum.

The actual calculation of the signal-to-error ratio is beyond the scope of this text, but it is approximately 6 dB per bit. So a maximum amplitude signal has a signal-to-error ratio of approximately 96 dB for 16-bit audio and approximately 144 dB for 24-bit audio. There are negative consequences to quantizing amplitudes, but the standard digital audio resolutions are generally sufficient to minimize these consequences.

Higher Resolutions

Just as sampling rates in recording are now typically greater than CD-quality, the resolution in recording has also increased beyond the CD-quality 16 bits per sample. The modern standard for recording is 24 bits per sample.

The increase in the resolution means that the noise due to the sampling error is far quieter compared to the overall signal, meaning the music can be recorded at a lower average level and still be far above the error noise. This becomes most valuable when the level of the signal falls quite low, as during soft passages in the music. The lower average recording level also allows the music to get significantly louder—more "headroom"—before the signal distorts, which can be valuable for music that has a wide dynamic range or sharp, sudden volume peaks. (See the next chapter, "Digital Audio Software," for further discussion of recording levels.)

The increase to 24-bit audio can also be seen in the same cultural light as the move to higher sampling rates—more is often perceived as better. However, while the value of recording at higher sampling rates is still disputed, it is generally agreed that recording at 24-bit is superior to recording at 16-bit, even if the final product is eventually distributed at 16-bit or as compressed audio.

"High-Definition" Audio

Audio at higher than CD-quality sampling rates and resolutions can be thought of as "high-definition" audio, by analogy with high-definition TV and video. Though **high-def audio** is becoming standard in the recording studio, there is some question as to its likely success as a consumer standard due to the combination of the typical listening environment and the typical audio playback equipment.

The typical listening environment is relatively noisy, surrounded as we usually are with talking roommates, whirring computer fans, or road and engine noise. The typical audio playback equipment is mediocre, whether a personal listening device with ear-buds or an inexpensive to moderately priced home or car stereo. Combined together, these factors yield a decidedly suboptimal listening experience in which you are unlikely to be able to appreciate a high-def recording. There is even some question as to whether the high-def difference is perceivable by most people even if the setting and the equipment are good. High-def recordings in the DVD-Audio or SACD formats may find a market primarily with the community of "audiophiles," who spend money and effort creating high-quality listening systems and environments.

High-def audio may find wider adoption on the Blu-ray disc, which has become the standard for high-def video and can support audio at the higher sampling rates and resolutions discussed above. Mid- to high-level home theater and gaming installations may well provide the environment and equipment needed to appreciate the audio quality improvements of high-def audio.

DIGITAL AUDIO FILE FORMATS

Once an audio signal has been digitized by the ADC, it is typically transmitted to a computer (over USB or FireWire) and stored in a computer file. As with any other type of data (text, pictures, videos), digital audio is stored in some **file format**, which determines what type of information is in the file and how it is organized on the disk. Clearly digital audio files contain digital audio, but there are a variety of ways for that audio to be encoded and stored.

When file formats were discussed in the chapter on computer software, a distinction was made between exclusive formats, which are used by one company or piece of software, and interchange formats, which can be read by software from more than one company. This distinction is still in place in the digital audio world, but a majority of the audio file formats are interchange file formats. For digital audio, probably the most important distinction to make is between **uncompressed** and **compressed files**.

Uncompressed File Formats

In uncompressed file formats, digital audio is stored as a series of 16- or 24-bit amplitude values or as 32-bit floating-point amplitude values—32-bit floating-point values are used for internal calculations within most audio recording software, but recording (ADC) and playback (DAC) are done with 16 or 24 bits. Chunks of data written at the beginning of the file indicate information such as the sampling rate, the resolution, the number of channels (two for stereo, six for 5.1 surround, etc.), and the length of the file. Some formats include other information as well, such as loop points for use by hardware or software samplers. Digital audio that is used by audio editing/processing/mixing software is stored in an uncompressed file format.

The two most prominent uncompressed file formats are **AIFF** (.aif) and **WAVE** (.wav). The Broadcast WAVE format (.wav), a variation on the WAVE format, is the default for many audio applications. In addition, formats such as Apple's **Core Audio Format** (.caf) and **Windows Media Audio format** (.wma) support both uncompressed and compressed audio. Each of the above file formats supports the full range of sampling rates and resolutions.

Calculating the size of an uncompressed digital audio file is straightforward and requires only the sampling rate, the resolution expressed in bytes (16 bits = 2 bytes,

24 bits = 3 bytes, 32-bits = 4 bytes), and some simple conversions. The approximate calculation for stereo, CD-quality audio is given below. The precise calculation is easy to make with a calculator, but the approximation is close enough (the symbol "≈" means "approximately").

44,100 samples/second × 2 bytes/sample = 88,200 bytes/second ≈ 90 kB/second
90 kB/second × 60 seconds/minute = 5,400 kB/minute ≈ 5 MB/minute
5 MB/minute × 2 channels (left and right) = *10 MB/minute*

There are many approximations in that calculation, but if you do it precisely using 1,024 bytes in a kilobyte and 1,024 kilobytes in a megabyte, the result is very close. This is the file size for *stereo* files. Mono audio files that are often used in audio recording projects will be half of that size.

To figure out the size of 24-bit, 96 kHz digital audio, you could either perform a similar calculation, or you could notice that 24 bits is 1½ times 16 bits and 96 kHz is approximately 2 times 44.1 kHz, making the product of those two numbers a factor of about three times the CD-quality standard. Similarly, a 24-bit, 192 kHz audio file would be about six times the CD-quality standard. Table 5.2 shows a variety of specifications for uncompressed audio and the resultant file sizes.

The CD distribution format (Red Book Audio) provides audio in an uncompressed format, and DVD-Video, DVD-Audio, and Blu-ray all allow for uncompressed or compressed audio, though audio on DVD-Video discs is often compressed. Audio on standard CDs is limited to 16-bit, 44.1 kHz, but DVD-Video, DVD-Audio, and Blu-ray support higher sampling rates and resolutions.

Table 5.2 **Approximate file sizes for uncompressed audio**

Audio specs	*Channels/tracks*	*Approx file size/min.*
16-bit/44.1 kHz (CD-quality)	2 channels (stereo)	10 MB
16-bit/48 kHz (video)	2 channels (stereo)	11 MB
24-bit/44.1 kHz	2 channels (stereo)	15 MB
24-bit/48 kHz (video)	2 channels (stereo)	16.5 MB
24-bit/96 kHz ("high-def")	2 channels (stereo)	33 MB
24-bit/192 kHz ("high-def")	2 channels (stereo)	66 MB
16-bit/44.1 kHz (CD-quality)	24 mono track recording	120 MB
16-bit/48 kHz (video)	24 mono track recording	132 MB
24-bit/44.1 kHz	24 mono track recording	180 MB
24-bit/48 kHz (video)	24 mono track recording	198 MB
24-bit/96 kHz ("high-def")	24 mono track recording	396 MB
24-bit/192 kHz ("high-def")	24 mono track recording	792 MB

Compressed File Formats

A file format is said to be compressed if some technique has been used to reduce the amount of data in the file as compared to the uncompressed file. It is worth noting that compression has at least two meanings in music technology. One pertains to the reduction in audio file size discussed here and the other refers to dynamic range compression, which is an audio processing function that will be discussed in the next chapter, "Digital Audio Software."

There are two basic types of audio file compression: lossless and lossy. **Lossless compression** reduces the size of audio files in such a way that the original data can be perfectly recovered. An example of lossless compression from the non-audio world is the .zip file, in which all the data from the zipped files can be fully recovered. **Lossy compression**, on the other hand, reduces audio file sizes by permanently and unrecoverably eliminating some of the audio information. Lossy compression typically achieves far greater reduction in audio file sizes than lossless compression.

Lossless Compression

Lossless audio compression achieves a reduction of about 50 percent, depending on the actual content of the file, without *any* loss of audio quality. There are a number of audio file formats that support lossless audio file compression. The **MP4 format** (.mp4 or .m4a) and the Apple Core Audio Format (.caf) both support Apple Lossless compression, the Windows Media Audio format (.wma) supports Windows Media Audio Lossless, and the **Ogg format** (.ogg or .oga) supports the Free Lossless Audio Codec (FLAC). Lossless compression is also used by the "high-def" audio distribution formats such as SACD, DVD-Audio, and Blu-ray.

Lossy Compression

The goal of lossy compression is to reduce the amount of data in an audio file so that it may be transferred (downloaded) more quickly and more files can be stored on a drive, such as a flash drive or personal listening device. It is simple to reduce the size of an uncompressed audio file, such as a WAVE or AIFF file, by cutting the sampling rate and reducing the resolution. Unfortunately, this simple solution results in poor-quality audio. Most lossy compression schemes utilize **perceptual encoding** to achieve file size reduction without a substantial loss in quality.

The term "perceptual encoding" encompasses a variety of techniques that use knowledge of the human auditory system to selectively remove elements that we wouldn't hear anyway. As an example, one of the auditory phenomena utilized by perceptual encoders is frequency **masking**. If two frequency components are close together, but one is of much higher amplitude, the higher-amplitude frequency component will mask (cover up) the small-amplitude frequency component (see Figure 5.6). In this case, there is no need to waste bits to represent the small-amplitude frequency

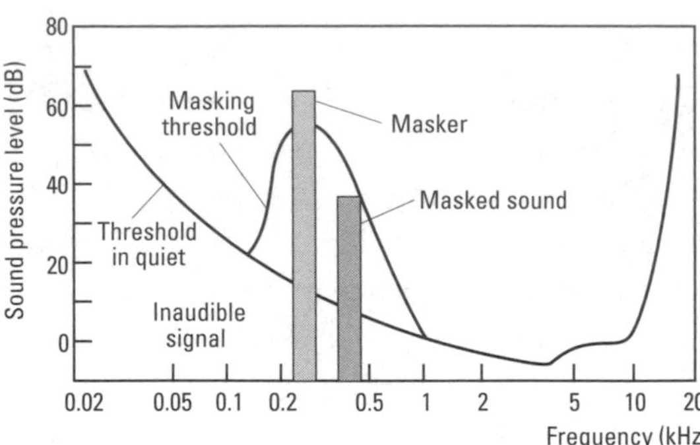

Figure 5.6 The threshold of hearing describes the softest sounds audible across the human hearing range. A masker tone or noise will raise the threshold of hearing in a local region, creating a masking curve. Masked tones or noise, perhaps otherwise audible, that fall below the masking curve during that time will not be audible. (From Ken C. Pohlmann's Principles of Digital Audio, 5th Ed. Copyright © 2005 by The McGraw-Hill Companies, Inc. Reproduced with permission.)

component. This type of "bit savings" is what allows a lossy compressed file to be as small as one-tenth the size of an uncompressed file and still sound acceptable.

The value of reducing the size of audio files for transmission and storage is clear, so the important question is whether the results are acceptable. As with many topics in music technology, the answer is: "it depends." It depends on the properties of the music that is being compressed, it depends on which compression scheme is used, and it depends on the specific settings for that compression scheme.

There are a number of file formats that support lossy compression, with the **MP3 format** being the most well known. Other file formats supporting lossy compression include the aforementioned MP4 format (.mp4 or .m4a), which supports AAC (Advanced Audio Coding) compression, the Windows Media Audio format (.wma), which supports a form of lossy compression, and the Ogg format (.ogg or .oga), which supports Vorbis compression. Apple's Core Audio Format (.caf) supports both AAC and MP3 compression. In addition, DVD-video utilizes lossy compressed audio.

You may notice that some formats support more than one type of audio. For example, the WMA and CAF formats both support uncompressed audio, losslessly compressed audio, and lossy compressed audio. In these situations, it is up to the audio software to determine how to decode the files and play them back.

When you save a file in a lossy file format, you choose a data rate, or **bitrate**, for the resultant file. Common bitrates include 128 kbps (kilobits per second) and 256 kbps. For many people, an MP3 or AAC encoded at 256 kbps will be largely indistinguishable from the original CD-quality recordings. In addition, noisy listening environments and mediocre-quality audio equipment make any compromise due to compression largely irrelevant for casual listening. However, in audio recording, editing, mixing, and mastering only uncompressed audio is used.

Approximate file sizes in megabytes per minute for lossy compressed audio can be calculated as follows:

$$\text{Bitrate in kbps} \div 8 \text{ bits/byte} \times 60 \text{ seconds/minute} \div 1{,}024 \text{ kB/MB}$$

Table 5.3 shows the approximate files sizes for compressed audio at various bitrates. The bitrates for uncompressed files are included as a reference. These are obtained simply by multiplying the sampling rate by the resolution expressed in bits and then multiplying by two channels for stereo.

Table 5.3 **Approximate bitrates and file sizes for stereo audio**

Audio specs	*Approx. bitrate*	*Approx. file size/min.*
MP3, AAC, WMA, Vorbis, etc.	128 kbps	1 MB
MP3, AAC, WMA, Vorbis, etc.	160 kbps	1.2 MB
MP3, AAC, WMA, Vorbis, etc.	192 kbps	1.5 MB
MP3, AAC, WMA, Vorbis, etc.	256 kbps	2 MB
MP3, AAC, WMA, Vorbis, etc.	320 kbps	2.4 MB
16-bit/44.1 kHz (CD-quality)	1,400 kbps	10 MB
16-bit/48 kHz (video)	1,500 kbps	11 MB
24-bit/44.1 kHz	2,100 kbps	15 MB
24-bit/48 kHz (video)	2,300 kbps	16.5 MB
24-bit/96 kHz ("high-def")	4,600 kbps	33 MB
24-bit/192 kHz ("high-def")	9,200 kbps	66 MB

Loops

In addition to the file formats discussed above, there are also several file formats for **loops**. The previous formats have all been associated with recording, distributing, or playing back audio, but loop formats are designed for composing with audio. The end result of a loop composition is eventually saved or exported in one of the formats discussed above. Loops can be run-of-the-mill AIFF or WAVE files, or one of the specialized loop formats such as Acid Loops, Apple Loops, or REX files.

A loop that is stored as a simple AIFF or WAVE file is not technically any different from any other AIFF or WAVE file. These files are only distinguishable from other AIFF or WAVE files in that they are designed to be repeated as a "loop" and are usually an integral number of bars long, such as two or four bars.

The specialized loop formats are a bit different. They are proprietary in that a single company controls each format—Sony controls the **Acid Loop format**, Apple controls the **Apple Loop format**, and Propellerheads controls the REX format (see below)—and they contain special data for use by the music creation software. Despite the proprietary control, these loop formats can be used in a variety of applications.

Both **Acid Loops** and **Apple Loops** are regular uncompressed audio files, WAVE and CAF or AIFF respectively, that include extra information, referred to as **metadata**, which contains the location of attacks, or transients, within the audio file (see Chapter 2, "Sound Properties and the Waveform View"). This information allows software to identify virtual slices of the audio file that can be made to line up with the bars and beats of a project, even if the project tempo is different from the original loop tempo. This is accomplished by automatically stretching or compressing the audio so that the beats of the loop line up with the project timeline. The software maintains this alignment even when the tempo is later adjusted by again stretching or compressing the audio.

Acid Loops were originally designed to be used with the Acid software, but can be used with other pieces of software as well. When WAVE files are turned into Acid Loops, they are referred to as "Acidized" WAVE files. Apple Loops are supported primarily by Apple's own software: GarageBand, Logic, and Soundtrack Pro. An Apple Loop that is created by a software synth in Apple's software can also contain information concerning which synth was used, what effects were applied, and the MIDI data that generated the loop.

REX files are a bit different from Acid or Apple Loops. A REX file starts as a regular file format (AIFF, WAVE, etc.), but is then processed using Propellerheads' Recycle software. When REX files are played back, instead of stretching or compressing the audio in between the transient markers, the slices are treated independently. When the project tempo is significantly slower than the original loop tempo, the slices are separated by silence, and when the project tempo is faster than the original loop tempo, the slices are overlapped. When REX files are played back in Propellerheads' Reason software, MIDI information is generated to trigger each of the slices. As a result, the slices can be reordered or reconfigured in Reason into an entirely new loop just by manipulating the MIDI messages.

Figure 5.7 shows the same loop as a WAVE file and as a REX file before and after a tempo change. In both (a) and (b), the WAVE file is on the top and the REX file is on the bottom. In 5.7a, the project tempo is the same as the original loop tempo and both loops sound fine. The REX file sounds continuous even though it is separated into slices, because the slices are right next to each other. In 5.7b, the project tempo has been reduced to about one-third of the original loop tempo. The WAVE file is still continuous, but because it has been stretched so much, the sound quality is severely degraded. In the REX file, each slice is unchanged in length so the slices are separated

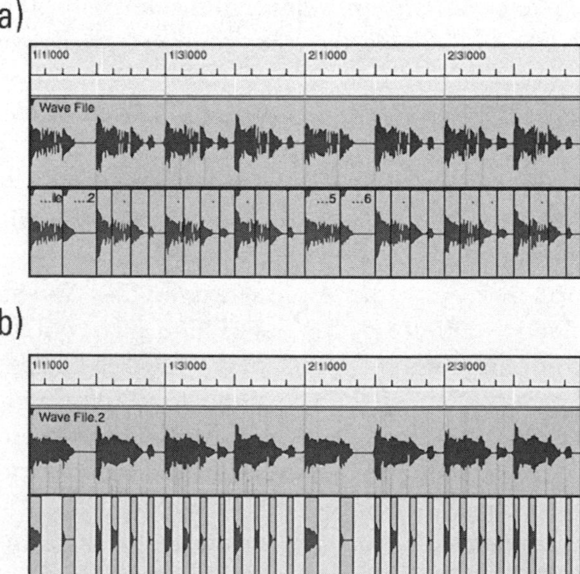

Figure 5.7 The same loop as a WAVE file and a REX file before and after a tempo change: (a) project tempo is same as original loop tempo; (b) project tempo is one-third of original loop tempo.

by silence. Each slice sounds good by itself, but the slices together sound unnatural because of the silence between them. For both file types, extreme changes of tempo result in sound problems.

REVIEW OF KEY TERMS

sampling 73	Core Audio Format 79
sample resolution 73	Windows Media Audio format 79
sampling rate 73	lossless/lossy compression 81
Nyquist frequency 74	MP4 format 81
sampling theorem 74	Ogg format 81
quantizing 75	perceptual encoding 81
sample width/bit depth 75	masking 81
bits 76	MP3 format 82
high-def audio 78	bitrate 82
file format 79	loops 83
uncompressed/compressed files 79	Acid Loop/Apple Loop formats 83
AIFF 79	metadata 83
WAVE 79	REX files 84

CHAPTER 6

Digital Audio Software: The Digital Audio Workstation

There are a variety of software applications that either generate or use digital audio. Software synthesizers and samplers generate digital audio; effects processors such as reverb units process and output digital audio; and computer-assisted instruction programs analyze digital audio to evaluate the pitch or rhythm of the input. However, by far the most common application is digital audio recording software.

A multi-track recording application that allows for editing, processing, and mixing audio is often referred to as a **digital audio workstation**, or **DAW**. The term is sometimes used to refer to the entire hardware and software system. Here we will use the term to refer to the software with the understanding that the software runs on a computer and requires hardware audio inputs and outputs in order to function.

In addition to audio recording, many DAWs also support MIDI sequencing and software synthesizers/samplers, making them full-featured recording and creation environments that can be used by engineers in a recording studio, pop or film composers in a project studio, or live performers and DJs. In general, the term "DAW" will be used when referring to the audio recording functions of such software and "sequencer" or "sequencer/DAW" when referring to the MIDI sequencing and softsynth hosting functions. MIDI sequencing and software synthesizers/samplers will be covered in later sections of this text.

There are many programs available that allow you to record, edit, process, and mix digital audio, ranging from free, open source programs to expensive professional-level DAWs. These programs also have a wide range of features, from simple two-track (stereo) recording and editing to unlimited tracks with many processing plug-ins and support for surround sound output. Despite the wide range of prices and features, there are several concepts and graphical interface conventions that are common to most of these programs.

COMMON DAW INTERFACE ELEMENTS

Transport

Among the most basic DAW interface features are the **transport controls**, including play, stop, pause, rewind, fast-forward, and record buttons. In the days of reel-to-reel recording—the 1940s to the 1990s—transport controls literally caused tape to be transported from one reel to another. Though no physical material is being moved by the transport controls now, the label has stuck. As you can see from Figure 6.1, transport controls from different DAWs are similar and share many of the same basic icons with CD players, iPods, cassette decks, and DVD players. When you use the transport controls, the results are reflected in the DAW's **main clock**.

A DAW's main clock can show time in a variety of formats, including real time, SMPTE time, and musical time. Real time is given in minutes, seconds, tenths of seconds, and hundredths of seconds; SMPTE, which stands for the Society of Motion Picture and Television Engineers, is given in hours, minutes, seconds, and frames; and musical time is given in bars, beats, and ticks.

The type of recording project will determine the appropriate time measurement. In a "pure" recording project in which all the audio is being recorded from external sources, the clock will usually show real time. In a project that is to be synchronized to video, such as sound effects editing, the clock will usually show SMPTE time. SMPTE time code divides a second into the number of frames at which the video was shot, which allows you to precisely synchronize elements of the project to the film. In a compositional project such as a song or a film score, the clock would usually show musical time in bars, beats, and divisions of a beat referred to as ticks, clicks, clocks, or units. This allows the audio to be integrated with MIDI-controlled software instruments. The divisions of a beat will be discussed in more detail in Chapter 10, "MIDI Sequencing."

Many DAWs allow you to display time in more than one format simultaneously using a secondary clock. This is particularly useful for projects such as film scoring, where musical time and SMPTE time are both important, and post-production sound editing, where real time and SMPTE time are both important.

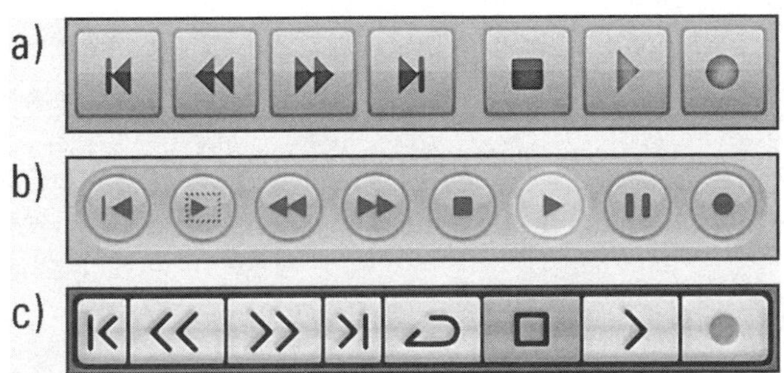

Figure 6.1 Transport controls from various DAWs: (a) Pro Tools LE 8 (courtesy of Digidesign); (b) Logic Pro 8 (screenshot reprinted with permission from Apple Inc.); and (c) Cubase Studio 4 (courtesy of Steinberg Media Technologies).

Figure 6.2 includes clocks from several different DAWs showing the same time in various formats. Figure 6.2a shows the clock from Pro Tools LE 8, with real time as the main clock and musical time as the secondary clock. The musical time indicates the last 32nd note of measure one, beat four. Figure 6.2b shows the clock from Logic Pro 8, with SMPTE time as the main clock and musical time as the secondary clock. The SMPTE time is offset to indicate a time of exactly one hour at the very beginning of the project. This is often done in video projects to allow for test tones and other material before the actual program material. The musical time in Figure 6.2b indicates the same point in the music as Figure 6.2a, but the time is given in bars, beats, 16th notes, and ticks rather than bars, beats, and ticks. Figure 6.2c shows the clock from Digital Performer 6, with real time as the main clock and SMPTE time (with no hour offset) as the secondary clock.

Tracks

In a DAW, you would create a separate **audio track** for each input source. If an instrument, such as a drum set, requires multiple microphones, you would create more than one audio track for that instrument. In addition, any imported audio or loops would require their own tracks. It is important to note that some DAWs have explicit limitations on the number of tracks that can be used in a project.

A track is usually represented as a horizontal strip in an **edit view** or a vertical strip in a **mix view**, where the interface is modeled after hardware mixers. Though these two views of a track allow you to perform different operations on the audio, they share common track controls, such as name, record-enable, play, mute, solo, input source, and output destination. Edit view and mix view will be discussed below.

Though not explicitly a track "control," each track has a name. This may seem trivial, but it's an important aspect of a project's organization. As you change from view to view, work on different phases of a project, or work on multiple projects at the same time, it becomes easy to lose track of just what audio is stored on a given track. A descriptive name like "drum set-kick drum" or "rhythm guitar-amp mic" can be very useful when working on a complex project or when coming back to a project after a period of time.

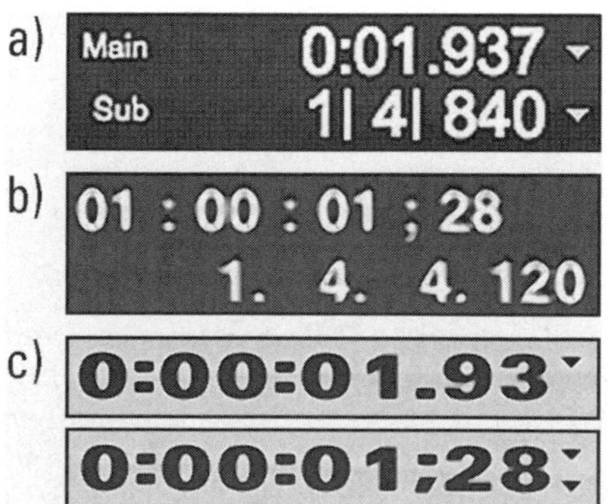

Figure 6.2 Clocks from various DAWs showing different ways of measuring time: (a) Pro Tools LE 8, with real time as the main clock and musical time as the secondary clock (courtesy of Digidesign); (b) Logic Pro 8, with SMPTE time as the main clock and musical time as the secondary clock (screenshot reprinted with permission from Apple Inc.); and (c) Digital Performer 6, with real time as the main clock and SMPTE time as the secondary clock (courtesy of MOTU).

In order to record on a track, you must **record-enable**, or "arm," that track. This is a safety feature that allows you to avoid accidentally recording over existing material. A track's **mute button** allows you to turn off various tracks so that they don't sound during playback. **Solo** is a complementary concept to mute where you can select specific tracks to sound during playback by clicking the individual solo buttons for those tracks. Solo allows you to isolate specific tracks so that you can perform certain editing operations or fix specific problems. It seems paradoxical, but you can actually "solo" more than one track at a time. In general, you would use mute when you want to hear all but a few tracks and solo when you want to hear only a few tracks.

Each track will have an **input assignment** and an **output assignment**. Input usually refers to the audio interface input for the source that is being recorded on a track, and output usually refers to the audio interface output. However, these can also be internal sources and destinations. This topic will be discussed later in the chapter under "Mixing."

Figure 6.3 shows basic track controls for Cubase Studio 4 (6.3a) and Digital Performer 6 (6.3b). In Figure 6.3a, the track inputs and outputs appear at the left and mute, solo, record, and input monitor icons are across the top. In Figure 6.3b, the input monitor, play/mute, and record icons appear across the top, and the output and input assignments appear below.

Edit View

The edit view for a track is used for just that: editing. In addition to the common track controls mentioned above, the edit view provides a timeline-based overview of the audio on the track with a graphic representation of its amplitude to facilitate finding appropriate edit points (see Figure 6.4). In addition to the transport controls mentioned above, the edit view's timeline provides alternate ways of navigating through a project, including moving the playback "head" and scrubbing.

The playback head, or playback wiper, indicates the current position on the project timeline. The transport controls change both the main clock and the position of the

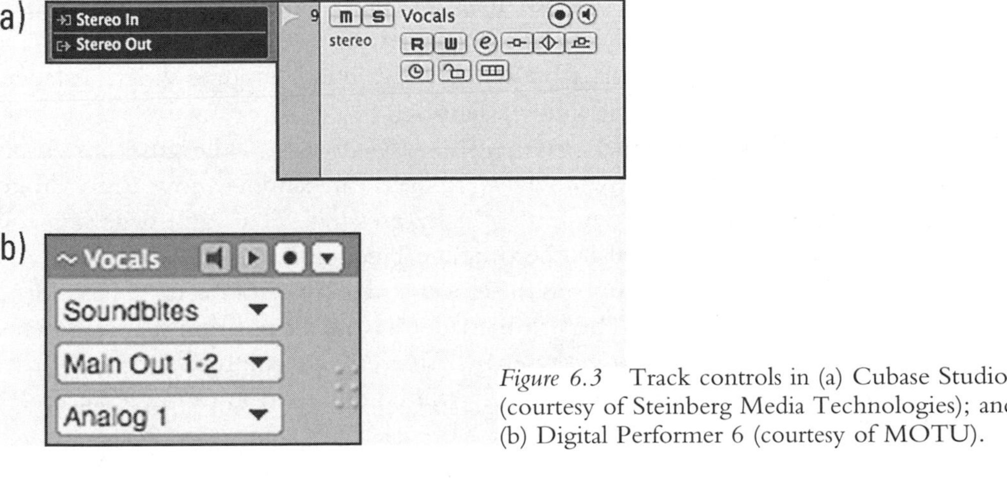

Figure 6.3 Track controls in (a) Cubase Studio 4 (courtesy of Steinberg Media Technologies); and (b) Digital Performer 6 (courtesy of MOTU).

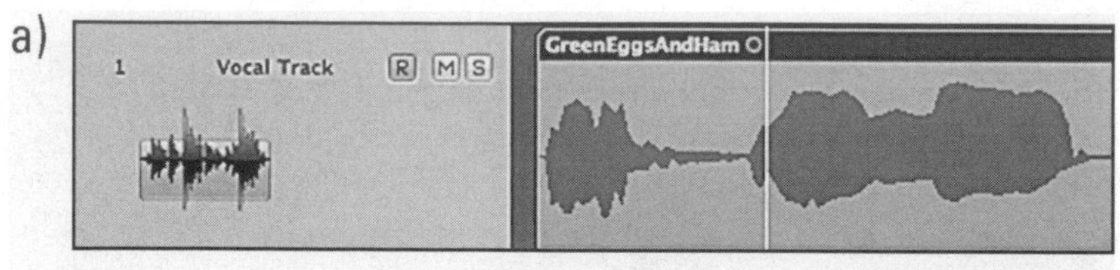

Figure 6.4 The edit view for tracks in (a) Logic Pro 8 (screenshot reprinted with permission from Apple Inc.); and (b) Cubase Studio 4 (courtesy of Steinberg Media Technologies).

playback wiper. You can typically drag the playback wiper to a desired location, or scroll to the desired point in the project and click or double-click on the timeline to move the playback wiper to that point. The clock will also change when the position of the playback wiper changes.

Scrubbing typically involves choosing a special scrubbing tool and then dragging the mouse along the audio. The audio under the cursor will play back giving you an idea of what part of the recording you're looking at. Often the audio will play back faster or slower, with the attendant higher or lower pitch, depending on how fast you move the mouse. This is similar to a practice from the era of reel-to-reel editing where the tape would be pressed up against the playback head as the reels were moved to determine location.

In addition to the waveform overview of the audio in a track, the edit view also typically shows any volume, pan, or effects automation present in the track. This will be discussed later in the chapter under "Mixing."

Mix View

Another common view of DAW tracks is the mix view, in which each track is represented by a fader strip designed to look like the channel strip of a hardware mixer (see Figure 6.5). In addition to the common track controls discussed above (mute, solo, record-enable, input/output), the mix view typically provides a volume slider, or fader, a pan knob, a place for insert effects, and auxiliary sends.

Each of the mix view interface components displays its state at the time shown on the main clock. There is no way in this view to see, for example, how the volume fader is going to change over time without actually pressing "play" and watching the fader move. This is very different from the timeline-based edit view discussed above.

As expected, the volume fader controls the amount of increase or decrease in volume of the audio recorded on the track. The volume fader has a 0 dB position that represents no change, a positive dB range that represents an increase in volume, and a negative dB range that represents a decrease. This aspect will be discussed in more detail under "Mixing."

Figure 6.5 The mix view for tracks in (a) Pro Tools LE 8 (courtesy of Digidesign); and (b) Logic Pro 8 (screenshot reprinted with permission from Apple Inc.). Effects inserts and sends are not shown.

The pan (panorama) knob positions the audio in the stereo field if the audio file has only one channel (mono) and adjusts the left-right balance if the audio file has two channels (stereo). In many DAWs, the pan knob is really a disguised pan slider. Because a mouse is not a great tool for moving in a small circle, often a DAW will allow you to click on the pan knob and drag up to move the pan knob clockwise or down to move the pan knob counter-clockwise. Some DAWs provide horizontal sliders for pan to avoid this potential confusion.

The effects inserts and auxiliary sends that are normally seen in the mix view are two different methods for applying effects to the audio in a track. Effects will be discussed further under "Mixing" later in the chapter.

RECORDING

The basic steps for recording, or "tracking," are straightforward:

1. Position the mics.
2. Connect the mics to the audio interface (we're assuming here that you're not using standalone preamps or a mixing board, though if you were, most of these concepts would remain the same).
3. Turn on phantom power on the interface if you're using condenser mics.
4. Set the appropriate inputs for your DAW tracks.
5. Record-enable those tracks.
6. Click the record button in the DAW transport controls.

With just these steps, you will end up with audio recorded to tracks in your DAW. However, it may not come out the way you want it. Proper recording technique is a very involved topic, but you can go a long way just by understanding recording levels and monitoring.

Recording Levels

Music seldom stays at the same dynamic level throughout an entire song. A vocalist may whisper during the introduction to a song and then switch to full-on screaming for the chorus, or a guitarist playing distorted power chords may suddenly switch to non-distorted picking. To accommodate this kind of volume range, you need to set the **trim/gain knobs**, on the audio interface so that the loudest sounds never

exceed the capacity of the digital system. If the input levels do exceed the capacity of the system, **clipping** occurs, which results in harsh digital distortion (see Figure 6.6). This kind of distortion is very different from the desirable distortion from an electric guitar.

Clipping occurs when an input level to your interface is too high, causing the ADC to assign maximum or minimum amplitude values to many samples in a row. This results in a waveform with a flat, or clipped, top and bottom that does not resemble the analog waveform that was being recorded. To avoid this, you need to watch the level meters in your DAW during sound check and recording. These meters display the levels of the incoming signals and turn red when a signal is being clipped. When clipping occurs, the solution is usually to turn down the trim/gain knob, on the audio interface and re-record the passage. If the gain for that input is all the way down and clipping is still happening, you may need to turn on a pad on that input which further reduces the level. Pads are often used for very loud instruments, such as kick drums and guitar amps.

The level meters in a DAW typically display the incoming level as **dBFS** (**decibels full scale**). Like all decibels, dBFS compares two values. In this case, those values are

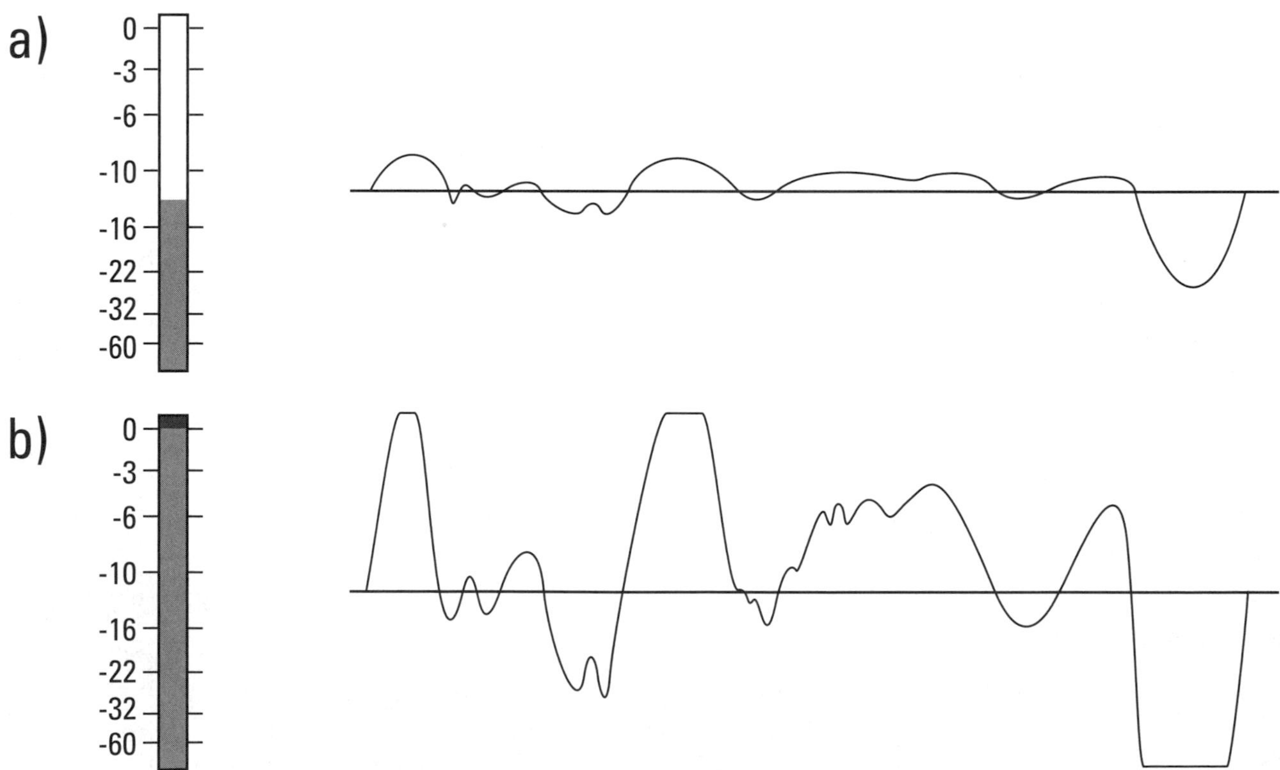

Figure 6.6 Two recording levels and the resultant waveforms: (a) good level and clean waveform, and (b) distorted level and clipped waveform.

the amplitude value of the sample being assigned by the ADC and the largest possible amplitude value, which is determined by the sample resolution (16- or 24-bit). The ratio of these two numbers is always less than or equal to one: the sample value being assigned is always less than or equal to the maximum value that can be assigned. The decibel equation produces negative values if the ratio is less than one and zero if the ratio is equal to one. Therefore, negative dBFS values are undistorted and a value of 0 dBFS indicates clipping.

As a result, when you're watching your DAW's level meters you want to be sure that the dBFS values are negative and don't reach zero. If they do, you need to turn down the trim/gain knob for that input on your interface or perhaps engage a pad. In general, when recording at 24-bit resolution, you should keep the average dBFS value at something like –18. Some engineers prefer –12 dBFS and others –24 dBFS. Average dBFS values in this range give you plenty of **headroom**, which is the amount of dBFS increase above the average level before clipping occurs, while still maintaining a good **signal-to-noise ratio**, which is the difference in dBFS between the signal and the noise in the system.

It's important to note that the decibels mentioned in the previous paragraphs are *not* the same as the dB SPL mentioned in the "Sound" section or the dBV and dBu mentioned in the "Audio Hardware" chapter. The decibel is an equation that involves the ratio of two values and is used in many different circumstances in music technology. When you see "dB," be sure you know what values are being compared.

Monitoring and Latency

During a recording session, it is standard practice for performers to be able to hear themselves along with the rest of the tracks through headphones. However, in digital systems there is a possible delay between when the performer makes a sound and when the sound reaches the headphones. The reason for this delay is that, after a signal has been digitized by your audio interface, the computer stores some number of samples in a **buffer** and then routes the output of the buffer to a track in your DAW software. To hear that audio back, the computer again stores samples in a buffer before sending them out to the audio interface. These buffers are necessary to avoid "dropouts" in the audio stream, which would be heard as pops or clicks. The delay caused by these buffers is called **monitoring latency**, and if it's too large, it can be very disconcerting to the performer.

To get around this, many audio interfaces have a **hardware monitoring** feature in which incoming audio can be routed directly from the hardware inputs to the hardware outputs without first going through the computer. This makes the monitoring latency almost zero for the performer. The drawback to this is that the performer's audio can't be routed through any effects in the DAW, such as reverb or EQ (equalization), during recording, though these effects can be applied later to the recorded audio.

Another solution to the monitoring latency problem is to lower the input/output buffer size to a small value. This makes the computer work harder because it has to prioritize handling sound samples so that there are no pops or clicks, but it can bring the latency down to a manageable level. With this strategy, you can pass the audio through the DAW's effects so that the performers can hear themselves with reverb and EQ, though these effects can also add to the latency (see Figure 6.7).

EDITING

Once the audio has been recorded, it can be edited and processed in a variety of ways. It's the editing process that allows you to cut out errors, combine multiple "takes" (versions) of a performance, and change the duration and pitch of the audio.

Non-destructive Editing

DAWs typically allow you to edit audio **non-destructively**. This means that the actual audio you've recorded isn't altered in the editing process. The DAW either creates new audio, as in the case of operations such as time stretching or pitch shifting, or changes the way it references the original file, as in the case of operations such as cutting and pasting. DAWs generally keep the actually audio files separate from the project file (but usually in the same project folder on the hard drive), so the audio that you "see" in the project file is merely a reference to that external file. These references to audio files are variously called regions, soundbites, clips, or events by different DAWs. We'll use "region" from now on for simplicity.

If you have a region that represents the entire soundfile you recorded, and you press play, the DAW will read the samples of the soundfile on the disk from beginning to end. If you select the end of that region and hit delete, that chunk of the soundfile will seem to disappear in the DAW. What really happens is that, when you press play again, the DAW will read the samples of the soundfile on the disk from the beginning until the point where the edited region ends, and then the DAW will stop reading the samples. The original soundfile hasn't been cut; the DAW just doesn't read the whole thing.

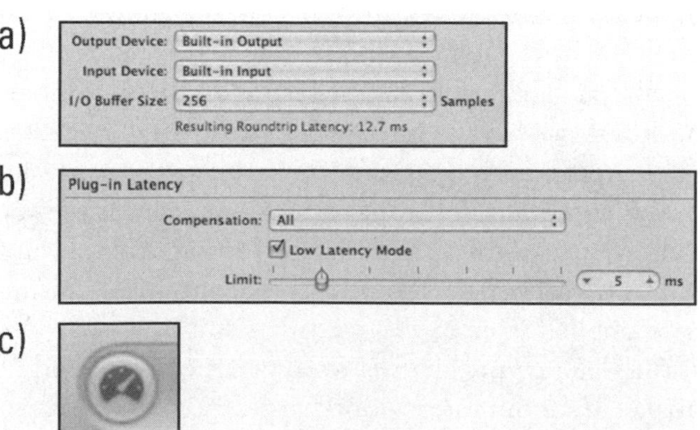

Figure 6.7 Latency-related settings in Logic Pro 8: (a) Input/output buffer size setting in samples; (b) plug-in delay compensation setting, which determines how Logic will shift tracks in time based on the delays caused by their plug-ins, and the "low-latency mode" setting; and (c) low-latency mode icon, which, when engaged, bypasses any plug-ins on the current track and its signal path that exceed the latency set in the preferences shown in (b)—this is useful when playing software instruments.

Similarly, if you copy a region and paste it elsewhere in a project, the DAW will simply read the same portion of the soundfile when it encounters the duplicated region. The same soundfile might be referenced by dozens of regions. Non-destructive editing is a very efficient and powerful way to edit. Many DAWs also have a destructive editor available, but it is typically used sparingly (see Figure 6.8).

Cut, Copy, Paste, Trim

Each DAW has its own terminology for ways of removing or copying parts of a region. The familiar cut, copy, and paste commands are usually available and operate on whatever region or portion of a region has been selected. Once you copy and paste part of a region, the pasted material becomes its own region which references the original audio file.

Another common way to edit a region is by editing its edge. Most DAWs have this feature, though they may each refer to it by a different name. For example, Digital Performer calls this function "Edge Edit," whereas Pro Tools calls it "Trim." This involves either using a special tool or positioning the mouse at a special place at the edge of a region and then dragging. This allows you to remove the beginning and/or end of a region (see Figure 6.9).

Removing all of a region *except* the part that is selected is another common editing function; it is the opposite of the "cut" or "delete" function. This involves selecting a portion of a region and then choosing the function from a menu or with a key command. Again, different DAWs use different names for this function. For example, Digital Performer calls this function "Trim," whereas Pro Tools calls it "Trim to Selection." This is a complementary function to edge editing. If you only need to *remove* a small portion at the beginning and/or end, you would use edge editing/trimming. If you only needed to *keep* a small portion of the region in the middle, you would use trim/trim to selection.

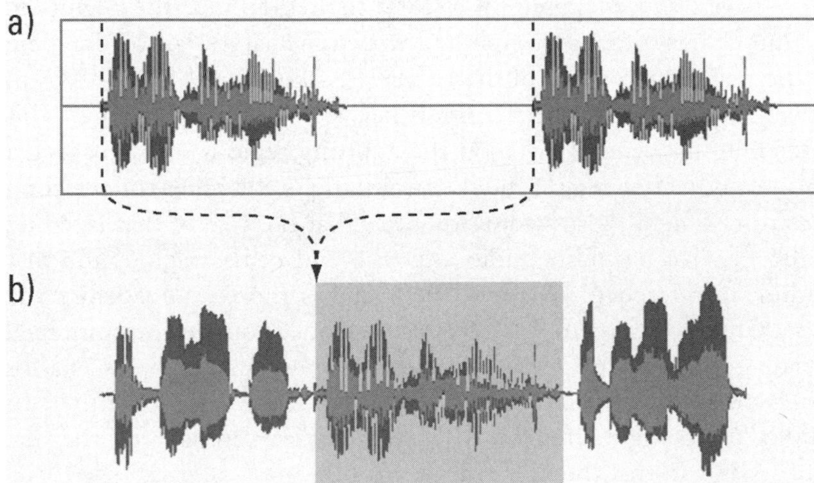

Figure 6.8 Non-destructive editing. The two events on the audio track shown in (a) both reference the same part of the audio file stored on the disk shown in (b).

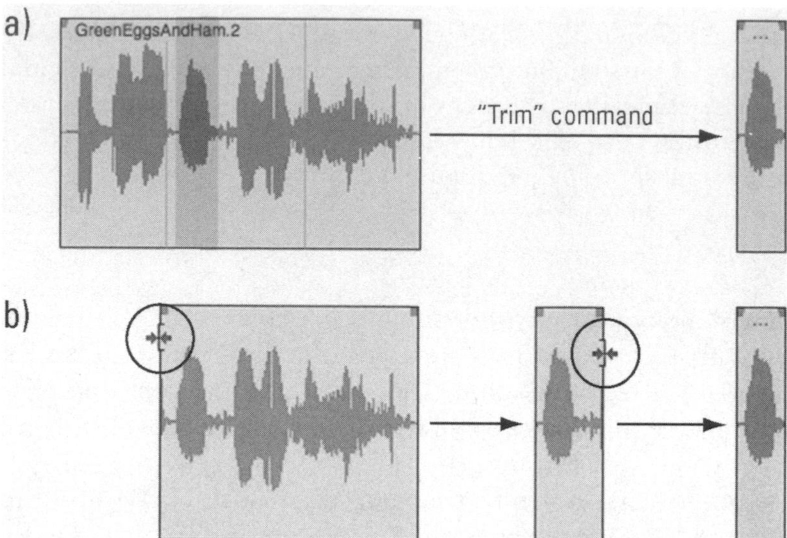

Figure 6.9 Using Trim and Edge Edit in Digital Performer 6 to achieve the same result: (a) the "Trim" command removes audio before and after the selection; (b) dragging the edge of a soundbite (region) removes that audio from the soundbite. (Courtesy of MOTU)

Aside from these common editing functions, each DAW has its own unique collection of functions that are designed to be efficient and useful in that particular DAW. Part of learning to edit or do anything else in a DAW is learning its terminology for common functions and learning the unique functions that represent that particular DAW's "spin" on editing.

Fades and Crossfades

A region that was cut, trimmed, or edge edited from another region often has sudden jumps in amplitude at the beginning and end. These sudden jumps typically sound like pops or glitches. One way of fixing these pops is to **fade** the region in at the beginning and fade it out at the end. This is often accomplished with a special tool or by dragging on a special place at the beginning or end of the region (see Figure 6.10).

A **crossfade** allows you to smooth the transition between adjoining regions. This is accomplished by dragging in a special place on the abutting regions or by making a selection that includes the end of one region and the beginning of the other and selecting a crossfade command from a menu. Crossfading requires that the region that is fading out references an audio file that has more audio after the end of the region, and that the region that is fading in references an audio file that has more audio before the beginning of the region. Crossfading, then, is really just a fade out of one region combined with a simultaneous fade in of another. One of the more common crossfading scenarios is when you want to combine the beginning of one take with the end of another. In that situation, the audio files being referenced will have similar material after the first region and before the second so that the crossfade is smooth.

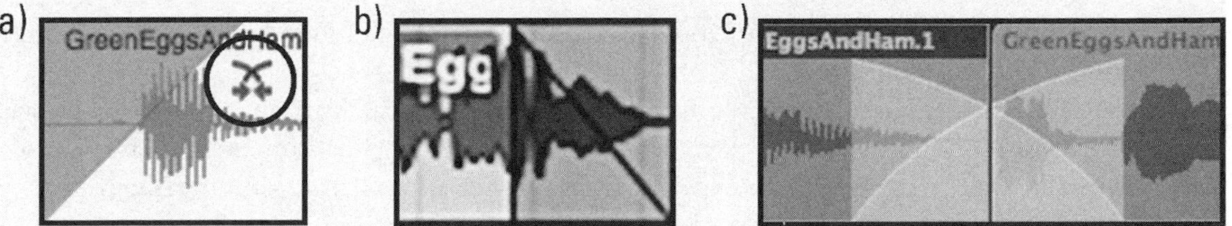

Figure 6.10 (a) Fade-in in Digital Performer 6—fade tool circled (courtesy of MOTU); (b) fade-out in Pro Tools LE 8 (courtesy of Digidesign); and (c) a crossfade between two regions in Logic Pro 8 (screenshot reprinted with permission from Apple Inc.).

The examples given above are linear fades: the lines are straight. Most DAWs allow you to change the shape of the fade depending on the desired affect. This is especially useful in crossfades, where linear fades can cause a drop in perceived volume in the middle of the crossfade. "Equal-power" fades can correct that drop in volume (see Figure 6.11).

Time Stretch and Pitch Shift

Two common ways of altering a region are to stretch it in time to make the region take more or less time and to shift its pitch to be lower or higher. In general, slowing down and speeding up a sound and changing a sound's pitch are inextricably linked together: lower and slower, higher and faster. Fortunately, DAWs have special time-stretch and pitch-shift functions that can be applied independently of one another. In

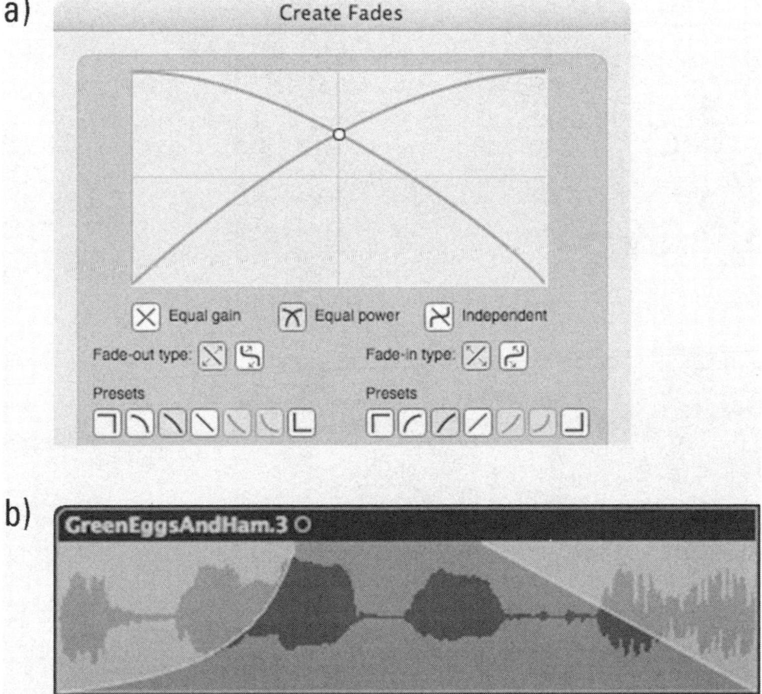

Figure 6.11 Variously shaped fades: (a) the "Create Fades" dialog in Digital Performer 6 with equal power crossfade selected (courtesy of MOTU); and (b) different fade-in and fade-out shapes in Logic Pro 8 (screenshot reprinted with permission from Apple Inc.).

fact, it can be difficult in some DAWs to perform the old-fashioned variety of combined pitch shift and time stretch.

The most famous application of **pitch shifting** is the currently ubiquitous vocal pitch-correction software known as Auto-Tune made by the company Antares. Auto-Tune involves detecting pitches in a recording or live audio stream and then pitch shifting them slightly to match desired pitches. This can be done automatically in real time or by hand after the recording has been completed. It is a controversial technique because it calls into question the extent to which a recording or performance reflects the skill of the engineer rather than the skill of the performer. Some performers have made extensive use of extreme settings in Auto-Tune to create an obviously processed sound (see Figure 6.12).

Pitch shifting is also used for transposing loops in music and for processing sound for film. Loops with pitched content can be transposed to match the current project's key using metadata in the loop soundfile to determine the key of the original. Pitch shifting like this generally works only for relatively small intervals, though the software is getting better at this all the time. Movie sound designers regularly speak of "pitching down" a recording to be used as an effect, such as lowering the pitch of a recording of a common animal to create the sound of a fantasy monster. This kind of pitch shift often uses the old-fashioned pitch shift/time stretch, in which lower and slower are linked (see Figure 6.13).

Time stretching is used in a variety of musical contexts. When a song is remixed, the remixer is usually supplied with the raw multi-track files. To sync up the original vocals with a new groove at a different tempo, the vocals may be time stretched. Another

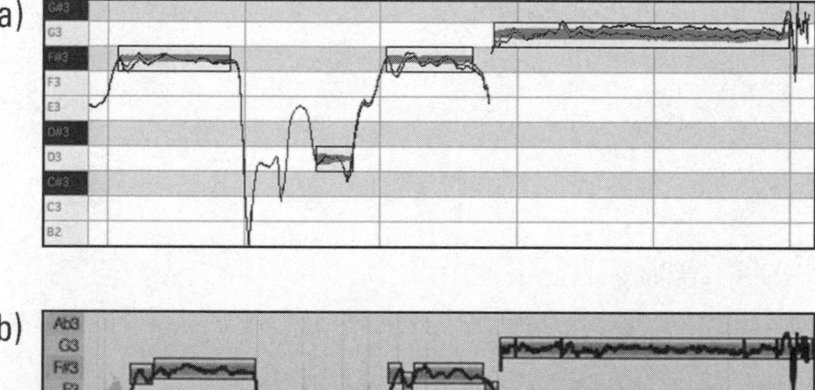

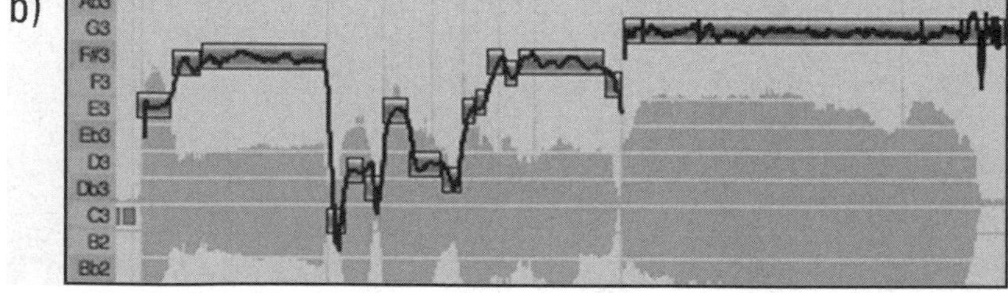

Figure 6.12 Pitch analysis and manipulation of digital audio using (a) Auto-Tune EVO (courtesy of Antares Audio Technologies); and (b) Digital Performer 6 (courtesy of MOTU).

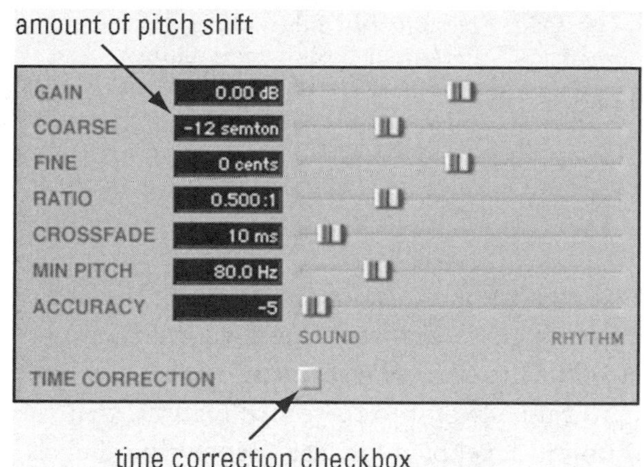

Figure 6.13 Pitch shift plug-in in Pro Tools LE 8 showing a pitch shift down of an octave and no time correction. The new region will be longer than the original. (Courtesy of Digidesign)

musical application of time stretching is composing with loops. When importing a loop into a project, that loop is seldom at the same tempo as the project. Using the metadata in the loop audio file, a DAW can time stretch it to sync it up with bars and beats of the project.

MIXING

Once all of the tracks have been recorded and edited, the mixing process begins. Mixing is a complicated topic, but it typically involves volume and pan automation and effects processing.

Volume and Pan

Volume and pan are fairly straightforward concepts. Nevertheless, proper setting of these parameters is a crucial task in mixing. Volume, pan, and effects parameters can all be automated in a DAW, which means that they can be made to change over time. You can see **automation** in action by watching the faders and knobs in the mix view or see the trajectories of these parameters in the edit view (see Figure 6.14).

In the mix view, there is usually a button or pop-up menu to enable writing automation and reading automation for a track. With automation in one of the "write" modes, you can press play and then move the volume fader or other control, and that gesture will be recorded. With automation "read" or "play" on, the recorded automation will control the audio on that track. Automation can also be turned off so that the track will play back as if there's no automation there. This can be useful for troubleshooting a mix.

As mentioned earlier in the chapter, the volume fader on a track controls the volume of the audio on the track relative to the level at which the audio was recorded. The volume fader's units are given in decibels (dB) of change, with 0 dB representing no change—the audio plays back at the same level at which it was recorded, positive dB representing a boost in volume, and negative dB representing a reduction in volume. If

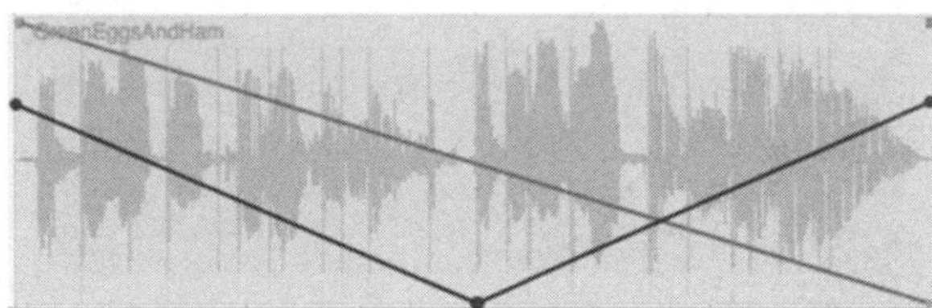

Figure 6.14 Edit view in Digital Performer 6, showing volume automation (dark line) and pan automation (lighter line). (Courtesy of MOTU)

the audio was originally recorded at a low level, a volume fader setting of 0 dB will pass that low level through with no change. In that circumstance, raising the fader into the positive dB range will increase the volume of the material we want to hear *and* the volume of any noise in the recording. If possible, it is usually best to re-record material that was recorded far too quietly rather than boosting its level by a lot. See “Recording Levels” on pages 91–93.

Effects

Effects processing is also an important part of the mixing phase. Common effects include dynamics processing, equalization (EQ), and time-based effects such as delay, flange, chorus, and reverb. There are also many other non-common effects that may be used for creative purposes, including granulation and decimation.

DAWs typically come with a variety of effect **plug-ins**. Plug-ins are parts of a program that perform specific functions and operate only within a host application—in this case a DAW. DAWs ship with some plug-ins already and there are many companies that make plug-ins for use with various DAWs. Those are referred to as “third-party” plug-ins.

When plug-ins are inserted in the mix view (see Figure 6.15), they are non-destructive in that their effects are calculated on the fly and the original audio file remains unchanged. Plug-ins can often be applied in the edit view as well by selecting a region or part of a region and choosing the plug-in from a menu. In that case a new audio file is created from the region with the applied effect.

Dynamics Processing

Dynamics processing refers to various ways of manipulating the overall dynamic range of a track. The dynamic range is the difference in loudness between the quietest part of the audio and the loudest part. This can vary quite a bit depending on the type of music. For example, pop music tends to have a fairly narrow dynamic range—even the singer’s breathing is loud—whereas classical music tends to have a very wide dynamic range from the softest oboe solo to the full blast of an orchestra. One of the most common dynamic processors is the **compressor**.

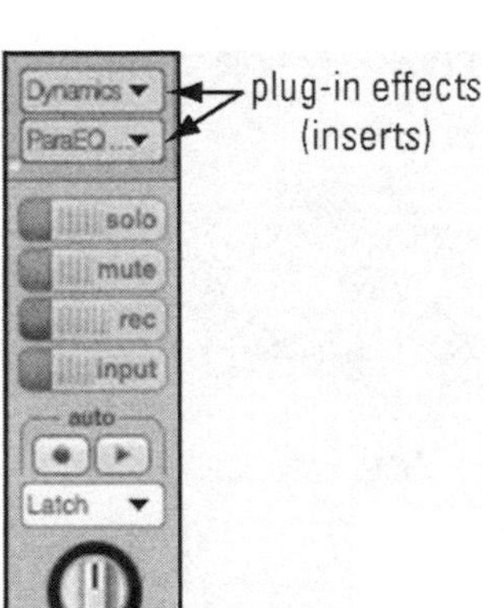

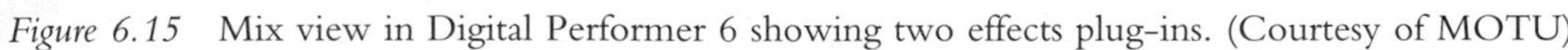

Figure 6.15 Mix view in Digital Performer 6 showing two effects plug-ins. (Courtesy of MOTU)

A compressor reduces the loud parts of an audio signal, thereby narrowing the dynamic range, and then typically boosts the entire signal so that everything is louder. As a result, the singer's breathing and the guitarist's power chords will be closer together in level, giving the music an "in your face" quality. Compression is used extensively, even excessively, in pop music and almost not at all in classical music. This is one of the reasons why it's so easy to hear all of a pop tune while driving in a car, but almost impossible to hear all of a classical piece in the same setting.

You can see an extreme example of compression in Figure 6.16. The original track as shown in Figure 6.16a has many dynamic peaks and valleys. Figure 6.16b shows the result of reducing the loud parts of an audio signal by a large amount; the loudest parts of the original audio signal are now almost the same as the quietest parts. Finally, Figure 6.16c shows the boosting of the entire signal back up to its previous maximum level. The dynamic peaks and valleys have compressed together, thereby drastically reducing the dynamic range of the audio.

Equalization

Equalization, or EQ, allows you to adjust the amount of energy in various regions of the spectrum, thereby changing the timbral quality of the audio. EQ is often used in a corrective fashion to boost part of an audio track's spectrum that is being covered up by audio on another track or cut out an unwanted hum at a particular frequency. EQ can also be used to shape the sound creatively to give a track or an entire mix a distinctive character. There are two basic types of EQ: graphic EQ and parametric EQ.

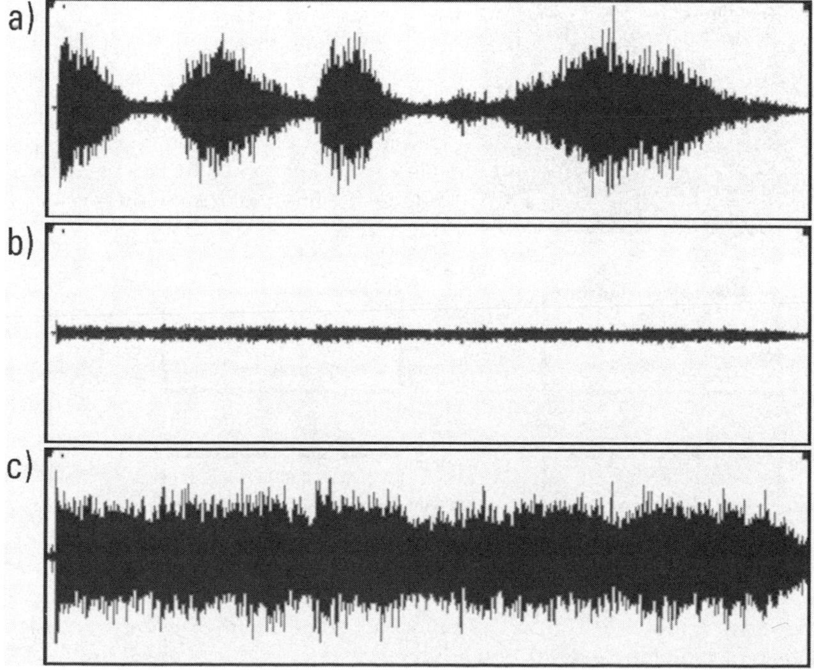

Figure 6.16 Dynamic range compression: (a) original track, (b) loud parts are reduced dramatically, and (c) entire track is boosted back to the original maximum level.

A **graphic EQ** divides the spectrum up into equal "bands" of frequency as specified by a musical interval, such as 1-octave bands, 2/3-octave bands, and 1/3-octave bands (see Figure 6.17). A professional graphic EQ typically has about 30-bands with each band being one-third of an octave. Many types of graphic EQs have far fewer bands, each covering a wider range of frequencies. Each band in a graphic EQ is given a slider that boosts or cuts that band by some number of dB, such as +/–6 dB or +/–12 dB.

A **parametric EQ** consists of one or more **filters** that boost or cut frequencies using one of the standard filter types, such as low pass, high pass, low shelf, high shelf, peaking, and notch (see Figure 6.18). The term "parametric" refers to the parameter(s) of the filter type that you control. Each filter type alters the spectrum in a different way.

Simple low pass and high pass filters are primarily controlled by the cutoff frequency, though they may also have a changeable slope. A **low pass filter** passes the frequencies below the cutoff frequency and cuts the frequencies above it. A **high pass filter** passes the frequencies above the cutoff frequency and cuts the frequencies below it.

Low shelf and **high shelf filters** are primarily controlled by two parameters: a cutoff frequency and a positive or negative gain. A low shelf filter boosts or cuts frequencies below the cutoff frequency evenly to create a raised or lowered "shelf" at the low end of the spectrum. A high shelf filter boosts or cuts frequencies above the cutoff frequency evenly to create a raised or lowered shelf at the high end of the spectrum.

Peak and **notch filters** are primarily controlled by three parameters: center frequency, bandwidth, and gain. A peaking filter boosts a band of frequencies (bandwidth) around the center frequency by some number of dB (positive gain). A notch filter

Figure 6.17 "Rane Series" graphic EQ plug-in by Serato has 30 1/3-octave bands. (Courtesy of Serato Audio Research)

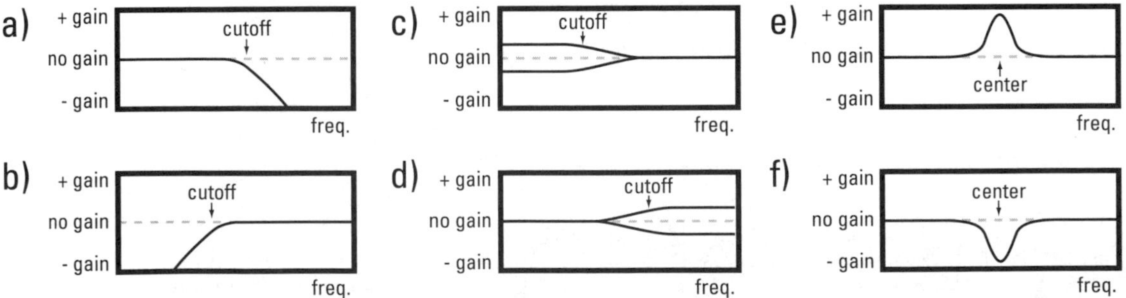

Figure 6.18 Filter types: (a) low pass, (b) high pass, (c) low shelf (gain determines whether it cuts or boosts), (d) high shelf (gain determines whether it cuts or boosts), (e) peak filter, and (f) notch filter.

attenuates a band of frequencies around the center frequency by some number of dB (negative gain). The size of the bandwidth is sometimes referred to as the "Q" of the filter.

Often a DAW will have a parametric EQ that consists of multiple different filters covering standard frequency ranges, such as low range, low midrange, midrange, high midrange, and high (see Figure 6.19).

Time-based Effects

Time-based effects are those that involve combining the original audio signal with delayed and modified copies of itself. These effects include delay, flange, chorus, and reverb. The most basic of these effects is a **delay**.

Delay involves storing the audio in a digital delay line for some amount of time and then playing back the stored audio combined with the undelayed signal. The delayed signal will naturally be "behind" the original. The length of the delay line determines the results of the effect. A delay line of about 100ms (one-tenth of a second) or more will create clear echoes of the original signal. A shorter delay time of around 10 to 50ms will give the sound some "thickness." Extremely short delay times of a few milliseconds or less produce effects similar to that of a "comb" filter, where evenly spaced frequencies in the spectrum are cut out. The output of a delay line can also be fed back to its input, resulting in a series of echoes that gradually die out or other effects if the delay time is very short (see Figure 6.20).

If we change, or modulate, the delay time periodically, the delayed signal will be shifted slightly up and down in pitch as well as being shifted in time relative to the original signal. One application of this time-varying delay line is a **flanger effect**. In

Figure 6.19 Masterworks parametric EQ in Digital Performer 6 (Courtesy of MOTU). There are five bands covering various frequency ranges plus high pass and low pass filters at each end of the spectrum.

a flanger, the modulation is centered around a relatively short delay time (less than about 20ms) with a modulation rate of less than about 10 Hz. Other parameters include the amount that the delay time changes, or the "depth," and the amount of feedback. A flanger imparts a swishing, swirling effect to the sound with a metallic edge when the feedback is high. If the modulation rate is kept low, it is possible to hear clearly the up and down shifting of the pitch. Another effect based on a modulated delay line is chorus (see Figure 6.21).

Figure 6.20 Delay with feedback: (a) delay plug-in from Cubase Studio 4 showing a long delay with 50 percent feedback (courtesy of Steinberg Media Technologies); and (b) an illustration of those echoes.

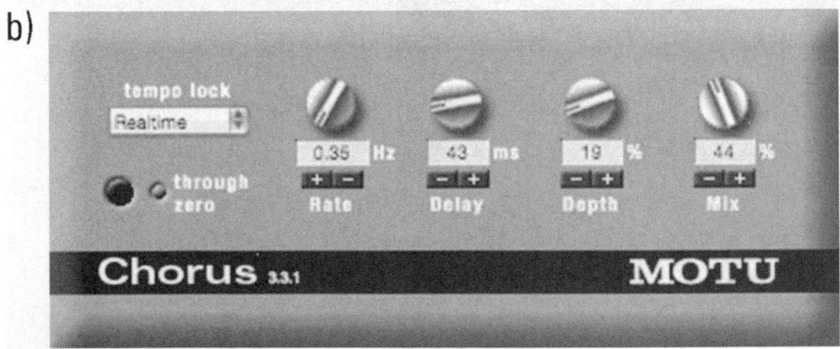

Figure 6.21 (a) Flanger plug-in, and (b) chorus plug-in, both from Digital Performer 6 (Courtesy of MOTU). Notice the flanger plug-in has a feedback control and smaller delay time than the chorus.

A **chorus effect** consists of multiple varying delays added together. In an actual choral ensemble, it is impossible for multiple singers on one part to produce exactly the same pitch at exactly the same time; they will each be slightly detuned in relation to one another. The same is true of any group of instruments playing the same part, such as the violins in an orchestra. The multiple time-varying delays when combined with the original signal simulate such an effect. To keep the effect subtle, the depth is usually modest and the modulation rate not very high.

Reverb can be thought of as many delays added together. When you perform in a room, whether a performance hall or your bathroom, the sound you produce bounces off the walls. Some of the bounces come directly back to you—these are referred to as "early echoes"—and some of the bounced signal bounces again off other surfaces and only eventually gets back to you. What you get back, then, are the early echoes followed by an increasingly dense and complicated series of other echoes that decrease in volume over time as the walls, seats, and audience members absorb the bouncing sound (see Figure 6.22).

Artificial reverb in software can be constructed from combinations of delays, and there are many plug-in reverbs that generate reverb that way. However, many DAWs now include a convolution reverb (see Figure 6.23).

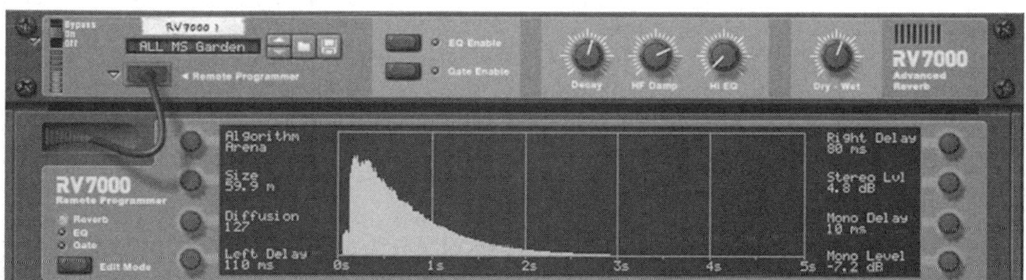

Figure 6.22 Reason's RV7000 reverb showing the density and shape of the reflections. (Screenshot copyright of Propellerheads. Used with permission)

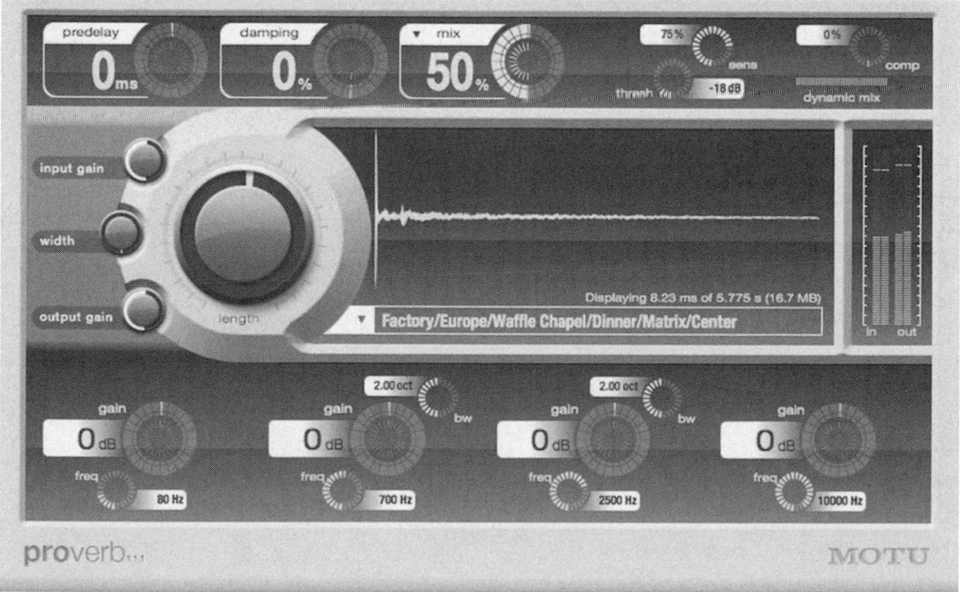

Figure 6.23 ProVerb convolution reverb from Digital Performer 6 (Courtesy of MOTU). The impulse response for this setting is shown in the middle.

A **convolution reverb** combines the audio signal with an **impulse response** audio file that was recorded in an actual acoustic space. An impulse response can be made by popping a balloon or shooting a starter pistol (the kind they use to start track and field races) on a stage and recording the results from somewhere in the hall (there are also more modern ways to generate impulse responses). The result of using a convolution reverb is that your audio sounds as if it was played in the hall that generated the impulse response. You can also use other soundfiles that are not actual impulse responses and sometimes get strange and interesting results.

BOUNCING DOWN

Once you have recorded, edited, and mixed a project in a DAW, the final step is to turn it into a single audio file that can be burned to CD or converted into a compressed file for distribution on the Internet. Commercial projects go through another step before bouncing, which is referred to as **mastering**. Mastering is usually performed by an audio engineer who specializes in the process.

Bouncing down a project is done differently in each DAW, but it typically involves just selecting the material to be bounced and choosing details like the output file format, sample rate, and resolution. If your project was recorded at 96 kHz and the final sample rate of the bounced audio is to be 44.1 kHz, then the DAW will "downsample" the project to the correct sampling rate. Similarly, if the project was recorded at 24-bit resolution and the resolution of the bounced audio is to be 16-bit, the DAW will convert the resolution.

REVIEW OF KEY TERMS

digital audio workstation (DAW) 86
transport controls 87
main clock 87
audio track 88
edit/mix views 88
record-enabling 89
mute/solo buttons 89
input/output assignments 89
trim/gain knobs 91
clipping 92
dBFS (decibels full scale) 92
headroom 93
signal-to-noise ratio 93
buffer 93
monitoring latency 93
hardware monitoring 93
non-destructive editing 94
fade/crossfade 96
pitch shifting 98
time stretching 98
automation 99
plug-ins 100
compressor 100
graphic/parametric EQs 102
filters 102
low pass/high pass filters 102
low shelf/high shelf filters 102
peak/notch filters 102
delay 103
flanger effect 103
chorus effect 105
reverb 105
artificial/convolution reverb 105
impulse response 106
mastering 106

CHAPTER 7

Audio—What Do I Need?

Now that we've covered the basics of hardware, data, and software, it's time to consider what hardware and software are necessary for a computer-based audio recording and editing system. It's important to recognize that a system should be designed according to your specific needs, and a given model system may be missing one or more components that you would find important. With that in mind, this chapter presents four digital audio systems of increasing complexity that could be found in a home or project studio. Expensive systems used in professional recording studios are beyond the scope of this chapter. (Links to the software and hardware discussed here are available on the book's website.)

AUDIO SYSTEM 0

The first audio system is really no system at all: just your computer and some freeware. I include this to emphasize that an audio system needn't be expensive and complex; it's possible to learn quite a bit about digital audio without purchasing anything aside from your computer. Creating work that you would want to present in public may require purchasing additional hardware and software, but initially Audio System 0 can be very useful.

Audio System 0 Hardware

- Computer (laptop or desktop) with built-in speakers and, preferably, a built-in microphone. A netbook may also work for this system.
- Headphones of any kind, though better quality headphones are desirable.
- Optional: a cable to connect the built-in computer output to your stereo system. One of the following cables will typically work for this:
  - A cable with one 3.5mm (also known as an ⅛-inch or mini-plug) TRS male connector on one end and two RCA male connectors at the other (see Figure 4.12 for images of various connector types).

  - A cable with male 3.5mm TRS connectors at each end. This cable is used if your stereo comes equipped with a 3.5mm input jack for connecting an iPod or other personal listening device.

Audio System 0 Software

- Free audio recording and editing software:
  - Free software that comes with your computer. For example, most new Macs come with GarageBand software, which has a number of powerful features for audio recording and editing.
  - Audacity, a free multi-track audio recording, editing, and processing program.
  - Other free software. Many a free software project is active for a time and then the developer tires of working on it or gets another job and the software becomes defunct. An Internet search and perusing user forums for audio recording and editing are the best ways to find current free software and evaluate whether it would be useful to you. (Links to some pieces of audio software are available on the book's website.)
- *Almost*-free audio recording and editing software:
  - There are several inexpensive audio recording and editing applications available, including Ardour (shareware) and Reaper (inexpensive personal license).
  - As with freeware, almost-free software comes and goes. Again, an Internet search and user forums will point you to current almost-free software.

AUDIO SYSTEM 1

Though Audio System 1 includes some purchases, it is still inexpensive and designed to allow you to learn audio concepts and techniques before spending significant amounts of money. This system avoids a full-blown audio interface, instead suggesting a USB microphone and, optionally, an instrument-to-USB guitar cable (see Figure 7.1).

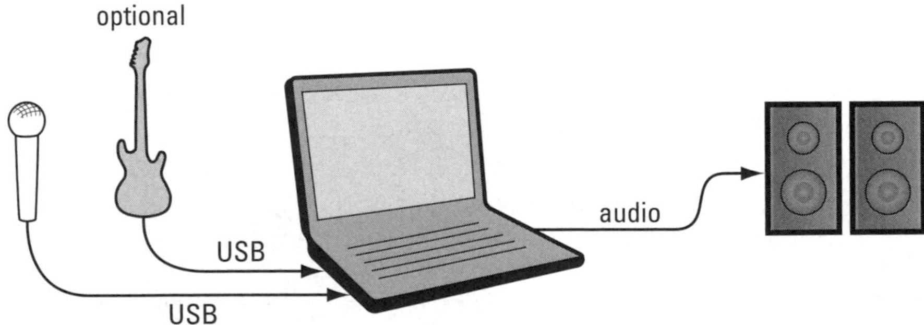

Figure 7.1 Audio System 1: USB microphone, powered monitors, and optional guitar-to-USB cable.

Audio System 1 Hardware

- Relatively recent computer (laptop or desktop) with more than the default amount of RAM (random access memory) sold with the system. It is unclear at the time of this writing whether netbooks would be suitable for any audio work; they are designed primarily to interface with network-based applications, but they may be powerful enough to handle this level.
- USB microphone.
- Good headphones.
- Powered monitors (speakers) that connect to the 3.5mm output of your computer (may require an adapter cable) or USB-powered monitors.
- Optional: Instrument-to-USB interface for a guitar or bass. These are small, cheap interfaces with a TS ¼-inch plug on one end and a USB "A" connector on the other. Though they look like merely cables, they have an embedded ADC. With both this and the USB microphone, you technically have two different audio interfaces; some operating systems or DAWs can "see" both simultaneously and some can only use one at a time.

Audio System 1 Software

The following are some options for recording and editing software:

- Free and almost-free audio recording and editing software. The software solutions discussed above, such as GarageBand, Audacity, Ardour, and Reaper, are all viable for this system.
- "Lite" versions of professional DAWs. Most DAWs, such as Logic Pro, Cubase, and Sonar, have less expensive versions of their full-blown systems. These include Logic Express, Cubase Studio, and Sonar Home Studio. Some have more than two levels of their products, requiring you to do some feature comparisons to see which version would work for you. As with the free and almost-free software, "lite" software can get you a long way before you have to upgrade to the more expensive professional versions.
- Educational versions/pricing of professional DAWs. In addition to the various levels of products discussed in the previous item, many DAWs have educational prices for both the full and lite versions of their products. For the most part, the lite versions will still be cheaper, but some companies discount aggressively to the education market.

AUDIO SYSTEM 2

This system is designed for semi-professional work in a home project studio (see Figure 7.2). Though not terribly expensive, this hardware should provide better sound quality and lower noise. One topic not addressed in the system below is the room itself.

In order to record with good quality, the room should be relatively isolated from noise, such as air conditioners and refrigerators, and not contain hard parallel surfaces that create strong reflections and color the sound. To reduce unwanted reflections, you can purchase acoustic foam that is typically attached to the walls and helps to absorb the sound.

Unless you create a separate recording room or use an isolation booth, computer fan noise is a persistent problem. One way to reduce, though not eliminate, computer fan noise is to use a microphone with a directional polar pattern, such as cardioid or hypercardioid, which strongly rejects sound coming from certain angles, and point the "null" of the pattern at the computer (see Figure 4.8).

Audio System 2 Hardware

- Relatively recent computer (laptop or desktop) with more than the default amount of RAM sold with the system.
- Audio interface with two inputs and two outputs:
  - Two inputs that can accommodate mic level, instrument level (High-Z) for guitars and bass guitars, and line level inputs for external processors or audio from hardware synthesizers.
  - Outputs can be balanced or unbalanced. Balanced is better for long cable runs between the interface and the speakers or if there is a lot of electro-magnetic interference from other equipment.

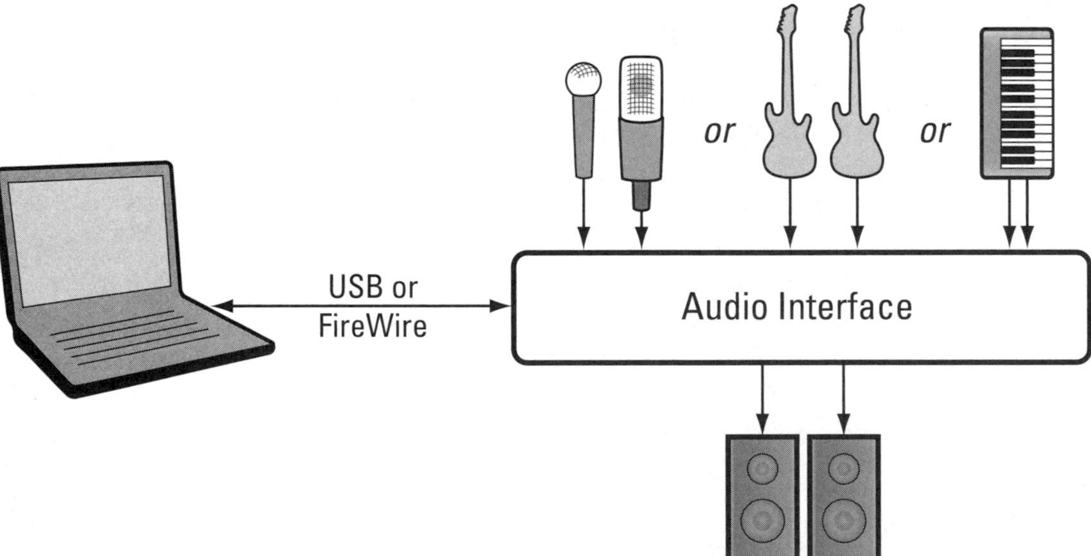

Figure 7.2 Audio System 2: a dynamic mic and a condenser mic as two possible inputs; audio interface with two inputs that can accommodate mic level, instrument level (High-Z), and line level; and powered monitors.

  - Can be USB or FireWire. The ability to be bus-powered is desirable if you want to be mobile with the interface and a laptop.
  - Phantom power for the condenser mic (discussed below).
  - Supports 44.1 kHz sampling rate and 16- and 24-bit resolutions. Higher sampling rates may be useful, but they are not necessary.
  - The interfaces discussed in Chapter 4 under "A Basic Audio Interface" fit this standard.
  - MIDI in and out jacks are desirable if you want to connect external MIDI devices.

- Two microphones, one dynamic and one large-diaphragm condenser, for recording various voices and instruments. Microphones can get expensive quickly, but a good microphone is crucial for converting acoustic vibrations into an electrical signal. Fortunately, there are good dynamic mics that are relatively inexpensive, such as the Shure SM57 or SM58. For a condenser mic, it's better to spend a little more at the outset for a good sounding microphone. You don't have to spend thousands, but you may well have to spend several hundred. A microphone such as the Rode NT1-A is a relatively inexpensive large-diaphragm condenser. As you upgrade to a more expensive system, you would naturally also upgrade your microphones. Various music technology publications such as *Mix*, *Sound On Sound*, or *Electronic Musician* regularly review current moderately priced microphones for project studios.
- Good headphones. Though at this level you want to avoid monitoring exclusively with your headphones, it may be necessary for practical reasons such as roommates or neighbors.
- Powered monitors of good quality. Monitors can also get expensive quickly, but you can find moderately priced monitors that are of good quality with decent bass response. The last part is important because this system does not include a subwoofer to handle low frequencies. Again, reviews of current monitors can be found in music technology magazines.

Audio System 2 Software

The following are some options for recording and editing software:

- Free software, almost-free software, lite versions of DAWs, or educational versions/pricing for DAWs are all workable options in this system, just as they were in Audio System 1. At this level, free and almost-free software may reveal their limitations.
- Full version of a DAW. Though the lite versions of many DAWs are still usable in this circumstance, you may find the features limiting. There is still the possibility of educational pricing for many of the full-featured DAWs, so this doesn't necessarily mean a very large expense. Full-featured DAWs include: Digital Performer (MOTU), Logic Pro (Apple), Sonar Producer (Cakewalk), Cubase (Steinberg), Live (Ableton), and Pro Tools LE (Digidesign). These are widely used DAWs, but there is a variety of others available.

- Optional: Various third-party plug-ins. All DAWs, both lite and full versions, come with a collection of plug-ins for dynamics processing, EQ, delay, chorus/flange, and reverb. However, there are companies that specialize in producing high-quality plug-ins, such as Waves, Universal Audio, and McDSP. You may find that, in some cases, those plug-ins are superior to the plug-ins that come with the DAW. In addition, there are specialized plug-ins that are not standard in DAWs, such as Antares' Auto-Tune.

AUDIO SYSTEM 3

This system is suitable for semi-professional and professional project studios and includes an audio interface with more inputs, a control surface, a variety of microphones, and a monitor system with a sub-woofer. I've chosen not to include a mixing board here and assume that all of the signal routing is happening within the DAW. However, there are a variety of different solutions at this level, including an analog mixing board that connects to the computer through an audio interface and a combination mixing board/interface (see Figures 7.3a, 7.3b and 7.3c).

Audio System 3 Hardware

- Newer, fast desktop computer with lots of RAM.
- Audio interface with eight inputs and eight outputs. More or fewer are, of course, possible, but ins and outs seem to come in units of eight.
  - Four to eight mic preamps that can also be used as line inputs and High-Z instrument inputs, either by using combo jacks or separate jacks for the same input. Remaining inputs, if any, are line inputs.
  - Eight line outputs for routing to monitors or a mixing board. Six of the outputs can be used for 5.1 surround sound.
  - S/PDIF digital inputs/outputs and, optionally, ADAT Lightpipe 8-channel digital inputs and outputs for routing audio to other digital equipment such as a digital mixing board.
  - Connection via USB, FireWire, or PCI card (made possible by the desktop rather than laptop system).
  - Phantom power for the condenser mics.
  - Interface should support at least 44.1 kHz, 48 kHz, and 96 kHz sampling rates and 16- and 24-bit resolutions. Examples include the M-Audio ProFire 2626 FireWire interface, the MOTU 896, and the Digidesign 003 Rack.
  - Optional: Higher-quality, and more expensive, mic preamps. The line level outputs of the preamps would be routed to line level inputs on the audio interface. In this case, the interface doesn't need to have as many preamps, so an interface like the MOTU 828 or 24I/O (PCI connection) would be appropriate.

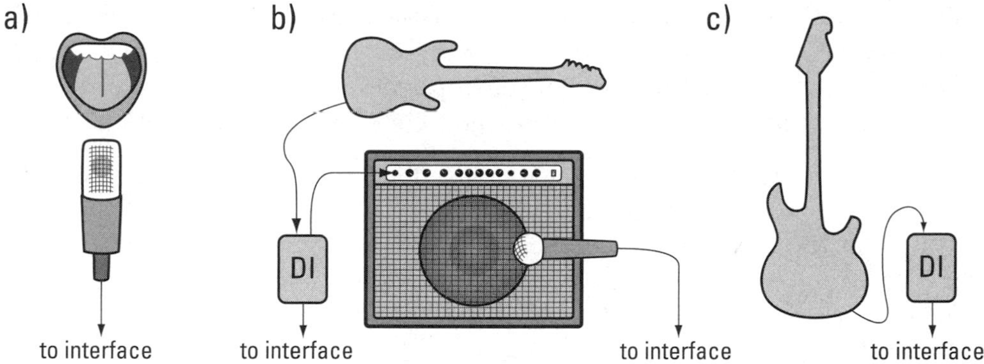

Figure 7.3a Audio System 3. Sample recording configuration: (a) large-diaphragm condenser mic for vocals, (b) guitar through DI box and dynamic mic on amp, and (c) bass guitar through DI box.

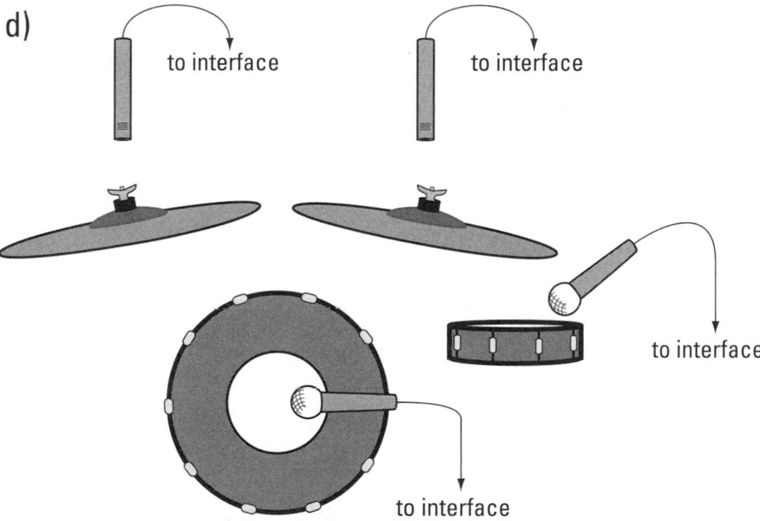

Figure 7.3b Audio System 3. Sample recording configuration for drums (simple): (d) large-diaphragm dynamic mic on the kick drum, small-diaphragm dynamic on the snare, and two small-diaphragm condenser mics on cymbals.

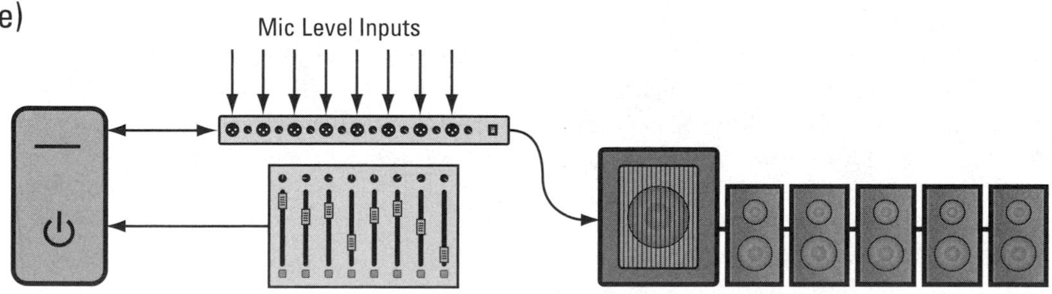

Figure 7.3c Audio System 3. Sample recording configuration: (e) sound sources input to mic preamps on an audio interface, a control surface for the DAW, and audio output to a 5.1 surround configuration.

- Several microphones of various types. The choice of microphones, of course, depends on the application and there are as many ways to mic a voice or instrument as there are microphones. In addition, microphones can vary widely in price, so your choice will be restricted by your budget. Here are some possibilities:
  - Dynamic instrument mics for guitar amps, horns, snare drum, toms. Examples include the Shure SM57 and Beta 57A.
  - Dynamic vocal mics. Examples include the Shure SM58 and Beta 58A.
  - Large-diaphragm dynamic mic for bass guitar amps and kick drums. Examples include the AKG D 112 and the Shure Beta 52A.
  - Small-diaphragm condenser mics for cymbal overheads, pianos, acoustic guitars, or other instruments. Examples include the Rode NT5 and the AKG C 451 B.
  - Large-diaphragm condenser mics for vocals and instruments. Examples include the Audio-Technica AT-4050 and the Rode NT1-A.
- Good headphones.
- Powered monitors in 2.1 stereo or 5.1 surround sound configuration. In this system, the quality of the monitors (and their price) would rise. The addition of the subwoofer will improve the performance of the monitoring at low frequencies and should make the bass and the kick drum clearer.
- High-quality cables. To reduce the overall noise in the system, high-quality cables should be used. They naturally cost more than bargain cables, but they can make a difference in a system like this. All connections should be balanced whenever possible, except guitars and many synths, which have unbalanced outputs.
- Miscellaneous equipment such as DI boxes.
- Optional: Headphone amplifier and headphones for use by performers while tracking.

Audio System 3 Software

The following are some options for recording and editing software:

- Full version of a DAW, perhaps with educational pricing. Full-featured DAWs include: Digital Performer (MOTU), Logic Pro (Apple), Sonar Producer (Cakewalk), Cubase (Steinberg), and Pro Tools LE (Digidesign). These are widely used DAWs, but there are a variety of others available.
- Various third-party plug-ins. Higher-end dynamics processing, EQ, and other types of processing plug-ins are available from companies such as Waves, Universal Audio, and McDSP. In addition, specialty plug-ins such as Auto-Tune from Antares and Pitch 'N Time from Serato Audio Research would be useful.

PRO TOOLS SYSTEMS

The well-known Pro Tools systems are widely used for studio recording and post-production sound for film and TV. The other DAWs mentioned above are full competitors to Pro Tools software in terms of features, but what makes Pro Tools distinct from those DAWs is that Pro Tools requires the use of an audio interface made by Digidesign or its sister company M-Audio. The other DAWs are more flexible and will accommodate a variety of interfaces.

There are two levels to Pro Tools software: LE/M-powered and HD. Pro Tools HD is an expensive professional option and is out of the range of the systems discussed here, so Pro Tools LE, used with Digidesign audio interfaces, and Pro Tools M-powered, used with certain M-Audio interfaces, are relevant to this chapter.

Pro Tools LE or M-powered is not a possibility as a DAW in Audio Systems 0 or 1 above, which don't require audio interfaces. The entry-level Digidesign Mbox interface or an M-Audio interface like the FireWire Solo, both shown in Chapter 4, are possible in Audio System 2. For Audio System 3, interfaces such as Digidesign's 003 or M-Audio's ProFire 2626 meet the requirements.

Section II
Further Reading

For a history of recording, Andre Millard's *America on record: A history of recorded sound* (2nd ed., 2005) provides an excellent, detailed overview of the topic from Edison's phonograph to the modern digital era. Mark Katz's fascinating book, *Capturing sound: How technology has changed music* (2004) approaches recorded sound by examining how it has changed the way we listen to, perform, and compose music. Katz examines a variety of "phonographic effects" as they have influenced the performance of jazz, the development of the modern violin vibrato, the emergence of turntablism, and other disparate musical phenomena.

For further exploration of audio recording, there are several good books available, including David Huber and Robert Runstein's *Modern recording techniques* (6th ed., 2005) and Francis Rumsey and Tim McCormick's *Sound and recording: An introduction* (5th ed., 2006). Both of those books thoroughly cover audio hardware and recording techniques. Daniel Thompson's *Understanding audio* (2005) delves more deeply into audio theory and includes excellent discussions of topics such as impedance and decibel levels.

For detailed, technical coverage of audio hardware, Glen Ballou's *Handbook for sound engineers* (4th ed., 2008) is a good resource. Ken Pohlmann's *Principles of digital audio* (5th ed., 2005) is an excellent technical resource for all aspects of digital audio.

Section II
Suggested Activities

This chapter provides some suggested activities relating to audio. For the software-based activities, you can use either your DAW or Audacity, the free audio editor, which can be found at: **http://audacity.sourceforge.net/**.

AUDIO HARDWARE: GET TO KNOW YOUR EQUIPMENT

If you have recording equipment of your own or equipment available in your school's studio, take some time to get to know the characteristics of each piece of gear. The best way to do this is to look at the manual or the specification sheet, which will provide many of the details discussed in this section. Many manuals for synthesizer equipment and audio interfaces have a page or two of specifications at the back. If you've misplaced the manual, many are available as PDFs online.

Answer the following questions for your equipment:

Microphones

Fill out for each one:

- Condenser or dynamic?
- Large diaphragm or small diaphragm?
- Polar pattern(s)?
- Other details (uses battery, stereo mic, etc.)?

Audio Interface

- Number of preamps?
- Phantom power for preamps?
- How much gain available using trim/gain knobs?

- Pads for preamps? If so, how many dB?
- High-Z instrument level inputs? How many?
- Line level inputs? How many?
- Line level input connectors?
- Line level inputs +4dBu or –10dBV?
- Line level inputs balanced, unbalanced, or either?
- How many simultaneous inputs?
- Number of line level outputs?
- Line level output connectors?
- Line level outputs +4dBu or –10dBV?
- Line level outputs balanced, unbalanced, or either?
- Digital inputs/outputs?
- Digital input/output type and connector?
- Support for direct monitoring?
- Other software control through provided driver or utilities?

Mixer

- Number of mic/line inputs?
- Number of line-only inputs?
- Number of buses?
- Number of outputs?
- Number of auxiliary sends?
- Number of auxiliary returns?
- Tape/phono in/out?
- Special features, such as effects?
- For each mic/line input:
  - Phantom power?
  - How much gain available using trim/gain knobs?
  - Pads on inputs? If so, how many dB?
  - Instrument level (High-Z) input available?
  - Number of aux sends?
  - Number of bands of EQ? Types and frequency range?
  - Mute and solo?
  - Output bus assignments besides mains?
- For each line-only input:
  - +4dBu or –10dBV?
  - Balanced, unbalanced, or either?
  - Connectors?
  - Mono or stereo?
  - Number of bands of EQ? Types and frequency range?

Synthesizers, Modules, Hardware Processors

- Input/output connectors?
- +4dBu or –10dBV?
- Balanced or unbalanced?

Monitors (speakers)

- Active or passive plus power amp?
- Two- or three-way?
- Bottom end of frequency range?
- Subwoofer?

DIGITAL AUDIO DATA: COMPRESSION TESTS

Compression percentages

To get a sense of how much a song or work is compressed by the different file compression types, take some CDs of various material, such as classical, rock, pop, and hip-hop, and rip a track from each as:

1. uncompressed WAVE or AIFF file;
2. losslessly compressed file (Apple Lossless, Windows Media Lossless, or FLAC);
3. AAC, WMA, or MP3 lossy compression at 256 kbps;
4. AAC, WMA, or MP3 lossy compression at 128 kbps.

You can do this on Mac or PC using Apple's iTunes or a variety of other programs. Fill out the table below to compare the amount of compression for each song or work.

Test of compression amount for different songs/works

Song/work				
Genre	*Classical*	*Rock*	*Pop*	*Hip-hop*
WAVE size				
Lossless size				
Lossless compression %				
Lossy 256 kbps size				
Lossy 256 kbps compression %				
Lossy 128 kbps size				
Lossy 128 kbps compression %				

Are there any significant differences between the songs/works that you chose in the compression achieved? The significant differences are likely to occur in the lossless compression because the data rate for the others is essentially fixed. It is important to note that you can't draw broader conclusions from this without a much more careful test.

To calculate the percentage of compression, first calculate the ratio of the size of the lossless or lossy compressed file to the uncompressed file:

R (ratio) = compressed size ÷ uncompressed size

and then use the following formula:

Percentage of compression = (1 – R) × 100.

For example, if a movement of a symphony is 80 MB uncompressed and 16 MB lossy compressed (AAC at 256 kbps), then R = 16/80 = 0.2, and the percentage of compression = (1 – 0.2) × 100 = 80% compression. The larger this number, the more compressed the file is.

Quality Loss Due to Compression Type

Using the same files you created in the last exercise, try to see if you can tell the difference between the files using one or both of the simple tests below. It is important to note that both of these tests are unscientific, though a more rigorous test can be devised using the second method.

Test 1

For one of the songs/works, listen carefully first to the WAVE file and then to one of the compressed files to see if you can perceive a loss in quality in the compressed files. Since you already know what each file is, partner up with a classmate and have the classmate play the files for you (first the uncompressed and then one of the compressed files). If one of you has better earphones, try switching earphones to see what difference that might make. Fill in the table below with "no difference" (sounds the same as the WAVE file), "a little" (sounds a little worse than the WAVE file), or "a lot" (sounds much worse than the WAVE file). The lossless compression should sound exactly like the WAVE file. Were some songs/works more sensitive to the compression?

Test of quality loss due to compression for different songs/works

Song/work				
Genre	*Classical*	*Rock*	*Pop*	*Hip-hop*
Lossless compression				
AAC/MP3 256 kbps				
AAC/MP3 128kbps				

Test 2

To eliminate some of the natural bias of the first test, you can try an "ABX" test, where your partner plays a portion of one of the files for a song/work (A), plays the same portion of a different one (B), and then plays either A or B (X). You would then say whether you can tell whether X was the A file or the B file.

DIGITAL AUDIO SOFTWARE ACTIVITIES

Many DAWs have extensive tutorial materials available either in a printed manual or online, so the first step in learning a DAW is to work through the tutorials. Once you've done that, there are several activities you can do before diving into a full-blown recording project.

Recording Activities

Microphone Types

If you have more than one microphone available to you, record an instrument or voice using different microphones to explore how each microphone "colors" what it captures. Try to use the same music for each microphone.

Levels and Clipping

- Record-enable an audio track in your DAW and set its input to that of your microphone.
- Watch the meters in your DAW as you sing or play into the microphone.
- Perform crescendos in different registers and various other changes in dynamic to see how levels are affected.
- Turn up the trim/gain knob for the preamp on the standalone preamp, audio interface, or mixer until some of your singing or playing causes the meter to go into the red (to clip).
- Record a passage of music without any clipping, then raise the trim/gain knob and record a passage of music with clipping.
- Play back to listen to the results and zoom on the waveforms to see the non-clipped and clipped waveshapes.

Monitoring and Latency

- If you're using an audio interface, turn off the direct monitoring feature if possible.
- Set an audio track to monitor the input, or record-enable a track and hit record.
- Listen for any time delay, or latency, between when you play or sing and when you hear yourself.

- Find the input/output buffer setting in your DAW and make the buffer large. Sing or play and listen for the latency.
- Reduce the input/output buffer size and listen again for latency.
- Continue this until the latency seems low enough so the delay doesn't bother you. Make a note of this setting for future reference.
- Turn the direct monitoring feature of your interface on and listen for any delay.

Editing Activities

Cut-up Speech

- Record or import some speech. There are many audio files of important political speeches on the Internet as well as sentences from commercials and other sources.
- Use your DAW's editing techniques, such as cut, copy, paste, edge edit, and trim, to create a new sentence with a different meaning.
- Use fades and crossfades to smooth out transitions.
- You can also pitch shift or time stretch various words to create a very different kind of sentence.
- You can use multiple tracks to create a synthetic conversation from a single recording. Use pitch shift and time stretch to change the "identity" of the person on each track.
- Notice that it can be very difficult to connect two words that were not originally spoken that way.

Re-groove Drums

- Import a short drum groove into your DAW. You can use a loop or record you or a friend playing a groove.
- Use your DAW's editing techniques to rearrange the elements of the groove to form a new one.
- The clock and timeline should measure time in bars and beats rather than real time or SMPTE time, so you can match up elements to beats or parts of a beat.
- Even if the groove was originally on one track, use a separate track for each element (kick drum, snare drum, cymbals, toms).
- Use fades and crossfades to smooth out transitions.
- You can also pitch shift or time stretch various sounds to create a very different kind of groove.
- You can use a different rearrangement of the drum elements to create a contrasting groove followed by a return to the original groove.
- Notice that some elements of a groove, such as the cymbals, may hang over into later elements and may sound cut off when moved.

Sound Groove

- Record or import several "non-musical" sounds. You can download these sounds or use sound effects CDs.
- Consider the variety of pitch, dynamic, timbre, and articulation in the collection of sounds.
- Use your DAW's editing techniques to create a 4- or 8-bar groove from these elements.
- The clock and timeline should measure time in bars and beats rather than real time or SMPTE time, so you can match up elements to beats or parts of a beat.
- Use a separate track for each sound.
- Remember to keep the groove changing to avoid static repetition.
- Use fades and crossfades to smooth out transitions.
- You can also pitch shift or time stretch various sounds to make them sound different.
- You can use a different arrangement of these elements to create a contrasting groove followed by a return to the original groove.

Sound Scene

- Record or import several "non-musical" sounds.
- Since you'll be creating a "scene" with these sounds, consider choosing sounds that would fit together in a scene, such as a "day at the beach" or "lunch in the food court." You can also make up improbable scenes, such as "lunch and a casual conversation in the middle of the freeway."
- Use your DAW's editing techniques to create a "scene" from these sounds using a separate track for each one.
- Try to shape the scene by increasing or decreasing the number of elements at various points either gradually or suddenly, and by delaying the entrance of one or more sounds so you can create some excitement in the piece.
- The clock and timeline should measure time in real time so you're not tempted to rhythmicize this activity.
- Use fades and crossfades to smooth out transitions.
- You can pitch shift or time stretch various sounds to make them sound different.

Mixing

Volume and Pan

- Choose one of the "Editing Activities" above and add volume and pan automation to each track.
- Try using the faders and knobs in the mix view as well as drawing the automation in the edit view.
- The "Sound Scene" would be appropriate for this activity because the scene would benefit from gradually changing volumes.

Compressor

- Choose one of the rhythmic "Editing Activities" above and insert a compressor plug-in in the mix view on one track.
- Solo the track with the compressor so that you can hear the effect clearly.
- If the plug-in has presets available, experiment with those first. You can turn the "bypass" for the plug-in on and off to hear the differences between no compression and compression.
- Set the initial compression parameters as follows: compression ratio 3:1, threshold –20 dB, attack time 20ms, release time 0.5 seconds, and makeup gain 0 dB. Your DAW's compressor may have more or fewer parameters.
- While playing the track back, modify the parameters one at a time and note their effects.
- The "Sound Groove" would be appropriate for this activity because the non-musical sounds may have a wide dynamic range.

Equalization

- Choose one of the "Editing Activities" above and insert a parametric EQ plug-in in the mix view on one track. Some DAWs have a multi-band EQ automatically on each track, so you would just need to activate it. For the purposes of learning EQ parameters, choose an EQ plug-in with the fewest bands that can take on any of the standard shapes (low pass, high pass, peak, notch, low shelf, high shelf).
- Solo the track with the EQ so that you can hear the effect clearly.
- If the plug-in has presets available, experiment with those first. You can turn the "bypass" for the plug-in on and off or bypass individual bands to hear the results of the effect.
- Bypass all but one band, select a shape and manipulate the parameters one at a time while the project is playing and note their effects. Repeat this for each shape.
- The "Sound Scene" project would be appropriate for this activity because the sounds are more likely to be long, rather than percussive, making it easier to hear the continuous changes.

Time-based Effects

- Choose one of the "Editing Activities" above and insert a delay plug-in in the mix view on one track.
- Solo the track with the effect so that you can hear the effect clearly.
- If the plug-in has presets available, experiment with those first. You can turn the "bypass" for the plug-in on and off to hear the results of the effect.
- Modify the effect parameters, such as delay time and feedback, one at a time while the project is playing back and note their effects.
- Repeat this for flange, chorus, and reverb.
- For the delay, one of the rhythmic projects might work best, but the "Cut-up Speech" and "Sound Scene" projects are also appropriate for the chorus and flange.

SECTION III

MIDI

OVERVIEW

MIDI (Musical Instrument Digital Interface), pronounced like "middy," allows synthesizers, computers, and other electronic musical devices to be physically connected together and exchange musical information such as pitch and volume. In the modern project studio, MIDI allows music keyboards to control software synthesizers and samplers and control surfaces to manipulate a DAW's onscreen faders and knobs. In addition, hardware synthesizers and many hardware audio processors can be controlled through MIDI by a computer, another synthesizer, or a control surface.

MIDI was developed in the early 1980s at roughly the same time as the personal computer and the inexpensive digital synthesizer became widely available. The confluence of these three technologies meant that you could play notes on a keyboard, record and edit them in a computer program, and then send those notes back to one or more synthesizers to be converted into sound. This seemingly simple arrangement formed the basis for the computer-based music technology that we use today.

The MIDI specification, often referred to as the "MIDI spec" (pronounced like "speck"), includes the means for connecting devices together (hardware) and the information that can be sent between these devices (messages). It is important to note that MIDI messages are *not* audio, but rather indicate which keys have been pressed on a keyboard and how hard, which knobs or sliders have been moved on a control surface and by how much, and what settings have been selected on a synthesizer or audio processor. These messages are then sent to other devices over MIDI connections. There they may be turned into sound by hardware or software synthesizers and samplers or may be stored in software and later sent to those synthesizers and samplers.

In the 1980s and 1990s, MIDI was at the center of an electronic or commercial composer's studio, which consisted of keyboard synthesizers and rack-mounted synthesizers connected together and to a computer by MIDI cables. Sound synthesis and sample playback has since largely migrated from hardware to software, making the "MIDI studio" a thing of the past. Nevertheless, MIDI lives on, playing an important role in controlling the sounds generated by software and allowing us to store and edit musical information in a sequencer to be played by those software synthesizers and samplers. In addition, MIDI is still the primary way of entering music into notation software and a useful way of interacting with computer-assisted instruction software (see Section V for a discussion of those applications).

As a result, it is important to understand MIDI hardware, MIDI messages, and the software sequencers that allow you to store, edit, and play back those messages.

WHAT'S IN THIS SECTION?

Chapter 8: MIDI Hardware

This chapter covers:

- a brief history of MIDI;
- controllers, modules, and keyboard synthesizers;
- workstations;
- basic MIDI connections;
- computer connections;
- alternate controllers.

Chapter 9: MIDI Messages

This chapter covers:

- MIDI channels;
- channel voice messages, including General MIDI;
- system messages;
- MIDI modes.

Chapter 10: MIDI Sequencing Software

This chapter covers:

- the standard user interface;
- MIDI input;
- MIDI editing;
- MIDI output;
- MIDI thru and local control;
- standard MIDI files;
- beyond sequencing.

Chapter 11: MIDI—What Do I Need?

This chapter describes the hardware and software components for several MIDI setups. Because MIDI and audio systems go hand in hand, these setups include the components found in the audio systems described in Section II:

- MIDI and Audio System 1: MIDI-based sequencing, notation, and computer-assisted instruction with a small USB controller, as well as recording, editing, and mixing with relatively inexpensive input and output devices.
- MIDI and Audio System 2: MIDI-based activities incorporating a keyboard synthesizer, as well as recording, editing, and mixing with a simple audio interface and a couple of microphones.
- MIDI and Audio System 3: MIDI-based activities incorporating a multiport MIDI interface, a keyboard synthesizer, and modules, as well as recording, editing, and mixing with a variety of microphones, a more complex audio interface, a control surface, and higher-quality components.

At the end of the section, there are suggestions for "Further Reading" and a list of "Suggested Activities" related to the material in this section.

CHAPTER 8

MIDI Hardware

As mentioned in the section overview, the MIDI (Musical Instrument Digital Interface) specification can be broken down into two parts: hardware and messages. The hardware portion of the MIDI spec describes cables, ports, computer interfaces, and various electrical details that allow for the communication of musical data between synthesizers, computers, and various other electronic musical devices. The messages portion of the MIDI spec describes what information can be communicated between such connected devices and what form the messages take. This chapter provides an overview of the hardware side of MIDI; MIDI messages will be taken up in the next chapter. However, before looking at current MIDI hardware, it is useful to understand a little bit about the history of MIDI and synthesizers in general.

A BRIEF HISTORY OF MIDI

MIDI was developed in the early 1980s by a consortium of synthesizer manufacturers to allow digital electronic musical devices from different manufacturers to communicate with and/or control one another. To understand MIDI fully it is useful to consider the development of synthesizers from the mid-1960s up to the early 1980s.

Analog Days: Synthesizers in the 1960s and 1970s

The early synthesizers developed by Robert Moog, Donald Buchla, and others in the mid-to-late 1960s were analog, modular, and voltage-controlled. **Analog** means that electrical signals in the synths consisted of continuous changes in electrical voltage rather than a discrete series of numbers as in modern digital synthesizers.

Modular means that the task of generating sound was distributed among separate hardware units called modules. One module might be responsible for generating an audio signal (an **oscillator**), another might be responsible for modifying the timbre of that audio signal (a **filter**), and still another might be responsible for modifying the overall amplitude of that audio signal (an **amplifier**). A single timbre, or "patch," consisted of these and other modules connected together with patchcords, which were similar to guitar cables, along with the various settings on each of the modules (see Figure 8.1).

Voltage-controlled means that devices such as keyboards, joysticks, and ribbon controllers were used to send control voltages to the modules to change their settings. For example, rather than turning the frequency knob on an oscillator module manually, you could connect an electronic musical keyboard that would output a different voltage for each key, resulting in the oscillator producing different pitches. The voltages from other devices, such as joysticks, ribbon controllers, and even other modules, could be connected to various modules to control parameters such as the cutoff frequency of a filter or the overall loudness.

This paradigm of analog keyboards and other devices controlling analog modules dominated synthesizer design into the 1970s. Even when synthesizers like the Minimoog abandoned the modular, patchable setup for a largely pre-patched, portable design, the voltage-control concept remained the same.

Providing all of the control voltages for the wide variety of modules in an early synthesizer was often too complex for one person; manipulating keyboards, joysticks, ribbon controllers, and module knobs required more than two hands. The need for some form of storage for control voltages was met by the development of analog sequencers in the late 1960s. Analog sequencers had a fixed number of "stages," each with several knobs for setting control voltages for the various modules used in a patch

Figure 8.1 Roland System 100M modular analog synthesizer (late 1970s–early 1980s). Rack shown includes a sequencer, a dual oscillator (VCO), a dual filter (VCF), a dual amplifier (VCA), and an output mixer.

Figure 8.2 Analog sequencer from the Roland System 100M. It features eight stages with two controls in each stage.

(see Figure 8.2). The sequencer would step through these stages at some tempo causing a series of notes—one note per stage—to be played on the synthesizer.

Digital Control, Digital Memory, and Digital Synthesis

As sequencers became more complex in the 1970s, digital versions were developed to store more stages and more parameters. Early digital sequencers included the Oberheim DS-2, the Sequential Circuits Model 800, and the Roland MC-8. This was a hybrid model of sound production with digital data controlling analog sound modules.

Another motivation for the development of digital control was the fact that analog synthesizers had no way to store the settings for different patches. Once the knobs and sliders on a synthesizer had been set to create a particular timbre, the only way to "store" that configuration was to write down the specifics on a piece of paper. Many synth manuals came with drawings of the front face of the synth that could be used to write down the settings for the knobs and sliders. With the advent of microprocessors, synthesizers such as the Sequential Circuits Prophet-5 could incorporate digital patch memory into an analog synthesizer.

Eventually, all-digital synthesizers were developed in which the control *and* the sound generation were digital (see Figure 8.3). Digital sound synthesis had been around since the late 1950s, but had been restricted to expensive mainframe and mini-computers

Figure 8.3 Yamaha DX7, an early all-digital, MIDI-compatible keyboard synthesizer (1983). At about $2,000, the DX7 was relatively inexpensive by early 1980s' standards.

that were unavailable outside of academic or corporate laboratories. Pioneering, but expensive, digital synthesizers and samplers such as the Synclavier paved the way for their less expensive counterparts in the early 1980s.

With the growing use of digital control and digital synthesis, manufacturers felt the need for a digital protocol to allow devices such as sequencers and synthesizers from different manufacturers to communicate with each other.

MIDI is Born

In 1981, representatives from several synthesizer manufacturers began discussing a communications standard for synthesizers. An initial proposal called the "Universal Synthesizer Interface," or USI, was presented in 1981 at a meeting of the Audio Engineering Society (AES). This was followed up by further meetings and alternate proposals, eventually leading to the **MIDI 1.0 Specification**, published in 1983 by the newly formed International MIDI Association. It is now published by the MIDI Manufacturers' Association and the Japan MIDI Standards Committee, which is part of the Association of Musical Electronics Industry (*sic*).

The first MIDI connection between synthesizers from different manufacturers occurred at the National Association of Music Merchants (NAMM) trade show in 1983 between a Sequential Circuits Prophet 600 and a Roland JP-6. Other synthesizer manufacturers quickly adopted the specification, making MIDI control a standard feature of the modern synthesizer.

The combination in the early 1980s of widely available microcomputers, widely available all-digital synthesizers, and the MIDI communications protocol to connect them was the "perfect storm" of modern music technology. This hardware configuration along with the newly emerging personal computer software industry inspired such programs as the Personal Composer notation program in 1983 and Opcode Systems' Sequencer program for MIDI sequencing in 1985.

CONTROLLERS, MODULES, AND KEYBOARD SYNTHESIZERS

Most of the MIDI-compatible devices available can be categorized as controllers, modules, or keyboard synthesizers.

A **controller** is a device that can *only* send MIDI messages when its keys are played and can't generate any sound of its own. With the migration of sound generation from hardware synthesizers and samplers to software synthesizers and samplers, a large market has developed for keyboard controllers, many with knobs and sliders for manipulating the parameters of software synthesizers. To match the portability of laptops, many of these keyboards are quite small, with only two octaves or so of keys (see Figure 8.4).

A **module** is a device that can generate sound when it receives MIDI messages but has no keys to play, and hence can't output MIDI messages. A module is usually designed as a rectangular box that can be installed in a rack for convenience in a studio or stage setting. Calling a device a "module" doesn't say anything about how it goes about producing sound. As we'll see later in the text, the two primary methods of producing sound electronically are **sampling** and **synthesis**. As a result, a module might produce sound via sampling, synthesis, or a hybrid of the two (see Figure 8.5).

The term **keyboard synthesizer** is ambiguous, but, for the purposes of this discussion, it refers to a device that can both send MIDI messages when its keys are played and generate sound when it receives MIDI messages. A keyboard synthesizer can be thought of as a controller and a module combined together (see Figure 8.6). It's worth noting that in this context "synthesizer" simply refers to an electronic sound-producing device and does not refer to the specific method by which the sound is generated. (See the "Synthesis and Sampling" section later in the text). The term "synth" will be also be used as a synonym for keyboard synthesizer.

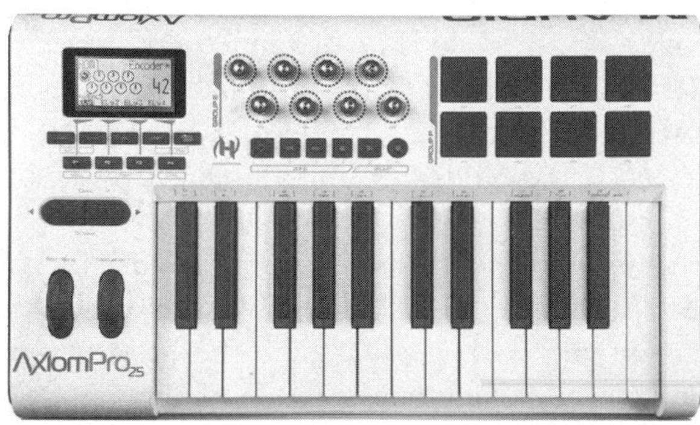

Figure 8.4 M-Audio Axiom Pro 25 keyboard controller. (Courtesy of M-Audio)

Figure 8.5 Roland Fantom-XR sound module. (Special thanks to Roland Corporation)

Figure 8.6 Yamaha S03 keyboard synthesizer. (Courtesy of Yamaha Corporation)

While "module" always refers to a rectangular box that generates sounds, "controller" can also mean the device in a project studio that is the primary means of MIDI input to the computer. For example, if you have a keyboard synthesizer attached to your computer, you could say that it is your "controller," even though it also generates sound.

WORKSTATIONS

Some keyboard synthesizers have additional features that elevate them to the level of a **workstation**. In addition to sending MIDI messages and producing sound, a keyboard workstation might include an onboard MIDI sequencer, multiple audio effects, and the ability to record digital audio samples or even entire tracks. It is important to note that the audio recording capacity available in keyboard workstations is more limited than that of a computer-based DAW.

With the combination of sequencing, sound generation capability, effects, and perhaps sound recording and playback, the keyboard workstation can be an all-in-one solution for creating and performing music (see Figure 8.7). In a home setting or a project studio setting, a computer would generally be used for MIDI sequencing, audio processing, and audio recording. However, in a live setting keyboard workstations offer an alternative to using a computer onstage. In addition, a keyboard performer may find a workstation to be more easily triggered and controlled than a live computer rig.

There are other hardware workstations that are not keyboard based, but instead use drum pads as their primary interface. The most famous example of this is the Akai MPC, which has been a staple of hip-hop production for a number of years (see Figure 8.8). The drum pads are used to trigger sampled sounds and the order in which the pads are pressed is stored within the device as part of a MIDI sequence. A device like an MPC can be used as a standalone workstation or in conjunction with a keyboard synthesizer, keyboard workstation, or computer.

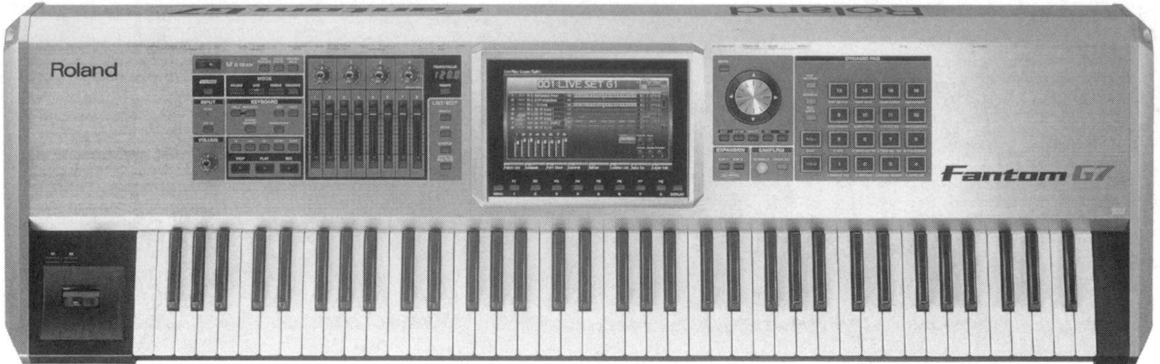

Figure 8.7 Roland Fantom G7 workstation keyboard. (Special thanks to Roland Corporation)

Figure 8.8 Akai MPC 5000 workstation. (Courtesy of AkaiPro)

BASIC MIDI CONNECTIONS: PORTS AND CABLES

Connecting devices together is MIDI's primary function and, in order to connect musical devices together, they must have the appropriate connectors. The MIDI spec requires a particular connector (a 5-pin "DIN") for the cables and the jacks on a MIDI-compatible device, which means that the connection hardware is independent of manufacturer—there is no "Yamaha MIDI cable" or "Korg MIDI jack." The jacks on a MIDI-compatible device are referred to as **ports**. The three standard ports are In, Out, and Thru, and each has a specific function (see Figure 8.9).

When you play a keyboard synthesizer, the MIDI messages that are generated by that keyboard, such as the message that indicates what note was played, are sent to the **Out Port**. Messages from another keyboard or computer arrive at the **In Port**. If you

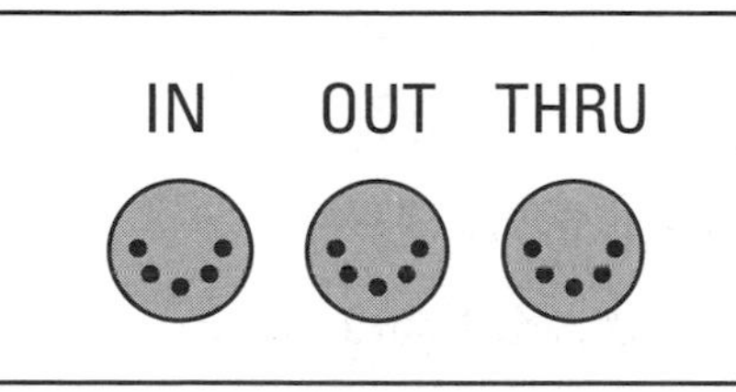

Figure 8.9 In, Out, and Thru MIDI ports found on most MIDI devices.

want to use one keyboard to control a second keyboard, you would connect a MIDI cable from the Out Port of Keyboard 1 to the In Port of Keyboard 2 (see Figure 8.10a). In this configuration, Keyboard 1 is referred to as the **master** and Keyboard 2 is referred to as the **slave**. Unlike most computer cables, MIDI cables are unidirectional instead of bidirectional, so you need separate cables for MIDI input and output. To avoid confusion when setting up MIDI connections, simply remember that Out Ports always connect to In Ports.

To reverse this arrangement and have messages from Keyboard 2 sent to Keyboard 1 instead, you would connect a MIDI cable from the Out Port of Keyboard 2 to the In Port of Keyboard 1 (see Figure 8.10b). Now Keyboard 2 is the master and Keyboard 1 is the slave. You'll notice that we haven't specified anything about these keyboards except that they're MIDI-compatible keyboard synthesizers. These connections are the same regardless of the manufacturer or type of keyboard.

The third common MIDI port, the **Thru Port** (yes, that's how it is spelled!) allows one keyboard to send messages to two or more other keyboards. If you want to play Keyboard 1 and have the messages sent to Keyboard 2 *and* to Keyboard 3, you would first connect the Out Port of Keyboard 1 to the In Port of Keyboard 2. Next, to pass

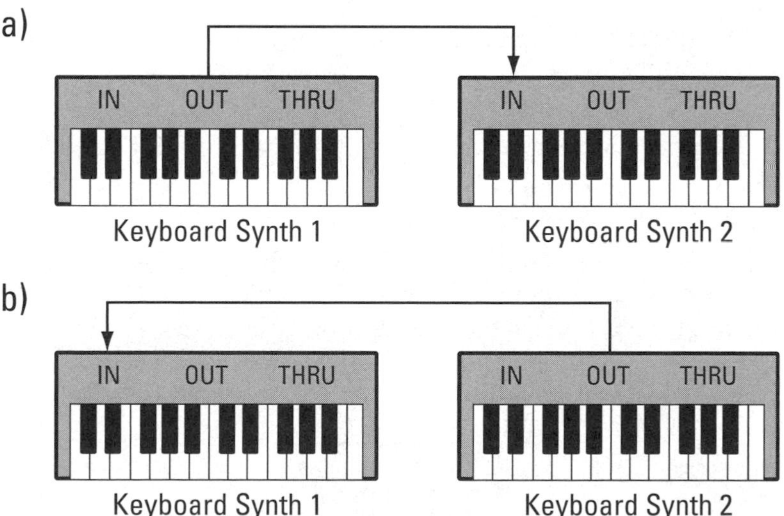

Figure 8.10 (a) MIDI connection that allows messages to flow from Keyboard Synth 1 (master) to Keyboard Synth 2 (slave); and (b) MIDI connection that allows messages to flow from Keyboard Synth 2 (master) to Keyboard Synth 1 (slave).

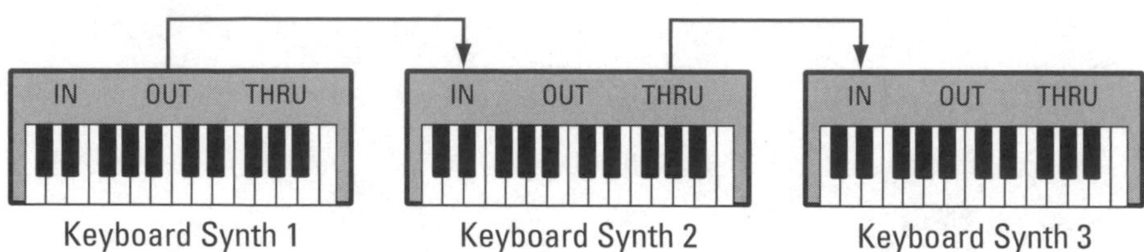

Figure 8.11 Daisychain MIDI connections that allow messages to flow from Keyboard Synth 1 (master) to Keyboard Synth 2 (slave) and Keyboard Synth 3 (slave).

on the messages received at the In Port of Keyboard 2, you would then connect the Thru Port of Keyboard 2 to the In Port of Keyboard 3 (see Figure 8.11). The Thru Port of Keybord 3 could then be connected to the In Port of another device and so on. To keep the function of the Thru Port straight, just remember: "whatever comes in goes thru."

Connecting multiple devices together in this way is referred to as **daisychaining**. This was a particularly important practice in the early days of MIDI, when daisychaining was the only way to control multiple MIDI synths from one synth or a computer.

So far, we've only discussed connecting synthesizers together, but a computer is often a central element in a MIDI network.

COMPUTER CONNECTIONS

Computers do not have MIDI jacks on them, so either the synth must be able to connect to a computer through a standard computer cable such as a USB cable, or a special interface must be used. Most controllers and many modules and keyboard synthesizers can connect to the computer directly through a USB cable. This arrangement is simple and is particularly useful for mobile music creation using a laptop and a small keyboard controller.

For MIDI devices that cannot connect to a computer via USB, a **MIDI interface** with standard MIDI jacks is needed (see Figures 8.12 and 8.13). The simplest of these interfaces connects to the computer via a USB cable and has one MIDI input port and one MIDI output port. To connect a controller or keyboard synth such that messages generated by the keyboard reach the computer, you would connect a cable from the Out Port of the controller or keyboard synth to the In Port of the interface. To connect

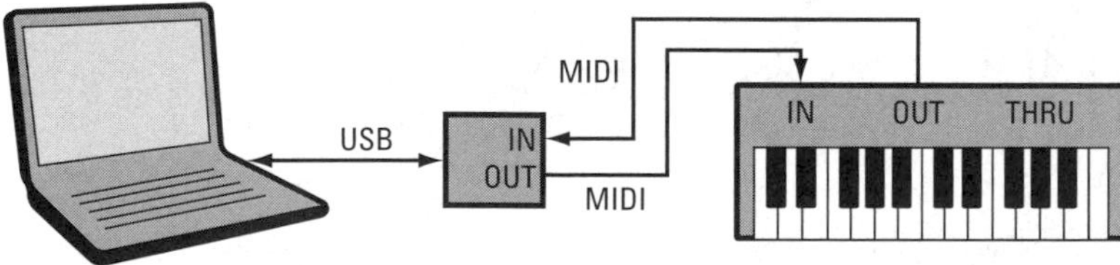

Figure 8.12 A computer and a keyboard synthesizer connected through a USB MIDI interface.

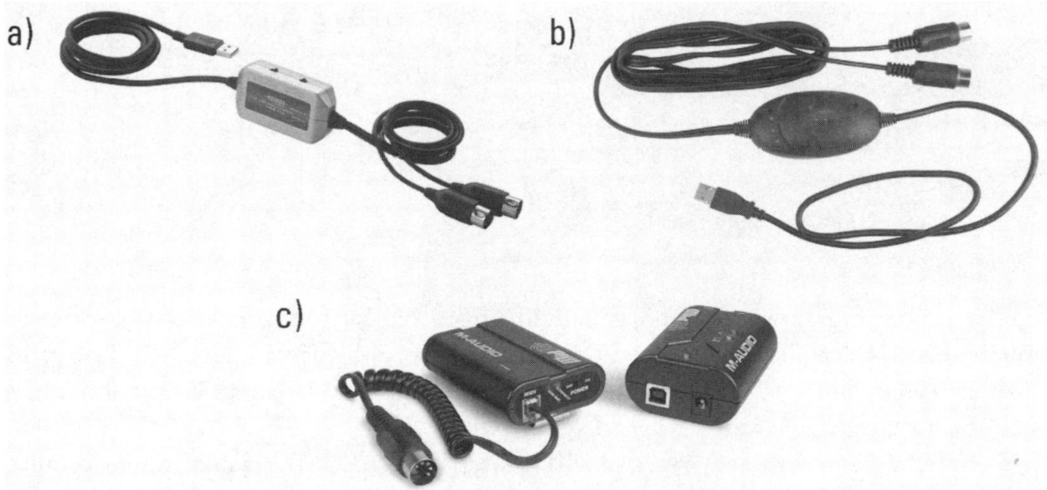

Figure 8.13 USB MIDI interfaces: (a) Edirol UM-1EX (special thanks to Roland Corporation); (b) M-Audio Uno; and (c) M-Audio MidAir wireless transmitter and receiver (both courtesy of M-Audio).

a keyboard synth or module such that it receives MIDI messages sent from the computer, you would connect a cable from the Out Port of the MIDI interface to the In Port of the keyboard synth or module.

In addition to these dedicated MIDI interfaces, many controllers, modules, and keyboard synths that connect directly to the computer via USB also have standard MIDI jacks, allowing you to connect other MIDI devices to the computer through those jacks. The same is true of external audio interfaces that have MIDI In and Out Ports. There are even MIDI controllers that connect to the computer, have standard MIDI jacks allowing other devices to connect to the computer, *and* act as simple audio interfaces all at the same time. These all-in-one keyboard controllers eliminate the need for a separate audio interface.

The various MIDI interfaces discussed so far have one MIDI input port and one MIDI output port. In order to connect more than one device to the computer, you would need a multiport MIDI interface.

A **multiport MIDI interface** is an external interface that possesses more than one In and Out Port. Although it is possible to connect a computer to more than one module or keyboard synthesizer through daisychaining as discussed above, it is not possible to have fully independent control over each device that way. To have independent control from the computer over a keyboard synth or module, a computer must be connected to that keyboard or module by a separate MIDI cable attached to a separate MIDI Out Port. A multiport MIDI interface provides this independent control over connected devices.

In the past, a project studio used by a commercial composer would have a MIDI interface with four or more inputs and outputs (see Figure 8.14), and larger studios would have 8-in/8-out interfaces or even multiple 8-in/8-out interfaces connected

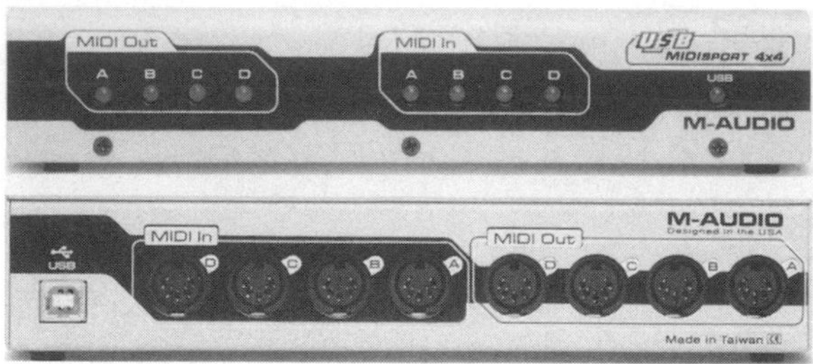

Figure 8.14 4-in/4-out multiport MIDI interface: M-Audio USB MIDISport 4×4. (Courtesy of M-Audio)

together. The migration of sound generation from hardware synthesizers to software synthesizers has significantly reduced the need for more than just a few MIDI ports in a project studio, and many require no MIDI ports at all, thanks to direct USB connection of controllers, modules, and keyboard synthesizers.

Peripheral devices such as external MIDI interfaces and USB keyboards may require the installation of driver software so that the operating system can communicate with the external device. However, many USB controllers are "class compliant" with the existing USB specifications and require no additional driver at all beyond the capabilities of the operating system. Audio interfaces that possess MIDI ports often require drivers, as do more complicated multiport MIDI interfaces.

ALTERNATE CONTROLLERS

The controllers that we've discussed so far have been keyboard controllers, but there are many other ways to provide MIDI information to a computer. A general definition for a MIDI controller is a device that converts physical actions into MIDI messages. There are many controllers modeled after non-keyboards that fit that definition, including guitar controllers, wind controllers, trumpet controllers, and percussion controllers (see Figure 8.15). For non-keyboard players, alternate controllers can be an excellent way to apply their particular performing skills to electronic performance and provide input to MIDI software.

Many of the instrument-style controllers have special sound modules that are designed to produce sounds that respond well to that instrument's control. For example, guitar controllers are usually sold along with guitar synthesizer modules that respond to each string individually and track guitar-specific gestures such as string bending, and wind synthesizer modules are often programmed to respond to parameters such as lip pressure and breath pressure.

There are also many control devices that don't look like musical instruments at all, but can be powerful controllers for shaping sound (see Figure 8.16). These include devices that allow for touchscreen control, infrared sensing, and various other physical sensors. In addition, many control devices that were designed for videogames make excellent musical input devices as well. These range from the standard joystick, which can be used to control the spatial position of sound, to game pads that have many buttons and small joysticks, to the Wii Remote which contains accelerometers and an infrared light detector.

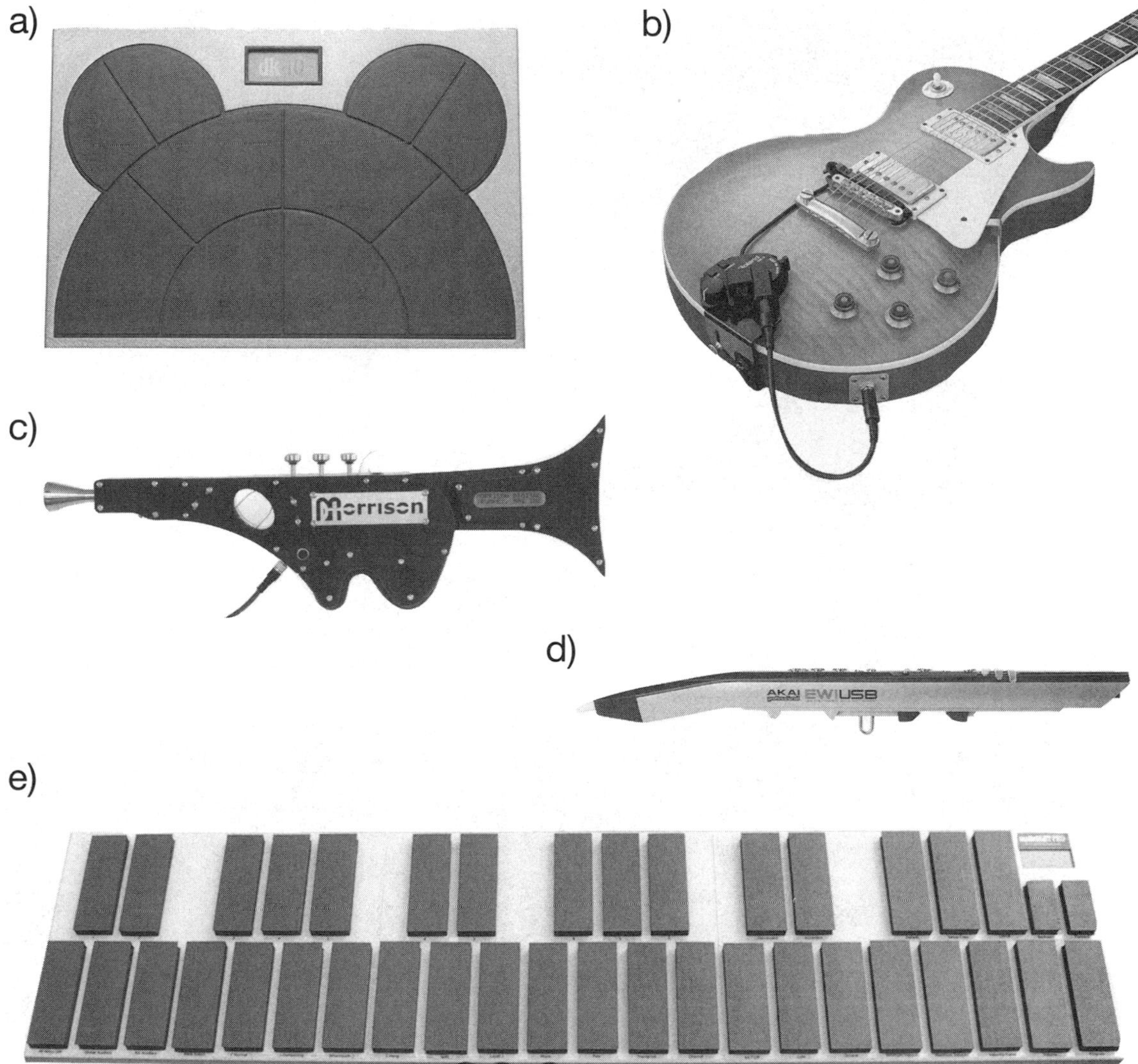

Figure 8.15 Non-keyboard instrument controllers: (a) Alternate Mode DK 10 percussion controller (courtesy of Alternate Mode, Inc.); (b) Roland GK-3 guitar converter (special thanks to Roland Corporation); (c) Morrison Digital Trumpet brass controller (courtesy of www.morrisondigitaltrumpet.com); (d) EWI USB wind controller (courtesy of AkaiPro); and (e) Alternate Mode MalletKat Pro mallet controller (courtesy of Alternate Mode, Inc.).

It is worth noting that, just as not every controller must be a keyboard, not every device that receives MIDI messages must be a sound generator. For example, there are theatrical lighting boards that can receive MIDI messages and change lighting scenes or intensities, software that causes visual images to respond to MIDI messages (used by "VJs" in clubs), and some experimental performers have even hacked devices such as a Roomba vacuum to respond to MIDI messages! Figure 8.17 shows a fountain that can be controlled by MIDI and thus can be synchronized to music.

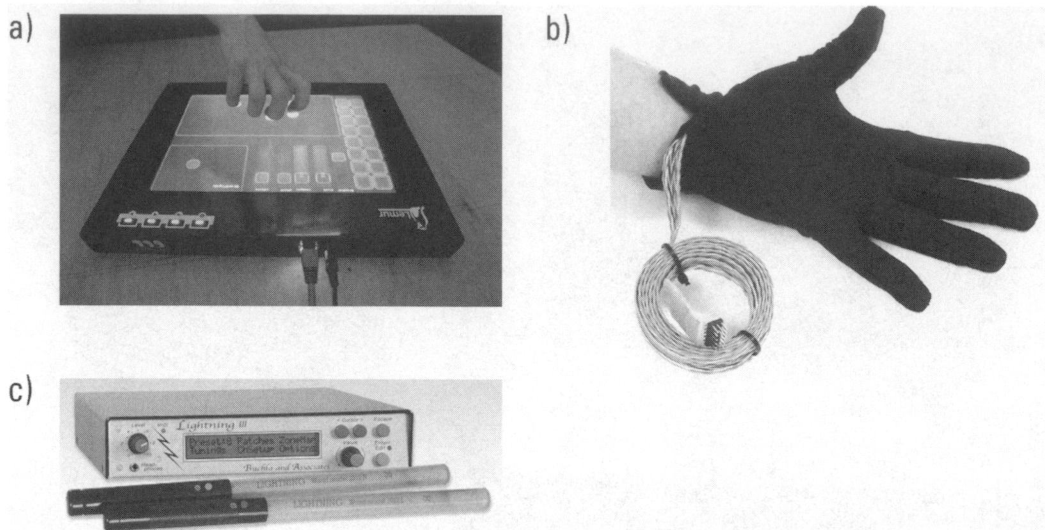

Figure 8.16 Alternate musical controllers: (a) JazzMutant Lemur multitouch controller (copyright © Yann Stofer, used with permission); (b) the TouchGlove sensor with six pressure-sensitive pads for the I-CubeX environment (courtesy of Infusion Systems Ltd, www.InfusionSystems.com); and (c) The Buchla Lightning III infrared wand controller (courtesy of Buchla and Associates).

Figure 8.17 A MIDI-controllable water fountain. (Courtesy of Erich Altvater, Atlantic Fountains)

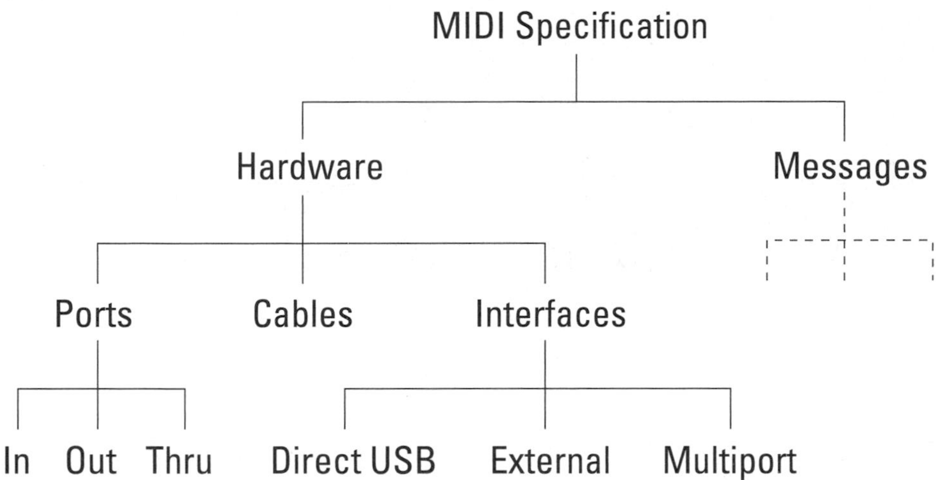

Figure 8.18 Summary of MIDI hardware.

REVIEW OF KEY TERMS

analog 128	synthesis 132
modular 128	keyboard synthesizer 132
oscillator 128	workstation 133
filter 128	ports 134
amplifier 129	Out/In Ports 134
voltage-controlled 129	master/slave 135
MIDI 1.0 Specification 131	Thru Port 135
controller 132	daisychaining 136
module 132	MIDI interface 136
sampling 132	multiport MIDI interface 137

CHAPTER 9

MIDI Messages

The last chapter focused on connecting MIDI hardware devices together. In this chapter, we will look in some detail at the MIDI messages used to control both hardware and software synthesizers. These messages are the information stored and played back by MIDI sequencing software; MIDI sequencing itself will be taken up in the next chapter.

MIDI messages are divided into two basic categories: **channel messages** and **system messages**. Channel messages are the most common messages and are used to send note, timbre, and expressive data to a receiving synthesizer—these are the "musical" messages. System messages are used to send information that can alter the configuration of the receiving synthesizer and synchronize the tempos of multiple devices, as well as a variety of other tasks. Channel and system messages will be discussed in more detail below, but, first, central to the function of MIDI channel messages is the concept of the **MIDI channel** itself.

MIDI CHANNELS

In the early days of MIDI, synthesizers could generally only produce one timbre, or "patch," at a time—they were "mono-timbral." To have more than one patch playing at the same time, such as a piano and a bass, you had to have a separate synthesizer for each patch and each synthesizer had to be set to a different channel. The concept of a MIDI channel is analogous to a broadcast television channel.

In order to watch two different TV shows at the same time, you have to have two separate TVs (receivers), each set to a different channel. What is shown on each TV depends on what is sent from the transmitter on that channel. Each TV "sees" only the information sent on its channel (see Figure 9.1a).

In the MIDI version of this, a computer is connected through a MIDI interface to Synthesizer "A," which is in turn daisychained using the Thru Port to Synthesizer "B." In this configuration, the computer is the master device (transmitter) and Synthesizers

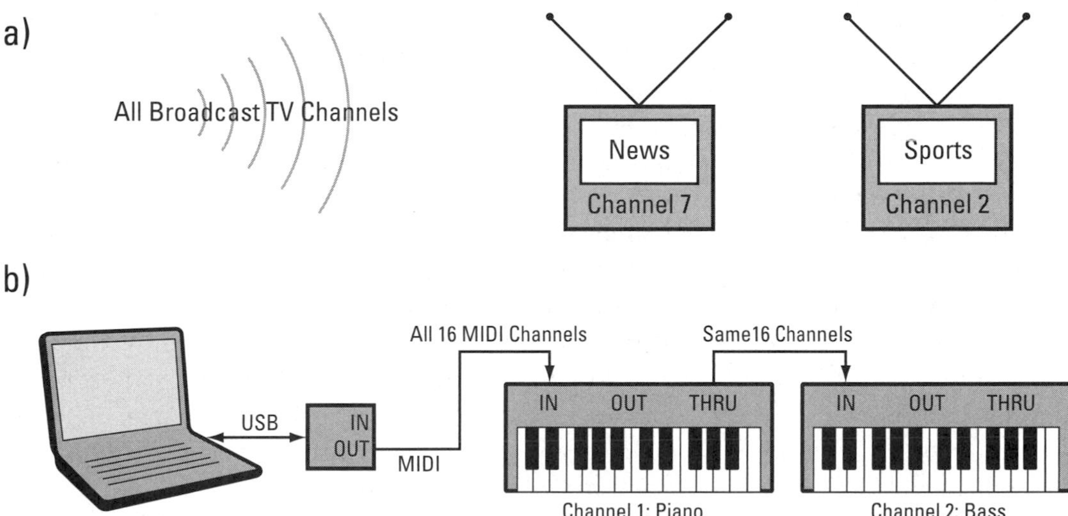

Figure 9.1 TV channels as an analogy for MIDI channels: (a) each TV tunes into a separate broadcast channel; and (b) each synth tunes into a separate MIDI channel.

A and B are the slave devices (receivers). If the synthesizers are set to receive on different channels and have different patches, you can choose which patch will be heard by sending a message from the computer on a particular channel.

If Synthesizer A is set to receive on Channel 1 and play a piano patch, and Synthesizer B is set to receive on Channel 2 and play a bass patch, a note message sent by the computer on Channel 1 will only be "seen" by Synthesizer A and a piano patch will be heard. On the other hand, if the computer sends a note message on Channel 2, it will only be "seen" by Synthesizer B and a bass patch will be heard. If the computer sends messages on both channels at the same time, piano and bass patches will be heard simultaneously (see Figure 9.1b).

Most modern synthesizers can play more than one timbre simultaneously—they are **multitimbral**. In order to accomplish this, a multitimbral synthesizer has internal channels, each with an independent timbre. If a computer is connected to a multitimbral synth, note messages sent by the computer to that synth on separate channels will be played on separate timbres (see Figure 9.2). The same is true if those messages are sent within the computer to a multitimbral software synthesizer.

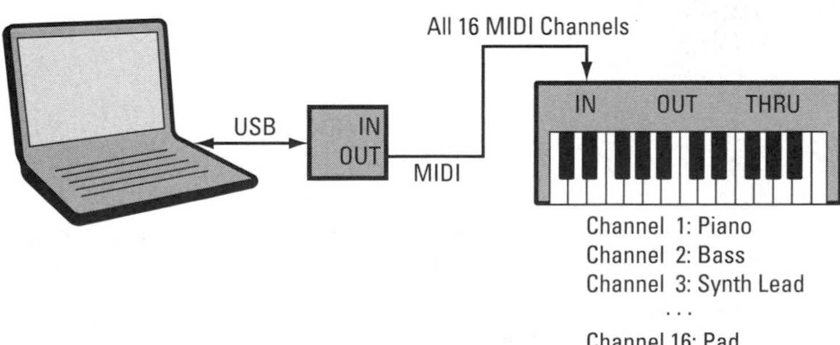

Figure 9.2 A computer connected to a multitimbral synth that can play a separate patch on each of the 16 channels.

Most synthesizers have a special mode for multitimbral response, which has various names, such as "multi" mode or "combi" mode, depending on the manufacturer. MIDI modes will be discussed later in the chapter.

There are 16 separate channels possible on one MIDI cable, so most synthesizers can play back 16 separate patches simultaneously. While this is quite a large number of patches, a simulated symphony orchestra or complex song would require many more than that. Even if we expand the system in Figure 9.2 by daisychaining several multitimbral synthesizers together using Thru Ports, the computer can still only send out messages on 16 total channels; the daisychained synths would share these 16 channels.

As we saw in the previous chapter, a **multiport MIDI interface** allows a computer to *independently* control each device attached to one of its Out Ports. In terms of MIDI channels, this means that the computer can send messages on 16 MIDI channels at the same time to *each* device allowing as many as 16 separate patches per MIDI Out Port (see Figure 9.3). A two-out multiport MIDI interface would allow for 32 separate channels (2 × 16), and thus 32 separate patches. An eight-out multiport MIDI interface would allow for 128 separate patches (8 × 16).

Though the preceding discussion was very hardware-centric, many of these same principles apply to software synthesizers. Even in software, MIDI channels are still used to route MIDI messages to synths, and most multitimbral software synths maintain the 16-channel limitation. Where more than 16 channels are available for a given software synth, they are usually in multiples of 16 (32, 48, 64).

CHANNEL VOICE MESSAGES

The most commonly used MIDI channel messages are the **channel voice messages**. The other category of MIDI channel messages—channel mode messages—will be described briefly later. Channel voice messages can be divided into three groups:

- note messages, which indicate that a note has been pressed or released;
- program messages, which specify what timbre those notes should play;
- expressive messages, which allow various properties of those notes to change over time.

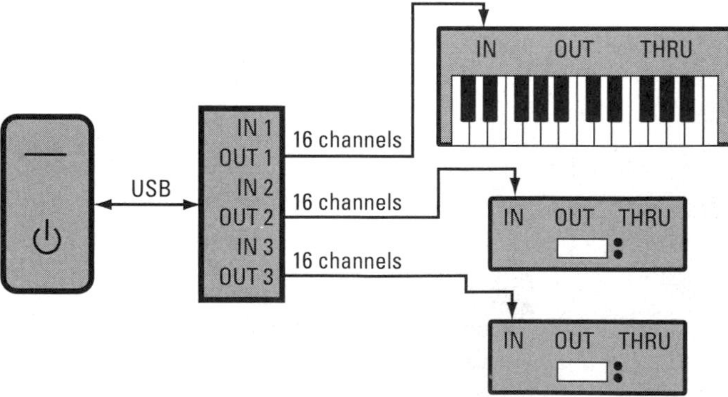

Figure 9.3 A computer connected to a 3-in/3-out multiport MIDI interface, which is connected to a keyboard synth and two modules. Each output can send messages on 16 channels for a total of 48 independent channels.

Note Messages

You can generate note messages by pressing a key on a keyboard, or they can be sent from MIDI software. Because MIDI was designed with keyboards in mind, a note message contains primarily information that a keyboard can send: what key was pressed and how hard it was pressed. These parameters are referred to as the **key number** and **velocity** respectively. The third piece of information in a note message is the channel (see "MIDI Channels"above), which allows notes with different channel numbers to play different patches.

MIDI key numbers range from 0 to 127 with key number 60 corresponding to middle C. While it might seem logical for keys to be numbered from 1 to 88 to correspond to the 88 keys on a piano, numbering systems in MIDI are derived from the binary system, or base 2. What this means is that most of the number ranges in MIDI are powers of two. For example, as we saw earlier, there are 16 MIDI channels, which is equal to 2 raised to the 4th power ($2^4 = 2 \times 2 \times 2 \times 2 = 16$). There are 128 key numbers (0 to 127), which is 2 raised to the 7th power ($2^7 = 2 \times 2 \times 2 \times 2 \times 2 \times 2 \times 2 = 128$). The figure 128 also happens to be the smallest power of two that is greater than 88.

Each half-step up in pitch increases the key number by one, and each half-step down lowers the key number by one. Since middle C is key number 60, C♯ is key number 61, D is key number 62, and so forth. Each octave spans 12 key numbers: one octave above middle C is key number 72 and one octave below middle C is 48. MIDI key numbers do not distinguish between enharmonic spellings of notes: The F♯ above middle C is key number 66 as is the G♭ above middle C. This fact explains the difficulty that computer notation programs occasionally have with properly spelling notes that are played on a MIDI keyboard.

While MIDI messages contain this key number—or rather its binary equivalent, software, such as MIDI sequencing programs, often represent key numbers using their pitch name and their register. This notation is commonly used in writings concerning musical acoustics and music theory, with middle C represented as C4, the major seventh above that as B4, the half-step above B4 as C5, and so on. The register designations change at the Cs.

A number of synthesizers and software programs in the world of MIDI offer a slight variant on this practice: middle C is often represented as C3 instead of C4. The designation of middle C as C3 may stem from the fact that, traditionally, most MIDI keyboards have 61 notes instead of 88. Labeling middle C as C3 makes the lowest C on a 61-note keyboard C1 rather than C2, which might seem odd. With middle C as C3 (see Figure 9.4), the lowest possible MIDI note, key number 0, is C2 and the highest possible note, key number 127, is G8. When working with a piece of MIDI hardware or software, it is important to establish what register it designates as middle C.

The velocity value that is transmitted as part of MIDI note message represents how quickly the key was depressed. On a piano, this translates directly to the loudness of a given note. On a synthesizer, this velocity could affect the resultant sound in a variety

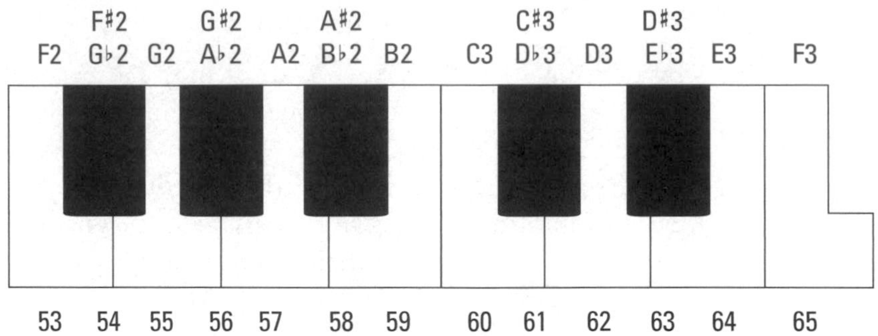

Figure 9.4 Some key numbers and their pitch-register designations (middle C is C3 here).

of ways, but loudness is still a standard mapping. As with key numbers, velocity values range from 0 to 127.

Figure 9.5 shows the mapping between velocity and dynamic level recommended in the MIDI spec. In practice the dynamic level for a given velocity value may vary from synth to synth, and even from patch to patch on the same synth. A note with a velocity of 80 could be fairly quiet on one synthesized patch and be unbearably loud on another. A change in velocity from 40 to 50 could be imperceptible on one synthesized patch and be too extreme on another. The only way to resolve this issue is to experiment with the patch you have chosen and modify note velocities according to what you hear.

There are at least two other aspects of a musical note that are *not* part of a MIDI note message: timbre and duration. A separate message, called a program change message (see below), addresses timbre, but duration is not dealt with at all. Let's consider this curious omission for a moment.

MIDI was designed originally as a real-time protocol to allow notes played live on one keyboard to trigger simultaneously notes from another keyboard. However, the actual duration of a note being played live, perhaps as part of an improvisation, cannot be determined until the note is over. If a master keyboard had to wait until the *end* of a note to send a note message, the slave device would never play at the same time as the master device. To solve this dilemma, the developers of MIDI split the note message into two separate messages: note-on and note-off. A keyboard sends a note-on message when a key is pressed down and a note-off when a key is released. The duration of the note, then, is simply the amount of time that elapses between the two messages.

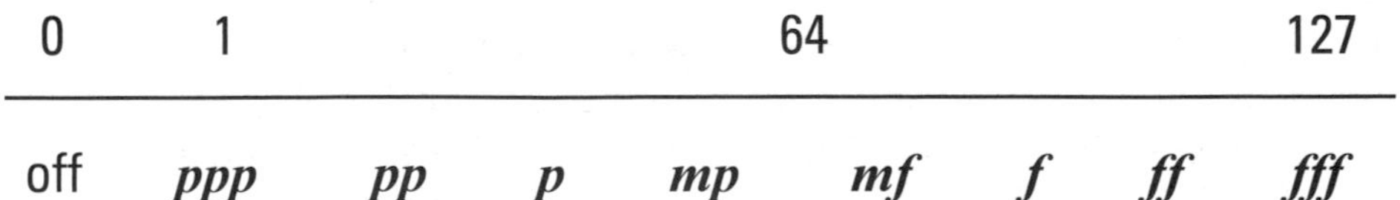

Figure 9.5 Suggested correspondence between velocity and dynamic level in situations where velocity is mapped to dynamic level (based on the MIDI 1.0 Specification).

A note-on message contains the channel, the key number, and the velocity. The corresponding note-off message contains the *same* channel, the *same* key number, and a release velocity value that corresponds to how quickly the key was released. In order to turn off a sounding note, the channel number in the note-off message must be the same as the channel in the note-on message, so that the correct timbre is turned off. In addition, the key number in the note-off message must be the same as the key number in the note-on message, so that the correct note being played on that timbre is turned off. A mismatch between either of these values would cause the note to keep playing—a "stuck" note—until you turned off the synth or sent an "All Notes Off" message from a MIDI sequencing program.

Program Messages

Program change messages—sometimes abbreviated as "**PC**" and also known as **patch change messages**—allow you to change the timbre of a synthesizer channel remotely. Note messages sent to that channel will then be played using the new timbre. This is especially useful when you're using computer software to control a multitimbral synthesizer, because you can change the patch on each of the synth's 16 channels from the computer. Without program change messages, you would have to select the patch for each channel directly from the front face of the synthesizer itself, which can be tedious and inefficient.

A keyboard synthesizer or module comes pre-programmed from the factory with specific patches, referred to as "factory presets," and many synthesizers allow users to create and store their own patches. Each of these patches, whether a factory preset or user-created, is stored in the electronic memory of the synthesizer and given a **program number** along with a name. For example, a patch might have a program number of "011" and the name "Funky Piano."

In addition, most synthesizers organize their patches into **banks** of 128 patches each, so a desired patch might have the full designation "Bank 02, Program 011, Funky Piano." Despite all of this information used to refer to a program location on a synthesizer, the MIDI program change message contains only two pieces of information: the channel and the program number. Issues relating to bank number and name will be discussed below.

The channel value allows you to select which channel of the synthesizer will receive the program change and the program number allows you to select the number of the desired patch. Like key numbers, program numbers range from 0 to 127 for a total of 128 different program numbers. This scheme has two drawbacks: (1) 128 values are inadequate to address the number of patches on modern synthesizers, which can range from several hundred to several thousand, and (2) the program number doesn't tell you *what* the patch will be, just its number.

At the time MIDI was developed, 128 program numbers were adequate to select any patch on a synthesizer, but this is no longer true. As with the 16-channel limitation that was bypassed by the development of multiport MIDI interfaces, the 128 program number limitation was addressed by the assignment of two control change messages (discussed later in the chapter) to be **bank change messages**.

A single bank change message, when combined with a program change message, would allow you to select first a bank of patches and then a program number within that bank. That would allow you to address over 16,000 patches (128 banks × 128 patches) instead of the original 128. With *two* bank change messages, you could address over two million patches (128 × 128 × 128)! Bank change messages solve the 128-program limitation, but they don't address the name issue.

The actual timbre called up by a particular program change number differs from synth to synth. On one synthesizer, a program number of 40 could call up a flute, whereas on another synthesizer, a program number of 40 could call up a helicopter sound effect. The fact that the program number gives no indication of the sound of the chosen timbre can be frustrating, but it is one of the compromises that allows MIDI to work with devices from any manufacturer. Since one of the selling points of a given synthesizer might be its unique set of patches, the MIDI program change message has to be generic so that it remains useful for all manufacturers. However, there are some instances where a predictable set of patches is desirable. This need is addressed by General MIDI.

General MIDI

General MIDI (also **GM**) is an addition to the MIDI specification that describes a minimum set of capabilities for a sound generator (whether hardware or software). The components of General MIDI include:

- a minimum number of simultaneous voices (polyphony): 24 overall or 16 for melody and 8 for percussion;
- support for 16 simultaneous MIDI channels (multimbral) with channel 10 devoted to drums/percussion;
- a minimum of 128 programs (patches) in which specific program numbers are mapped to specific program names (see Table 9.1);
- a minimum of 47 preset percussion sounds conforming to the "GM Percussion Map" (see Table 9.2).

It is worth noting that the only guarantee for a GM patch number is that the patch *name* will be the same. All GM patches with a particular name will sound *approximately* like that instrument, but, since General MIDI doesn't specify *how* the sound is to be produced (a particular synthesis method or sample playback), General MIDI sounds will vary, possibly dramatically, from GM synth to GM synth.

General MIDI is most useful in settings where the predictability of patches is a central concern, such as playback in music notation programs, in the exchange of MIDI files, and in music education. Music education settings typically require this consistency so that computer-assisted instruction software can predictably access appropriate sounds.

A computer-based lesson about the sound of a saxophone wouldn't be very effective if the synth was playing a trombone patch!

You may notice that the GM patches in Table 9.1 are numbered from "1" to "128," whereas it was mentioned above that the program change numbers range from 0 to 127. This "off-by-one" issue stems from the different methods of counting used by computers and people. Computers are more than happy to start counting with the number zero, but people are more inclined to count items starting with one. The actual numerical values sent down a MIDI cable as program change numbers start with 0 and go to 127, but they are often shown in lists, like the one in Table 9.1, as people would count them.

The off-by-one problem crops up in other places when dealing with MIDI. For example, it was mentioned above that there are 16 MIDI channels labeled as "1" to "16." However, the actual numerical values for channel numbers sent in MIDI messages range from 0 to 15. This apparent discrepancy again stems from our distaste for uttering phrases like "channel zero."

The General MIDI System Level 1 (GM or **GM1**) was adopted in 1991. Additional components were later added and defined as the General MIDI System Level 2 (**GM2**, adopted in 1999). The GM2 components include:

- an expansion of the original 128 GM1 patches to 256 patches using bank change messages to select variations on the original GM1 patches;
- an increase in the polyphony from 24 voices to 32 voices;
- expansion from one drum kit at a time to two by defining channel 11, in addition to GM1's channel 10, as a drum/percussion channel;
- nine new drum kits, in addition to the standard GM1 kit;
- 14 additions to the GM1 drum map.

If a synth is GM or GM2 compatible, that does not necessarily mean that it only has 128 or 256 patches or is only 24 or 32 voice polyphonic. Many synths have a GM bank or GM1/GM2 banks plus one or more other banks containing patches not covered by those specifications. This allows a synth to be GM1/GM2 compatible when needed, but also to have unique features and patches that can appeal to professional markets.

Expressive Messages

So far we have program change messages for choosing a synthesizer patch and note messages for starting and stopping notes. However, these two kinds of messages don't allow for any changes in the sound *during* the note. For example, while the velocity value in a note-on message can set the initial loudness of a sound, it cannot influence the loudness after that. Expressive MIDI messages were designed for just such purposes.

There are four separate messages that can be described as **expressive messages**: control change, channel pressure, polyphonic key pressure, and pitch bend. This simplicity is a bit misleading, though, because there are many different types of control change messages.

Table 9.1 **The General MIDI Patch Map**

Program #	*Patch name*	*Program #*	*Patch name*
	Piano Instrument Group		**Reed Instrument Group**
1	Acoustic Grand Piano	65	Soprano Sax
2	Bright Acoustic Grand Piano	66	Alto Sax
3	Electric Grand Piano	67	Tenor Sax
4	Honky-tonk Piano	68	Baritone Sax
5	Electric Piano 1	69	Oboe
6	Electric Piano 2	70	English Horn
7	Harpsichord	71	Bassoon
8	Clavi	72	Clarinet
	Chromatic Percussion Group		**Pipe Instrument Group**
9	Celesta	73	Piccolo
10	Glockenspiel	74	Flute
11	Music Box	75	Recorder
12	Vibraphone	76	Pan Flute
13	Marimba	77	Blown Bottle
14	Xylophone	78	Shakuhachi
15	Tubular Bells	79	Whistle
16	Dulcimer	80	Ocarina
	Organ Instrument Group		**Synth Lead Instrument Group**
17	Drawbar Organ	81	Lead 1 (square)
18	Percussive Organ	82	Lead 2 (sawtooth)
19	Rock Organ	83	Lead 3 (calliope)
20	Church Organ	84	Lead 4 (chiff)
21	Reed Organ	85	Lead 5 (charang)
22	Accordion	86	Lead 6 (voice)
23	Harmonica	87	Lead 7 (fifths)
24	Tango Accordion	88	Lead 8 (bass + lead)
	Guitar Instrument Group		**Synth Pad Instrument Group**
25	Acoustic Guitar (nylon)	89	Pad 1 (new age)
26	Acoustic Guitar (steel string)	90	Pad 2 (warm)
27	Electric Guitar (jazz)	91	Pad 3 (polysynth)
28	Electric Guitar (clean)	92	Pad 4 (choir)
29	Electric Guitar (muted)	93	Pad 5 (bowed)
30	Overdriven Guitar	94	Pad 6 (metallic)
31	Distortion Guitar	95	Pad 7 (halo)
32	Guitar Harmonics	96	Pad 8 (sweep)

	Bass Instrument Group		**Synth Effects Group**
33	Acoustic Bass	97	FX 1 (rain)
34	Electric Bass (finger)	98	FX 2 (soundtrack)
35	Electric Bass (pick)	99	FX 3 (crystal)
36	Fretless Bass	100	FX 4 (atmosphere)
37	Slap Bass 1	101	FX 5 (brightness)
38	Slap Bass 2	102	FX 6 (goblins)
39	Synth Bass 1	103	FX 7 (echoes)
40	Synth Bass 2	104	FX 8 (sci-fi)
	String Instrument Group		**Ethnic Instrument Group**
41	Violin	105	Sitar
42	Viola	106	Banjo
43	Cello	107	Shamisen
44	Contrabass	108	Koto
45	Tremolo Strings	109	Kalimba
46	Pizzicato Strings	110	Bag pipe
47	Orchestral Harp	111	Fiddle
48	Timpani	112	Shanai
	Ensemble Instrument Group		**Percussive Instrument Group**
49	String Ensemble 1	113	Tinkle Bell
50	String Ensemble 2	114	Agogo
51	SynthStrings 1	115	Steel Drums
52	SynthStrings 2	116	Woodblock
53	Choir Aahs	117	Taiko Drum
54	Voice Oohs	118	Melodic Tom
55	Synth Voice	119	Synth Drum
56	Orchestra Hit	120	Reverse Cymbal
	Brass		**Sound Effects Instrument Group**
57	Trumpet	121	Guitar Fret Noise
58	Trombone	122	Breath Noise
59	Tuba	123	Seashore
60	Muted Trumpet	124	Bird Tweet
61	French Horn	125	Telephone Ring
62	Brass Section	126	Helicopter
63	SynthBrass 1	127	Applause
64	SynthBrass 2	128	Gunshot

Source: Based on The Complete MIDI 1.0 Detailed Specification.

Table 9.2 **The General MIDI Percussion Map for Channel 10**

Key #	*Drum sound*	*Key #*	*Drum sound*
35	Acoustic Bass Drum	59	Ride Cymbal 2
36	Bass Drum 1	60	Hi Bongo
37	Side Stick	61	Low Bongo
38	Acoustic Snare	62	Mute Hi Conga
39	Hand Clap	63	Open Hi Conga
40	Electric Snare	64	Low Conga
41	Low Floor Tom	65	High Timbale
42	Closed Hi Hat	66	Low Timbale
43	High Floor Tom	67	High Agogo
44	Pedal Hi-Hat	68	Low Agogo
45	Low Tom	69	Cabasa
46	Open Hi-Hat	70	Maracas
47	Low-Mid Tom	71	Short Whistle
48	Hi Mid Tom	72	Long Whistle
49	Crash Cymbal 1	73	Short Guiro
50	High Tom	74	Long Guiro
51	Ride Cymbal 1	75	Claves
52	Chinese Cymbal	76	Hi Wood Block
53	Ride Bell	77	Low Wood Block
54	Tambourine	78	Mute Cuica
55	Splash Cymbal	79	Open Cuica
56	Cowbell	80	Mute Triangle
57	Crash Cymbal 2	81	Open Triangle
58	Vibraslap		

Source: Based on The Complete MIDI 1.0 Detailed Specification.

A **control change** message, abbreviated as **CC**, includes three pieces of information: the channel, the control number, and the control value. Including the channel in the message means that control change messages affect only the timbre assigned to that channel. This allows, for example, different volume changes (crescendos/diminuendos) to be applied to different timbres.

The **control number** allows the user to change various expressive characteristics independently and simultaneously. While control numbers can take on values between 0 and 127, in practice only a handful of control numbers are regularly used, including modulation wheel (CC1), channel volume (CC7), expression (CC11), pan (CC10), and sustain pedal (CC64). The two bank change messages mentioned earlier are CC0 and CC32. The **control value** determines the value of the parameter indicated by the control number.

The **modulation wheel** controller (CC1) is usually activated by a wheel or joystick on the left side of a keyboard. As the mod wheel (or joystick) is rotated away from the user, the keyboard sends out a series of CC1 messages with increasing control values (see Figure 9.6). The control values for CC1 and every other control number range from 0 to 127.

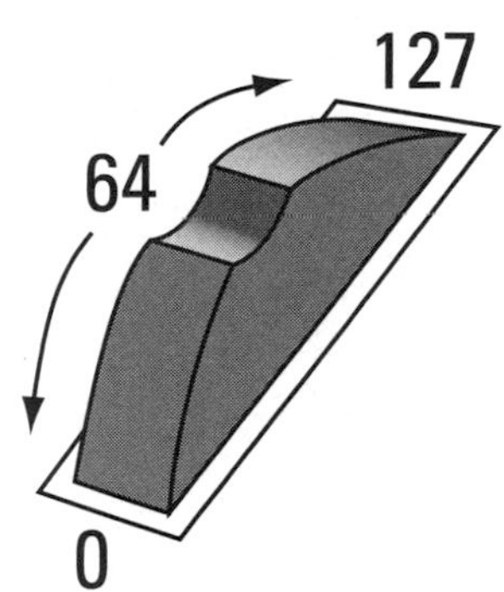

Figure 9.6
A modulation wheel sends out CC1 messages with values between 0 and 127.

The effect of CC1 is entirely determined by the receiving synthesizer. Often CC1 messages change the amount of vibrato that is added to the chosen patch, but a receiving synth can be programmed to interpret CC1 control values in a variety of different ways, including opening/closing a filter and changing the pitch of all or part of the patch (even though there is a dedicated message just for pitch bend). The quickest way to tell the effect of the mod wheel on a given patch is to experiment.

The **channel volume** controller (CC7) sets the volume for a given channel on a synthesizer. This allows you to manage the volume for each of the 16 MIDI channels independently. Unlike the mod wheel messages, there is not necessarily a dedicated knob, wheel, or slider that sends out the main volume message; CC7s are most often manipulated in a sequencing program. The control value for CC7 determines the volume setting, with 0 being silent and 127 being maximum.

The **expression** controller (CC11) works in conjunction with the channel volume controller (CC7). Where CC7 is used to set the overall volume for a channel, CC11 is used to modify that volume temporarily, allowing you to create crescendos and diminuendos. For example, using a MIDI sequencing program, a CC7 message could be sent to a given channel on a synth with a value of 64, and then a series of CC11 messages could be sent to create a crescendo from a CC11 value of 97 to a CC11 value of 127. This might result in a crescendo from *piano* to *mezzo forte* (see Figure 9.7a).

If you decided that the notes playing on that channel needed to be louder overall, you could change the CC7 value to 96 and the same CC11 crescendo (97 to 127) would now result in a dynamic crescendo from *mezzo forte* to *forte* (see Figure 9.7b). The actual dynamics will vary from patch to patch and from synth to synth, but this example should give you the general idea of the relationship between CC7 and CC11.

a) CC7 64		b) CC7 96	
	CC11 97		CC11 97
	CC11 103		CC11 103
	CC11 109		CC11 109
	CC11 115		CC11 115
	CC11 121		CC11 121
	CC11 127		CC11 127
p	***mf***	***mf***	***f***

Figure 9.7 The change in CC7 from (a) to (b) causes different beginning and ending dynamics for the crescendo created by the CC11 messages. The jumps between CC11 values are for graphical convenience.

This arrangement allows you to change the relative mix between channels by sending CC7 messages while leaving the crescendos and diminuendos unchanged. CC7 is widely supported, but CC11 is not supported by every hardware or software synth. In situations where CC11 is not supported, CC7 would be used for both the overall channel volume and for crescendos and diminuendos.

The **pan** controller (CC10) sets the position of the timbre in the left–right stereo field for a given channel (pan is short for "panorama"). This allows you to manage the stereo position of the timbres assigned to each of the 16 MIDI channels independently. There is seldom a knob or slider for pan, so CC10 messages are most often sent using a sequencing program. The control value for CC10 ranges from 0 to 127 with 0 typically being left, 64 middle, and 127 right. Some software programs and synthesizers display pan positions as –63 for left to +63 for right or 63L to 63R.

The **sustain pedal** controller (CC64) determines whether the notes on a given channel are held after their keys have been released. In other words, if the sustain pedal on a synthesizer is depressed while the performer is holding down one or more keys, those notes will continue to sound after the performer has released those keys until the sustain pedal is released. This is referred to as a damper pedal on an acoustic piano because the pedal causes the dampers to be held away from the strings.

CC64 is a different type of controller from CC1, CC7, CC11, and CC10. Those controllers are referred to as **continuous controllers** because their control values can range from 0 to 127. CC64 is a **switch controller**: it is either on (control value 127) or off (control value 0). The values between 0 and 63 are interpreted as "off" by a receiving synth, and the values between 64 and 127 are interpreted as "on." As many pianists have noticed, this is a less refined control than the damper pedal on an acoustic piano, which allows half-pedaling and gradual pedaling.

Another type of expressive message is the **channel pressure** message, also known as **aftertouch** or monophonic aftertouch, which is sent out when the performer strikes a key and then presses down. This message contains only two pieces of information: the channel and a pressure value. It's called "channel" pressure because there is only one **pressure value** for the entire channel regardless of how many notes are sounding; this is also why it is sometimes referred to as "monophonic" aftertouch.

As with the previous messages, the pressure value ranges from 0 to 127. Like the mod wheel (CC1), channel pressure has no predefined effect on the destination synthesizer. It is often used to add vibrato, but could also be used to open or close a filter or make some other modification to the sound.

The advantage in performance of aftertouch is that the performer doesn't have to give one hand up to activate the control—he or she can play the keyboard with both hands and still be able to modify the notes while they are sounding. Aftertouch could also allow a keyboard player to play notes with the right hand, open and close a filter using aftertouch, and add vibrato with the mod wheel using the left hand.

Polyphonic key pressure is a form of aftertouch that allows the performer to send a separate pressure value for each key—hence the name "polyphonic." Polyphonic key pressure messages contain three pieces of information: channel, key number, and pressure value for that key. Poly pressure messages can be used to control the same kinds of effects as channel pressure, such as vibrato amount or filter cutoff frequency, but have the added feature of allowing those effects to be different for *each* note. In practice, poly pressure is seldom used: only the more expensive controller keyboards transmit poly pressure and most synthesizers aren't programmed to respond to it.

The last expressive message type is probably the most familiar: **pitch bend**. Like the modulation wheel controller, pitch bend is usually associated with a specific physical control that is either a wheel, a joystick, or part of a combination modulation/pitch bend joystick. Pitch bend controls go both up and down, and "snap back" to the zero position (no pitch change) when you release the wheel or joystick. The nearly universal effect is, of course, to bend the pitch of the note or notes playing on a given channel. The actual musical range of the pitch bend is determined by the receiving synth, but the typical default is a maximum up or down of a major second. The pitch bend range is programmable on most synthesizers.

The pitch bend message consists of three pieces of information: a channel, a coarse bend value, and a fine bend value. Up to now, the range for most of the values in a MIDI message (key number, velocity, control number, control value, pressure value, etc.) has been from 0 to 127. Pitch bend, however, combines two values—**coarse bend** and **fine bend**—to create a much larger range.

Two numbers, each ranging from 0 to 127 (128 values), taken together might seem to create a composite value of 0 to 255 (128 + 128 = 256 values), but, because pitch bend combines the binary digits of the two values together, you get 128 × 128 = 16,384 values. This is usually represented as –8,192 when the pitch bend wheel is all the way down, to +8,191 when the pitch bend wheel is all the way up (see Figure 9.8).

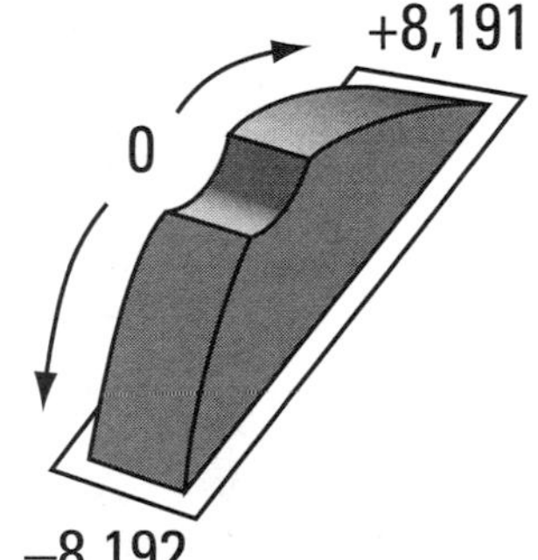

Figure 9.8 Pitch bend wheel sends out values between –8,192 and +8,191.

It turns out that we are far more sensitive to changes in pitch than to changes in many other musical parameters, so a mere 128 values (0 to 127) over whatever pitch bend range is defined by the receiving synth might cause us to hear steps between the values, instead of a smooth bend. This effect would be magnified if the pitch bend range on the receiving synth were set to a large value such as two octaves (down one octave to up an octave).

SYSTEM MESSAGES

Unlike channel voice messages, MIDI system messages are not directed at a specific channel, but rather apply to the entire receiving MIDI device. System messages are used for a wide variety of purposes, such as communicating messages to a specific synthesizer (System Exclusive), receiving time code from external sources such as video decks (MIDI Time Code), and transmitting timing messages between MIDI devices (MIDI Timing Clock).

System messages can be quite powerful, but they have not been used as frequently in recent years, particularly with the proliferation of software-based synthesizers and

Table 9.3 **Summary of channel voice messages**

Message type	*Information in message*		
Note-on	Channel	Key number	Velocity
Note-off	Channel	Key number	Release velocity
Program change	Channel	Program number	[nothing else]
Control change	Channel	Control number	Control value
		1 = Modulation wheel	
		7 = Main volume	
		11 = Expression	
		10 = Pan	
		64 = Sustain pedal	
		0 = Bank change 1	
		32 = Bank change 2	
Channel pressure	Channel	Value	[nothing else]
Poly key pressure	Channel	Key number	Value
Pitch bend	Channel	Fine bend value	Coarse bend value

samplers, many of which don't need these specialized messages. For the purposes of this text, it is sufficient to recognize the existence of system messages and note the few functions mentioned in the previous paragraph.

MIDI MODES

Thus far it has largely been assumed that synthesizers receiving MIDI messages are ready to respond appropriately and independently on any channel. However, there are a number of different ways for a synthesizer to respond to incoming messages, which are referred to as **modes**. Modes are not really hardware or messages, but they play a prominent role in the MIDI specification in describing how hardware synthesizers respond to messages.

Omni On/Off

Omni On and Omni Off modes determine whether a synthesizer "tunes in" to all channels at the same time or just one. In **Omni On mode**, messages received on any channel are played using the same patch. This is a useful mode for making sure that the synthesizer and the connections work regardless of channel settings, and it is the mode recommended by the MIDI spec for a synthesizer when it first powers up. In **Omni Off mode**, a synthesizer only responds to those messages on its single "receive channel." This was an important mode when synthesizers were largely mono-timbral. In the modern **multi mode**, a synthesizer behaves as if it were made up of 16 Omni Off synthesizers in the sense that it can respond independently with a separate patch on each MIDI channel. Multi mode is also referred to as combi or performance mode by various manufacturers.

Poly/Mono

Poly and mono modes refer to the number of simultaneous voices that a synthesizer can play. **Polyphonic** (poly) **mode** indicates that the synthesizer can play more than one "note" at a time, whereas **monophonic** (mono) **mode** indicates that the synthesizer can play only one voice at a time. Poly is the most common mode for synthesizers, but mono is useful for patches that mimic vintage analog synths, which were monophonic.

A vast majority of the synths made today are polyphonic and multitimbral. Rather than change an entire synth (all 16 channels) to mono mode for an analog lead sound, modern synths allow this to be changed on a patch-by-patch basis.

Channel Mode Messages

Channel mode messages are used to switch the receiving synth into one of the modes discussed above, turn sounding notes off, or reset the controller values. These messages are technically control change messages, but control numbers 120–127 have been dedicated to these channel mode functions.

SPLITS AND LAYERS

In addition to the various ways in which a synthesizer can respond to incoming MIDI channel messages, there are also several ways in which a synthesizer can respond to a direct performance on the keys. The simplest of these performance modes is the **patch mode** in which there is one patch heard across the entire keyboard. However, in some performance situations, it is useful to have more than one patch accessible from the keys at a time. The two standard modes for playing more than one patch at a time are split mode and layer mode (see Figure 9.9). As with multi mode, these modes are not part of the MIDI specification; they have been developed over the years by manufacturers to meet a variety of user needs.

In **split mode**, part of the keyboard plays one patch while the other plays a different patch. The key at which this transition is made is referred to as the **split point**. One typical application of this is to have an accompanying patch, such as a guitar, assigned to the keys below, say, middle C, and a

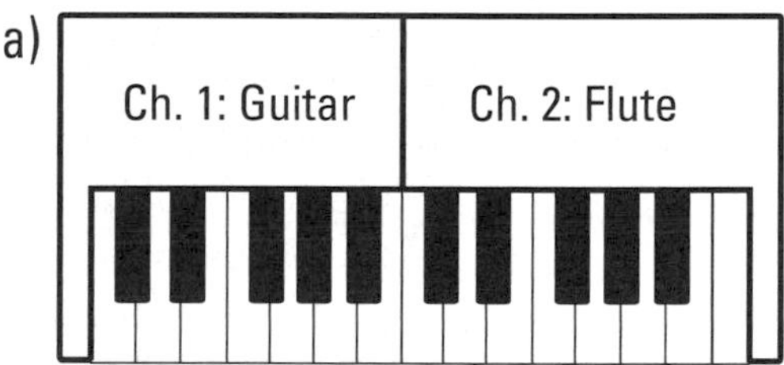

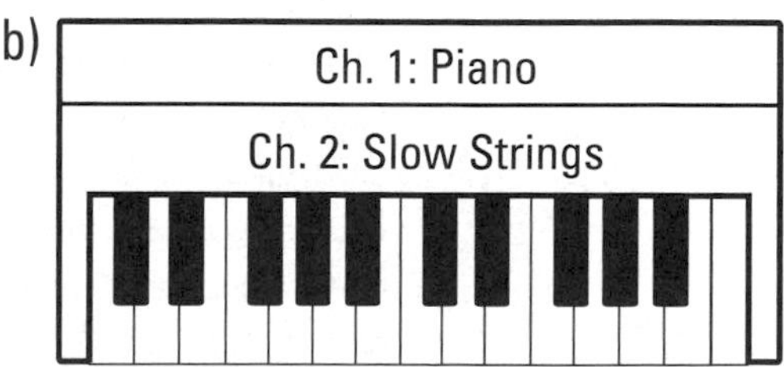

Figure 9.9 (a) Keyboard in split mode with a split point at middle C; and (b) keyboard in layer mode.

melodic patch, such as a flute, assigned to keys above that split point. This allows the performer to play both melody and accompaniment from the same keyboard.

In **layer mode**, the same key plays more than one patch at the same time, thus "layering" the two patches together. A typical application of layering would be to combine a patch that has a sharp attack, such as a piano, with a patch that has different characteristics, such as slowly attacking strings. The layering of these two patches provides the bite and definition of the piano sound with the lushness of the strings that enter when notes are held.

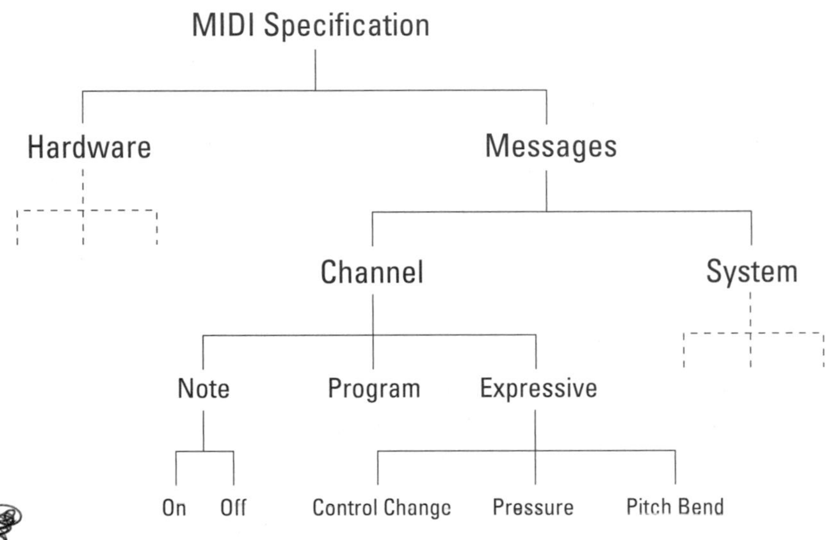

Figure 9.10 Summary of MIDI messages.

REVIEW OF KEY TERMS

channel/system messages 142	expression 153
MIDI channels 142	pan 154
multitimbral 143	sustain pedal 154
multiport MIDI interface 144	continuous controllers 154
channel voice messages 144	switch controllers 154
key number/velocity 145	channel pressure/aftertouch 154
program/patch change (PC) messages 147	pressure value 154
program number 147	polyphonic key pressure 154
banks 147	pitch bend 155
bank change messages 148	coarse/fine bend 155
General MIDI (GM) 148	modes 156
GM1/GM2 149	Omni On/Off modes 156
expressive messages 149	multi mode 157
control change (CC) 152	polyphonic/monophonic modes 157
control number 152	channel mode messages 157
control value 153	patch mode 157
modulation wheel 153	split mode/point 157
channel volume 153	layer mode 158

CHAPTER 10

MIDI Sequencing

MIDI technology is used in a wide variety of contexts, including computer notation, computer-assisted instruction, and multimedia authoring. One of most important applications for MIDI in a creative context is **MIDI sequencing**. "Sequencing" in the general sense involves organizing objects or information in some kind of order. A sequence of driving directions involves organizing a group of instructions in general time order: first turn left, then drive 5 miles, and finally turn right. DNA sequencing involves examining DNA components (A, G, C, T) and putting the symbols in a row that represents the spatial organization of the components. MIDI sequencing involves organizing MIDI messages—note messages, program messages, expressive messages, and system messages—in time.

The purpose of MIDI sequencing is to create performances on hardware or software synthesizers and samplers. Creating nuanced performances on a synth requires careful attention not only to notes and rhythms, but also to expressive characteristics such as dynamics and vibrato. The art of MIDI sequencing involves taking the raw materials of MIDI—the messages—and using them to create the subtle expressive changes that live performers execute naturally.

The term "MIDI sequencer" is misleading nowadays in the sense that few, if any, sequencers deal only with MIDI. Most allow the user to combine MIDI, digital audio, software synthesis and sampling, and digital video in a single software environment, though the video is seldom editable within the sequencer. The term **digital audio workstation** (**DAW**), which was used in the "Audio" section of this book, is equally misleading in that only a few DAWs deal only with digital audio. In practice, the terms "sequencer" and "DAW" are often used interchangeably, with "sequencer" more likely to be used in the context of composing/arranging music and "DAW" more likely to be used in the context of audio recording and editing.

The purpose of this chapter is to provide an overview of the MIDI features that can be found in most standard sequencer/DAWs. Fortunately, most sequencers operate in a similar manner, so once you learn a sequencer, changing to another is largely a matter of learning new menus, buttons, and key commands for already familiar functions.

MIDI sequencing involves inputting MIDI messages, organizing and editing MIDI messages, and outputting MIDI messages, all discussed in detail below. However, it is useful to first look at the user interface features common to most sequencers.

THE STANDARD USER INTERFACE

Multi-track Audio Recording Paradigm

The standard interface for MIDI sequencing is derived from **multi-track audio recording**. Multi-track audio recording, of course, involves recording *audio* from different instruments on separate tracks so that they can be edited and processed separately and later mixed together. MIDI sequencers organize MIDI messages on separate **tracks**, with the output of each track assigned to a monotimbral instrument or a **MIDI channel** on a multitimbral instrument, and a patch (see below) chosen for that instrument or channel. Tracks and channels are *not* one and the same. The output of one track can be usually assigned to multiple MIDI channels and/or multiple tracks can be assigned to the same channel. Tracks can be thought of as purely organizational elements, allowing you to store and edit various MIDI messages and then output them to a monotimbral synth or one or more MIDI channels on a multitimbral synth.

Also by analogy with audio recording, each MIDI track typically has a record-enable button, a mute button, and a solo button (see Figures 10.1a and 10.1b). Those features will be covered later when MIDI playback is discussed. Though this interface paradigm originated when sequencers were MIDI only, it is particularly convenient now that MIDI and digital audio regularly coexist in the same piece of software and even in the same window.

Another sequencer interface feature that was derived from audio recording practice comprises the transport controls, consisting of play, stop, pause, rewind, fast-forward, and record (see Figure 10.2). Transport controls were also covered in Chapter 6 when discussing digital audio recording.

Patchlists

As mentioned above, tracks are assigned to monotimbral instruments or MIDI channels on multitimbral instruments, and **patches** are then assigned to those outputs. For software synthesizers it is common to choose the patch directly from the softsynth's window instead of from the sequencer track. For hardware synths, it's possible to set the patches for each channel on the synthesizer itself, but it is often more convenient to choose patches in the sequencer by name from a pop-up menu. However, as you saw in Chapter 9, "MIDI Messages," program (patch) change messages and bank change messages specify patches by number, not by name.

The mapping between a patch name chosen in a sequencer and bank change/patch change numbers that are sent to a synthesizer is handled by a **patchlist**. A patchlist is a file on the computer that contains a list of patches by name on a synthesizer and the

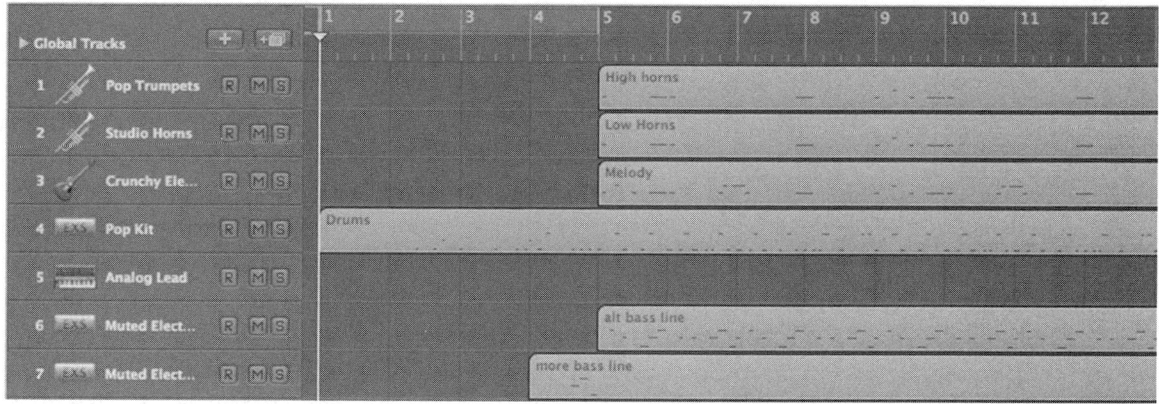

Figure 10.1a Arrange window from Logic Pro 8. (Screenshot reprinted with permission from Apple Inc.)

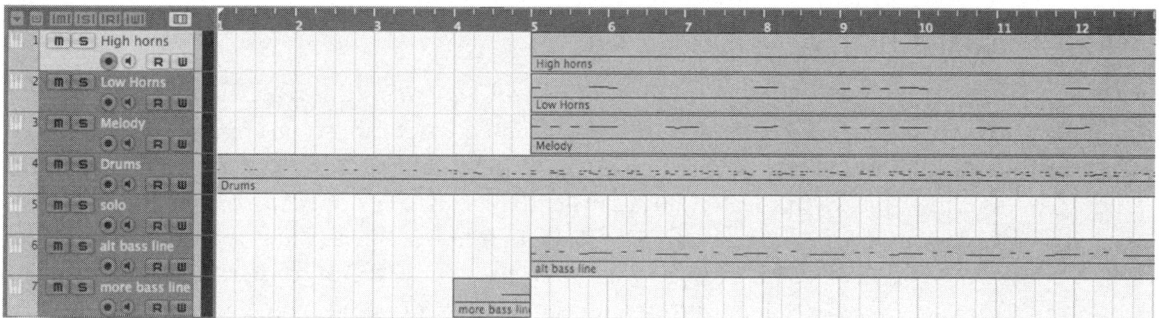

Figure 10.1b Tracks window from Cubase Studio 4. (Courtesy of Steinberg Media Technologies)

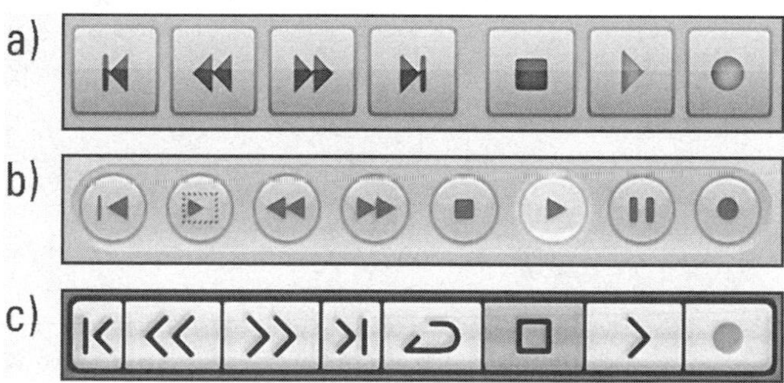

Figure 10.2 Transport controls from various sequencer/DAWs: (a) Pro Tools LE 8 (courtesy of Digidesign); (b) Logic Pro 8 (screenshot reprinted with permission from Apple Inc.); and (c) Cubase Studio 4 (courtesy of Steinberg Media Technologies).

bank change and program change numbers that are associated with those patches (see Figure 10.3). When you choose a patch in a sequencer, the sequencer looks up the proper bank and program numbers and sends those to the synthesizer.

Different sequencers often have different ways of formatting patchlists and different ways of making those lists available to the sequencer. You can often find any patchlists that are not automatically installed with your sequencer by searching the Internet, or

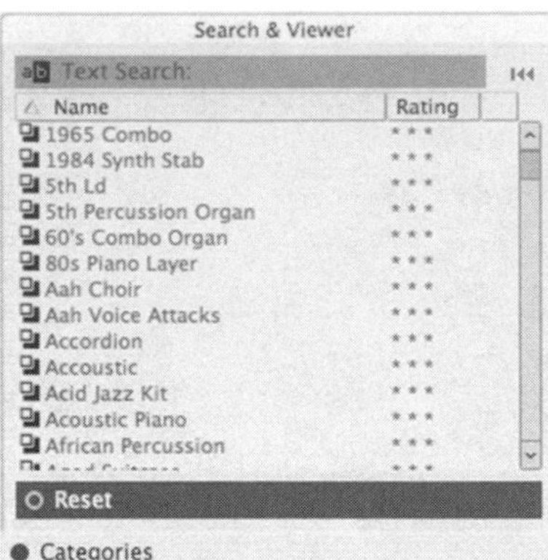

Figure 10.3 Patchlist Viewer in Cubase Studio 4. (Courtesy of Steinberg Media Technologies)

you can make them with a text editor or a special piece of software for making patchlists (there are several freeware/shareware patchlist makers available).

Measuring Time

Another important feature of the common sequencer interface is the method for measuring time. When a sequencer is being used to compose or arrange, the preferred time format involves measures and beats. In addition, some system is needed for subdividing beats so that note values smaller than a quarter note can be represented. Some sequencers divide the beat directly into some number of "ticks," also referred to as "units" by some sequencers. This division is referred to as the **PPQN**, or parts per quarter note. PPQN varies from sequencer to sequencer and can usually be changed by the user.

One possible PPQN is 480. This means that a quarter note would get 480 ticks, an eighth note 240 ticks, a sixteenth note 120 ticks, and so on (see Table 10.1). Many sequencers can be set to have a PPQN in the thousands. This may seem like an inhumanly precise measurement of time, but it allows the MIDI messages to be aligned precisely with both audio and video events (see Figure 10.4).

Table 10.1 **Tick values of note durations for a PPQN of 480**

Musical duration	*# of ticks*
Quarter note	480
Eighth note	240
Sixteenth note	120
Dotted eighth	360
Eighth-note triplet	160
Quarter-note triplet	320
Half note	960
Whole note	1920

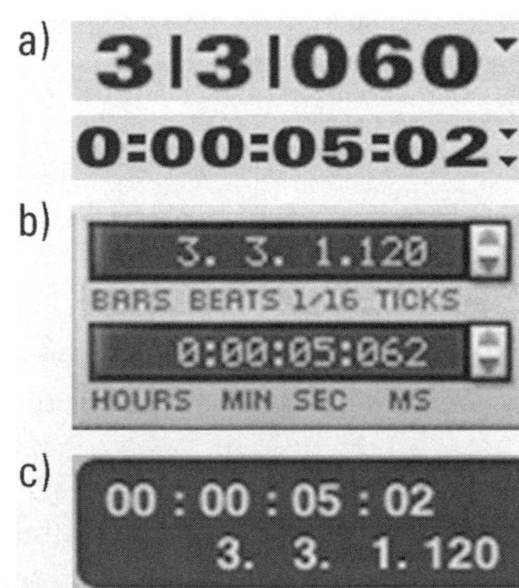

Figure 10.4 Clocks from various sequencers showing the same time: (a) Digital Performer 6—measure time and SMPTE time (courtesy of MOTU); (b) Reason 4—measure time and real time (courtesy of Propellerheads); and (c) Logic Pro 8—SMPTE time and measure time (screenshot reprinted with permission from Apple Inc.).

Another variation on this measurement in musical time is to first subdivide the beat into sixteenth notes and then divide those sixteenth notes into some number of ticks. If the number of ticks per sixteenth note were 240, it would be equivalent to a PPQN of 960.

As you saw in Chapter 6, "Digital Audio Software," sequencer/DAWs can display time in a variety of other ways as well, including real time for recording projects and SMPTE time code for synchronizing with digital video. See Figure 6.2 (page 88) for other clock examples.

Displaying Pitch

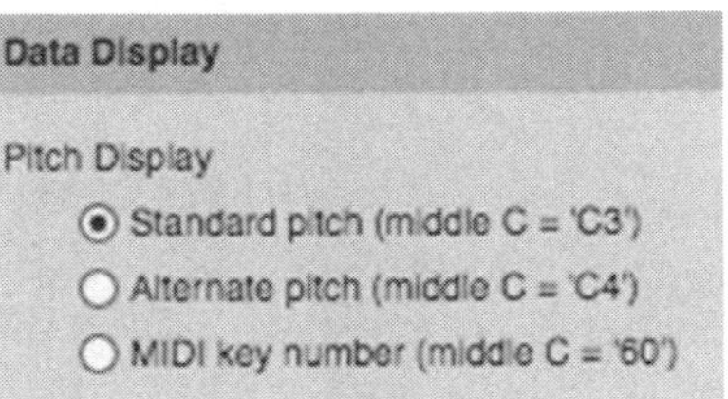

Figure 10.5 Pitch preferences in Digital Performer 6. (Courtesy of MOTU)

The pitch in a MIDI note message is transmitted as a numerical value (the key number), but it is displayed in various windows in a MIDI sequencer in pitch-register notation (see Figure 10.5). In many MIDI applications and MIDI devices, middle C (key number 60) is represented as C3, as opposed to the C4 that is the standard in other areas of music and acoustics. The register numbers change at the Cs: a half step below C3 is B2 and an octave above C3 is C4.

MIDI Editors

The term **editor** in a sequencing program refers to a particular view of the MIDI information. You've already seen one of the standard MIDI editors, the **tracks editor**, also called the arrange window or the project window. The tracks editor is useful for manipulating one or more tracks of a sequence on the timescale of a measure or more. You don't typically edit notes themselves in this view, though some sequencers allow you to zoom in from the tracks view and edit individual notes.

Aside from providing a "birds-eye" view of your sequence, the tracks editor is also typically where you specify the output instrument or MIDI channel(s) on a multitimbral instrument for a track and assign a patch to that instrument or channel. In addition, you can set the track to be record-enabled and control playback functions such as mute and solo. Many of these settings can also be selected in other editors.

To edit MIDI messages more precisely, there are a variety of common "note-level" editors that show each note in a track or in multiple tracks. Most sequencers have a similar set of editors, though a given sequencer may have an additional editor that is unique or only one or two of the standard editors. It is important to note that the editors all access the same MIDI messages: if you change a note in one editor, it will change in all of the other editors that display note information as well.

The choice of which editor to use depends on the editing tasks that you wish to perform. Often, any one of two or three editors would serve your purposes just fine, in which case the choice of editors becomes one of personal preference.

One of the most common note-level editors is the **piano roll editor**, also referred to as the graphic editor or the key editor (see Figure 10.6). The piano roll editor shows

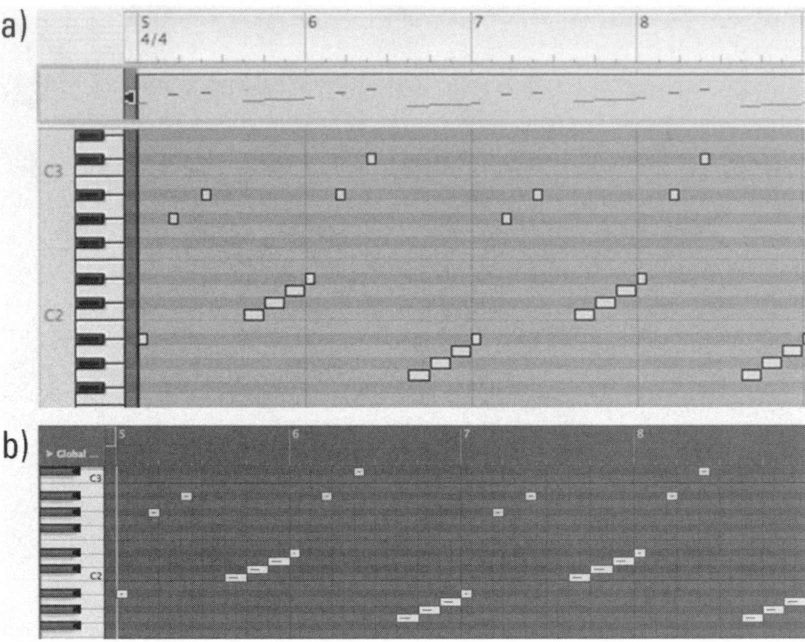

Figure 10.6 Piano roll-style editors in (a) Reason 4 (courtesy of Propellerheads); and (b) Logic Pro 8 (screenshot reprinted with permission from Apple Inc.).

MIDI notes as horizontal bars whose height represents pitch and whose length represents duration. Piano roll editors may also show controllers and other MIDI messages as well.

Another common note-level editor is the **list editor**, which displays MIDI information as a list of messages (see Figure 10.7). This editor is the most precise editor in that every MIDI message has its own line and each piece of information in the message can be changed individually. The list editor is one of the best editors for troubleshooting a sequence that isn't behaving as you expect, because all messages are clearly displayed.

A **drum editor** is similar to a graphic editor, but it specializes in collecting together notes that represent drum kit elements and displaying them in such a way that drum patterns become clear. Figure 10.8 shows the same information displayed in a piano roll editor and a drum editor.

A **notation editor** allows you to see information in standard music notation (see Figure 10.9). For many musicians new to sequencing this is the preferred note editor because it takes advantage of years of musical training. A notation editor is an excellent view for seeing and editing pitch, but usually a poor view for rhythm. Traditional notation in a sequencer works best when information falls on a time grid of quarter notes, eighth notes, and sixteenth notes. However, because sequencers are primarily designed to produce *performances* on electronic instruments, it is seldom desirable to have all of the musical events happen perfectly on a grid. A good groove may require that, say, the snare drum on the second and fourth beats of a measure be a little late, or that the downbeat be slightly anticipated by the horns. This makes performance sense, but

a)

Position	Status	Ch	Num	Val	Length/Info
5. 1. 1. 0	Note	4	A#1	80	.. .. 1. 0
5. 1. 4. 0	Note	4	G#2	120	.. .. 1. 0
5. 2. 3. 0	Note	4	A#2	120	.. .. 1. 0
5. 3. 3. 0	Note	4	C2	80	.. .. 2. 0
5. 4. 1. 0	Note	4	C#2	79	.. .. 2. 0
5. 4. 3. 0	Note	4	D2	79	.. .. 2. 0
6. 1. 1. 0	Note	4	D#2	80	.. .. 1. 0
6. 1. 4. 0	Note	4	A#2	120	.. .. 1. 0
6. 2. 3. 0	Note	4	C#3	120	.. .. 1. 0
6. 3. 3. 0	Note	4	G1	80	.. .. 2. 0
6. 4. 1. 0	Note	4	G#1	80	.. .. 2. 0
6. 4. 3. 0	Note	4	A1	80	.. .. 2. 0
7. 1. 1. 0	Note	4	A#1	80	.. .. 1. 0
7. 1. 4. 0	Note	4	G#2	120	.. .. 1. 0
7. 2. 3. 0	Note	4	A#2	120	.. .. 1. 0
7. 3. 3. 0	Note	4	C2	80	.. .. 2. 0
7. 4. 1. 0	Note	4	C#2	80	.. .. 2. 0
7. 4. 3. 0	Note	4	D2	80	.. .. 2. 0
8. 1. 1. 0	Note	4	D#2	80	.. .. 1. 0
8. 1. 4. 0	Note	4	A#2	120	.. .. 1. 0
8. 2. 3. 0	Note	4	C#3	120	.. .. 1. 0
8. 3. 3. 0	Note	4	G1	80	.. .. 2. 0
8. 4. 1. 0	Note	4	G#1	80	.. .. 2. 0

b)

```
5|1|000 ♪ Bb1 ↓ 80 ↑ 37 ↔ 0|120
5|1|360 ♪ Ab2 ↓ 120 ↑ 32 ↔ 0|120
5|2|240 ♪ Bb2 ↓ 120 ↑ 33 ↔ 0|120
5|3|240 ♪ C2 ↓ 80 ↑ 58 ↔ 0|240
5|4|000 ♪ Db2 ↓ 80 ↑ 46 ↔ 0|240
5|4|240 ♪ D2 ↓ 80 ↑ 55 ↔ 0|240
6|1|000 ♪ Eb2 ↓ 80 ↑ 21 ↔ 0|120
6|1|360 ♪ Bb2 ↓ 120 ↑ 46 ↔ 0|120
6|2|240 ♪ Db3 ↓ 120 ↑ 45 ↔ 0|120
6|3|240 ♪ G1 ↓ 80 ↑ 57 ↔ 0|240
6|4|000 ♪ Ab1 ↓ 80 ↑ 32 ↔ 0|240
6|4|240 ♪ A1 ↓ 80 ↑ 41 ↔ 0|240
7|1|000 ♪ Bb1 ↓ 80 ↑ 37 ↔ 0|120
7|1|360 ♪ Ab2 ↓ 120 ↑ 32 ↔ 0|120
7|2|240 ♪ Bb2 ↓ 120 ↑ 33 ↔ 0|120
7|3|240 ♪ C2 ↓ 80 ↑ 58 ↔ 0|240
7|4|000 ♪ Db2 ↓ 80 ↑ 46 ↔ 0|240
7|4|240 ♪ D2 ↓ 80 ↑ 55 ↔ 0|240
8|1|000 ♪ Eb2 ↓ 80 ↑ 21 ↔ 0|120
8|1|360 ♪ Bb2 ↓ 120 ↑ 46 ↔ 0|120
```

Figure 10.7 List editors showing the same messages in (a) Logic Pro 8 (screenshot reprinted with permission from Apple Inc.); and (b) Digital Performer 6 (courtesy of MOTU).

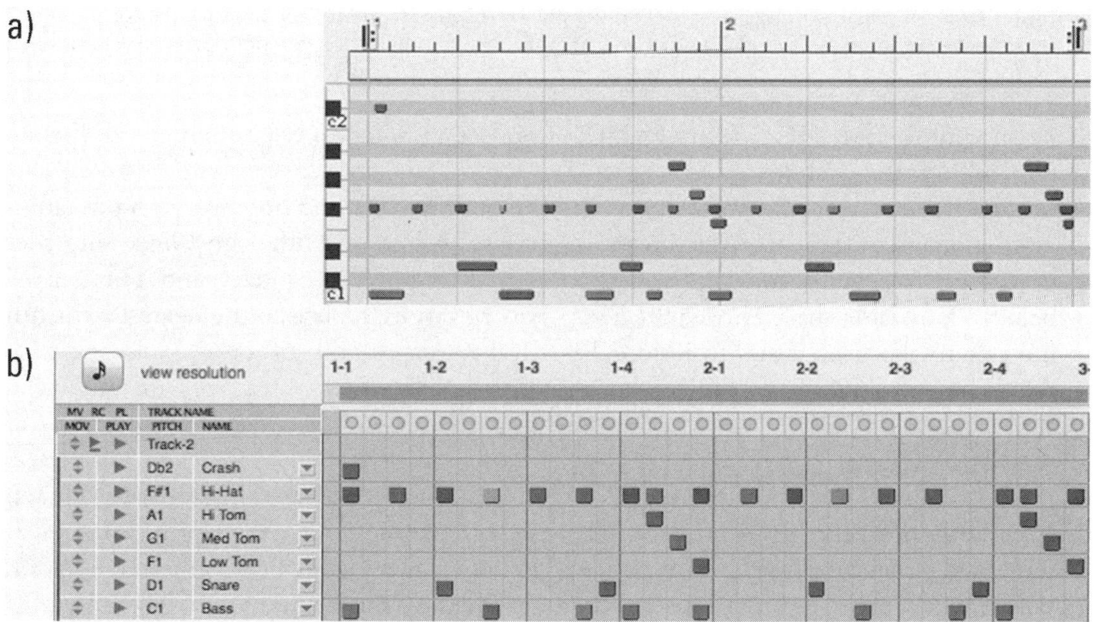

Figure 10.8 The same drum pattern shown in (a) the piano roll editor, and (b) the drum editor in Digital Performer 6. (Courtesy of MOTU)

Figure 10.9 The same music shown in (a) the piano roll editor, and (b) the notation editor in Digital Performer 6 (courtesy of MOTU). Notice how this passage is better represented piano roll-style than in notation.

not notation sense—the last thing you want to see in notation is a bunch of 128th-note rests and dotted 64th notes.

To accommodate the distinction between performance and notation, most notation editors quantize the events in time—force them to line up with a grid line—in order to display acceptable-looking notation (see "Transpose, Quantize, and Humanize" below). You can usually choose the level of quantization, such as to the nearest sixteenth note or to the nearest eighth note. The MIDI messages will still be played back with the un-quantized timing, and the other editing views will display the un-quantized timing, so the notation editor is the only view that doesn't show the actual timing of the MIDI events.

Notation editors in sequencers have become quite sophisticated in recent years, such that they can display such notation elements as dynamics and articulations. However, sequencers specialize in performance, suggesting that high-quality computer notation will still be carried out in a separate program for the time being.

The **mixer window** in a sequencer is somewhat different from the other editors. The previous editors show MIDI messages organized in time. A mixer window provides a graphical representation of volume, pan, and a few other settings only for the time currently shown on the sequencer's clock (see Figure 10.10).

Figure 10.10 The mixer window showing MIDI tracks in Digital Performer 6. (Courtesy of MOTU)

The strength of the mixer window is that it provides you with an intuitive interface for entering volume and pan information. In addition to a slider to control volume and a knob or slider to control pan, a mixer window usually provides you with a way of capturing the movements of these sliders and knobs in real time while the sequence is playing. After capturing these movements, the faders and knobs move automatically while the sequence plays back. As a result, the volume and pan messages when viewed this way are referred to as **automation**.

As mentioned above, many of these editors display the same information, just in different ways. Notes are displayed in the piano roll, list, and notation editors. Controller information can be seen in the piano roll and list editors and in the mixer window. Which editor is chosen for a particular task is typically a matter of personal preference, though it is a good idea for you to attempt to accomplish tasks in multiple views to experience the advantages and drawbacks of each.

MIDI INPUT

There are a variety of ways to input MIDI messages into a sequencer, including real-time entry, step-time entry, and manual entry. In addition, there are a number of entry modes that affect what happens to existing data or where in time the recording takes place.

Real-time entry

Real-time entry involves playing live to a metronome while the sequencer is recording, often with a one- or two-bar countoff before the recording starts. Of course, you don't have to line up to the beat at all; you could turn off the click and countoff and play freely while the sequencer records. It won't look "right" according to the bar-beats-ticks grid, but the sequencer will happily record the information and play it back. Some sequencers have a feature that allows you to align the grid to notes that you have recorded without a click by tapping a key along on the keyboard as the sequencer plays back. This would allow you to record with rubato and still line up other parts to it later. This will be discussed under "Tempo Changes" later in the chapter.

Real-time entry can also be used with other MIDI messages besides just note messages. For example, you may want to add pitch bend or vibrato with the mod wheel to a passage you've sequenced. Both of those message types are associated with either wheels or a joystick on a keyboard and can be performed live either while you're playing the notes or after the notes have been entered using overdub mode (see "Entry Modes" below). In addition, any other knob or slider on a keyboard or controller that sends MIDI messages can also be recorded in real time in the same way.

The advantage to real-time entry is that it allows you be expressive in your playing style in terms of articulations and timing (swing or some other groove). Since sequencing is most concerned with what is heard—the performance—this is a very important feature. The drawback to real-time entry is that every wrong note or misplayed rhythm is also recorded along with your expressive performance. Fortunately, you can edit the pitches and timing in one of the editors or apply one of the "corrective" functions discussed below in "MIDI Editing" to clean up the performance.

Step entry

Step entry involves selecting the pitch and the duration separately so that the notes are put in step by step. To step enter notes, you choose the duration using a letter or a number on the computer keyboard and play the pitch on a MIDI keyboard (see Figure 10.11).

Because you are not actually performing the music while entering it, you need to be conscious of the desired performance results during and after step entry. For example, notes with articulations that affect the note duration, such as staccatos, are step-entered by modifying the selected duration of the note. In the case of staccato, this means reducing the duration of the note. Passages that are entered with step entry can sound overly precise and often require further editing to create an effective performance.

Manual Entry

Manual entry involves inputting data using a virtual tool such as a "pencil" tool. While this method of entry is occasionally useful for adding in a note or two, it is most widely used to enter automation information such as pan, volume, mod wheel, and pitch bend

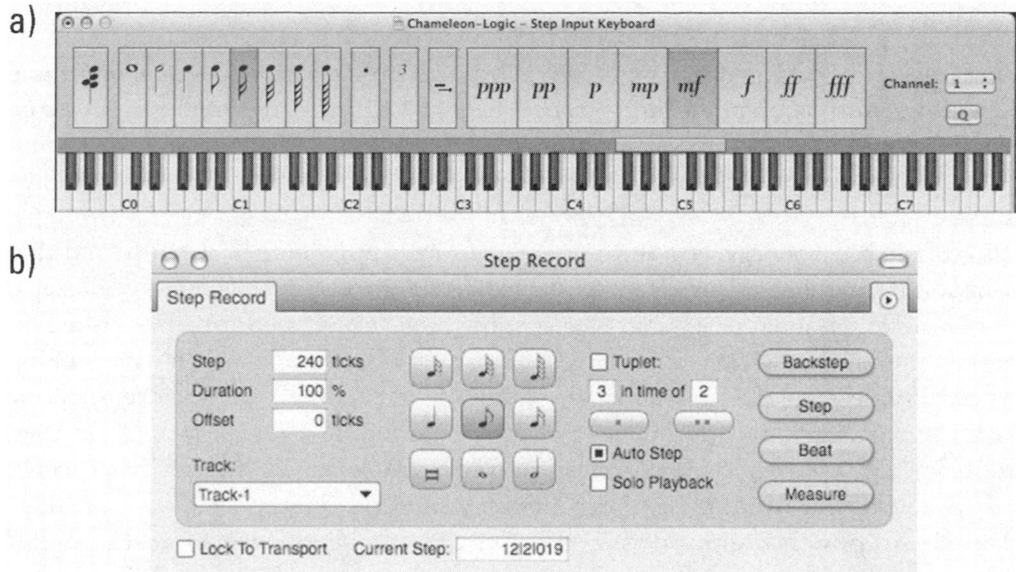

Figure 10.11 Step entry windows in (a) Logic Pro 8 (screenshot reprinted with permission from Apple Inc.); and (b) Digital Performer 6 (courtesy of MOTU).

(see Figure 10.12). Typically a pencil tool will have a parameter that specifies what data is being entered and the type of line that is to be entered, such as straight, curved, or freehand. The piano roll editor and the drum editor are typical editors for manual entry. Additionally, a drum editor may have a manual entry tool that works with patterns of notes rather than single notes.

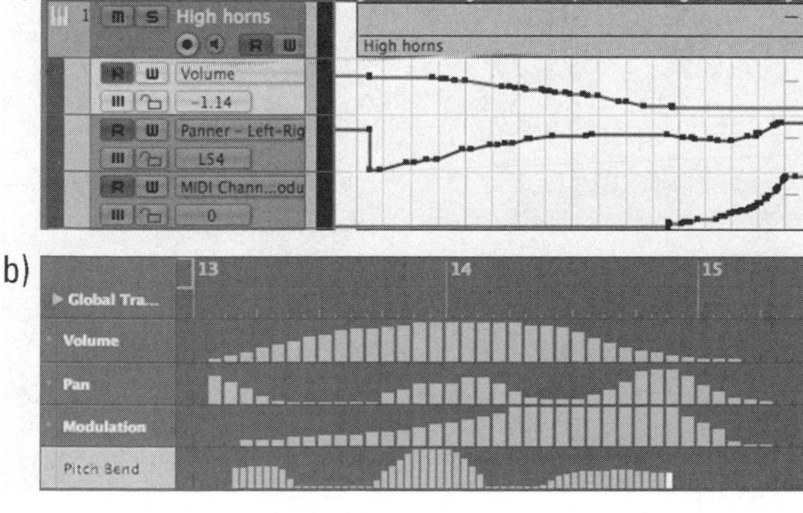

Figure 10.12 Manual entry windows for volume, pan, and mod wheel controllers in (a) Cubase Studio 4 (courtesy of Steinberg Media Technologies); and (b) Logic Pro 8 (screenshot reprinted with permission from Apple Inc.).

Entry Modes

For both real-time entry and step entry, there are several different modes that determine how existing information in the target track is handled. The simplest of these is **replace mode**. In this mode, old information is deleted when new MIDI messages are being recorded. Various sequencers have different names for these modes, but they work in a similar way.

In **overdub or merge mode**, the new information is merged with the existing information. "Overdub" in this instance means nearly the opposite of what it means in audio recording. In audio recording, overdubbing refers to one performer recording on more than one track, such as a guitarist recording a rhythm track and then overdubbing a solo on another track. In sequencing, overdubbing refers to recording more than one pass on the *same* track, so you might first record the left hand of the piano and then overdub (merge) the right hand of the piano on that same track. "Merge" is probably the better term, but "overdub" is also commonly used (see Figure 10.13).

Punch-in/punch-out mode is also derived from audio recording, and its MIDI implementation is closer to the audio implementation than overdub. Punch-in/punch-out allows you to specify which part of a track can be recorded on and which can't. To use this mode, you define two points in time: a punch-in point and a punch-out point. Before the punch-in point, nothing can be recorded, even if the track is record-enabled and you've pressed the record button in the transport controls, and after the punch-out point nothing can be recorded. Between the punch points anything goes. Punch-in/punch-out can be utilized either in replace mode or in overdub (merge) mode with the part of the track between the punch points being the only location affected by those modes (see Figure 10.14).

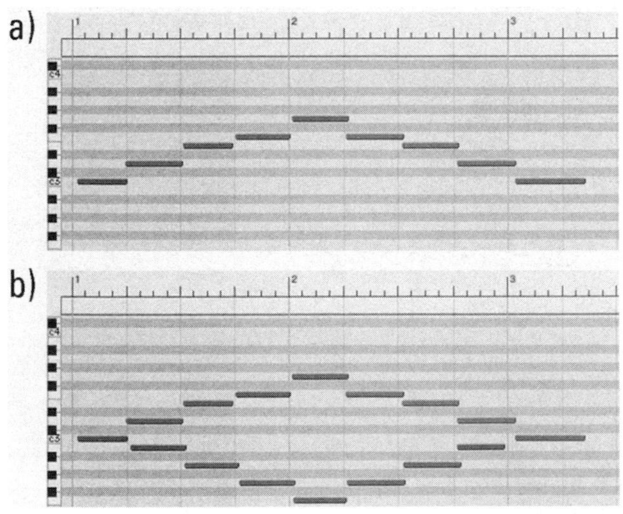

Figure 10.13 Overdub in piano roll editor of Digital Performer 6: (a) first recording, and (b) after overdub. (Courtesy of MOTU)

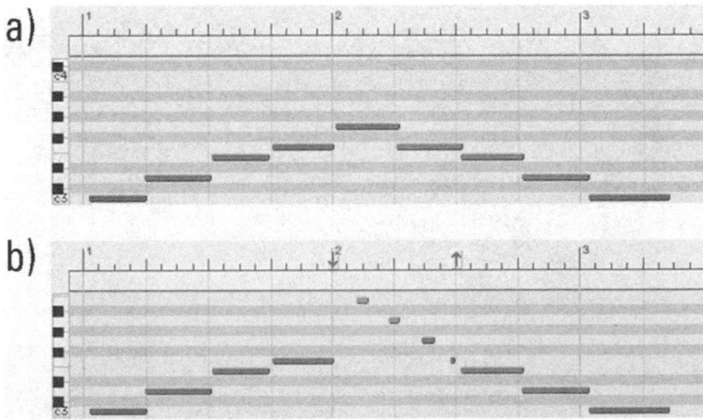

Figure 10.14 Punch-in/punch-out in piano roll editor of Digital Performer 6: (a) first recording, and (b) after punch-in. The arrows in the timeline in the second image indicate the punch-in/punch-out points. (Courtesy of MOTU)

Loop mode allows you to specify a range of measures (or portions of a measure) that will repeat continuously while you're recording. This is different from looping part of a track for playback, which will be discussed below. By itself, loop mode could be used to record, say, a solo over and over until you get it just right. Some sequencers allow each pass to be stored as a separate "take" so that you can choose the best take later.

Loop mode is particularly useful when combined with overdub/merge, which allows you to add elements to a track on each pass (see Figure 10.15). For example, this would allow you to build up a complex drum pattern. On the first recording pass you might play the bass drum and the snare drum, during the second pass you might play the hi-hat and crash cymbals, and during the third recording pass you might add drum fills and other miscellaneous percussion. Loop mode can also be useful during editing, when you want the sequencer to repeat the same portion of the song while you make edits.

MIDI EDITING

Once MIDI messages have been entered into a sequencer, you can **edit** them to create the performance that you desire. There are many different editors and editing functions that you can use to manipulate MIDI messages. Each of these allows you to edit either the components of the MIDI messages, such as the key number and velocity in note messages, the organization of these messages in time, or both.

Cut, Copy, and Paste

To operate on the data, you must first select it. The typical selection strategies are available in sequencers just as they are in other programs such as word processors: click once to select, shift-click to select more than one item, and drag-enclose to select a group of

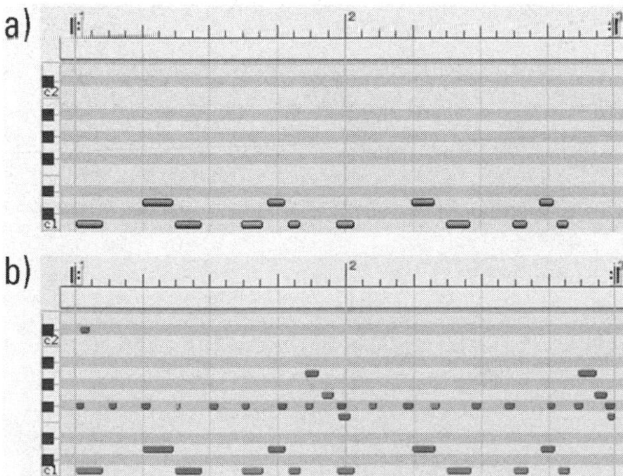

Figure 10.15 Loop-overdub in the piano roll editor of Digital Performer 6: (a) first time through, and (b) after two more passes. The repeat marks in the timeline indicate the loop points. (Courtesy of MOTU)

items or all items in a certain time range. The editing functions **cut, copy,** and **paste** are also available, though there are more graphically oriented ways of accomplishing these same tasks, such as dragging selected messages for cut-and-paste and dragging selected items with a modifier key pressed, such as option or alt, for copy-and-paste.

In a time-based program such as a sequencer, there are typically some extensions to the cut, copy, and paste paradigm. For example, a normal cut or delete command will get rid of the selected messages, but the time that they occupied is still there, leaving a gap in the sequence. A different version of cut, called **snip** by some sequencers, removes both the messages *and* the time that was selected thereby closing the gap (see Figure 10.16). Just as snip is an extension of cut, **splice** is an extension of paste, in which the previously cut or copied messages push the existing messages later in time. If the regular paste function is used, time is not inserted in the track along with notes.

With a regular paste, the merge versus replace issue discussed under "Entry Modes" becomes important. "Paste" could mean replace the existing messages with the pasted messages *or* merge the pasted messages with the existing messages on the track. Some programs rename the paste function to reflect either replace or merge and add another editing function to take care of the other mode.

When dragging selected messages it is often useful to **constrain dragging** to either the vertical direction—changing pitch when dragging notes—or the horizontal direction—changing position in time. This is usually accomplished by dragging the selected items with the shift key held down. In addition, it is often useful to limit horizontal position changes to only multiples of a selected musical duration. For example, if you're moving a group of notes from one beat to the next, you might want to set the **edit grid** to a quarter note, so that the notes will only move in multiples of quarter notes. You can turn the grid on or off to meet your editing needs.

Transpose, Quantize, and Humanize

The pitch and timing of groups of MIDI messages can be modified by a variety of editing functions, including transpose, quantize, and humanize. MIDI note messages can be **transposed** by interval quite easily by simply adding a number of semitones to each key number. You can also make more complex pitch changes, such as changing the mode from major to minor or combining the transposition by interval

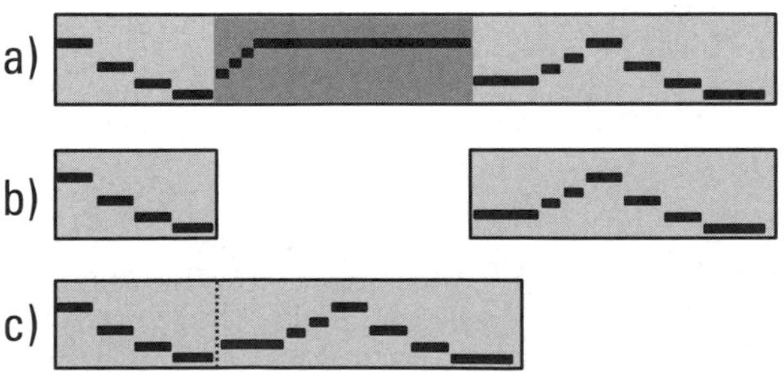

Figure 10.16 "Cut" versus "snip": (a) original segment, (b) hole left by "cut," and (c) removal of time by "snip."

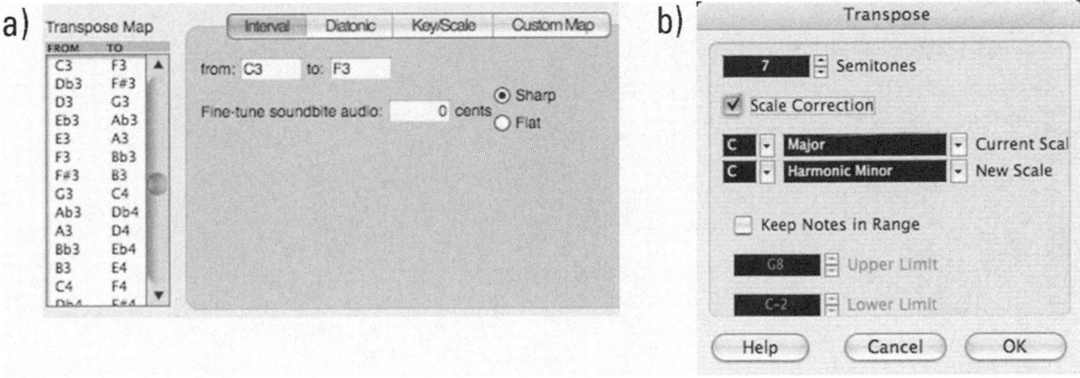

Figure 10.17 Transpose windows in (a) Digital Performer 6 showing simple transposition by interval (courtesy of MOTU); and (b) Cubase Studio 4 showing transposition and change of scale type (courtesy of Steinberg Media Technologies).

and **mode change** to transpose a sequence from, say, C major to G harmonic minor (see Figure 10.17).

The reason why pitch changes in MIDI are so straightforward is that, unlike digital audio, the pitch (key number) is directly encoded into the MIDI note message. In fact, it is possible to have the sequencer create an analysis of the selected notes and identify their tonic and mode, though few sequencers have such features.

The timing of MIDI messages can be altered in a variety of ways, such as shifting all selected messages early or later in time, creating a backward version (retrograde) of selected messages, or by **quantizing** the selection. Quantizing involves automatically "correcting" the timing of MIDI messages that were entered in real time by moving selected messages to the nearest time point on a specified grid. If you play a downbeat a little late, you can use the quantize function with the grid size set to a quarter note to "snap" that note to the downbeat. This function is related to the constrained grid dragging discussed above.

You have to be careful when quantizing a real-time performance, because you can easily eliminate the expressive characteristics you were trying to obtain by recording in real time. In fact, one sequencer refers to this strict form of quantizing as **over-quantizing**. Most quantize functions have one or more parameters that allow you to decide the strength of the quantization, which means that you can cause selected notes to move *toward* a grid point, but not all the way *to* a grid point. Other parameters allow you to focus the quantization on notes near beats and ignore notes that lie in between and vice versa (see Figure 10.18).

A variant on quantization is **input quantize**. With input quantize active, the correction of the notes to the grid happens while the notes are being entered. This can save some time, but is not very flexible since the variations in timing in the performance are eliminated before the MIDI messages are even being recorded.

In addition to quantizing to a regular grid, it is possible to quantize to an uneven grid to create effects like shuffle or swing. **Swing quantize** takes notes of a specified

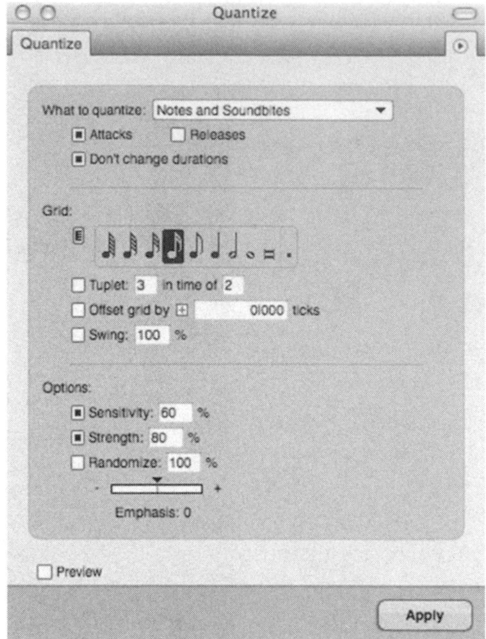

Figure 10.18 Quantize window in Digital Performer 6. In addition to a simple grid, swing can be applied and quantization can be modified with various options. (Courtesy of MOTU)

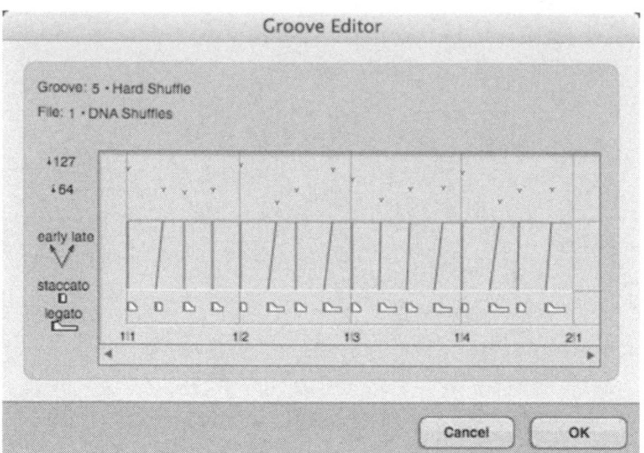

Figure 10.19 Groove quantize window in Digital Performer 6. Groove quantize alters the velocity, timing, and duration of selected notes according to the pattern shown. (Courtesy of MOTU)

value (usually eighth notes) and delays the second note to create the characteristic uneven eighth notes of swing. Other quantize patterns are possible as well, and can be combined with velocity patterns to create **groove quantize**, in which the note timings are shifted in a pattern throughout a measure(s) and the velocities of the notes are changed to create different emphases than the original messages (see Figure 10.19).

Quantize can be applied destructively or non-destructively. In **destructive quantizing**, the original placement of the notes is lost and only the quantized version remains. On the other hand, **non-destructive quantize** changes the timing and velocity only while the song is playing back and leaves the notes in their original locations. This allows for a great deal of experimentation over time with the proper quantize settings. Non-destructive quantize settings are usually track-wide settings since the function no longer applies to just a selected group of notes.

Some sequencers have a feature that is the opposite of the quantize function: **humanize**. Where quantize is used to "correct" MIDI messages that were input in real time, humanize can be used to selectively "mess up" MIDI messages that were entered through step entry. For example, some sequencers use the same velocity value for all step-entered notes. This kind of precision can sound machine-like and can be disturbing when machine-like is not the desired aesthetic.

To correct the constant velocities, humanize can change the velocities of selected notes by varying them randomly within a certain range. This function could be applied to a group of notes that all have a velocity of 80 by giving them random variations in velocity of +/−5, so the resultant velocities would be somewhere between 75 and 85. Similarly, the timing of step-entered notes can be varied randomly within certain limits to remove the mechanical sensation of inhuman precision.

There are many more editing functions that allow you to move MIDI messages in time, such as shift and retrograde, or change message components, such as setting velocity and scaling control values. Each sequencer will have its own "spin" on these functions, so it is useful when you are first learning a sequencer to experiment with the functions that are available, as they are the tools that allow you to shape the electronic performance of your music.

MIDI OUTPUT

At its simplest level, MIDI **output** involves rewinding a sequence back to the beginning and pressing play in the transport controls. Other common playback features include the ability to mute and solo tracks and to change tempo.

Mute and Solo

When sequencing, it is often useful to either silence a few tracks or to hear only a few parts. Silencing a part or parts is referred to as **muting**. This is usually a straightforward process and involves clicking on a button labeled "M" or clicking on a "play-enable" icon to turn it off. When you prefer to hear only one or a few parts, it is cumbersome to mute all of the other parts, so you would use the complementary solo function. **Soloing** is usually a matter of clicking a button labeled "S" on a track or enabling the solo function generally and then choosing which tracks to solo. Ironically, you can "solo" more than one part at a time. Regular use of mute and solo can improve the efficiency of creating and editing a complicated sequence.

Tempo Changes

Tempo can be static for the entire sequence, set by entering a number into a tempo field, or can be changed dynamically by using a special **tempo track**. In addition to traditional expressive uses, tempo changes can be used to align the bars and beats of the sequence with the bars and beats of an audio track or with specific events in digital video.

There is an inherent bias in sequencers toward strict tempos: it's difficult to perform a natural rubato when the metronome click is hammering away at a steady tempo. Rubato can be added to a strict-tempo performance afterward by changing the tempo track, but it can be difficult to achieve a natural result. In most sequencers, you can record MIDI in real time without the metronome and afterward adjust the bars and beats to the rubato tempo.

Many sequencers allow you to "tap" in the tempo while the sequence is playing back or drag the beats or barlines to match up with the performance. These tempo changes now form a **tempo map** of the rubato passage. Once the changing tempo of the sequence matches the performance, other MIDI parts can be sequenced using the metronome click that now follows these tempo changes (see Figure 10.20).

The same techniques can be used to match bars and beats to audio files that have been imported into a sequence. It is simple to match the tempo of an audio file that contains only fixed-tempo material, but if the tempo of the audio material varies, the tap tempo and/or drag bars and beats techniques could be used.

Video is somewhat different in that you only rarely want downbeats or accents in the music to line up with video events. Otherwise, you are said to be "mickey-mousing" the video. The first step in creating a video tempo map is to place **markers** in the sequence at time locations that match events of interest in the video. The sequencer can then calculate a tempo that will make a certain number of measures fit in that time or find a tempo that generally matches the markers.

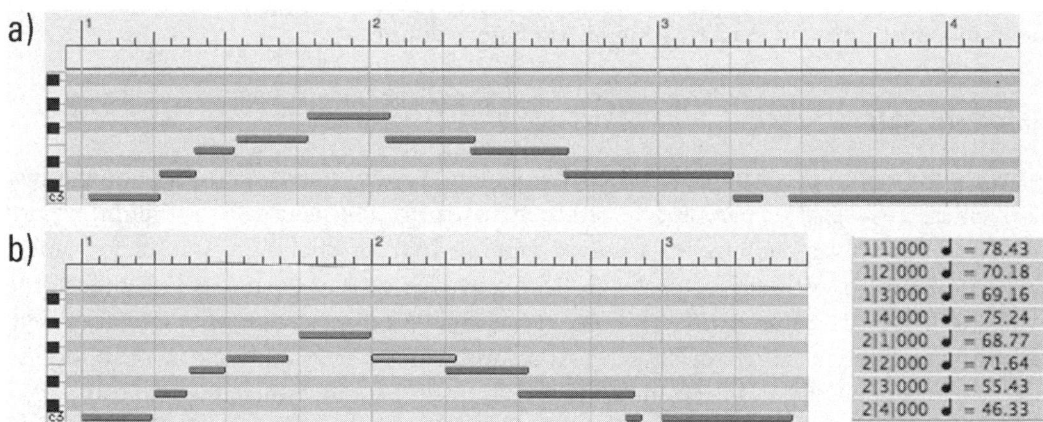

Figure 10.20 Demonstration of aligning a sequencer's time grid with a free recording by tapping in the tempo after the recording: (a) original free recording, and (b) time grid aligned with recording along with the resultant tempo changes.

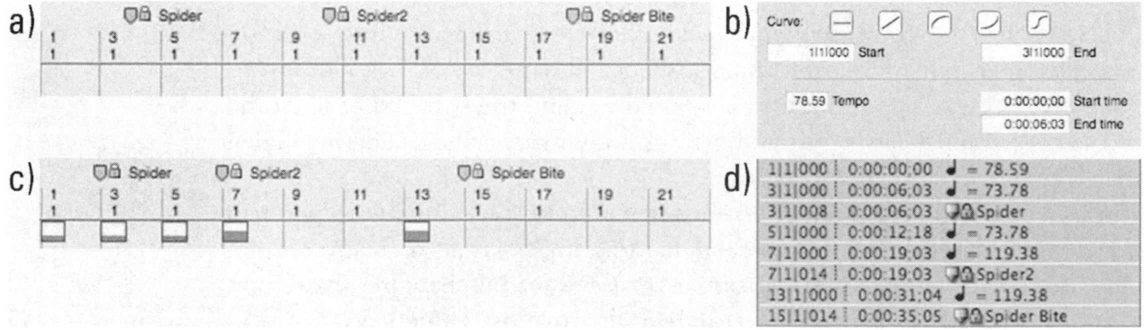

Figure 10.21 Demonstration of adjusting a sequencer's tempo to markers when working with video: (a) original timeline with unaligned markers, (b) change tempo window, (c) new timeline with aligned markers, and (d) required tempo changes.

Figure 10.21 shows an example of a video tempo map. In Figure 10.21a, the sequence is at a fixed tempo and the markers at the top indicate important video events. Figure 10.21b shows the change tempo window in Digital Performer 6, which allows you to specify beginning and ending measures along with beginning and ending times; the sequencer figures out the required tempo. Figure 10.21c shows the alignment of the measures with the markers due to the tempo changes that are shown in 10.21d.

MIDI THRU AND LOCAL CONTROL

When you connect a keyboard synth or controller to a computer and begin recording on a sequencer track, you want the notes that you play on the keyboard to sound like the patch you've chosen for the track. For this to happen, the sequencer must route the MIDI messages generated by your keyboard to the output device for the selected sequencer track.

When the output is a software instrument, the MIDI messages are passed to the software synth internally. When the output is a hardware synth, the messages are routed to the MIDI output of the computer. The process of taking in MIDI messages and routing them to an internal softsynth or an external hardware synth is referred to as **MIDI Thru** (not to be confused with the Thru port on a synth). The MIDI Thru function is used by a variety of programs, including sequencers and notation software (see Figure 10.22).

If you're sequencing using a keyboard synth—meaning that it both generates MIDI messages from its keys *and* converts incoming MIDI messages into sound—you have to be concerned about the keyboard synthesizer's **Local Control** setting. When you purchase a keyboard synthesizer, plug it in, and turn it on, it will generate sound when you play the keys. This happens because there is a direct connection between the keys and the "sound engine"—the part of the synth that converts MIDI messages into sound. This direct connection is referred to as the Local Control and, in this case, the Local Control is "on."

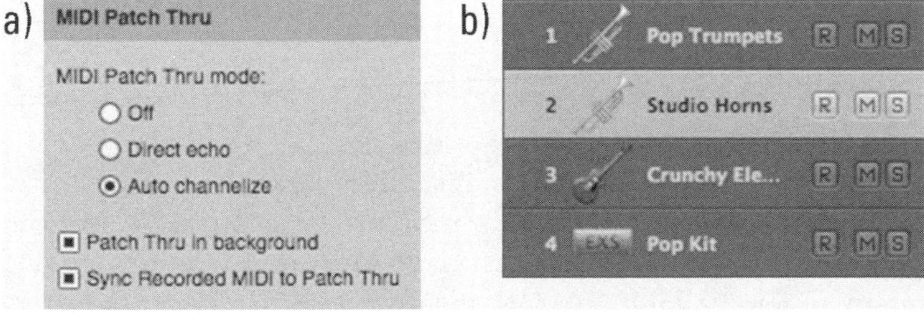

Figure 10.22 (a) MIDI Patch Thru preference window in Digital Performer 6 (courtesy of MOTU); and (b) track selected for patch thru in Logic Pro 8 (screenshot reprinted with permission from Apple Inc.).

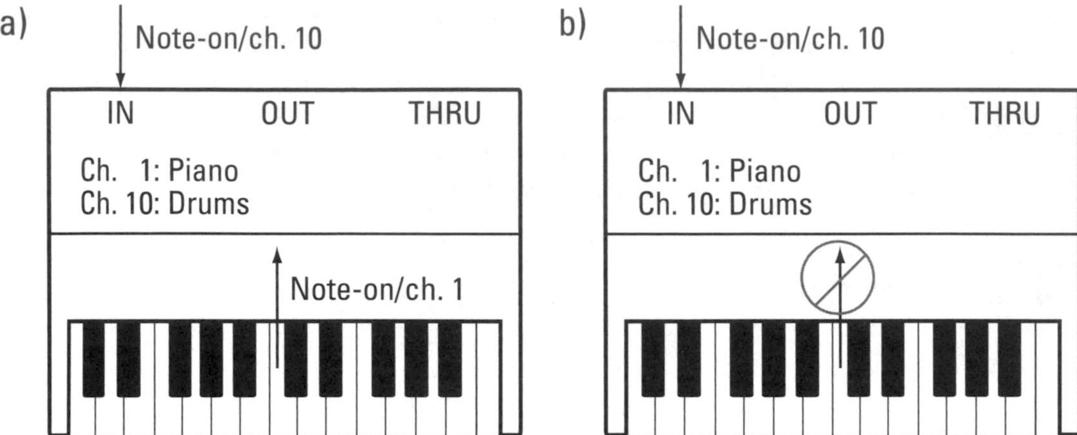

Figure 10.23 (a) A key played on a keyboard synth results in two note messages being sent to its sound engine: one directly from the key via Local Control and the other from the sequencer via MIDI Thru. Both drum and piano patches are heard. (b) With the Local Control "off," a key played on a keyboard synth results in only one note message being sent to its sound engine from the sequencer via MIDI Thru. Only the drum patch is heard. This is the desired setting for sequencing.

If you connect this synth to a computer running a sequencer and record-enable a track whose output is a channel on the same synth, then the synth will receive two note-on messages for each key that you play. One note-on message will come directly from the key via the Local Control. The second note-on message will come from the sequencer via MIDI Thru. Depending on the output channel setting on the sequencer track, the two note-on messages may be on different channels, resulting in two different patches being heard for every key that is played. This can be distracting if, for example, you're trying to sequence drums, but you're also hearing a piano patch due to the Local Control.

To avoid this problem, you need to turn the Local Control "off" on the keyboard synth so that the sound engine only receives the messages coming through your sequencer via MIDI Thru. Local Control "off" is the desired setting for sequencing with a keyboard synthesizer (see Figure 10.23). Local Control is not an issue when using a hardware module or purely software sound sources.

STANDARD MIDI FILES

Sequencer/DAWs typically save their data in an exclusive **file format**. These file formats contain the MIDI messages, but also include information specific to that sequencer, such as track settings, mixer settings, information on audio files used in the project, and audio processing plug-ins. Table 10.2 lists several sequencer/DAWs and their associated file extensions.

In general, one program can't read another's exclusive file format, so it is necessary to have an interchange file format that can allow you to transfer data from one program to another. The **Standard MIDI File** (**SMF**, file extension .mid) serves this function for programs that deal with MIDI data, including notation programs and sequencers.

SMFs come in three types:

- Type 0: All data is stored in one track. Simplest, most transferable format.
- Type 1: Data is stored in multiple tracks. Used for most situations.
- Type 2: Contains one or more independent single-track patterns. Seldom used.

Table 10.2 Sequencer file extensions

Sequencer/DAW	*File extension*
Logic	.logic
Digital Performer	No extension
Cubase	.cpr
Pro Tools	.ptf
Sonar	.cwp

Type 0 SMFs are useful for simple MIDI players, both hardware and software. Type 1 SMFs are used by music applications that organize MIDI messages into separate tracks, including sequencing and notation programs. If you're going to transfer a file from one MIDI application to another, you will generally use a Type 1 SMF.

SMFs can store all of the MIDI messages discussed previously, but they also store information such as track names, tempo, time signature, key signature, and the amount of time between events. SMFs do *not* store information concerning audio files, plug-ins, or any data that is specific to a particular sequencer/DAW. As a result, an SMF represents only a portion of the data used in many projects. Nevertheless, it is very useful for transferring MIDI data between software.

In addition to sequencers, notation programs also support SMFs. However, SMFs store data that is most useful to performance programs such as sequencers and omit data that is important to notation programs. For example, the SMF doesn't store articulations, slurs, crescendos, or page layout information. SMFs won't even indicate the difference between a G♯ and an A♭ because the notes are stored as note-on/note-off messages that indicate pitch with a key number, which would be the same for both of those spellings. If you save a notation file as an SMF and then import it back into the same program, all of that information will be lost. Increasingly, notation programs support another interchange format, MusicXML, which supports notation-specific data. This will be discussed further in Chapter 15, "Computer Notation."

BEYOND SEQUENCING

Sequencers provide you with a powerful platform for creating performances on electronic instruments. However, once the tracks are recorded and edited, the performance is essentially static—press play and there it is. Because MIDI is a real-time protocol, there is no reason why MIDI messages can't be generated, manipulated, and played back on the fly as part of a live performance.

There are a variety of applications that have been designed for such purposes, and most include live audio processing, synthesis, and sampling in software. Three such applications showing the great variety of approaches to live performance with software will be discussed below: Max/MSP, Live, and MainStage.

Max was first created in the 1980s to control the parameters of an experimental synthesizer in real time, and was released commercially in 1990. Instead of a track-based paradigm, Max used objects to receive MIDI messages from a controller, such as a keyboard, wind controller, or control surface, process those messages, and send them to a hardware or software synthesizer to be converted into sound. This was a radical departure from the sequencer approach to MIDI, and was clearly designed as a real-time performance environment.

In Max, a group of objects connected together to execute an input–processing–output function is referred to as a "patch." The simple Max patch shown in Figure 10.24 brings in MIDI controller information from a modulation wheel (CC1, here on channel 1) and uses the control values from the mod wheel as key numbers for a note message. The newly created note messages are then sent to a synthesizer, thus creating a "note generator" out of your mod wheel.

As computers became powerful enough in the 1990s to process and synthesize digital audio, a new group of audio objects was added to Max to form **Max/MSP**. The basic approach of connecting objects together to form patches remained, but the new objects also processed or generated audio instead of just processing or generating MIDI. Objects designed to manipulate images and video were added in the 2000s to form **Max/MSP/Jitter**. This program is a powerful visual programming environment for the real-time manipulation of all types of media.

The Max/MSP patch shown in Figure 10.25 stores an audio file in a buffer called "igor," and plays it back using the "groove~" object, which allows for looping and variable speed/pitch playback. The "dac~" object represents the audio output of the computer.

A similar program called **PD** (for **Pure Data**), created by Miller Puckette, who was the original programmer of Max, is available as an open source/freeware application. It lacks some of the bells and whistles of Max/MSP, but it can be used to create similar interactive MIDI and audio works.

Another application that breaks somewhat with the sequencing paradigm is **Ableton's Live**. Live can act as a straightforward sequencer/DAW that integrates MIDI, digital audio, and software synthesizers/samplers just as other sequencer/DAWs do.

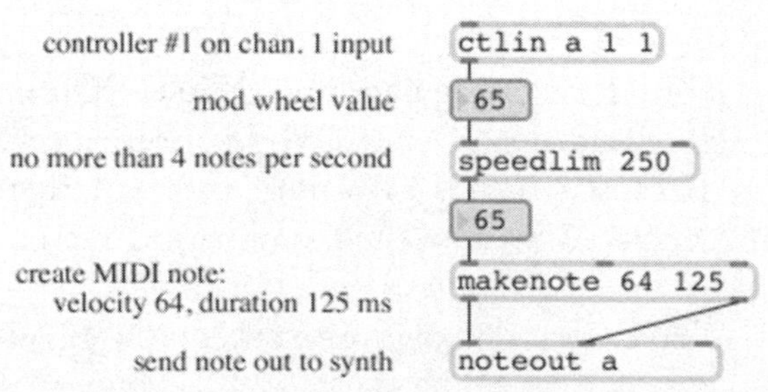

Figure 10.24 A Max patch that converts incoming CC1 messages into notes. (Courtesy of Cycling74, Inc.)

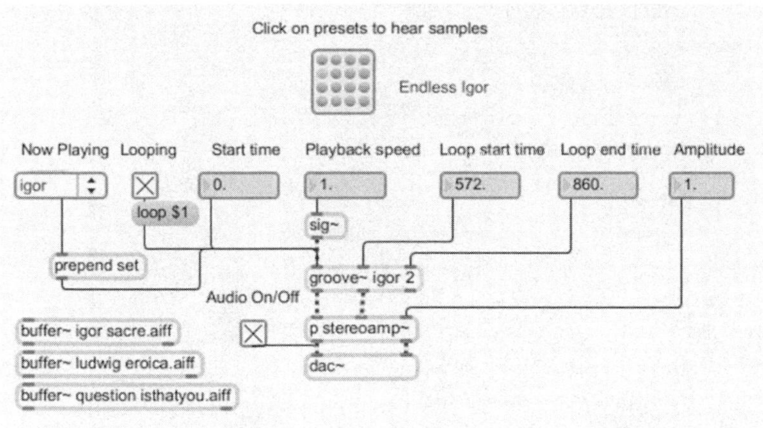

Figure 10.25 A Max/MSP patch that plays back a stored sample with variable looping and playback speed/pitch. (Courtesy of Cycling74, Inc.)

However, Live uses a "clip"-based paradigm in which some number of measures of MIDI or digital audio can be organized and triggered independently on the fly. It can also take in MIDI and audio and process it in all in real time.

This allows Live to be a unique performance or compositional tool. To make matters more complex, Live can incorporate Max/MSP patches with its "Max for Live" addition. The Live screenshot in Figure 10.26 shows the "session" view, in which each vertical track has a number of clips. Live's "arrange" view is very similar to the standard tracks editor discussed previously. In the session view, each track is represented by a vertical strip. Each set of horizontally aligned slots in the upper portion of the strip corresponds to a "scene," and various "clips" of audio or MIDI data are placed in those scenes. A scene can be made up of everywhere from a clip in one track to clips in each track.

To perform these scenes, you could step through them one at a time activating all the clips in the scene's horizontal row, or you could turn the clips on and off individually regardless of the scene to which they belonged to create a unique, changing mix of clips.

Apple's **MainStage**, a program that ships with Apple's sequencer/DAW **Logic Pro**, is a tool designed for live performance. MainStage allows you to process input audio from a microphone, guitar, or other source, and play software instruments from a MIDI controller. In MainStage, MIDI is used to control aspects of the sound processing, using such controls as sliders, knobs, and foot pedals, and to control the sound generation by software instruments.

The MainStage screenshot in Figure 10.27 shows an audio processing setup for guitar audio input in which an external MIDI pedal controls the vibrato rate. Other MainStage setups use MIDI input to control the pitch of software synthesizers and other performance parameters.

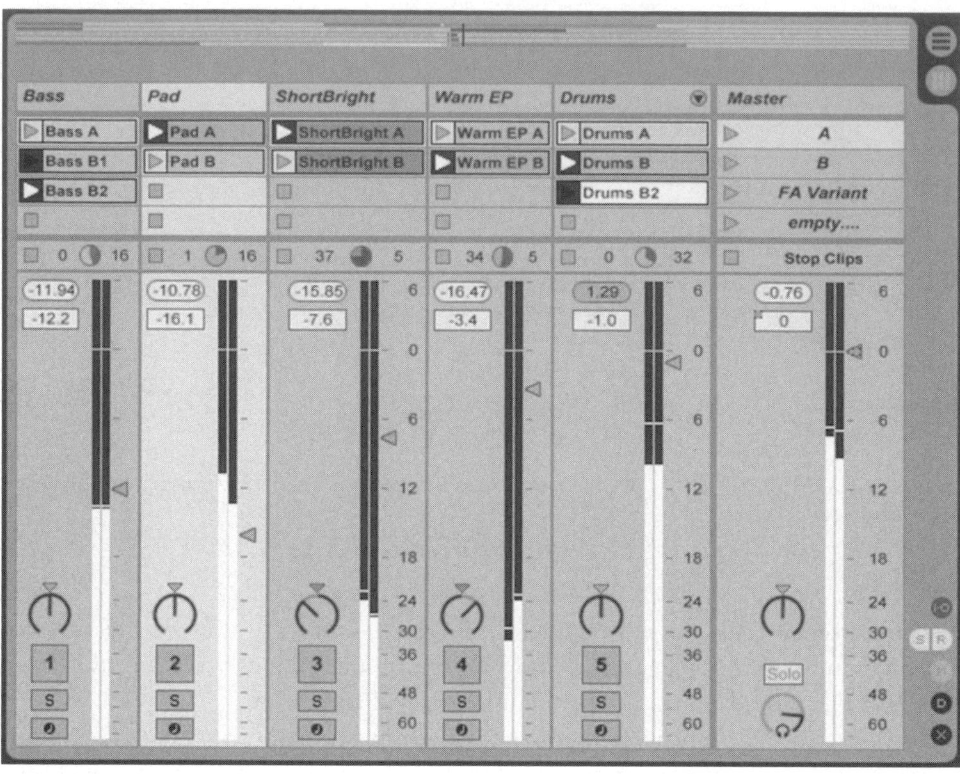

Figure 10.26 A portion of the session view in Ableton's Live 8 showing five tracks, each with two or three clips. (Courtesy of Ableton)

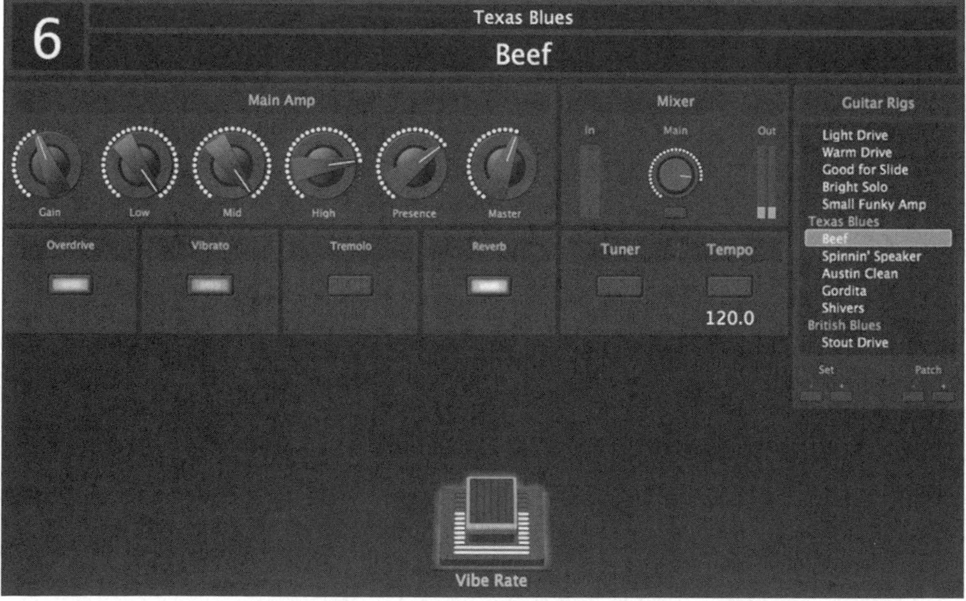

Figure 10.27 A patch in MainStage that processes incoming guitar audio and can be controlled by MIDI controllers. (Screenshot reprinted with permission from Apple Inc.)

REVIEW OF KEY TERMS

MIDI sequencing 159
digital audio workstation (DAW) 159
multi-track audio recording 160
tracks/MIDI channels 160
patches 160
patchlists 160
PPQN 162
editor 163
tracks editor 163
piano roll editor 163
list editor 164
drum editor 164
notation editor 164
mixer window 166
automation 167
real-time entry 168
step entry 168
manual entry 168
replace mode 170
overdub/merge mode 170
punch-in/punch-out mode 170
loop mode 171
editing 171
cut/copy/paste/snip/splice 172
constrain dragging 172
edit grid 172
transposing 172
mode change 173
quantizing 173
over-quantizing 173
input/swing/groove quantize 173–174
destructive/non-destructive quantize 174
humanize 174
output 175
muting 175
soloing 175
tempo track/map 175–176
markers 176
MIDI Thru 177
Local Control 177
file format 178
Standard MIDI File (SMF) 179
Max and Max/MSP 180
Max/MSP/Jitter 180
PD (Pure Data) 180
Ableton's Live 180
MainStage 181
Logic Pro 181

CHAPTER 11

MIDI—What Do I Need?

Now that we've covered the basics of MIDI hardware, messages, and sequencing, it's time to consider what hardware and software is necessary for MIDI sequencing. It's important to note that modern sequencer/DAWs combine MIDI with audio recording, audio loops, and software synthesis and sampling. As a result, there is significant overlap with the audio systems discussed in Chapter 7. This chapter presents three MIDI and audio systems of increasing complexity that could be found in a home or project studio. Since the audio components of such systems were discussed in Chapter 7, we will focus on the MIDI components here. (Links to the software and hardware discussed here are available on the book's website.)

MIDI AND AUDIO SYSTEM 1

This system takes Audio System 1 from Chapter 7 and adds a USB MIDI keyboard controller (see Figure 11.1). In addition to the audio recording applications discussed in Chapter 7, this system is capable of MIDI sequencing using software synthesizers and

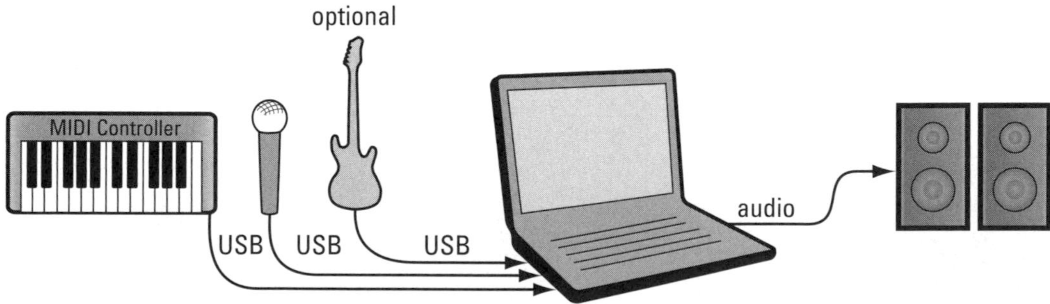

Figure 11.1 MIDI and Audio System 1: USB controller, USB microphone, powered monitors, and optional guitar-to-USB cable.

samplers, as well as other applications that use MIDI input, such as computer notation and computer-assisted instruction. Like Audio System 1, this system is relatively inexpensive.

MIDI and Audio System 1 Hardware

- All of the components of Audio System 1 discussed in Chapter 7.
- MIDI keyboard controller that connects to the computer through USB:
  - Can be either bus-powered through USB or have a separate power supply.
  - Various sizes from 2-octave keyboards to full 88-key controllers.
  - A variety of knobs and sliders are useful for controlling software synths and samplers, though this is not strictly necessary.
  - Small, bus-powered keyboard controllers are suitable for mobile music creation.

MIDI and Audio System 1 Software

The following are some options for recording and editing software:

- Some free and almost-free programs have MIDI and softsynth capabilities, such as GarageBand and Reaper.
- All of the professional DAWs mentioned in Chapter 7— Digital Performer (MOTU), Logic Pro (Apple), Sonar Producer (Cakewalk), Cubase (Steinberg), Live (Ableton), and Pro Tools LE (Digidesign)—whether in their full or "lite" versions, have MIDI sequencing capabilities and can host software synthesizers and samplers. Software synths and samplers are needed in this MIDI and audio system because no hardware sound generator is included.
- All of these sequencer/DAWs ship with some software synthesizers and samplers. The number and usefulness of these software synths and samplers differ from program to program, but they are generally good enough to get you started.

MIDI AND AUDIO SYSTEM 2

This system takes Audio System 2 from Chapter 7 and adds a keyboard synthesizer for hardware sound generation (see Figure 11.2). It is important to note that a hardware synthesizer is not necessarily superior to a software synthesizer. Instead of a keyboard synth, you may want to purchase a keyboard controller with more keys, weighted action, or more knobs and sliders.

Keyboard synths are useful in performance situations, and the sound set may be a useful addition to the software synths. Unlike softsynths, hardware synths don't take up any CPU (central processing unit) power, so they provide additional voices above those provided by softsynths. Because the keyboard synthesizer is generating sound rather than the computer, its audio outputs will have to be routed to inputs on the audio interface.

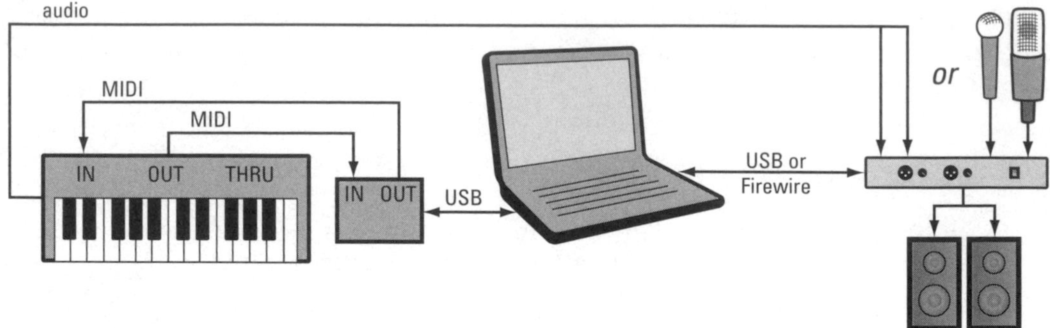

Figure 11.2 MIDI and Audio System 2: a keyboard synth, an external MIDI interface, an audio interface, and powered monitors. The keyboard synth, the microphones, or guitars into the High-Z inputs (not shown) are the possible inputs to the audio interface.

MIDI and Audio System 2 Hardware

- All of the components of Audio System 2 discussed in Chapter 7.
- Keyboard synthesizer:
  - May connect to the computer through USB or through MIDI cables attached to a MIDI interface. If the audio interface in this system doesn't have MIDI In and Out Ports, a separate simple USB MIDI interface is needed.
  - Audio outputs may be unbalanced or balanced. These will be connected to the inputs on the audio interface. If the interface has just two audio inputs, you may have to switch off between the keyboard synthesizer and any microphones you're using.
  - May be of any size, but 61-, 76-, or 88-note keyboards are common. May have weighted action (like a piano) if desired, but that will increase the price.
  - Number of banks and patches and method of sound generation will be a matter of personal preference and budget. The more features the keyboard synth has, the more expensive it is likely to be.

MIDI and Audio System 2 Software

The following are some options for recording and editing software:

- All of the sequencer/DAWs mentioned in MIDI and Audio System 1 above will be sufficient for this system.
- Additional software synthesizers and samplers and/or additional sample libraries may be desirable here. This will be discussed in more detail in Section IV, "Synthesis and Sampling."

MIDI AND AUDIO SYSTEM 3

This system takes Audio System 3 from Chapter 7 and adds a multiport MIDI interface, a keyboard synthesizer, and two hardware modules (see Figure 11.3). As with MIDI and Audio System 2, the hardware devices are not necessarily superior to software, and a keyboard controller plus some sample libraries could provide more flexibility. The advantages to hardware include substantial polyphony (64 voices, 128 voices, or more per device) that doesn't depend on the computer's CPU. The keyboard synth and two modules will take up six analog inputs on an audio interface, which may necessitate a larger interface or trading off between input sources.

MIDI and Audio System 3 Hardware

- All of the components of Audio System 3 discussed in Chapter 7.
- Multiport MIDI interface with at least three ins and outs.
- Keyboard synthesizer (same as MIDI and Audio System 2 above).
- Hardware modules:
  - May generate sound in a variety of ways. Because software sample libraries are available for many commonly used timbres, such as orchestral timbres, hardware modules with unique sounds or methods of sound generation may be desirable. These include MIDI-controlled analog synthesizers, such as Dave Smith Instruments' Evolver, and synthesizers designed for non-keyboard controllers, such as the Yamaha VL-70m, designed for wind controllers, or the Roland GR-20, designed for guitar controllers. This will depend, naturally, on your timbral needs.

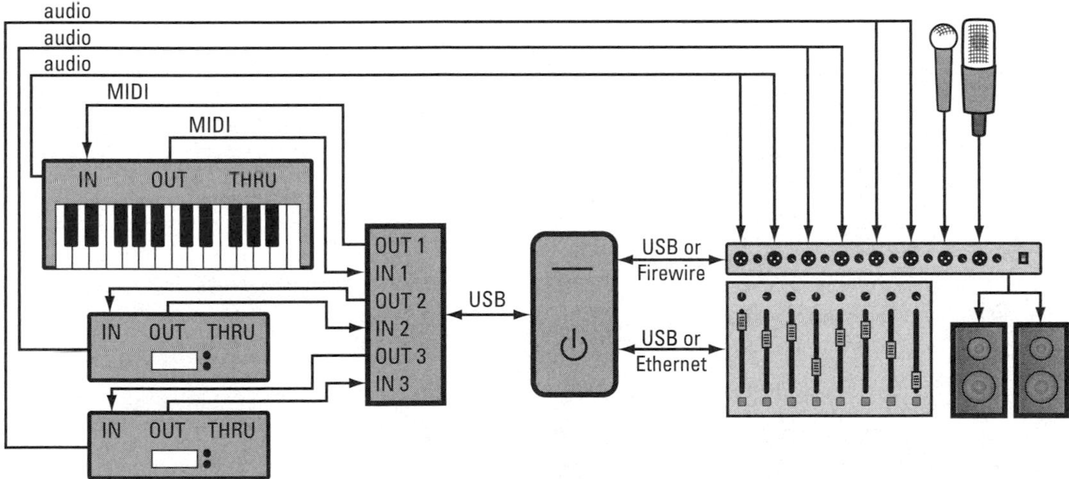

Figure 11.3 MIDI and Audio System 3: a keyboard synth, two modules, a multiport MIDI interface, an 8-input audio interface, a control surface, and powered monitors. The keyboard synth and modules, along with microphones or guitars (not shown), are the possible inputs to the audio interface.

- Audio outputs may be unbalanced or balanced. These will be connected to the inputs on the audio interface. Between these inputs and your other input sources, you may exceed the inputs on your interface, necessitating an interface with more inputs or trading off between inputs.
- Some modules and keyboard synths have digital outputs that can be connected to the digital inputs of an audio interface or digital mixing board. This eliminates any system noise from the analog cable runs.

MIDI and Audio System 3 Software

The following are some options for recording and editing software:

- Full version of a sequencer/DAW, perhaps with educational pricing. Full featured sequencer/DAWs include: Digital Performer (MOTU), Logic Pro (Apple), Sonar Producer (Cakewalk), Cubase (Steinberg), and Pro Tools LE (Digidesign). These are widely used sequencer/DAWs, but there are a variety of others available.
- Additional software synthesizers, a software sampler, and various sample libraries, such as orchestral sample libraries. This will be discussed in more detail in Section IV, "Synthesis and Sampling."

Section III Further Reading

For a history of analog and digital synthesizers, including the development of MIDI, Peter Manning's *Electronic and computer music* (rev. ed., 2004) provides a detailed overview, as does Thom Holmes's *Electronic and experimental music* (3rd ed., 2008). Joel Chadabe's *Electric sound* (1997), in addition to providing an overview of synthesizers and MIDI, includes many "eye-witness" accounts from the participants in these developments. For further exploration of analog synthesizers, Mark Vail's *Vintage synthesizers* (2nd ed., 2000) provides details and anecdotes about many historically important synths.

Andrea Pejrolo and Richard DeRosa's *Acoustic and MIDI orchestration for the contemporary composer* (2007) integrates a practical study of orchestration with a detailed discussion of the MIDI messages and MIDI sequencing techniques necessary to create MIDI realizations of orchestrated music. For further exploration of MIDI, there are several books that go through the MIDI specification in some detail, including Robert Guerin's *MIDI power! The comprehensive guide* (2nd ed., 2005) and Paul D. Lehrman and Tim Tully's *MIDI for the professional* (1993).

The definitive technical resource on MIDI is the MIDI spec itself: *The Complete MIDI 1.0 Detailed Specification* (MIDI Manufacturer's Association, 2006). This document provides the specifications for General MIDI 1 and Standard MIDI Files as well.

Section III
Suggested Activities

This chapter provides some suggested activities relating to MIDI and MIDI sequencing. These activities can be carried out in any sequencer and with any sound sources. Even though different sequencers share many interface elements and concepts, each has its own terminology and procedures for various actions. If your sequencer's documentation includes tutorials, it is valuable to go through those first before engaging in the activities listed here, so that you can translate the instructions here into your sequencer's "language." These activities also assume that you have a controller or a keyboard synthesizer hooked up to your computer through USB or some form of external MIDI interface.

EXPLORING MIDI MESSAGES

To explore the MIDI messages sent by your keyboard synthesizer or controller, you can use a piece of software known as a "MIDI monitor." There are several available for Macs and PCs as freeware. (See the book's website for links to some MIDI monitor software.)

With the MIDI monitor software running:

- Play Middle C and notice the key number and velocity that you produce. The preferences in the MIDI monitor software may allow you to choose how the data is displayed.
- Play a series of notes with a variety of velocities. Note the effort required to generate a velocity of 127 (maximum) and the restraint required to generate a velocity of 1 (or at least in the single digits).
- Move the modulation wheel/joystick and notice the CC1 values. Move the wheel/joystick as little as possible and notice the difference in values. In many cases, it is not possible to change the mod wheel value by just one with the physical wheel/joystick.

- Move the pitch bend wheel/joystick and notice the values when the wheel is all the way down and all the way up. The minimum value should be –8,192 and the maximum value should be 8,191.
- Move any other sliders or knobs on your keyboard synth/controller to see what MIDI messages they send and what their values are.

RECORDING NOTES

Using your sequencing software, explore the various modes of note entry.

Step Recording

Choose a piece of music with several voices—a selection from the keyboard music of J.S. Bach would be appropriate.

- Add a track to your sequencer for each of the voices in the piece. The tracks can be MIDI tracks for controlling a keyboard synth or tracks for software instruments.
- Choose the name, output channel, and patch for your track. For software instrument tracks, you might choose the patch directly from the front panel of the software instrument itself rather than in the tracks view.
- Step record each part in turn. The process for step recording is different for each sequencer, so you will need to consult the manual for your sequencer.

Real-time Recording

Choose a piece of music with a melody, chords, and bass whose style would benefit from the flexibility of real-time recording—a jazz or pop tune would be appropriate.

- Add a track to your sequencer for each of the voices in the piece. The tracks can be MIDI tracks for controlling a keyboard synth or tracks for software instruments.
- Choose the name, output channel, and patch for your track. For software instrument tracks, you might choose the patch directly from the front panel of the software instrument itself rather than in the tracks view.
- Choose the recording tempo, which can be different from the final playback tempo, and activate the metronome and countoff.
- Record the melody, chords, and bass parts one at a time. Be sure to play with the necessary "feel," such as swing, while recording the melody. Depending on your keyboard skills, you may need to simplify the bass and chords parts.

Recording Modes and Quantization

Use the sequence that you recorded in real time and explore the following features:

- Experiment with the overdub/merge and punch-in/punch-out recording modes to see where they might be useful.

- Create a drum part of modest length (two or four bars) using the loop-overdub/merge feature. On the first pass, enter the kick drum and snare; on the second, the hi-hats and crash cymbal; and on the third, enter fills with the tom-toms.
- Select the melody part and experiment with the quantize function. Notice how strict quantization cleans up the performance, but also removes the expressive feel that you added during recording. You may want to solo the melody track for this.
- If there are additional parameters to your sequencer's quantize feature, such as "strength," experiment with those to see if they improve the results of the quantization.
- If your sequencer has a "swing" quantize and/or a "humanize" function, try first quantizing the melody strictly and then using these functions to try to re-create a natural feel to the melody.

EDITING AND ARRANGING

You can make fairly elaborate arrangements starting with just melody, chords, bass, and drums and using cut, copy, and paste along with selective deleting and transposition. Using one of the sequences you created through step recording or real-time recording, create a more extensive arrangement of about ten tracks. The jazz or pop tune used in the real-time recording example might work best here.

Here are some simple arranging procedures and suggestions:

- Look for places in the piece where new musical features enter and take that opportunity to copy a part into a new track to change the instrumentation. Repetitions are a good place to change instrumentation.
- Occasionally layer different instruments together to create a composite sound.
- Add instruments over the course of a section of music to build up the texture, or remove instruments to simplify it.
- Use unusual instruments occasionally to spice up or emphasize a line or chord.
- All the notes of a chord needn't be played by the same instrument—try splitting harmonies between instruments. For example, you can copy the chords to a track and then delete all but one of the notes of the chord so that a trumpet can play one note, do the same for another track so a saxophone can play the second note of the chord, and so on.
- Copy the melody into another track, transpose it up an octave, and selectively delete many of these notes so that the new track acts as a punctuation to the existing melody, similar to the function of a horn section in funk or jazz-rock.
- Take care not to have all of the tracks going all of the time—that is a recipe for a muddy arrangement. Try to vary the overall texture and number of simultaneously playing tracks and use the build-up of texture and number of voices to emphasize important points in the piece.

EXPRESSIVE SEQUENCING

In the last exercise, you created a sequence through cut, copy, and paste along with transposition and selective deleting. Now it's time to enhance the expressiveness of the arrangement using expressive messages such as control change messages and pitch bend. You can enter expressive messages while recording in real time, with a mixer view, or manually using a pencil tool. Each method has its advantages and drawbacks. In practice, you should become comfortable entering and manipulating expressive messages in all three ways.

Record Controllers in Real Time

- For each instrument/patch, determine the effect of the controllers that can be manipulated from your keyboard synth or controller by record-enabling each track in turn and playing some notes while manipulating the wheels, knobs, and sliders. The mod wheel and pitch bend wheel are the most common controls.
- Record-enable a track to which you want to add expressive messages, make sure that overdub/merge mode is active, click record, and manipulate the controls in real time as the sequence is playing. Some sequencers have dedicated controller tracks that can be record-enabled independently from the track, eliminating the need to use overdub/merge.
- Repeat this for each type of expressive message you wish to add to that track.
- Repeat the previous two steps for other tracks to which you want to add expressive messages.

Record Automation in the Mixer View

- Open the mixer view and enable automation write/record for a given track. Automation record is different from the record-enable button used for recording notes or overdubbing/merging controllers.
- While playing the sequence, move the volume fader for that track to create the desired changes in volume.
- Rewind and play again. This time move the pan knob for that track to move the sound around in the stereo field. Note that many pan "knobs" are really hidden sliders that you drag straight up for clockwise and straight down for counter-clockwise.
- Repeat these steps for each track that you wish to automate.
- To manipulate the volume more than one track at a time—for example, to fade them all down—use fader groups in the mixer view.

Enter Expressive Messages Manually

- Most sequencers allow you to draw in expressive messages using a pencil tool. This can be accomplished in a variety of ways depending on the sequencer. This may be done in an extension of the tracks view, in the piano roll editor, or in a view specially designed for this.
- Manual entry allows you to draw very precise curves for the data.
- Choose a track and an expressive message to enter, such as modulation wheel. Select the pencil tool and draw the values for that message in the track.
- Repeat the previous step for each type of expressive message you wish to enter, such as pitch bend, volume, or pan.
- Repeat the previous two steps for each track you want to modify.

SECTION IV

Synthesis and Sampling

OVERVIEW

The two primary ways for electronic musical devices and software to produce sound are through synthesis and sampling. Synthesis involves creating sound from the ground up using simple waveforms combined and manipulated according to an algorithm, or recipe. Synthesis techniques can produce rich, unusual sounds, can attempt to produce realistic instrumental or vocal sounds, or can morph between the unusual and the realistic.

Sampling, on the other hand, involves using pre-recorded sounds played back in response to MIDI messages. The greatest advantage to sampling is the potential for realism, since it can incorporate recordings of actual acoustic instruments. As such, sampling is currently the dominant electronic sound production technology for music where realism is paramount. For example, film and television composers use sampling technology extensively either to demonstrate their music to directors and producers using realistic sounds, or to actually serve as the final product.

Sampling, however, is even more pervasive than that. Because sampling can utilize sounds recorded from any source, samples can include recordings of non-musical sounds (cars, jet engines, gardening tools) as well as recordings of sounds produced by a synthesizer, causing sampling and synthesis to get tangled up with one another.

SYNTHESIS AND SAMPLING: WHAT DO I NEED?

In the previous two sections, "Audio" and "MIDI," there were separate chapters concerning what hardware and software is necessary to carry out activities at various levels. Hardware and software that generate sound using synthesis and/or sampling require MIDI communications and audio input and output. As a result, the physical systems needed for synthesis and sampling are the same MIDI and audio systems discussed in Chapter 11, so there is no need for a separate chapter to discuss those systems in this section. For synthesis and sampling, any of the MIDI and audio systems are sufficient, with the same advantages and disadvantages covered in that chapter. For controlling softsynths it is useful to have a keyboard controller with a variety of knobs and sliders for adjusting parameters.

The advantages and disadvantages of hardware versus software synthesizers and samplers are discussed in Chapter 12, but software is increasingly dominant so that will be the focus here. Which specific software synth or sampler you need is highly dependent on the specific projects that you wish to undertake. Most sequencer/DAWs ship with at least a few softsynths, enabling you to experiment with various sound production methods before purchasing additional software.

If you are going to create music with a wide array of synthetic sounds, you may find it desirable to purchase additional softsynths or download freeware employing various synthesis techniques to increase the timbral resources at your disposal. Considerations for a softsynth include compatibility with your sequencer/DAW (plug-in format, ReWire), the synthesis method(s) employed, and the degree to which it is programmable. In terms of programmability, most softsynths provide a series of knobs and sliders for altering parameters; some, such as Propellerheads' Reason, allow you to also interconnect several synthesizers; and a few, such as Native Instruments' Reaktor or Cycling74's Max/MSP, allow you to design your own synthesizer almost from scratch, complete with a custom set of knobs and sliders to control your creation. A program such as Max/MSP/Jitter or PD/GEM can also allow you to manipulate other media, such as images or video, in real time.

If you are interested in simulating acoustic instruments or otherwise using samples, you may find it desirable to purchase some sample libraries. Most sample libraries come with their own sample player software so that purchasing and installing the library is all that you need to do to access your new samples. Otherwise, you may need to purchase a full-blown software sampler, such as MOTU's MachFive or Native Instruments' Kontakt, in order to load your sample library and play it back from your sequencer/DAW. An additional advantage to a full-blown sampler such as MachFive, Kontakt, Logic's EXS24, or Reason's NN-XT is that you can record your own unique samples and set them up to be played back by a sequencer or keyboard in the studio or in live performance.

WHAT'S IN THIS SECTION?

Chapter 12: Electronic Sound Production

This chapter covers:

- an overview of synthesis and sampling;
- a basic synthesis model, including an oscillator, a filter, and an amplifier;

- dynamic sound elements, including envelopes and LFOs;
- basic synth examples;
- hardware versus software;
- plug-ins, ReWire, and standalone softsynths;
- software latency, polyphony, and multitimbral capacity.

Chapter 13: Synthesis Methods

This chapter covers:

- wavetable synthesis;
- additive synthesis;
- subtractive synthesis;
- frequency modulation;
- physical modeling;
- granular synthesis/processing;
- example softsynths for each method;
- non-commercial software synthesizers.

Chapter 14: Sampling Methods

This chapter covers:

- sampling techniques, including keymapping, multisampling, velocity switching, looping, and key switching;
- sampler patches and sample libraries;
- soundware;
- library formats;
- samplers, sample players, and ROMplers.

At the end of the section, there are suggestions for "Further Reading" and a list of "Suggested Activities" related to the material in this section.

CHAPTER 12

Electronic Sound Production

SYNTHESIS AND SAMPLING

The various methods for producing sound electronically can be grouped into two primary categories: synthesis and sampling.

Synthesis refers to any method that generates sound "from the ground up" according to some recipe, or **algorithm**. For example, to re-create the sound of a trumpet using a synthesis method, you could use software that adds together simple sine waves whose frequencies, amplitudes, and phases match the partials that are present in a trumpet sound. This particular method is referred to as additive synthesis and will be discussed in more detail in the next chapter along with a variety of other synthesis methods.

Sampling uses stored digital audio triggered by MIDI messages to generate sound. For example, to re-create the sound of a trumpet using sampling, you would make separate recordings of a trumpet being played at various pitches, dynamic levels, and articulations, and then import those recordings into a software or hardware **sampler**. The sampler would then play one of those recordings when it received an appropriate MIDI note message from a controller or a sequencer. Sampling will be discussed more fully in Chapter 14. Naturally, it is possible to combine sampling and synthesis to create hybrid sampling-synthesis methods.

Most hardware "synthesizers" today use sampling as their primary sound production method. The term "synthesizer," then, is often used to mean any "electronic sound-producing device," rather than a device whose primary method of sound production is synthesis. In the software realm, there are many software synths that use samples and many that employ one or more synthesis methods, including "analog-modeling" synthesis, in which the inherently digital software emulates the sound production methods of analog synthesizers.

Sampling is commonly used to re-create existing instrumental timbres, as is the case in many electronically produced television and film scores. However, even when the desire is not to emulate perfectly a real instrument or voice, but to produce an unusual sound of some sort, sampling can be a useful method. Sampling adds a built-in "realism" to even a heavily modified or processed sound, because the natural fluctuations of the physically produced sound are captured in the sample.

Synthesis methods are commonly used to create sounds that are decidedly "electronic," such as those found in dance music, pop music, or experimental electronic music. Even with synthesized sounds, it is usually desirable to modify, or modulate, the sound to provide some of the realistic fluctuations found in sampled sounds. There are only a few situations where it is aesthetically desirable to have a pure, unmodulated synthetic timbre. To make things more complicated, many synthesizers that utilize sampling methods provide sampled "electronic" sounds recorded from vintage synthesizers or synthesized by software and then saved as a sample. Many synths that provide "vintage" synth sounds base them on samples.

A BASIC SYNTHESIS MODEL

In order to understand synthesis and sampling methods, we'll start with a basic model of the electronic sound production process and refine and expand from there in the following chapters. One useful model can be drawn from analog synthesizers whose sound functions were separated into separate hardware boxes called "modules" that were then patched together to create electronic timbres. This "modular" approach allows us to consider each step in the electronic sound production process separately (see Figure 12.1). Our basic model has three modules:

- The **oscillator** provides a basic waveform (timbre) at a particular frequency (pitch).
- The **filter** modifies the spectrum (timbre) of the basic waveform.
- The **amplifier** applies an envelope to the amplitude of the audio (loudness and articulation).

Notice that these three synthesizer elements generate most of the sound properties discussed in Chapter 2, "Sound Properties and the Waveform View."

While analog synthesis is generally a thing of the past, analog-*modeling* synthesis—software or hardware digital synthesis that emulates analog techniques—has become

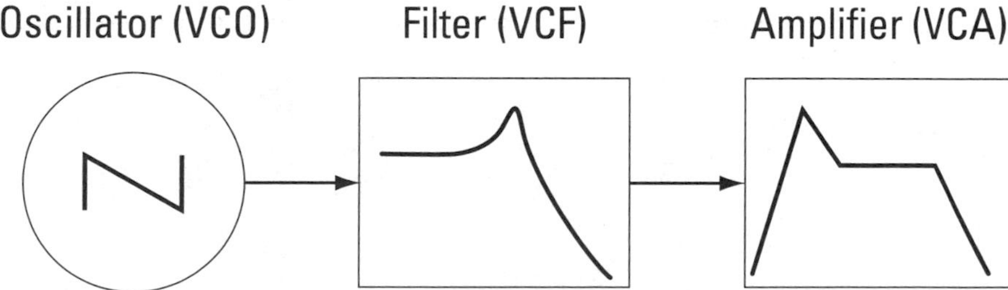

Figure 12.1 A basic synthesis model based on analog synthesis.

pervasive, particularly in the realm of electronic pop and dance music. In analog synthesizers, the oscillator was referred to as a VCO (voltage-controlled oscillator), the filter as a VCF (voltage-controlled filter), and the amplifier as a VCA (voltage-controlled amplifier). "Voltage control" is a largely obsolete term, but it is still occasionally used to describe these modules even in a digital context. In addition, there are several companies that make actual analog synths, in which case the "VC" terminology is accurate. Some digital synths explicitly refer to these components as DCO, DCF, and DCA, substituting "digitally controlled" for "voltage-controlled."

This model of synthesis is often referred to as "subtractive" because the filter removes some of the partials from the waveform. Other forms of subtractive synthesis will be covered more fully in the next chapter, "Synthesis Methods." Next, we'll consider each of the modules of the basic synthesis model in turn.

PITCH AND TIMBRE SOURCE: THE OSCILLATOR

Basic Waveforms

The oscillator's primary job is to generate a waveform at a particular frequency. The most basic oscillator takes one cycle of a waveform and repeats it over and over at the rate determined by the MIDI key number (see Figure 12.2).

In the digital realm, this is a type of sound generation known as fixed waveform synthesis, or **wavetable synthesis**. This form of synthesis can produce any timbre that can be stored as a single cycle, but the waveform stays the same throughout a note, unlike acoustic sounds. Other forms of synthesis that can act as the basic pitch and timbre source in a synthesizer will be discussed in the next chapter.

There are several essential waveforms that derive from the waveforms that were typically available in analog synthesizers. The sine, triangle, sawtooth, square, and pulse waveforms are shown in Figure 12.3. These waveforms and their spectra were discussed earlier in Chapters 2 and 3.

Noise

One important source for synthetic timbres is not a "waveform" at all: noise. **Noise** is characterized by *not* having a periodic shape and comes in several "colors," such as **white noise** and **pink noise**, that indicate the way that energy is distributed in the spectrum.

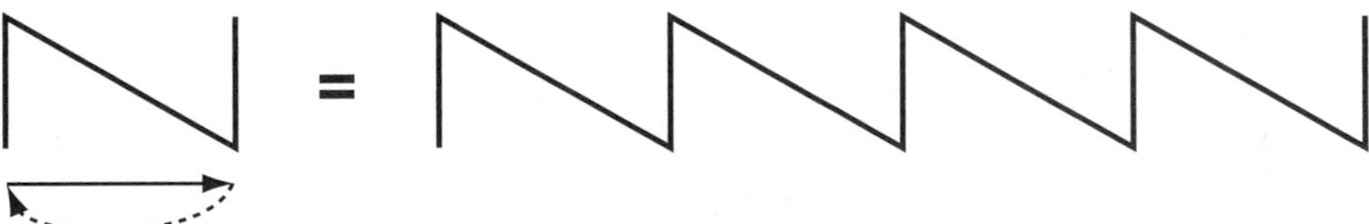

Figure 12.2 Wavetable synthesis: a single cycle of a waveform (here a sawtooth) is looped at a rate equal to the desired fundamental frequency to produce a basic timbre.

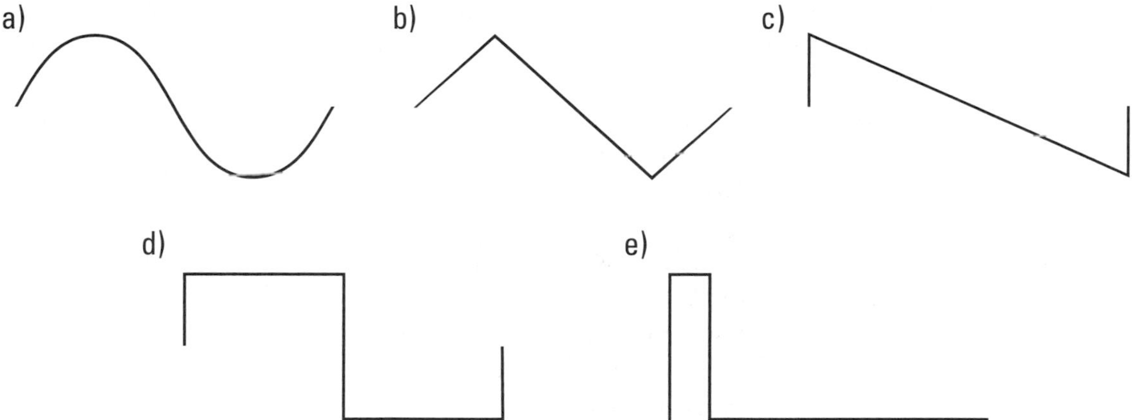

Figure 12.3 Basic waveforms: (a) sine, (b) triangle, (c) sawtooth, (d) square, and (e) pulse.

In a synthetic timbre, noise is often layered with another waveform to create a percussive attack. As discussed in the "Sound" section, the attack portion of a sound is often richer in partials than the sustain portion, and noise can be used to enrich a sound artificially during the attack. The noise would fade quickly after the attack, leaving the other waveform(s) to sound during the sustained portion of the note.

Pitch

Pitch seems like an obvious characteristic of an oscillator: play an A above middle C on the keyboard and hear the pitch A with a frequency of 440 Hz. This is, in fact, how most oscillators respond to the key number of a MIDI note-on message. However, one of the great promises of electronic music when it was first being developed was that it would allow us to transcend the limitation of 12 equal-tempered notes to the octave (see the "Tuning and Temperament" section in Chapter 3, pages 35–37). It is possible in some synths to map the incoming key number to any desired frequency, including microtonal frequencies that fall in between the traditional equal-tempered frequencies. Most synths utilize equal-tempered pitches, but allow for various amounts of detuning.

TIMBRE MODIFICATION: THE FILTER

The filter's job is to modify the timbre (spectrum) of the source waveform by boosting or cutting some of its partials. In Chapter 3, "The Overtone Series and the Spectrum View," and Chapter 6, "Digital Audio Software," you saw that EQ, or equalization, is a common application of filters in stereos and recording software. Equalization comes in two primary forms: graphic EQ and parametric EQ. The filters in a synthesizer or sampler are related to parametric EQ. However, while EQ filters are typically designed to correct some problem in recorded sound and often remain "invisible," filters in synthesizers are designed to modify timbre creatively and contribute noticeably to the overall synthesized sound.

The **low pass filter** is the basic filter type in our synthesis model. There are a variety of other filter types that were introduced in Chapter 6, "Digital Audio Software," and will be discussed further in Chapter 13, "Synthesis Methods." A low pass filter passes the low frequencies largely unchanged and cuts the high frequencies. You can simulate the effect of a changing low pass filter with your mouth by saying "ah" and then smoothly changing to "oh."

The primary parameter of a low pass filter is its **cutoff frequency**, which determines where in the spectrum the partials start to be reduced in amplitude. Changing the cutoff frequency of a low pass filter alters the brightness of the tone—lowering the cutoff frequency makes the timbre darker. One of the differences between a low pass filter that would be used in an EQ and a low pass filter used in synthesis is **resonance**.

Resonance in a low pass filter takes the form of a boost in the frequencies right at the cutoff frequency. What this means is that, as the cutoff frequency changes, the boost at that frequency makes the change clearly audible. Since the cutoff frequency of a filter in a synthesizer often changes during the course of a note, the resonance makes that filter change more noticeable. Resonance turns the synthesizer filter into an active participant in the sound.

Figure 12.4 shows the effect of a low pass filter with resonance. The original spectrum shown in 12.4a is passed through the filter in 12.4b whose cutoff frequency is 660 Hz. Figure 12.4c shows the result. Notice the frequencies below 660 Hz are unchanged, the frequencies above 660 are cut, and the frequency right at 660 Hz is boosted by the resonant peak of the filter (indicated by the arrows).

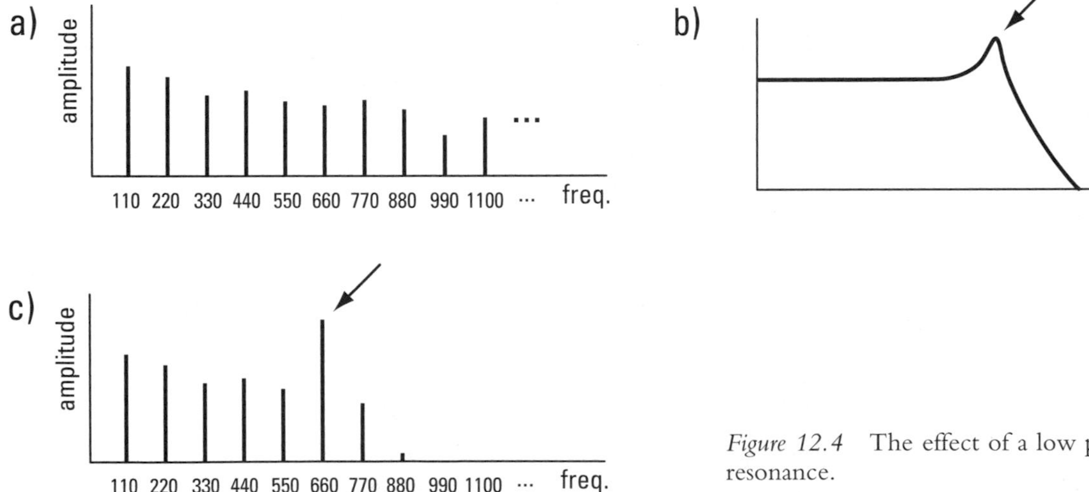

Figure 12.4 The effect of a low pass filter with resonance.

LOUDNESS MODIFICATION: THE AMPLIFIER

The amplifier's job in a synthesizer is similar to that of a stereo or guitar amplifier: to increase or decrease the amplitude of the audio. We saw previously that the key number of an incoming MIDI note-on message is used to determine the frequency of the waveform produced by the oscillator. The other important number in that note-on message is the velocity, which can be used to control the output level of the amplifier. This is a useful function, but it only allows the amplifier to set the overall amplitude—it doesn't shape the amplitude in any way over the course of the note. This is where an amplitude envelope comes in.

Applying Articulation with an Envelope

In the discussion of articulation in Chapter 2, we saw that the amplitude envelope of a sound determines its articulation (see pages 28–29). In a synthesizer, an envelope generator allows the amplifier both to determine the maximum amplitude of the sound and to shape the amplitude over the course of a note. A simple model for an envelope that has proven useful is the **ADSR envelope**: **a**ttack time, **d**ecay time, **s**ustain level, **r**elease time. In a softsynth, these values are set with sliders or knobs. The amplifier of a synthesizer uses the envelope as follows:

- When the synth receives a MIDI note-on message, the **attack** segment of the amplitude envelope causes the amplitude to rise from zero to a maximum amplitude determined by the velocity value in the note-on message (see Figure 12.5). The duration of this segment is determined by the setting of the Attack slider or knob.
- Immediately after the attack segment concludes, the **decay** segment of the envelope reduces the amplitude to a percentage of the maximum amplitude determined by the Sustain slider. The duration of this segment is determined by the setting of the Decay slider or knob.
- The amplitude level stays the same during the **sustain** segment, which lasts until the synth receives a MIDI note-off message. The duration of this segment is determined by the amount of time between the note-on message and the note-off message. There is no actual sustain "time" that is set. The Sustain slider or knob determines the percentage of the maximum amplitude that is maintained during the sustain segment of the envelope.
- During the **release** segment of the envelope, the amplitude falls from the sustain level to zero. The duration of this segment is determined by the setting of the Release slider or knob.

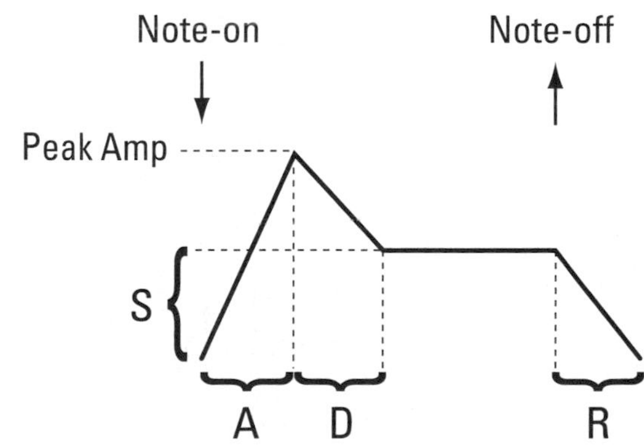

Figure 12.5 ADSR envelope also showing the peak amplitude determined by the note-on velocity.

The envelope is **gated** by the note-on and note-off messages, meaning that the note-on message starts the envelope ("opens" the gate) and the note-off message causes the envelope to conclude ("closes" the gate). This is sometimes called **triggering**, but a trigger typically starts a process like an envelope, which then proceeds without further control. A typical synthesizer envelope requires the note-off message to complete the envelope.

In Chapter 2, "Sound Properties and the Waveform View," we identified two basic kinds of instrument articulations and their associated envelope types. Bowed or blown instruments are associated with an ADSR envelope, and struck or plucked instruments are associated with an AR envelope. Many synthesizers provide just one type of envelope, such as the ADSR. The values for the segments of that envelope can be set to emulate the desired acoustic envelope.

Many programmable synthesizers (particularly software synthesizers) provide sliders or knobs to control each of the basic components of an ADSR envelope. These sliders can be set to simulate many of the common instrumental articulations. Figure 12.6 shows a variety of ADSR settings and the envelopes that they generate.

Other envelope shapes, with more sections and/or curved line shapes, can be found in many synthesizers, but the ADSR remains in widespread use. Envelopes can also be used to control dynamically other aspects of a synthetic sound besides the amplitude.

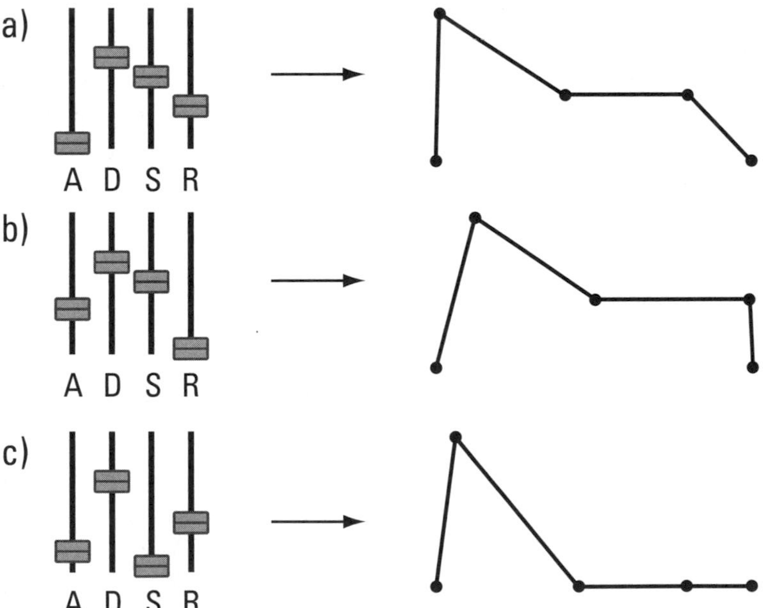

Figure 12.6 Various ADSR controls and their resultant envelopes: (a) sharp attack, (b) sudden release, and (c) struck/plucked shape.

DYNAMIC SOUND

The primary drawback to the wavetable synthesis technique used by the oscillator in the basic synthesis model is that the timbre doesn't change during the sound. The sound properties of natural timbres change constantly, particularly when the sound is getting louder or quieter. When a natural sound gets louder, as it does during the attack phase of a note, the timbre gets brighter because the increase in energy in the system excites the higher partials. The reverse occurs when a sound gets quieter, with the higher partials fading faster than the lower ones.

This type of dynamic change is present in all facets of acoustically produced sound: the pitch is never perfectly steady, the amplitudes of the partials don't remain the same, the overall amplitude fluctuates, and so on. To re-create the realistic fluctuations of acoustically produced sounds, it is necessary to introduce changes to the basic synthesis parameters throughout the course of a note. Modification of a synthesis parameter is referred to as **modulation**. The changeable synthesis parameters in the basic synthesis model are:

- oscillator: pitch and waveform;
- filter: filter type, cutoff frequency, and resonance;
- amplifier: overall level and attack-decay-sustain-release parameters.

Of these parameters, pitch, cutoff frequency (both discussed earlier), and overall level are most commonly modulated over the course of a single note or series of notes. There are three basic ways to control these parameters: through **direct control**, with an **envelope**, and with a **low frequency oscillator** (**LFO**).

Direct Control of Synthesis Parameters

Controlling the pitch, cutoff frequency, and overall level can be accomplished by manipulating wheels, sliders, and knobs on a hardware synth/controller, or virtual wheels, sliders and knobs with a mouse in a softsynth. This can be very effective, but you are limited in the number of parameters you can change while you are also playing notes in live performance. However, if you are using a sequencer to control a hardware or software synth, you can use a variety of expressive MIDI messages such as control change, aftertouch, and pitch bend to control simultaneously multiple synthesis parameters.

You can directly control pitch with pitch bend messages, the cutoff frequency with aftertouch or modulation wheel (CC1) messages, and the overall level with control change number 7 (CC7) and/or number 11 (CC11) messages. Direct control via MIDI messages in a sequence works best when you want to modify synthesis parameters for occasional notes or across many notes, but if you want the synthesis parameters to change in a particular way during each note, an envelope is a better solution.

Modulation with Envelopes

The basic synthesis model includes an envelope to control the overall level, which is the most fundamental application of an envelope. However, envelopes can, in theory, be applied to any synthesis parameter, including filter cutoff frequency and pitch. Which synth parameters can be controlled by envelopes differs somewhat from synth to synth.

An envelope applied to the cutoff frequency of a low pass filter is particularly useful for simulating the brightening of a sound during the attack of a note and the darkening of a sound as the sound dies away. The envelope applied to the cutoff frequency can be a simple ADSR envelope or something more complex depending on what type of envelope is available in the synth (see Figure 12.7).

An envelope can also be applied to the pitch of an oscillator (see Figure 12.8). The pitch would start at the frequency determined by the MIDI key number and rise (A), fall (D), sustain (S), and finally return (R) to that original pitch. This can generate siren sounds and other such special effects. However, a pitch envelope is often applied with no attack, a small decay, no sustain, and no release. In this configuration, the pitch envelope applies an almost imperceptibly fast drop from a high pitch to the pitch of the key number right at the beginning of a note, creating a bit of complexity in the sound right at the beginning of the attack of the note. This serves the function of giving the note a more complex timbre during its attack, which, in its perceived effect, helps to mimic natural instrument behavior.

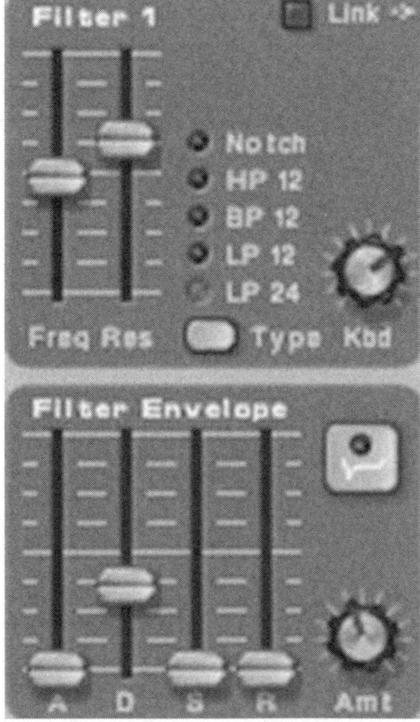

Figure 12.7 The filter and filter envelope sections from Reason's Subtractor. (Courtesy of Propellerheads, Inc.)

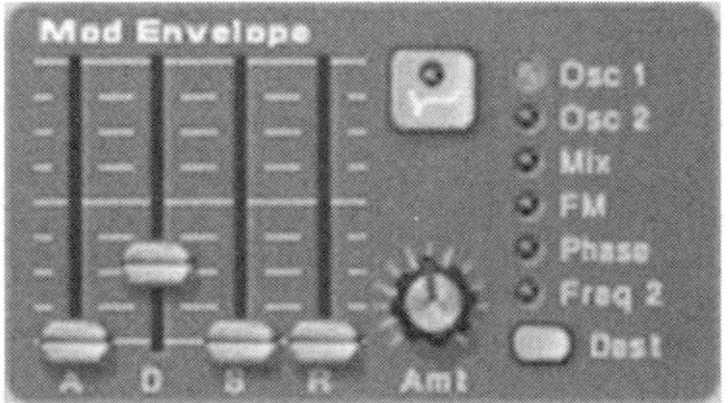

Figure 12.8 An envelope assigned to the pitch of the oscillator ("Osc 1") in Reason's Subtractor. (Courtesy of Propellerheads, Inc.)

Modulation with LFOs

In addition to direct control and envelope control of synthesis parameters, it is often useful to alter synthesis parameters using a varying signal generated by a low frequency oscillator, or LFO. These oscillators are "low" frequency because they operate below the range of human hearing, below 20 Hz. In that frequency range, waveforms can't be heard directly as pitches. Instead, an LFO is used to modify, or modulate, another synthesis parameter. An LFO has three basic parameters: **waveform**, **rate**, and **depth**. In a regular oscillator, these correspond to waveform, frequency, and amplitude. The change of terminology when discussing the LFO reflects its use as a modulator of other synthesis parameters.

If an LFO is applied to the pitch of an oscillator, it will produce a periodic variation in frequency above and below the frequency indicated by the MIDI key number. At the proper rate—approximately 5–10 Hz—this periodic fluctuation is heard as **vibrato**. The depth of the LFO corresponds to how "wide" the vibrato is, and the waveform indicates how the pitch changes. A relatively smooth waveform such as a sine wave or triangle wave will work best for vibrato.

If an LFO is applied to the cutoff frequency of a low pass filter, it will vary the cutoff frequency above and below the cutoff frequency value set by a slider. This will cause a periodic change in the brightness of the sound. You can simulate this with your mouth by repeating "wah-wah-wah . . .," which is, of course, a **wah-wah** effect, similar to the effect of a guitar wah pedal if the guitarist is rocking his or her foot steadily.

If an LFO is applied to the output level, it will vary the volume above and below the volume set by a slider or by the MIDI note-on velocity. This will cause a periodic change in the loudness of a sound that is referred to as **tremolo**. Tremolo is also the effect created by the motor on a vibraphone. The vibraphone's motor causes small discs in the resonators to revolve, periodically opening and closing the mouth of the resonator, thus creating the vibraphone's characteristic "pulsing" effect.

BASIC SYNTH EXAMPLES

There are a great many softsynths available that follow the basic analog synthesis model described in this chapter. Two examples will be described here: one fairly simple and one of moderate complexity.

MOTU's BassLine, which ships with their sequencer/DAW Digital Performer, is a relatively simple analog-modeling synth (see Figure 12.9). It features one oscillator that can be a sawtooth, square, or hybrid waveform, one low pass filter with resonance, and an amplifier that features an overdrive control. The register for the oscillator is given in terms of organ pipe lengths with longer lengths indicating lower pitches. This is a curious practice, but it is fairly common.

Each of the three basic components (oscillator, filter, amplifier) has a single modulation source. The oscillator has a glide, or portamento, control, the filter has an envelope that is essentially an AR (attack-release) envelope, and the amplifier also has

Figure 12.9 MOTU's BassLine softsynth, which ships as part of Digital Performer. (Courtesy of MOTU)

an AR envelope with a zero attack. An AR envelope makes sense in the case of an instrument called "BassLine," because a bass falls into the "plucked or struck" articulation category.

The Subtractor synth that is part of Propellerheads' Reason is somewhat more complex (see Figure 12.10). In the oscillator section, there are two independent oscillators and a noise source. Each oscillator can be set to any one of 32 waveforms and can be tuned by octaves, semitones, and cents. The decay of the noise can be set along with its relative level and "color." The filter section has two filters that can be linked together, one of which can be switched among many different filter types. Each filter also has a resonance control. The amplifier section features a simple level control.

Figure 12.10 The Subtractor softsynth that is part of Propellerheads' Reason. (Courtesy of Propellerheads, Inc.)

There are many modulation options for creating dynamic sound. There are direct control settings for controlling the effect of the MIDI note-on velocity, the modulation wheel, and other sources. There are dedicated ADSR envelopes for amplitude and filter cutoff frequency and another envelope that can be routed to many different parameters including pitch. In addition, there are two LFOs that can be routed to various parameters.

HARDWARE VERSUS SOFTWARE

Now that we've examined a basic synthesis model, it is useful to consider the various ways that we can access synthesis and sampling.

The earliest commercial digital synthesizers were self-contained keyboards or rack-mounted units. At that time, personal computers lacked the processing power to synthesize sound in real time. As a result, computers were used for MIDI sequencing, which requires much less processing power, and the external hardware synthesizers generated the actual sound.

The increase in the processing power of personal computers in the intervening decades has led to the wide availability of software for real-time sample playback and synthesis (see Figure 12.11). Increasingly, project studios are moving to software-only solutions for sound generation, using keyboards only as controllers. Some large software-only project studios use multiple computers, one for sequencing and one or more for software sound generation. Throughout these chapters, the term "softsynths" will be used to refer to both software synthesizers and software samplers. This is similar to the

Figure 12.11 A variety of software synthesizers: Native Instruments' Kontakt (courtesy of Native Instruments GmbH, Germany), Combinator from Propellerheads' Reason (courtesy of Propellerheads, Inc.), Native Instruments' FM8, EXS24 from Apple's Logic (screenshot reprinted with permission from Apple Inc.), Modulo from MOTU's Digital Performer (courtesy of MOTU), and Kjaerhus Audio's Spectra (courtesy of Kjaerhus Audio).

practice of calling a keyboard that generates sound a "synthesizer" even if it uses samples as the basis for its patches.

While software synthesizers and samplers are beginning to dominate the project studio environment, hardware synths are still valuable in live performance settings due to their durability and reliability. As a result, a keyboard synth and perhaps a rack-mounted module or two will be found in a number of project studios into the near future.

Hardware synthesizers and samplers interact with sequencer/DAWs through MIDI interfaces. Software synthesizers, however, interact directly with sequencer/DAWs within the computer. Software synths and samplers can act as plug-ins to sequencer/DAWs, as ReWire slaves to sequencer/DAWs, or as standalone software controlled by an external MIDI source.

Plug-in Softsynths

As a plug-in, a softsynth is fully integrated into the sequencer/DAW and loads when the project file loads. The sequencer/DAW in this situation is referred to as the **host application**. This is usually the easiest type of softsynth to use from the end-user standpoint. Some sequencer/DAWs load a softsynth plug-in on an "instrument" track and require a MIDI track or tracks to store MIDI messages that are then sent to the plug-in on the instrument track. In other ways, the instrument track acts like an audio track, allowing for volume and pan changes, effects inserts and sends, and so on.

There are a variety of **plug-in formats** for softsynths and each sequencer/DAW supports one or more of them. The most common plug-in types are Apple's Audio Units (**AU**), Microsoft's DirectX Instrument (**DXi**), Steinberg's Virtual Studio Technology instrument (**VSTi**), and Digidesign's Real-Time Audio Suite (**RTAS**). The formats supported by your sequencer/DAW dictate which plug-in formats you can use. VSTi softsynth plug-ins are probably the most widely supported, with AU common on Apple computers, DXi in a number of Windows programs, and RTAS plug-ins being used by Pro Tools software. There are several other formats that are usually used in more specialized circumstances: TDM plug-ins for the high-end Pro Tools HD systems, and DSSI and LV2 plug-ins for the Linux operating system. In addition, there are a variety of **plug-in wrappers** that allow one type of plug-in to work on a system that doesn't accept that type. For example, a VST-to-RTAS wrapper would allow you to use VST instruments within Pro Tools LE.

ReWire Softsynths

Some softsynths aren't available as plug-ins, so the sequencer/DAW must communicate to the softsynth in another way. **ReWire** is a technology developed by the company Propellerheads, primarily as a way for sequencer/DAWs to communicate with Propellerheads' softsynth rack, Reason, which is not available as a plug-in. However, ReWire can be used by other softsynths as well.

If two pieces of software are connected via ReWire, one is referred to as the **ReWire master** and the other as the **ReWire slave**. This is similar to the host/plug-in relationship discussed above, except that the ReWire master and slave are running as separate applications. ReWire allows audio and MIDI to be exchanged between the two applications as well as synchronization information. If both ReWire applications have transport controls, pressing "play" in one app will cause the other to play as well. One of the more typical scenarios is that the ReWire master is a sequencer/DAW in which MIDI information is sequenced and sent via ReWire to a ReWire slave. The ReWire slave is a synthesizer/sampler that receives the MIDI messages and generates sound. The sound is passed back from the ReWire slave to the ReWire master and can then be mixed and processed using the sequencer/DAW's capabilities (see Figure 12.12).

Standalone Softsynths

Some softsynths run in a **standalone mode** in which they are simply independent applications. Two applications connected via ReWire are running separately, but the ReWire technology creates a special connection between them. Often a synth can run either as a plug-in or in standalone mode depending on the needs of the user. A sequencer/DAW can send MIDI messages to a standalone softsynth through a special inter-application connection that is either built into the system, such as the Mac's Inter-application Communications bus (IAC bus), or is supplied by third-party software such as SubtleSoft's MIDIPipe or the Maple Virtual MIDI Cable.

You might run a softsynth as a standalone application because the MIDI messages are coming from outside the computer from a controller keyboard or from another computer. As mentioned above, some project studios use separate computers for sequencing and sound generation. This configuration is shown in Figure 12.13. In this configuration, a sequencer/DAW on one computer is sending MIDI messages out through a MIDI interface. The Out Port of that interface is connected to the In Port of a MIDI interface connected to a second computer. Those messages are received by a softsynth running as a standalone application on the second computer, which then generates audio. Since sampling is one of the dominant ways of electronically producing sound, these standalone softsynths are likely to be samplers.

Frequently, the audio from the softsynth is sent out of its computer through an audio interface to an audio interface connected to the sequencer/DAW's computer.

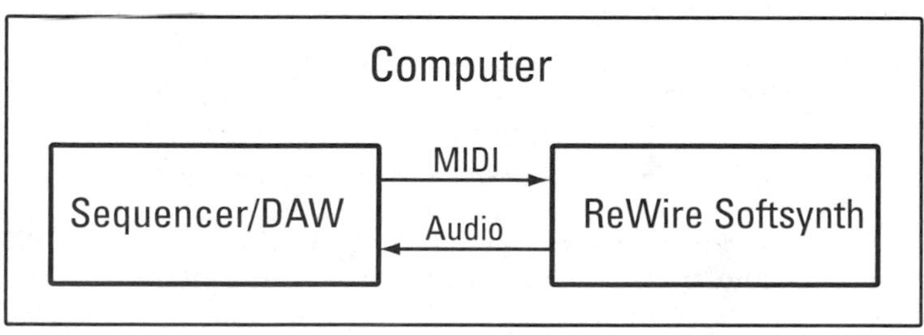

Figure 12.12 Two programs on one computer communicating through ReWire. MIDI messages flow from the ReWire master to the ReWire slave and audio flows back from the ReWire slave to the ReWire master.

This audio can then be mixed and processed in the sequencer/DAW. In this scenario, the computer on which the softsynth is running as a standalone application dedicates its processing power and RAM only to the generation of sound and not to sequencing, mixing or processing, which is taken care of by the first computer. For situations involving a large number of samples or complex sound synthesis that requires a great deal of CPU power, this configuration can be very useful (see Figure 12.13).

Latency

One important factor for all software synths is **latency**. Latency was discussed in Chapter 6, "Digital Audio Software," in the context of audio recording and monitoring. Latency in the context of softsynths refers to how long it takes from the time you press a key on an external controller to the time you hear the sound. For live performance situations or for recording softsynth tracks, this latency must be kept low—it is very difficult to perform properly when the sound is delayed by a perceivable amount. Any delay of more than about 10–15ms is likely to be perceivable, depending on the timbre.

The main source of latency here is the **output buffer** that is set in your sequencer/DAW. Software that plays back audio doesn't send individual samples directly to the DAC, because if a sample is delayed coming from a softsynth it will produce an unpleasant pop or a dropout in the audio. Instead, some number of samples are first stored in an output buffer and then sent to the DAC. Now if a sample is delayed coming from the softsynth, there are other samples ahead of it in the buffer, so the DAC always gets a steady stream of samples. The size of this output buffer determines the delay.

When you're recording softsynth tracks, this buffer has to be small enough for you not to perceive the latency, or at least for it not to bother you. The drawback to small buffer sizes is that your computer has to work harder and thus has less power to devote to audio processing plug-ins and other tasks. As a result, you may want to record softsynth tracks using a small output buffer (low latency) and then raise the buffer size (higher latency) when you're done (see Figure 12.14).

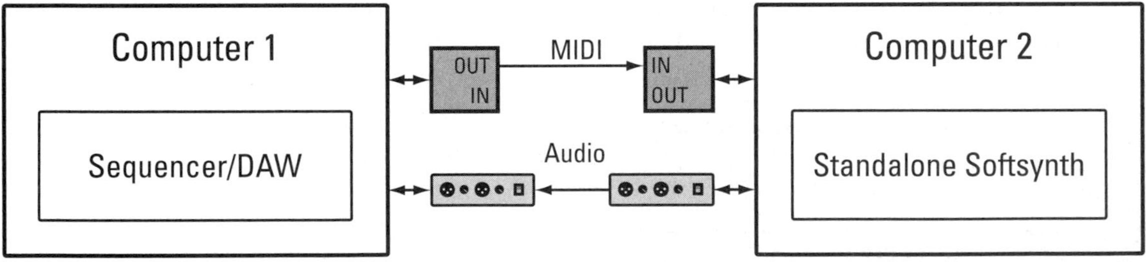

Figure 12.13 Two programs on separate computers. MIDI messages flow from the sequencer/DAW computer to the softsynth computer through MIDI interfaces, and digital audio flows back from the softsynth computer to the sequencer/DAW computer through audio interfaces.

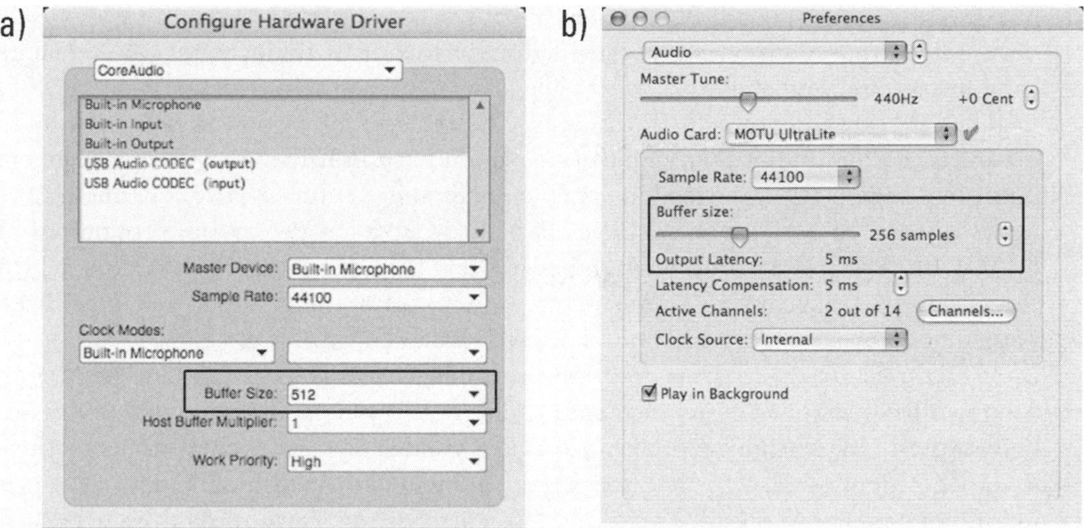

Figure 12.14 Audio configuration windows in (a) Digital Performer 6 (courtesy of MOTU); and (b) Reason 4 (courtesy of Propellerheads). The rectangles highlight the buffer settings.

POLYPHONY AND MULTITIMBRAL CAPACITY

Digital hardware synthesizers are really specialized computers. They have CPUs of sorts that coordinate the receiving and sending of MIDI data, sound generation, and user interaction—just don't try to type a paper on them! Software synthesizers, of course, use the processing power of the host computer's CPU to perform such tasks. While the "power" of a multi-purpose computer is measured either as instructions/operations per second or by benchmarks, the computing power of a synthesizer can be measured by the number of simultaneous notes it can produce and the number of simultaneous timbres that can sound. These two important concepts in electronic sound production are **polyphony**—the ability of a synthesizer to produce more than one voice at a time, and **multitimbral capacity**—the ability of a synthesizer to produce more than one timbre at a time.

The General MIDI (GM) standard discussed in Chapter 9, "MIDI Messages," requires at least 24 voices of polyphony and the newer GM2 standard requires at least 32 voices of polyphony. However, most modern hardware synthesizers have the capacity to produce 64, 128, or more voices simultaneously. This appears at first to allow for as many as 128 notes at once, but "voices" and "notes" are not identical. Depending on the synthesizer and the patch, each note may require two or more voices of polyphony. In practice, you have to learn to listen for notes that cut off unnaturally, notes that play late, or even notes that don't play at all, to tell if you've exceeded your synth's polyphony.

Softsynths don't necessarily have a fixed polyphony, since their polyphony is based on the available CPU power. This gives softsynths more flexibility to take up only the CPU power that is needed at a given moment in the music. Demanding software setups, though, can quickly tax a CPU, particularly if the computer is a laptop or a modestly powered desktop. Such situations have led some to run their softsynths on a separate computer as discussed above.

The GM1 and 2 standards discussed in Chapter 9 require compatible synths to be at least 16-part multitimbral (16 simultaneous timbres). Most hardware synthesizers adhere to this standard and don't exceed it, largely because this is sufficient to allow one timbre on each of the 16 MIDI channels that can be addressed across one cable connected to the MIDI In Port. There are a few synthesizers that have more than one In Port, which allows them to have more simultaneous timbres, and there are a few specialized synthesizers that allow for only one or a few simultaneous timbres.

While software synthesizers do not have to adhere to the same numeric limitations in terms of the number of simultaneous timbres (16), most still retain the vestiges of their hardware incarnations. For example, when you load a multitimbral softsynth plug-in into a sequencer/DAW, it often shows up with 16 available channels (16-part multitimbral) and you must load another "instance" of the software synth to get access to another 16 channels.

REVIEW OF KEY TERMS

synthesis 198
algorithm 198
sampling/sampler 198
oscillator 199
filter 199
amplifier 199
wavetable synthesis 200
noise 200
white/pink noise 200
pitch 201
low pass filter 202
cutoff frequency 202
resonance 202
ADSR envelope 203
attack/decay/sustain/release 203
gating/triggering 204
modulation 205
direct control 205
envelope 205
low frequency oscillator (LFO) 205
waveform/rate/depth 207
vibrato 207
wah-wah 207
tremolo 207
host application 210
plug-in formats 210
AU/DXi/VSTi/RTAS 210
plug-in wrappers 210
ReWire 210
ReWire master/slave 211
standalone mode 211
latency 212
output buffer 212
polyphony 213
multitimbral capacity 213

CHAPTER 13

Synthesis Methods

In the basic synthesis model described in the last chapter, the oscillator is responsible for generating the initial sound from a small collection of basic waveforms such as sine, triangle, sawtooth, square, and pulse. While this is a good starting point, we would soon grow tired of just those few basic sounds. Fortunately, there are a great many methods, or **algorithms**, for synthesizing sounds that can produce a wide array of interesting and unusual timbres. There are too many algorithms to cover in detail here, so this chapter will examine a collection of algorithms that demonstrates the variety of approaches that can be taken to synthesizing sound.

WAVETABLE SYNTHESIS

We've already seen fixed waveform **wavetable synthesis** at work in the oscillator of the basic synthesis model in the previous chapter. To create a sound in this manner, a synthesizer starts with one cycle of some waveform stored in memory. This single cycle need not be one of the basic waveforms that have been discussed so far; a single cycle of any shape will do. As we learned in Chapter 2, "Sound Properties and the Waveform View," the shape of the waveform determines its timbre, so we can generate a different timbre simply by using a different stored shape. To generate a particular frequency using the stored waveform, the synthesizer repeats the waveform over and over at that frequency: to create sound with a frequency of 440 Hz, the synthesizer repeats the stored waveform 440 times per second (see Figure 13.1).

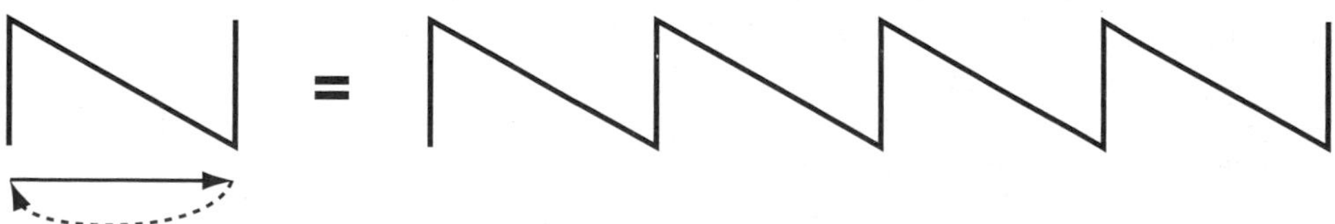

Figure 13.1 Wavetable synthesis: a single cycle of a waveform (sawtooth) is looped at a rate equal to the desired fundamental frequency to produce a basic timbre.

Fixed waveform wavetable synthesis is a very efficient method of producing sound, requiring very little processing power and very little memory. It was historically used in devices that didn't have much memory, such as synthesizers built into computer soundcards. It is now primarily found in the oscillators of analog-modeling synthesizers, both hardware and software.

The drawback to fixed waveform wavetable synthesis is that, from the beginning of the note to the end of the note, the timbre stays the same—the spectrum is static. One way of alleviating this static character is to utilize a filter and amplifier along with direct control, envelopes, and LFOs, discussed in the previous chapter under "Dynamic Sound" (pages 205–207).

ADDITIVE SYNTHESIS

Additive synthesis is an algorithm in which many simple waveforms are added together to produce a complex timbre (see Figure 13.2). At the heart of additive synthesis is the sine wave. As you recall from the discussion of basic waveforms and their spectra in Chapter 3, "The Overtone Series and the Spectrum View," a sine wave has only one partial in its spectrum. In order to build a complex spectrum consisting of many partials, each with its own frequency and amplitude, an additive synthesizer uses one sine wave for each of the partials and then adds all of those sine waves together. The resultant spectrum now has all of the desired partials with the correct amplitudes.

Additive synthesis is also known as **Fourier synthesis** after the nineteenth-century French mathematician, Jean Baptiste Joseph Fourier. Fourier proposed that any periodic function, such as a waveform produced by a musical instrument, could be expressed as a sum of sine waves given appropriate frequencies and amplitudes (the actual theory is somewhat more involved than this). In theory, additive synthesis can perfectly re-create any periodic sound for which we have the necessary data for all of the partials. In practice that is a tremendous amount of data. Not only does each partial change in amplitude

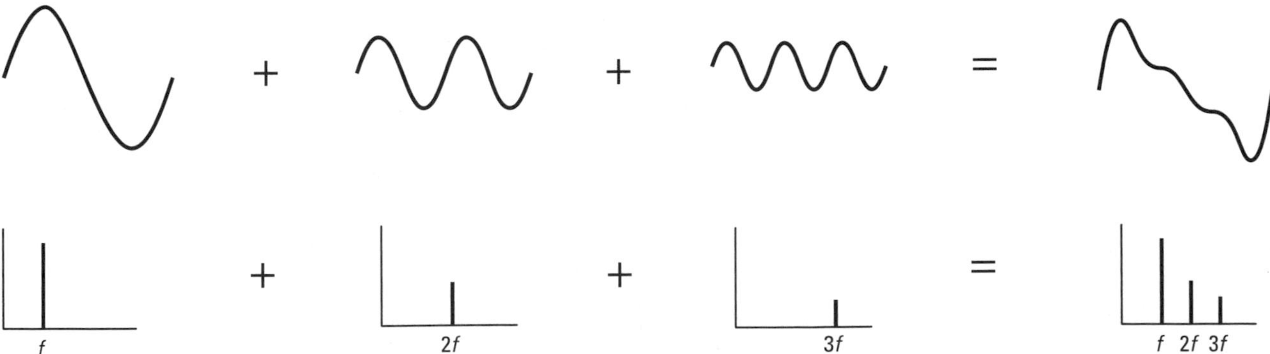

Figure 13.2 Waveform and spectrum view of three sine waves adding together to form a more complex waveform. If enough partials are added in these proportions, a sawtooth wave will be formed.

over the course of a note, but it may also change in frequency, and start with a different phase than the other partials. To perfectly re-create a sound, the synthesizer would have to have all of that data for each partial of a note at each point during the course of a note—and that's just for one timbre!

In addition to the problem of needing tremendous amounts of data, additive synthesis is also computationally intensive. It can require dozens of oscillators producing sine waves to create the spectrum generated by one wavetable oscillator. On the plus side, additive synthesis can generate new timbres that change in interesting ways over time.

Because of the large amount of data necessary and the required computational power, additive synthesis has not been a common synthesis technique in commercial hardware or software synths. However, there have been a few additive hardware synths over the years and there are a number of softsynth plug-ins available that utilize this technique or a variant of it.

Additive Synthesis Example

Throughout this chapter, we will see examples of software synths that utilize the synthesis technique under discussion. This is not meant to be an endorsement of these products. They were chosen because they represent clear examples of the synthesis techniques—there are likely to be other software synths or hardware synths that perform similar functions. (Links to other software or hardware synths that utilize these synthesis techniques are available on the book's website.)

Ideally, an additive synthesizer would give you control over the frequency, amplitude, and phase of each partial. Most synths that utilize additive synthesis create a limited implementation of it to make the task of creating and modifying patches less daunting. For example, Spectra by Kjaerhus Audio restricts the partials to integer multiples of the fundamental (following the overtone series). Figure 13.3 shows Spectra's "Harmony Inspector," where you can choose the amplitude for each harmonic partial. Despite the fact that the partials necessarily lie in the overtone series, you can create many unusual timbres through unique combinations of partials.

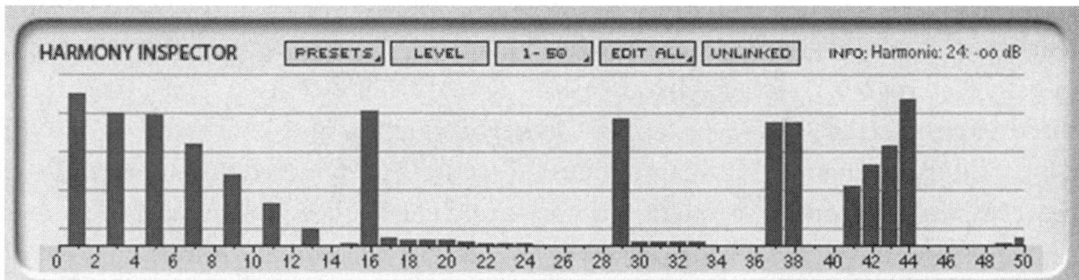

Figure 13.3 The "Harmony Inspector" from the Spectra softsynth allows the user to control independently the amplitude for each partial in the overtone series. (Courtesy of Kjaerhus Audio)

SUBTRACTIVE SYNTHESIS

Subtractive synthesis is an algorithm that produces sound by subtracting frequencies from an already "rich" spectrum. A rich spectrum simply means that there are many partials in the initial waveform. A buzzy sawtooth waveform is a good candidate for subtractive synthesis, as is noise. We've already discussed the components of a synthesizer that remove portions of a spectrum: **filters**. In fact the basic synthesis model that was discussed in the last chapter can be considered a "subtractive" model, which is typical of analog-modeling synthesis.

Filter Types

The **low pass filter** with **resonance** that was discussed in the last chapter is the most commonly used filter in analog-modeling synths, but there are several others that are also common in subtractive synthesis.

A **high pass filter** is the opposite of a low pass filter. The high pass filter passes the frequencies above the **cutoff frequency** and cuts the frequencies below the cutoff frequency. Where a low pass filter changes the brightness of a sound from bright to dark as its cutoff frequency is lowered, a high pass filter removes the "body" of a sound as its cutoff frequency is raised, leaving only the higher partials. A high pass filter in a synth can also have a resonance parameter that behaves in a similar manner to the resonance of a low pass filter.

A **band pass filter** allows only a range, or band, of frequencies to pass, and cuts frequencies outside of this band. The band pass filter is different from the peaking EQ discussed in Chapter 6, "Digital Audio Software," because a peaking filter passes frequencies outside the peaking band with no change and a band pass filter cuts frequencies outside the pass band. The key parameters for a band pass filter are the **center frequency** and the **bandwidth**. The bandwidth determines the size of the range of frequencies that are passed and the center frequency positions that pass band in the frequency spectrum. A bandpass filter with a narrow bandwidth can pick out individual partials of a sound as the center frequency changes. If the center frequency is "swept," or moved across the spectrum, with a small bandwidth, it can create a glassy, otherworldly sound.

A **band stop filter**, also called a **notch filter**, allows all frequencies to pass through without change *except* for a narrow band of frequencies that is cut. A band stop filter has the same parameters as a band pass filter: center frequency and bandwidth. As with the band pass filter, the bandwidth can be altered to affect a wider or smaller range of frequencies. When the center frequency of the band stop filter is swept, the timbre changes subtly depending on which partials are being cut or partially cut.

These four filter types—low pass, high pass, band pass, and band stop/notch—are the simplest models for filters used in synthesizers (see Figure 13.4). Many analog-modeling synths use these directly and may allow them to be combined in parallel or in series ("cascaded"). Other synths may use filters whose pass and cut characteristics are quite complicated. Nevertheless, these filters provide a good foundation for understanding other, more complex filters.

The Voice Model

Noisy and buzzy sounds shaped by filters can serve as a good model for the most common of sounds: speech. Physically, we produce speech by forcing air through our vocal folds that then open and close as described in Chapter 1, "What is Sound?" The sound produced by this process is essentially a buzz.

That buzzy waveform proceeds through a series of chambers including the throat, mouth, and nasal cavity (see Figure 13.5). The sizes and shapes of these chambers alter the spectrum of the buzzy sound and create the basic timbre of our voices, just as the barrel and bell of a clarinet and the sound box of a violin create the basic timbres of those instruments. In other words, these chambers in our bodies filter the buzz produced by our vocal folds—we are all living, breathing subtractive synthesizers!

Different vowel sounds are produced by slightly different configurations of our throat, mouth, and nasal cavities. Each of these cavities creates a peak in the spectrum, called a **formant**, whose position and amplitude changes as we move our mouth and throat

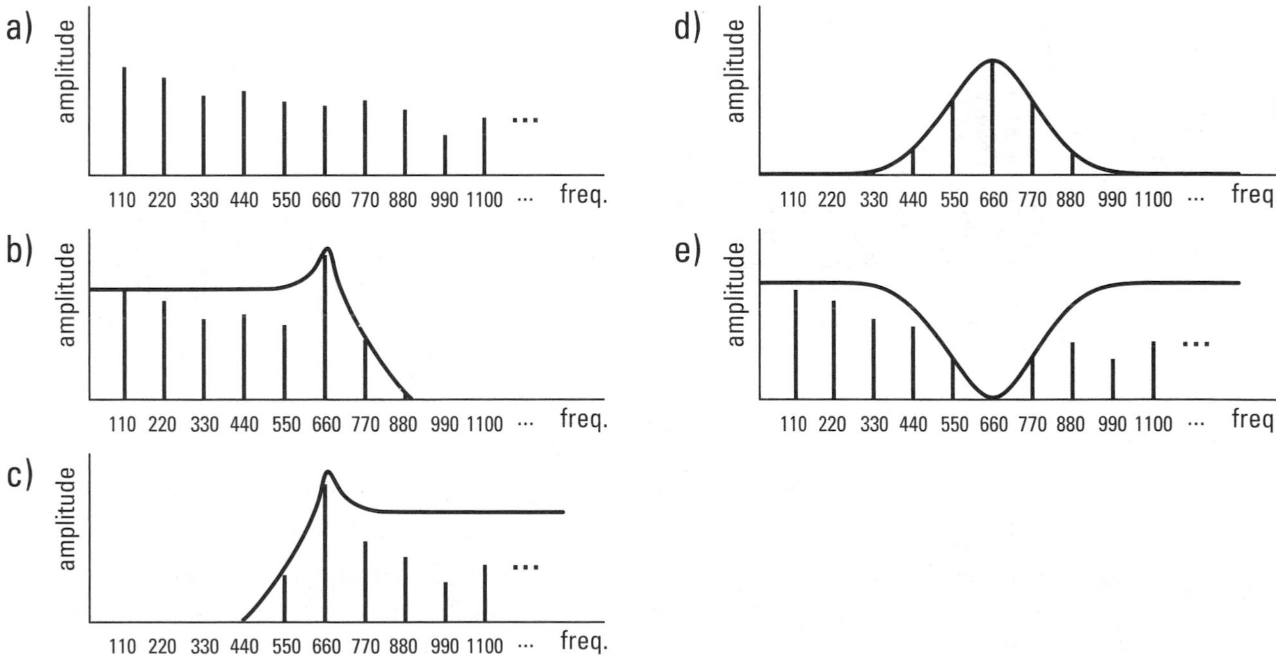

Figure 13.4 The effect of various filter types on a spectrum: (a) original spectrum, (b) low pass filter with resonance, (c) high pass filter with resonance, (d) band pass filter, and (e) band stop, or notch, filter.

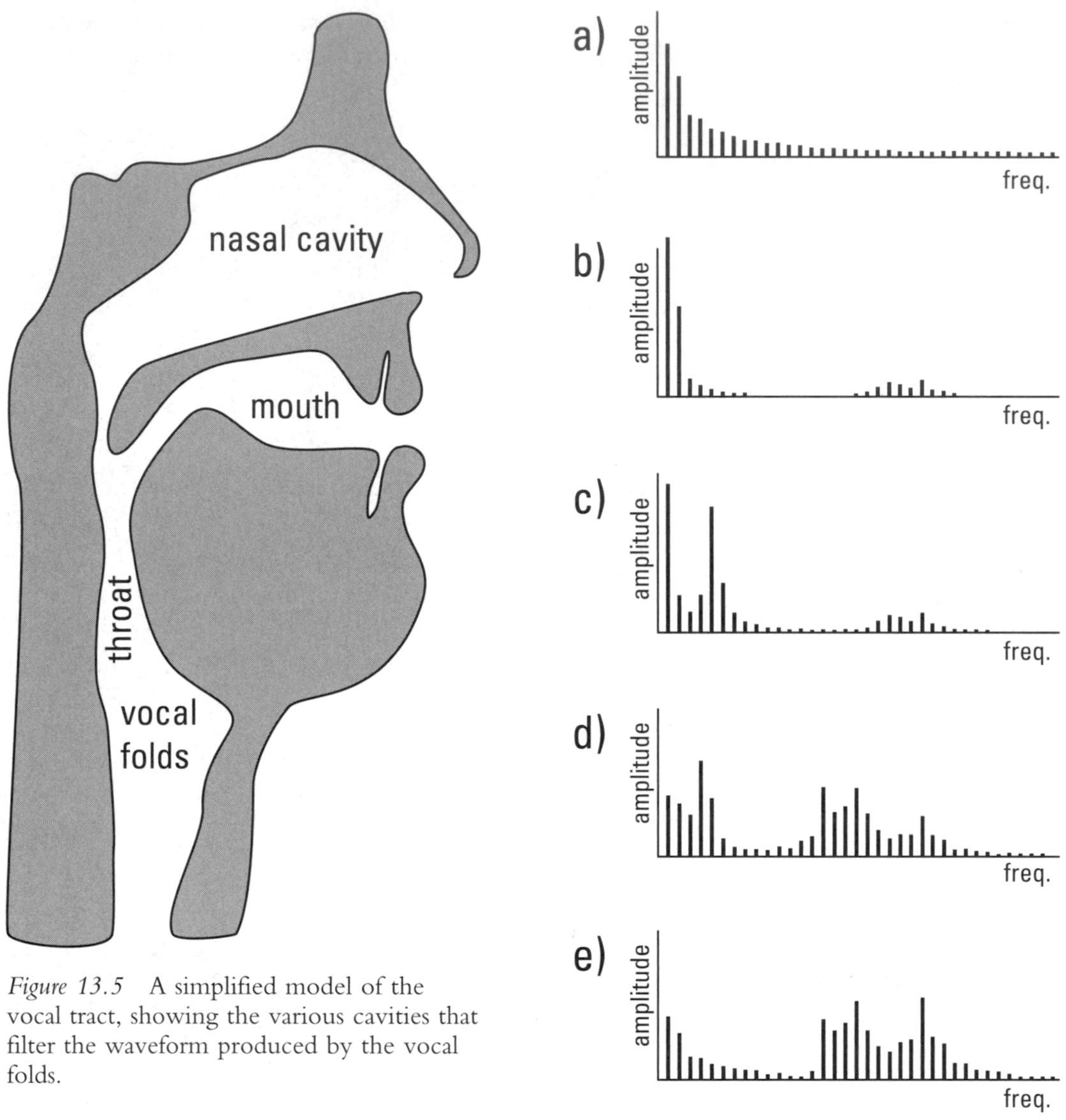

Figure 13.5 A simplified model of the vocal tract, showing the various cavities that filter the waveform produced by the vocal folds.

Figure 13.6 A sawtooth wave processed by the formant filter in Reason's Thor synthesizer: (a) unchanged sawtooth, and (b) through (e) various filter settings that yield progressively brighter vowel-like spectra.

to make different sounds: each vowel that we speak has unique formant locations and amplitudes. A spectrogram of various vowels can be seen in Figure 3.3 (page 39). Figure 13.6 shows the spectra that result from a simulation of the vocal tract using a sawtooth wave and a formant filter from the Thor synthesizer in Propellerheads' Reason softsynth rack. Notice that each setting results in a different shape to the spectrum, reflecting the different formant locations and amplitudes.

Talk Boxes and Vocoders

Subtractive filtering based on the human voice can be found in two applications from popular music: the guitar talk box and the vocoder. The **guitar talk box** has been used prominently by such rock guitarists as Peter Frampton ("Show Me The Way"), Joe Perry of Aerosmith ("Sweet Emotion"), and Joe Walsh ("Rocky Mountain Way"). The technique involves taking the output of an amplifier and connecting it to a device that consists of a small speaker (a compression driver) connected to a tube, which is run up a mic stand and positioned next to a microphone. The performer then places the tube in his or her mouth and changes the shape of their mouth, neck, and nasal cavities as if talking while playing the guitar. The spectrum of the guitar sound is shaped by those cavities and then picked up by the microphone.

A **vocoder** processes signals by applying the spectrum of one audio signal to another. In this respect a vocoder is similar to the talk box in that the spectrum of the one signal (the voice) is applied to another signal (the guitar). The signal providing the spectrum in a vocoder is referred to as the modulator and the signal being shaped is referred to as the carrier. In many vocoder applications, the modulator is a live voice or a soundfile of a voice that is split up by the vocoder into some number of frequency bands. The changing amount of energy from the modulator in each of the frequency bands is then applied to the carrier sound. A common carrier sound is one with a rich spectrum such as a synthesizer pad. The synthesizer pad is then made to "talk" by the vocoder.

Subtractive Synthesis Example

Any synthesizer that includes a filter can be considered subtractive, such as the examples presented at the end of the last chapter, so we'll focus on a vocoder example instead.

The BV512 vocoder that is part of Propellerheads' Reason is shown in Figure 13.7. The screen labeled "modulation levels" shows the instantaneous amplitude levels for each of the 16 frequency bands that the modulator signal was split into. The back panel

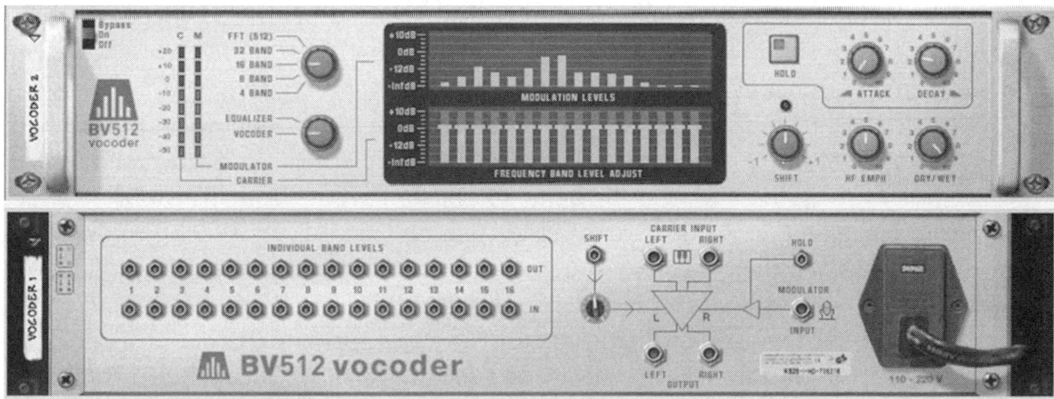

Figure 13.7 The BV512 vocoder from Propellerheads' Reason. (Courtesy of Propellerheads, Inc.)

allows you to connect a stereo carrier input and a mono modulator input. The carrier input could come from any one of Reason's synth modules (such as the Maelström or Thor synthesizers). To use a voice recording as the modulator, one of Reason's sample playback modules—the NN-19 or NN-XT—is used.

FREQUENCY MODULATION

In additive and subtractive synthesis, the algorithms involve direct construction (or deconstruction) of the desired spectrum. In additive synthesis, each new sine wave adds a partial to the spectrum, while in subtractive synthesis filters emphasize or de-emphasize a portion of the spectrum. In contrast, in **frequency modulation**, or **FM**, synthesis the components of the algorithm interact in a more complex way to produce the resultant spectrum.

FM synthesis is closely related to vibrato. To create vibrato on a musical instrument, you periodically raise and lower the pitch being played. A violinist accomplishes this by shaking the finger stopping the string, thereby periodically increasing and decreasing the length of the string. A trombonist accomplishes this by moving the slide back and forth, thereby periodically increasing and decreasing the length of the air column.

In normal vibrato, the speed of the vibrato is slow relative to the frequency of the pitch being played. A normal instrumental or vocal vibrato is in the range of 5–8 Hz, whereas the pitch being played is typically in the hundreds of hertz (remember, the "tuning A" is 440 Hz). In synth terms, the performer is "modulating" the pitch (frequency). In a synthesizer, this modulation would be handled by an LFO as discussed under "Dynamic Sound" in the previous chapter (see pages 205–207).

However, if the vibrato rate increases from the normal instrumental/vocal vibrato rate into the audible range, above 20 Hz, we stop hearing the modulation as vibrato and instead hear a new timbre. FM synthesis, then, is generated by one oscillator modulating the frequency of another oscillator, with this modulation taking place above 20 Hz. The frequencies of the partials in this new timbre are determined by the **carrier frequency**, which is the frequency of the oscillator that is being modulated, and the **modulating frequency**, which is the frequency of the oscillator doing the modulation. The modulating frequency would be called the vibrato rate if the frequency were below the audible range. It is important to note that the carrier and modulator are different in FM than they are in a vocoder even though the same words are being used.

Sounds produced by FM can be quite bright and range from harmonic to very inharmonic. Because FM was able to produce such rich sounds with such simple means (only two oscillators), the Yamaha Corporation licensed the technology from Stanford University in the 1970s and eventually released the FM-based Yamaha DX7 in 1983. The DX7 used six separate oscillators in various configurations rather than the two described above. The DX7 was one of the first inexpensive digital synthesizers (around $2,000) and came out at just about the same time as MIDI and the personal computer. The confluence of these three innovations helped to fuel the growth of the electronic musical instrument and music software industries in the 1980s and fostered the widespread use of music technology in schools and private homes.

In the simple version of FM, where one oscillator is frequency modulating another, the resultant spectrum contains partials, referred to as **sidebands**, which are spaced out on either side of the primary frequency, called the carrier frequency. The spacing of the partials is determined by the modulating frequency. The number of partials on either side of the carrier frequency is determined by the depth of the "vibrato," which is used to calculate a parameter called the **index of modulation**. To create a timbre with some number of partials spaced out by a certain amount, the synthesizer programmer has to determine the carrier frequency, the modulating frequency, and the index of modulation.

Figure 13.8 shows the spectrum produced by a single modulator and a single carrier. The carrier frequency is indicated by f_c and the modulating frequency is indicated by f_m. As a result of the frequency modulation process, partials are produced above and below the carrier that are f_m Hz apart. The index of modulation here produces three sidebands above the carrier and three sidebands below the carrier. If f_c and f_m are chosen carefully, the partials can end up being whole-number multiples of a fundamental, resulting in a harmonic spectrum. In Figure 13.8, an f_c of 440 Hz and an f_m of 110 Hz produce sidebands that form an overtone series with a fundamental of 110 Hz. As you can see, this is a very different way of creating a spectrum than additive or subtractive synthesis. With more oscillators, very complex spectra can be generated.

The advantages of FM synthesis over synthesis algorithms prior to its development included its ability to create complex timbres whose spectra changed over the course of a note with a minimum of processing power. FM can create a spectrum with two oscillators that would require more than a dozen oscillators in additive synthesis. FM also gives you the ability to create sounds that not only change in brightness, but also change from one timbre to another, by altering the relationship between the carrier and modulating frequencies.

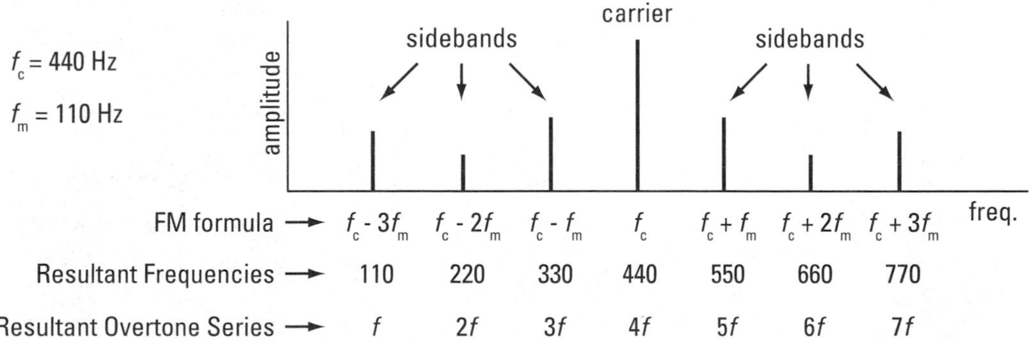

Figure 13.8 The harmonic spectrum that results from simple FM, where the carrier frequency is 440 Hz and the modulating frequency is 110 Hz and the value of the index of modulation causes three sidebands to be generated on each side of the carrier frequency.

Frequency Modulation Synthesis Example

Though the hey-day of frequency modulation has passed, FM lives on as an additional sound design technique in software and hardware synthesizers or as the primary technique in a few specialized softsynths. The most prominent of the specialized softsynths is Native Instruments' FM8, the first version of which was called FM7 as a link to the DX7. FM8 is a fully realized six-operator (oscillator) FM synth.

Figure 13.9 shows the spectrum/waveform view from FM8 that is available as one of the "expert" views. FM8 has several other views, including an "Easy/Morph" page that allows you to manipulate intuitive parameters without delving into the depths of FM programming. The rightmost section of Figure 13.9 shows the six operators, labeled A through F, plus two "special-case" operators, X and Z, that allow for processing not available on the original FM synths. A patch is formed from the interconnection of these operators. In the figure, operators B and F are ultimately carriers (though carriers can modulate other operators) and connect to the audio output. The other operators act as modulators. The operators can be controlled by envelopes in another of the expert views, which allows you to create timbres that vary dynamically over time.

The middle section of Figure 13.9 shows the spectrum (top) and the waveform (bottom) of the resulting timbre. As you can see, this particular arrangement of operators creates quite a dense and complex spectrum.

PHYSICAL MODELING

The goal of each of the previous synthesis techniques is to create a specific spectrum resulting in the desired timbre. **Physical modeling synthesis**, on the other hand, seeks

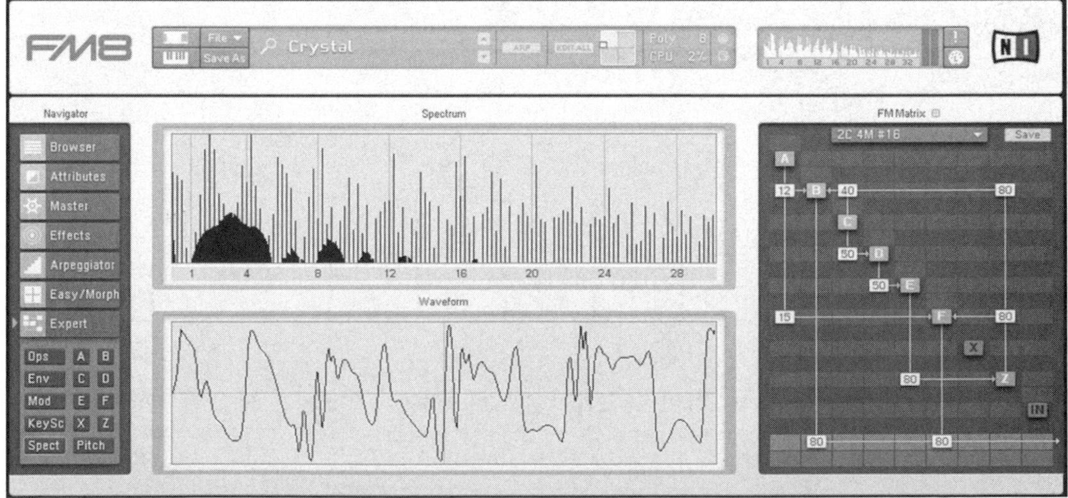

Figure 13.9 The spectrum expert view in Native Instruments' FM8 softsynth, showing the arrangement of the operators as well as the resultant spectrum and waveform. (Courtesy of Native Instruments GmbH, Germany)

to mathematically re-create, or model, the physical mechanism by which an instrument produces sound with the hope that the mathematical result of that modeling process will be closely related to the sonic result of playing the actual instrument. In the end, the desired spectrum is produced, but almost as a "side effect" of the modeling process.

The idea behind physical modeling is that each individual part of an instrument is modeled mathematically and the results are fed into the next part. For example, to model a clarinet, one would first model the behavior of the mouthpiece—a flexible reed with air blowing across it. The mathematical result of the mouthpiece would then serve as the input to a model of the barrel of the clarinet, which in turn would serve as input to a model of the bell. Each element influences the next, but may also change the behavior of the previous element, making the model more complex. In the case of a clarinet, the characteristics of the barrel and the fingering actually determine the frequency of the reed's vibration.

There are a variety of techniques for modeling instruments, such as digital waveguide synthesis, that use common digital signal processing functions such as delay lines and filters. These methods depart somewhat from the pure modeling of an instrument's physical behavior, but they have the advantage of taking much less computing power to calculate.

Figure 13.10 shows a simplified model of a clarinet consisting of two elements: an excitation source and a resonator. The complex signal from the reed/mouthpiece element is passed to a resonator that represents the barrel. The barrel element provides feedback to the reed/mouthpiece element, which models the actual behavior of the clarinet, where the length of the air column in the barrel determines the pitch produced by the mouthpiece.

Even with these simplifications, the inputs to a physical model are intuitive physical characteristics such as breath pressure, the stiffness of the reed, and the length of the barrel. The output of the physical model is similar to the original instrument and the

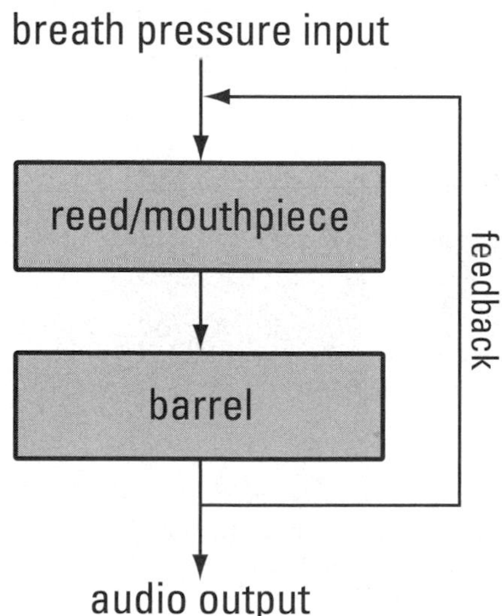

Figure 13.10 A simplified physical model of a clarinet consisting of an excitation source, a resonator, and feedback between the elements. (McIntyre, Schumacher, and Woodhouse, 1983, adapted from *The Computer Music Tutorial* by Curtis Roads, 1996, courtesy of The MIT Press)

model responds to inputs such as breath pressure in a manner similar to the instrument. Having direct control over physical aspects of an instrument model can yield not just accurate re-creations, but also unusual new creations, such as a clarinet with a 20-foot barrel or a plucked marimba.

Physical modeling's primary disadvantage in its pure form is that it requires quite a bit of processing power to perform the necessary calculations in real time. It wasn't until the development of simplified, computationally efficient methods that physical modeling became practical. Even then, only a few hardware synthesizers, such as the VL series that Yamaha released in the 1990s, adopted physical modeling as their primary sound generation method, and those synthesizers could only play one or two notes at a time. Like FM, physical modeling has found a second life in software.

Physical Modeling Synthesis Example

There are several softsynths that use physical modeling as their primary synthesis technique. Some support multiple physical models that can be combined in various ways, while others model just one type of instrument, such as strings. Among the more flexible of the physical modeling softsynths is Applied Acoustics Systems' Tassman, which allows you to build your model from a variety of generators and resonators.

Apple's Sculpture softsynth, which comes with their sequencer/DAW Logic Pro, uses a physical model of a string as its basis (see Figure 13.11). You can choose the material for the string itself with a two-dimensional virtual "pad" that allows you to mix four materials: steel, nylon, wood, and glass. This pad alters the stiffness of the string and the amount of damping due to the material of the string. Damping is a measurement of how quickly the string stops "ringing" after it is plucked. You can also choose an amount of damping due to the medium in which the string vibrates.

Once you've selected the material of the string and the way it vibrates, you choose the way that the string is excited, such as being plucked, struck, or bowed. There are three "objects" that can excite the string or disturb it while it's vibrating at variable positions along its length. The objects have "strength" factors that determine how they affect the string. Another physical element that can be controlled is the positioning of

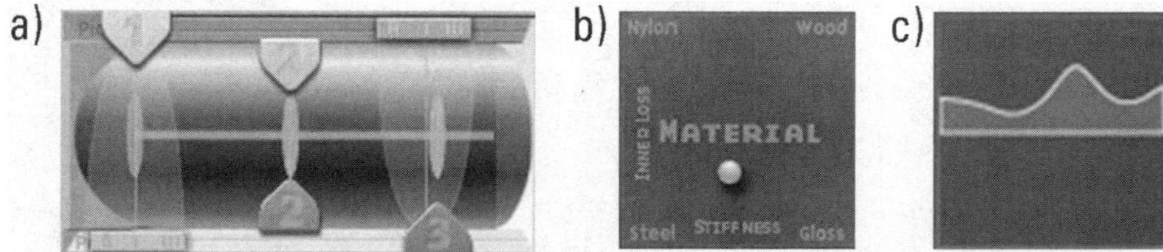

Figure 13.11 Elements from Apple's Sculpture physical modeling softsynth: (a) excitation of a modeled string by up to three objects numbered 1, 2, and 3, with two movable "pickups" labeled A and B; (b) the material pad for choosing the string material; and (c) the result of the body resonance controls on the spectrum. (Screenshot reprinted with permission from Apple Inc.)

two virtual "pickups." This affects the resultant timbre just as the position of the pickups on an electric guitar does. The relationship of the pickup positions to the positions of the exciting objects also has a strong influence on the sound. The output of the sound is further modified by the "Body EQ," which acts as a resonating body similar to the sound box of a guitar or violin.

GRANULAR SYNTHESIS AND GRANULAR PROCESSING

Granular synthesis is an unusual synthesis technique in which an overall sound is constructed out of a large number of short bursts of sound called grains. A grain of sound at its simplest consists of an enveloped waveform of very short duration, approximately 5 to 50 milliseconds. To get a sense of how short this is, a 32nd note at quarter note equals 120 and is about 63ms long. By itself a grain sounds like a small "pop," but with a density that might reach thousands of grains per second, a granular "cloud" can sound like an avalanche of sound.

There are a great many varieties of granular synthesis that can be obtained by changing the grain itself—the waveform, the frequency of the waveform, the length of the grain, the shape of the envelope—and by changing the way the grains are arrayed in time—the density of the grains, the regularity or irregularity of their occurrence, and so on. Granular clouds can sound like anything from a gritty, irregular noise mass ("asynchronous" granular synthesis) to a decent imitation of the human voice ("synchronous" granular synthesis and FOF synthesis). Granular synthesis can be a processor-intensive activity requiring the generation of up to hundreds or thousands of particles of sound per second.

Figure 13.12a shows the basic anatomy of a grain with a waveform of some shape and frequency enclosed in a short envelope. Figure 13.12b presents a possible grain cloud in which many grains are arrayed in a variety of ways in pitch and time. Different shades of the grains represent different waveforms. In this cloud, a few sparse grains become denser and more widely spaced in pitch until they separate into three coherent

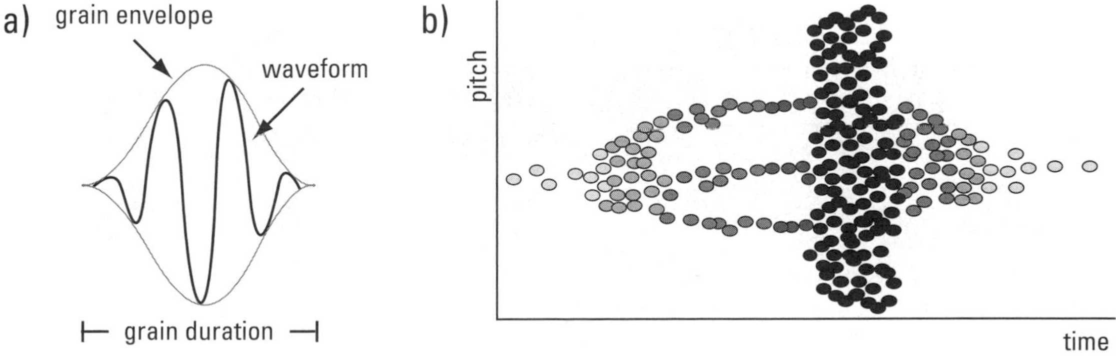

Figure 13.12 (a) An individual grain, and (b) a cloud of grains showing a variety of shapes over time.

strands. The strands are interrupted by a dense collection of grains that soon thin out back to the original few sparse grains. Even with these few parameters, the number of possible grain clouds is enormous and varied.

Granular techniques can also be used for processing soundfiles or live sound. In **granular processing**, the sound to be granulated is cut up into grains by multiplying successive portions of the sound by the same granular envelopes described above. As the sample is "granulated," the grains can be played more slowly or more quickly, thereby time-stretching/compressing the sound without changing the pitch, and the bits of sound within the grains can be sped up or slowed down, thereby pitch-shifting the sound without changing the time relationship of the grains to each other. At the same time, the quality of the sound can be changed in remarkable ways by altering the density of the grains and introducing randomness into the placement of the grains in time.

Granular Processing Example

There are many pieces of software that implement granular synthesis and/or granular processing, though only a few are part of commercial software packages.

Native Instruments' Reaktor is a programmable synthesis environment in which you can build synthesizers and processors from individual modules (it also has many "pre-built" synths). Reaktor has an environment for choosing modules and creating connections between them as well as an interface, or panel, view that lets you change parameters with knobs and sliders.

Reaktor's "Grain Cloud" module processes stored samples using granular techniques. Figure 13.13 shows the performance panel of Reaktor's "Grain Osc" instrument, which utilizes the Grain Cloud module. This panel allows the user to manipulate parameters

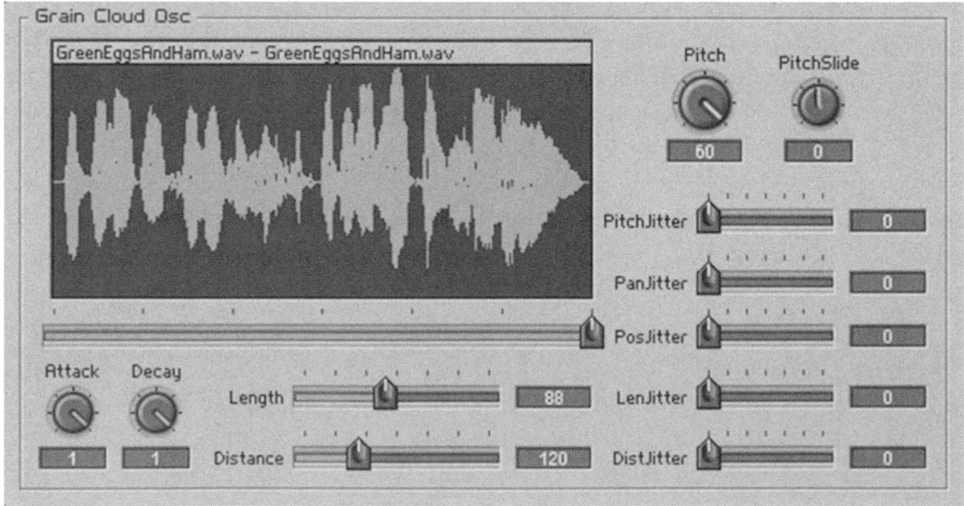

Figure 13.13 The panel view of the Grain Osc instrument in Reaktor. (Courtesy of Native Instruments GmbH, Germany)

of the grain and the grain cloud, including pitch, grain length, the distance between grains, and the position of the grains in the soundfile. For each of these parameters, there are corresponding "jitter" parameters that allow those values to be randomized to varying degrees. It's this jitter that allows the cloud of grains to vary so widely in texture from a focused stream to an incoherent mass.

. . . AND MANY MORE

There are many other synthesis techniques that have been used in the past, are currently in use in commercial and non-commercial hardware and software, or are being developed and tested by researchers in commercial and academic settings. The important thing to understand when encountering a new synth is that each synthesis algorithm has a particular way of generating sound with parameters that can be controlled by composers and performers. With that mindset, each new synth becomes an opportunity to explore new ways of creating and controlling sound that can contribute to your musical goals. In addition, many new synths utilize existing synthesis techniques that are repackaged with new features or a new interface, so understanding the basic synthesis model from the last chapter and the synthesis techniques from this chapter can help you when you encounter something new.

NON-COMMERCIAL SOFTWARE SYNTHESIZERS

The examples of synthesis techniques in action presented above have been drawn from commercially available software synthesizers. However, there are a great number of software synthesizers available that are freeware or shareware. Some of this software is the result of a programmer's hobby and some is a result of academic research. Other software got its start in an academic or personal setting and has since become an open source project that is contributed to by a large group of people. These types of software are not backed by a company, don't come with tech support, and are often not available as plug-ins to a standard sequencer/DAW. However, they are often quite stable, very powerful, free, and have substantial user communities.

Some of the synthesis methods discussed above that are sparsely represented in commercial software, such as granular synthesis, are widely available in non-commercial software, and many of these packages can be programmed to use almost any type of synthesis. For some of them, the operative word is "program." While few require writing code in a language as complex as C++ or even Java, most require more effort to realize a synthesis algorithm than is needed to set sliders and knobs in a commercial softsynth. However, with a little extra effort, these synths can generate exciting, surprising, and unique results.

The program **Csound**, created by Barry Vercoe at MIT in the 1980s, is a direct descendant of the first computer music program written at Bell Labs in the 1950s. Csound is now maintained and augmented by a community of programmers as free, open source software.

Csound utilizes two user-created text files or one file that combines the two. The "orchestra" file consists of lines of text that represent "unit generators" and their interconnections. Unit generators are functions that create audio or control signals such as oscillators, LFOs, and envelopes. These lines of text are grouped into "instruments," and there can be many different instruments in the orchestra file.

The "score" file consists of note start times, durations, pitches, and other data that are linked to parameters in the orchestra file. The Csound program takes these two text files and generates a soundfile. This style of "compiling" a soundfile from two data files reveals Csound's origins in a non-real-time computing environment in which compiling one second of sound could take considerably longer than one second. In recent years, various programmers have created real-time versions of Csound in which the score is replaced by real-time control such as MIDI.

Figure 13.14a shows an excerpt from a Csound orchestra file. Everything after a semicolon is a comment and will not be interpreted by Csound. The first two lines (excluding the comment lines) assign parameters (p4 and p5) from the score file to variable names. The third line utilizes the "linen" unit generator to create a linear envelope that rises over 50ms to the amplitude specified in the score (iamp), sustains at that level, and then falls to zero over 200ms. The total duration for the note is determined by a parameter in the score (p3). The next line utilizes the "oscil" unit generator to create a repeating waveform with an envelope defined by the previous line (kenv), a frequency specified in the score (icps), and a waveform defined by a function specified in the score (f1). The next line utilizes the "moogladder" unit generator to filter the waveform created in the previous line (aosc) with a cutoff frequency of 1760 Hz and a resonance value of 0.9. The final line sends the filtered signal (ares) to the left and right output channels.

Figure 13.14b shows a simple Csound score file for use with the orchestra in 13.14a. The first line (excluding the comment lines) defines a function (f1) that is a sum of sine waves with relative amplitudes of 1, 0.5, 0.33, 0.25, etc. The next line is a note statement directed to instrument 1 (i1), that starts at time 0, is 5 seconds long, has a peak amplitude of 25,000 (the full range is 32,767), and a frequency of 220 Hz. This score is compiled along with the orchestra file by Csound to produce an audio file.

The example in Figure 13.14 is extremely simple and is meant to relate Csound's functions to familiar synthesis functions found in other softsynths. Csound has a tremendous variety of unit generators that can be used to realize essentially *any* synthesis algorithm, including additive, subtractive, frequency modulation, granular synthesis, physical modeling, scanned synthesis, wave terrain synthesis, phase vocoding, and linear predictive coding. Its power lies in that extreme flexibility. (The book's website contains links to more powerful Csound examples and other Csound resources.)

Other programs that utilize the unit generator concept include James McCartney's SuperCollider (free/open source), RTcmix, written originally as CMIX by Paul Lansky (free/open source), and Roger Dannenberg's Nyquist (free/open source). Supercollider and RTcmix in particular are specifically designed for real-time usage. In addition, both

a)
```
; basic parameters from score
iamp      = p4            ; amp is 0 to 32,767
icps      = p5            ; freq in Hz

; simple amplitude envelope
kenv      linen           iamp, .05, p3, .2

; oscillator - envelope, freq, waveform table
aosc      oscil           kenv, icps, 1

; low pass filter - signal, cutoff freq, resonance
ares      moogladder      aosc, 1760, .9

; output of instrument, same signal left and right
          outs            ares, ares
```

b)
```
; sawtooth wave with 10 partials

f1 0 1024 10 1 .5 .33 .25 .2 .17 .14 .13 .11 .1

; play a note
; Note parameters:
;    1. inst #
;    2. start time
;    3. duration
;    4. amplitude
;    5. frequency
i1 0 5 25000 220

; end score
e
```

Figure 13.14 Example Csound files: (a) an orchestra file excerpt consisting of an oscillator, a filter, and an amplitude envelope; and (b) a score file consisting of one waveform table (sawtooth) and one note statement.

Csound and RTcmix are available as objects for use within Max/MSP, which was discussed in the "Beyond Sequencing" section of Chapter 10 (see pages 179–182).

Several programs mentioned previously in this text, such as Reaktor and Max/MSP, have an environment in which you graphically place and connect objects to create synthesis algorithms. An example of a non-commercial visual programming environment is Miller Puckette's **PD** (**Pure Data**). Miller Puckette was the creator of the Max program in the 1980s and many of his sound generation objects have been the source of similar objects in Max/MSP. Because of this close connection, PD operates in a similar fashion to Max/MSP. The primary difference lies in Max/MSP's abundance of interface objects and other graphically oriented features such as its "presentation mode."

Figure 13.15 shows a PD patch that performs simple frequency modulation synthesis. The three labeled number boxes provide the basic values for the carrier frequency, modulating frequency, and modulation depth (related to the index of modulation). The output of the modulating oscillator with a frequency of 110 Hz is multiplied by a modulation depth of 150 and then added to the carrier frequency of 440 Hz. This sum is the frequency for the carrier oscillator, whose amplitude is then multiplied by 0.3 (1.0 is the maximum). The result is sent to both output channels through the "dac~" object. The spectrum for this example is shown in Figure 13.8 (page 223). Notice the similarity between the way that PD patches are constructed and the way Max/MSP patches are constructed as shown in Figures 10.24 and 10.25 (pages 180 and 181). As with the Csound example, this is a very simple patch and PD (and Max/MSP) is capable of much more complex synthesis.

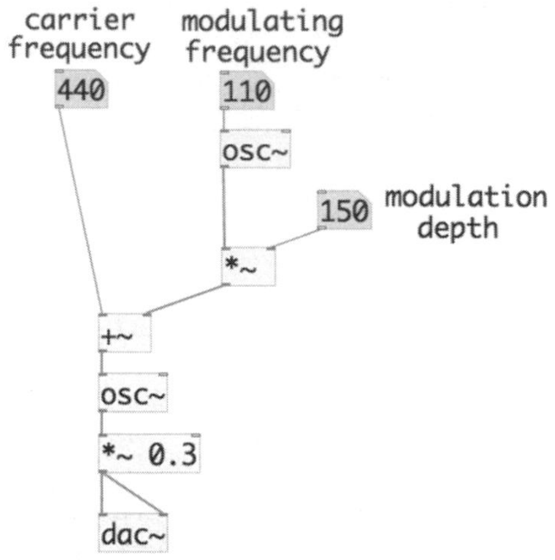

Figure 13.15 A PD (Pure Data) patch that performs simple frequency modulation synthesis.

REVIEW OF KEY TERMS

algorithms 215
wavetable synthesis 215
additive synthesis 216
Fourier synthesis 216
subtractive synthesis 218
filters 218
low pass/high pass filters 218
resonance 218
cutoff frequency 218
band pass filter 218
center frequency 218
bandwidth 218
band stop/notch filter 218
formant 219
guitar talk box 221
vocoder 221
frequency modulation (FM) 222
carrier/modulating frequency 222
sidebands 223
index of modulation 223
physical modeling synthesis 224
granular synthesis 227
granular processing 228
Csound 229
PD (Pure Data) 231

CHAPTER 14

Sampling Methods

The basic synthesis model discussed in Chapter 12, "Electronic Sound Production," includes an oscillator, a filter, and an amplifier. In the last chapter, "Synthesis Methods," you saw that you could replace the simple oscillator of the basic model with a timbre generated by synthesis techniques, such as additive synthesis, subtractive synthesis, frequency modulation, physical modeling, and granular synthesis. In this chapter we will discuss yet another substitute for the simple oscillator: samples.

As with the synthesis methods in the last chapter, a software or hardware instrument that generates sound primarily through sampling methods can still be processed by filters and amplifiers and modulated by envelopes and LFOs. Most of the material in Chapter 12, "Electronic Sound Production," still applies to samplers.

As mentioned previously, "sampling" can be a somewhat confusing term in music technology as it has at least three distinct meanings:

1. a measurement of an analog waveform by an analog to digital converter (ADC) (see Chapter 5, "Digital Audio Data");
2. the recording of individual single notes played by an instrument;
3. the "borrowing" of a segment of musical material as found in genres such as hip-hop.

In this chapter, we'll focus on the second meaning of the term. Samples are the primary way of imitating acoustic instruments in software or hardware and music produced this way is found in all forms of popular media from pop music to music for TV and film.

BASIC SAMPLING METHODS

Keymapping

The first step in reproducing an acoustic instrument tone through sampling is to record a musician playing individual notes on an instrument. Let's take the re-creation of a trumpet sound as an example.

In a recording studio, we would ask a trumpet player to play a single note at some dynamic level for some length of time. For our example, let's imagine that we asked the performer to play an A440, or A3 (we'll use standard MIDI register numbers where middle C is C3 here), at *mezzo forte* for about three seconds with no special articulation (no accent or staccato). Figure 14.1 shows such a note as seen in an audio editor. Notice the deviation in amplitude envelope from the idealized ADSR.

Now that we have the audio for a genuine trumpet note, we have to set up the sampling software or hardware to play that sample when it receives an incoming MIDI note. Since the pitch of the note sampled was A3, it makes sense to assign that sample to the MIDI key number 69, which corresponds to A3. This key number is referred to as the **root key** of the sample—the key number that will trigger the sample to be played back without any pitch modification. This is an example of **keymapping**: the mapping of a sample to a particular key number or range of key numbers.

At this point, we have a sampled instrument that can play back a single note—a good start, but not terribly useful yet. It is possible to allow several key numbers, a **key range** or **key zone**, to trigger the playback of this sample and alter the pitch of the sample to match the incoming key number. The simplest way to do this would be to have key numbers above the root key to cause the sample to be played faster, thereby transposing the pitch up, and key numbers below the root key to cause the sample to be played back slower, thereby transposing the pitch down.

In Figure 14.2, a single trumpet sample is shown with a key range that spans the full range of the trumpet from E2 to D♯5 (where middle C is C3)—some trumpet players can play higher than this and others not as high, but this is a good general range. The root key is A3, so notes at the extreme ends of the range will be transposed by about an octave and a half.

These screenshots are from Native Instruments' Kontakt 3 software sampler. For convenience and clarity, we will use this same sampler to illustrate many of these concepts. This is not necessarily an endorsement of this software: there are many software samplers with similar capabilities.

This would seem to give us a sampled trumpet instrument that covers the full range of the acoustic instrument. However, the particular transposition technique mentioned above—playing the sample faster or slower—creates a big problem. When the sample is played faster, the sample becomes shorter, and when the sample is played slower, it becomes

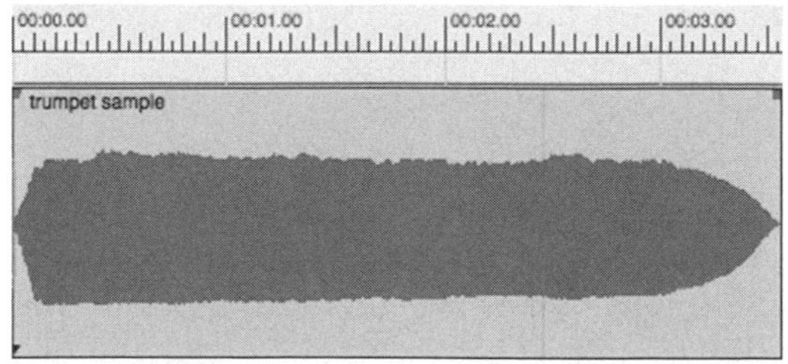

Figure 14.1 A three-second trumpet sample at A440 (A3), *mezzo forte*.

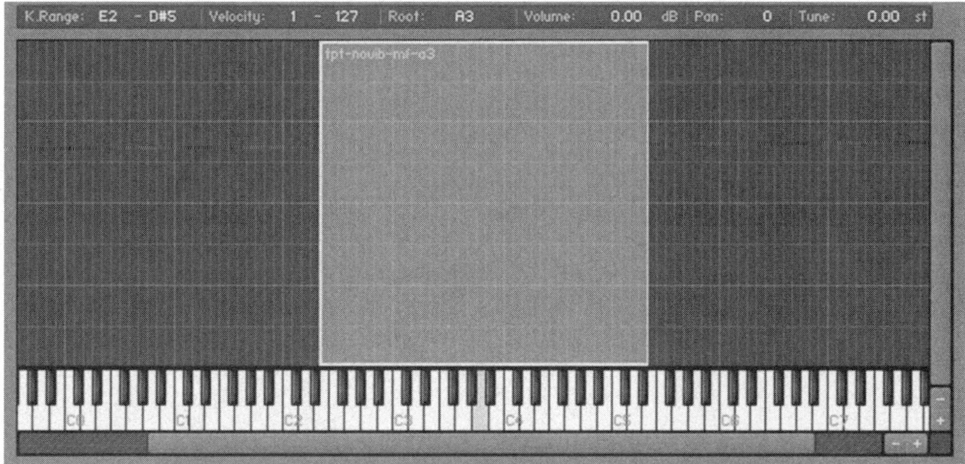

Figure 14.2 A single trumpet sample keymapped to the full range of the instrument shown in the Mapping Editor of Native Instruments' Kontakt. (Courtesy of Native Instruments GmbH, Germany)

longer (higher and faster, lower and slower). There are more sophisticated techniques in use by modern samplers that avoid the linked time-and-pitch change, but they share a similar problem with the faster/slower playback technique: they are only useful for some small number of semitones either way before the sample starts to sound unnatural.

Multisampling

The simplest way to solve the transposition problem is to bring our trumpet player back into the studio and ask him or her to play some more notes. This is **multisampling**: the act of recording representative notes of an instrument across its full range and assigning each sample to a key range.

Figure 14.3 shows five trumpet samples across the range of the instrument. Each sample has a key zone of seven semitones (the top zone is eight semitones wide) with the root key in the middle. This is an example for illustration purposes only; seven semitones is a wide key range by modern standards.

At its most extreme, multisampling involves recording each note of an instrument throughout its range, referred to as **chromatic sampling**, resulting in a key range of one semitone for each sample. Since sampling involves recording digital audio, the more samples that are recorded and the higher the sampling rate and resolution, the more storage and RAM space is required. However, RAM has increased steadily in size and modern software samplers stream most of the audio from disk rather than loading all the samples into RAM. Chromatic sampling is a common technique in many high-end sample libraries (see pages 241–242), particularly with piano samples. Figure 14.4 shows a chromatically sampled piano. When chromatic sampling is not desirable, samples are assigned to a key range of about a few semitones, though this varies by instrument, register, and sample library.

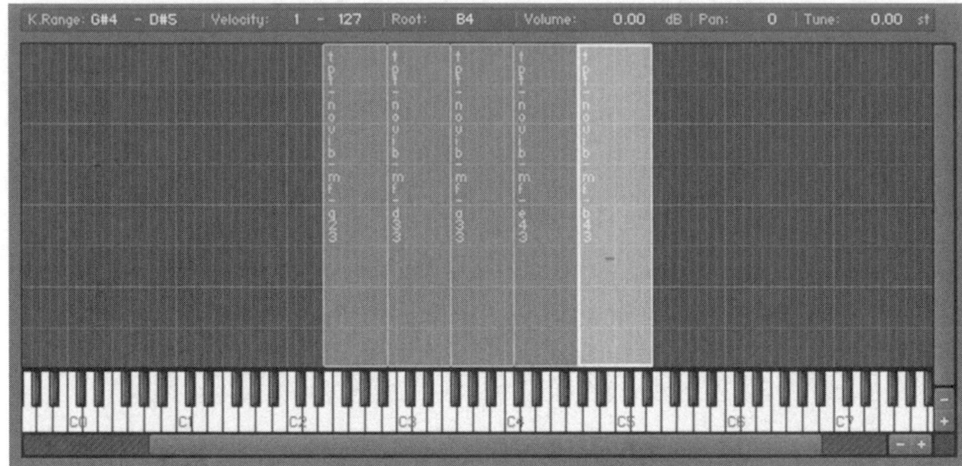

Figure 14.3 A multisampled trumpet. Five trumpet samples cover the full range of the instrument with key zones of seven semitones. One key zone is highlighted showing that it is being played.

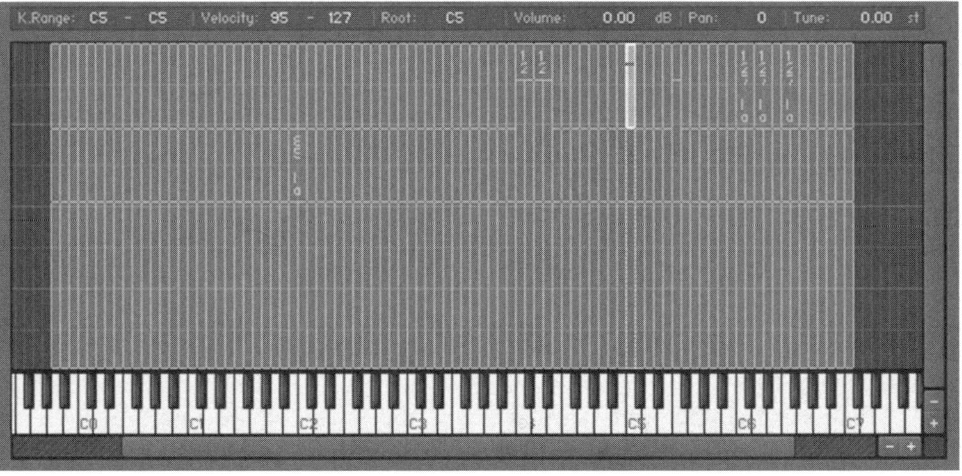

Figure 14.4 A chromatically sampled piano with three velocity zones. One of the key/velocity zones is highlighted, showing that it is being played.

Chromatic sampling may not be used in some cases due to disk space or RAM considerations. Another reason that chromatic sampling may not be used in some cases is that it can be difficult to get a performer to play each different note with the same attack, loudness, and brightness, leading to chromatic multisamples whose timbres are inconsistent from note to note. With some modification, pianos can be played via MIDI, allowing for precise control of each note and therefore greater consistency from note to note if each and every note is sampled. Even without such modification, consistency is possible on keyboard instruments. This consistency is more difficult for wind and string samples, though careful recording and editing can mitigate the inconsistencies.

With keymapping and multisampling techniques, we have an instrument that can play any pitch in a desired range with good sounding timbre. At this point, however, each sample plays back with exactly the same volume and timbre no matter how high the velocity in the MIDI note-on message—the velocity is completely ignored. The simplest solution is to increase the volume of a sample as the velocity increases, but this doesn't take into account the fact that, as natural instruments get louder, their timbres get brighter. One solution to this problem is to use velocity switching.

Velocity Switching

Velocity switching uses the velocity value of the MIDI note-on message to choose between multiple samples for each key number. This requires that we drag our trumpet player back into the studio to play each sample at a variety of dynamic levels (naturally, these recordings would all be done at the same session). We then import those recordings into our sampler and choose the velocity at which the sampler switches to a sample that was recorded at a different dynamic level.

In Figure 14.5, there are three velocity zones analogous to the key zones or key ranges discussed above. The samples in the first velocity zone were recorded at the dynamic of *piano*, the samples in the second velocity zone were recorded at the dynamic of *mezzo forte*, and the samples in the third velocity zone were recorded at the dynamic of *forte*. If the sampler receives a MIDI note-on message with a key number of 77 and a velocity of 110, it will use the key number to select a sample in the key zone that has a root key of E4, and will use the velocity to choose the sample in that key zone that was performed at the *forte* dynamic. Within each velocity zone, the note-on's velocity will increase the overall loudness of the sample as well. Figure 14.4 also shows velocity switching.

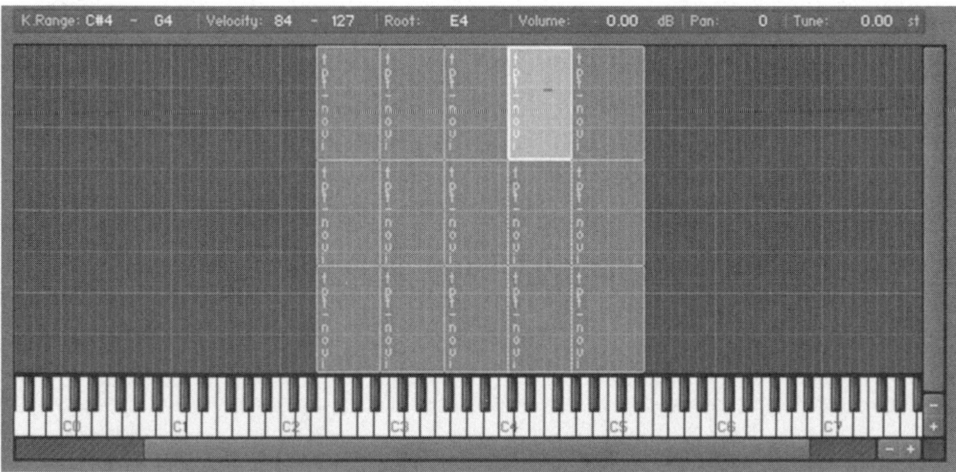

Figure 14.5 A multisampled, velocity-switched trumpet with three velocity zones. One of the key/velocity zones is highlighted, showing that it is being played.

Velocity switching is the commonly used method to achieve a linkage between loudness and brightness of timbre. However, in situations where RAM is limited, a low pass filter can also be used to simulate this linkage. A low pass filter avoids any inconsistencies in the transition from one sample to another, but lacks some of the desired natural quality that velocity-switched samples provide.

Another feature that many samplers have that is designed to enhance naturalness is the ability to select from several different samples when a note is repeated. Essentially the same note at the same dynamic level is recorded a second time, third time, and so on. These samples are then "stacked" on top of each other and, if a key is repeated with a velocity in the same velocity zone, the sampler will **round robin** (cycle) through the available samples. This way the same sample isn't heard many times in a row; exact repetition is a dead giveaway that it is a sample-based performance.

With keymapping, multisampling, and velocity switching, we have an instrument that can play any pitch in a desired range and whose timbre changes with loudness. However, at this point any MIDI note that is longer than the sample we've recorded (3 seconds in this example) will simply stop sounding once the sample length has been reached. The solution to this problem is looping.

Looping

Looping is also a term that has multiple meanings in music technology. The most common use of the term refers to repeating a segment of musical material in conjunction with the third definition of sampling above (the "borrowing" of a segment of musical material). As discussed in Chapter 5, "Digital Audio Data," loops can also be considered a distinct digital audio file format. In the case of the single note samples that we're dealing with here, looping refers to the technique of repeating part of the sustained portion of the sample in order to lengthen it. Figure 14.6 shows the loop overview in Native Instruments' Kontakt sampler, indicating the specific points in the soundfile for the start and end of the loop.

When a note-on message is received, the hardware or software sampler plays back the beginning of the soundfile until it gets to the loop section and then repeats that specified portion. When a note-off message is received, the sampler proceeds to the end of the soundfile. The trick to looping, of course, is getting the right loop points so that the looped sample sounds natural. If the beginning point of the loop and the end point of the loop have different amplitudes, the resultant looped sample will have a "pop" at each repeat of the loop. Typically, the beginning and end of the loop will be placed on zero crossings (where the waveform crosses the horizontal line) to avoid such pops. Even with the loop points at zero crossings, the overall amplitudes at the beginning and end of the loop have to be similar to avoid a pulsing effect on every loop repeat.

Figure 14.7 shows the beginning and ending points of the loop from Figure 14.6. The end of the loop is shown to the left of the center line and the beginning of the loop is shown to the right of the center line, so the center line represents the moment

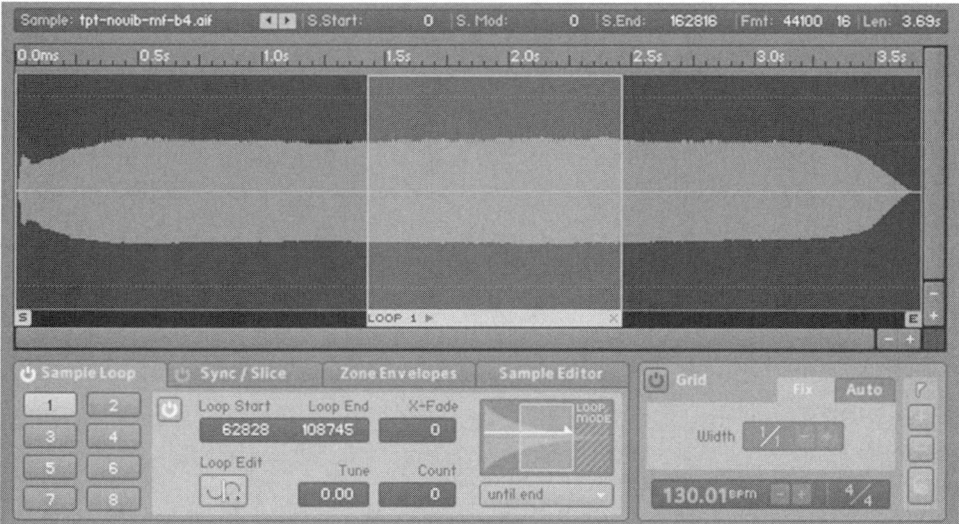

Figure 14.6 A looped sample. The start and end times of the loop are expressed precisely as the number of audio samples from the start of the soundfile.

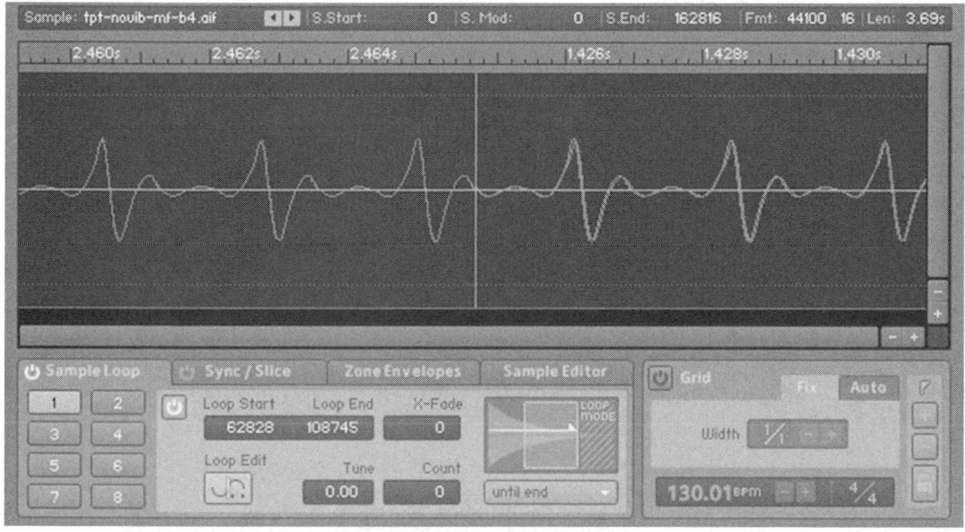

Figure 14.7 The loop point shown in Kontakt's loop editor. The beginning of the loop is to the right of the center line and the end of the loop is to the left of the center line.

at which the loop repeats. Note that the loop points are placed at zero crossings and the amplitudes at the beginning and end of the loop are similar.

Some samples are difficult or even impossible to loop. We've been assuming all along that there *is* a sustained portion to the sample. However, many percussive sounds have only attack and release portions, so the loop points will always have mismatched amplitudes. There are a number of tricks that samplers use to create smooth loops, such as playing the loop forward and then backward and then forward again or crossfading between the end of the loop and the beginning of the repetition of the loop. Nevertheless, some samples aren't properly loopable.

With keymapping, multisampling, velocity switching, and looping we now have a complete sampled instrument loaded in the sampler ready to receive MIDI messages from a keyboard or sequencer.

Key Switching

The methods described thus far can provide a fairly realistic MIDI-controlled sampled instrument. However, the sample set will have only one type of articulation. Some instruments, particularly strings, require several different articulations (*arco*, *pizzicato*, *sul ponticello*) in order to be fully emulated.

The easiest way to accomplish this would be to have separate multisampled, velocity-switched sample sets for each articulation type and simply assign each to a different MIDI channel. However, from the composer's point of view, having to switch sequencer tracks just to add a note or two of *pizzicato* (plucked) strings in a longer passage that's mostly *arco* (bowed) is a bit awkward. A composer is more likely to think of these two articulations as coming from one instrument than as the output of separate instruments.

Some sample libraries combine multiple articulations into one set by using **key switching** to select the articulation. Key switching works by assigning a specific MIDI key number to each articulation type; the key number is typically outside the playable range of the particular instrument and is not assigned to a sample. When the sampler receives a number defined for key switching, it switches to a separate multisampled, velocity-switched sample set responding on the same channel as the previous sample set. The key number is then included in the sequence along with the sounding notes, creating an easy way for a composer to select the desired articulation. The key switches effectively act like patch change messages in that they can allow a single track in a sequencer to play different timbres at different points in a sequence (see Figure 14.8).

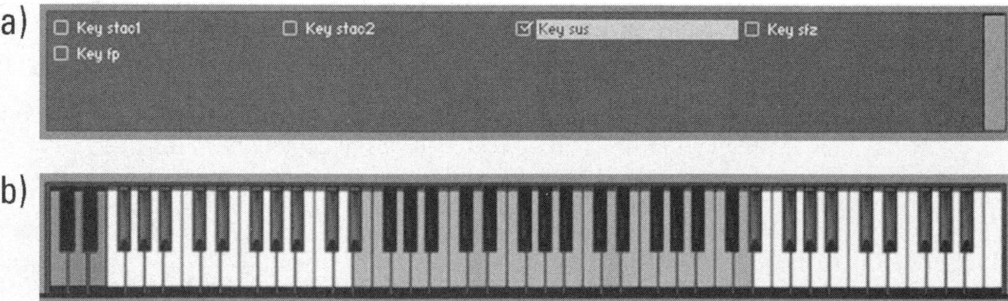

Figure 14.8 A key-switched sample set: (a) the Group Editor in Kontakt showing the available trumpet articulations for this particular sampler patch; and (b) keyboard showing the key switches for the patch on the keys C0 to E0 and the samples mapped to the keys E2 to D♯5.

SAMPLER PATCHES AND SAMPLE LIBRARIES

A multisampled, keymapped, velocity-switched, and looped sample set is the basis for a **sampler patch**. A sampler patch at its simplest consists merely of this sample set. However, most samplers and sample players allow all of the modification and modulation associated with synthesis to be used with samples, including filters, amplitude envelopes, filter envelopes, pitch envelopes, and LFOs.

Figure 14.9 shows Kontakt's modulation window displaying a volume envelope, a filter envelope, and an LFO assigned to pitch (vibrato). The envelopes here have an additional "hold" segment making them attack-hold-decay-sustain-release envelopes. The plateau in the displayed envelopes is the "hold" segment of the envelope.

A sampler patch, then, is the sample set plus any modifications and modulations, and may also include other sample sets accessed via key switching. For acoustic instrument imitation, many modification and modulation features will probably be lightly used, but for sample sets that are reproducing vintage synth sounds or just unique, non-imitative sounds, these features may be called upon more.

Multiple sampler patches can be said to form a **sample library**. It's possible (and even fun!) to create your own sample libraries, but there are a variety of companies that sell these (see also "Library Formats" below).

SOUNDWARE

As you can see from the above discussion, creating high-quality sampled instruments is a *lot* of work and requires excellent recording engineering skills, audio editing skills, sample setup skills, and access to high-quality instruments, performers, facilities, and

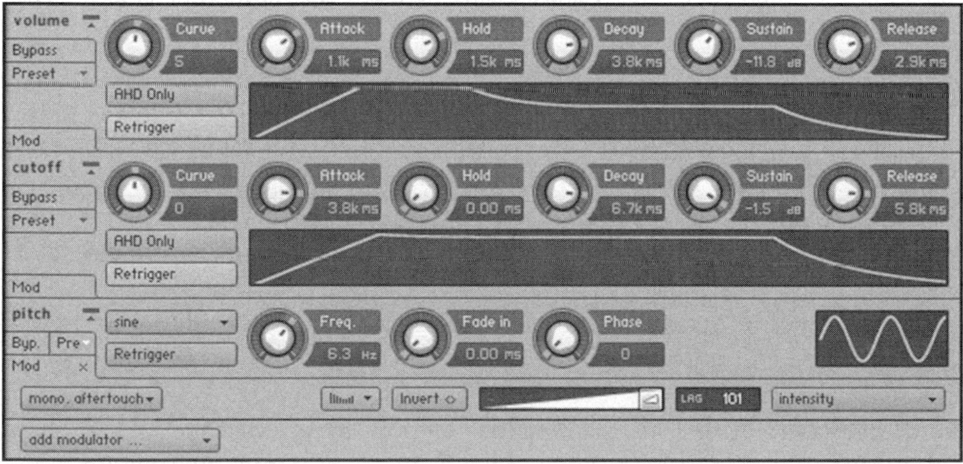

Figure 14.9 The modulation window in Kontakt showing some synthesizer elements assigned to modify sample playback, including a volume envelope, a filter envelope, and an LFO assigned to pitch (vibrato).

equipment. Because of this difficulty and the popularity of sampling in electronic sound production, an entire industry, sometimes referred to as the **soundware** industry (by analogy with *soft*ware), has sprung up around this need.

Soundware companies produce sound libraries of various instruments and sounds ranging from analog synthesizers to acoustic instruments to soda cans. Many sample libraries provide not just notes, but also a variety of timbral effects, such as *sul ponticello* for strings, a variety of playing styles, such as flutter tonguing for wind instruments, and even a variety of complete musical gestures, such as harmonic glissandos for strings.

Prices for these libraries can range from under a hundred to several thousand dollars depending on the number of velocity zones, lengths of the samples, quality of the samples, numbers of articulations, and so on. Many of these soundware companies create loops as well as sampled instruments and the line between the two can be pretty thin when the samples include full rhythmic grooves and other musical gestures. Purchasing a sample library that can emulate a high-quality symphonic sound can get quite expensive, but this level of quality has come to be expected in commercial music fields such as film scoring. Even in cases where the final product will be a recording of a live ensemble, the preliminary stages of the work are usually carried out using high-quality sample libraries.

Library Formats

Sample libraries typically come either with their own plug-in instrument "player," or are formatted for use by a particular software or hardware sampler. They may also be available in both manners. A plug-in sample player is usually available in one or more of the plug-in formats discussed in Chapter 12, "Electronic Sound Production": VSTi, AU, DXi, and RTAS. These plug-in formats determine the compatibility of that library with a given sequencer/DAW. For example, if your sequencer/DAW can't handle VST instruments, then a sample library that comes with only a VST plug-in player wouldn't be compatible with that sequencer/DAW.

Sample libraries that don't have their own players will be formatted to work with one or more software or hardware samplers. There are many software samplers and hardware samplers in existence and many require a slightly different format for the keymapping, multisampling, velocity switching, and looping information. These formats include Kontakt, Logic/EXS24, MachFive, Halion, NN-XT, Roland, Akai, and many, many others. Some samplers can handle the conversion from one library format to another or directly support multiple library formats. In addition, some kinds of sample libraries are also available in one or more of the loop formats—Acid, Apple Loops, REX—though the loop formats are not necessarily designed to be controlled by MIDI messages in the way that regular sample libraries are.

There are a couple of formats that straddle the line between wavetable synthesis and full-blown sample playback: the SoundFont 2 (SF2) and Downloadable Sounds 2 (DLS 2) formats. Sound banks in these formats include samples, but were developed primarily for wavetable synthesis. These formats are supported by many software samplers as well as a number of software synthesizers.

SAMPLERS, SAMPLE PLAYERS, AND ROMPLERS

When sampling first became widely available in the 1980s as an electronic sound production technique, computers were not fast enough to handle digital audio, so **samplers** were built into hardware keyboards or modules that were connected to the computer through a MIDI interface. Also at that time, audio editing on computers wasn't as commonplace as it is now, so samplers themselves allowed the user to record and edit samples as well as create loop points. As a result, the term "sampler" came to mean a device that could record, edit, and loop samples, then set them up for playback through keymapping and velocity switching. A "**sample player**" referred to a device whose stored samples were unchangeable.

Samplers are now largely software. Since programs for recording, editing, and looping samples are commonplace, those functions are not typically found in software samplers. The term "sampler" has come to mean software whose samples can be changed by loading sample libraries or loading individual samples and keymapping them, velocity switching them, and so on. A "sample player" in the software sense is software that can play back a given sample library (as discussed above in "Library Formats"), but either can't load new libraries or can't set up keymapping, velocity switching, and looping for new samples.

In the hardware sense, sample players are synths or modules that use fixed samples stored in ROM as the basis for their patches. These devices are sometimes referred to as **ROMplers**, for ROM-based sample players. Many hardware synths and modules are ROMplers. Despite the implication that the samples in ROMplers can't be changed, some synths and modules allow you to buy new ROM cards to plug into specialized slots on the system. These cards provide additional samples for the system as well as the program information to make these samples available as a patch (the same sample set can be used by many different patches). The term ROMpler is also sometimes applied to software sample players that use a fixed collection of waveforms.

As mentioned in Chapter 12, "Electronic Sound Production," in some settings, a separate computer is used to play back the sample libraries so that the computer running the sequencer/DAW can be dedicated to sequencing and audio processing. In that case, the sample computer is equipped with a MIDI interface to receive MIDI messages from the master computer and an audio interface to send audio back to the master computer (see Figure 12.13, page 201). In a sense, the sample computer becomes a hardware synth, albeit one that runs a full-fledged operating system capable of letting you check your email.

REVIEW OF KEY TERMS

root key 234	key switching 240
keymapping 234	sampler patch 240
key range/zone 234	sample library 240
multisampling 235	soundware 242
chromatic sampling 235	samplers 243
velocity switching 237	sample players 243
round robin 238	ROMplers 243
looping 238	

Section IV
Further Reading

Each commercial softsynth and sampler is accompanied by a physical or electronic manual and perhaps some tutorials. These resources are of great practical value for you to get up and running and make sound with your software. Some of these manuals also provide valuable, though usually limited, information about the various synthesis or sampling methods used by the software. In addition, many softsynths are the subject of books published separately from the manual that can also be useful. However, the manuals and tutorials seldom provide the important technical and historical information that is essential in order to understand properly what you're doing.

For a historical view of the development of synthesis and sampling technologies, Peter Manning's *Electronic and computer music* (revised ed., 2004), Thom Holmes's *Electronic and experimental music* (3rd ed., 2008), and Joel Chadabe's *Electric sound* (1997) are excellent resources.

Samuel Pellman's *An introduction to the creation of electroacoustic music* (1994) provides a nice overview of both analog synthesis methods and a variety of digital synthesis methods. The age of Pellman's book means that it misses the softsynth revolution, but the concepts involved in the synthesis methods are still valid, as are the musical examples discussed. Jim Aikin's *Power tools for synthesizer programming* (2004) provides a practical overview of analog-modeling synthesis methods as well as a very short introduction to other synthesis methods.

The most comprehensive text available on synthesis and sampling methods is Curtis Roads's 1,000+ page *The computer music tutorial* (1996). Though Roads's book is over ten years old, it is written in such a way that it is still applicable to current technology. Charles Dodge and Thomas Jerse's *Computer music* (2nd ed., 1997) also provides a detailed look at the synthesis and sampling techniques discussed in this section. Both of these books come out of an "academic" tradition and are more readily applicable to synthesizing sound in programs such as Reaktor, Csound, SuperCollider, Max/MSP, and PD than in most commercial softsynths. However, they provide critical background and theory on the synthesis and sampling methods used in commercial softsynths. Learning to move knobs and sliders is relatively easy; understanding how to move them effectively to produce interesting results is much harder. Books such as those by Roads and Dodge and Jerse allow you to understand these concepts at a deep level.

There are also a number of specialized books that apply to a particular program or synthesis method. Richard Boulanger's *The Csound book* (2000) is naturally concerned with using Csound, but it also contains a great deal of detailed information on a wide variety of synthesis methods, because it is necessary to understand those methods deeply before programming them in Csound. Curtis Roads's *Microsound* (2001) is an in-depth look at the many forms of granular synthesis and processing. Perry Cook's *Real sound synthesis for interactive applications* (2002) covers many synthesis techniques, including physical modeling in some detail, though it includes some math relating to digital signal processing and physics. A number of other books relevant to this section can be found in the bibliography.

Section IV
Suggested Activities

This chapter provides some suggested activities relating to synthesis and sampling.

Most sequencer/DAWs come with at least a few softsynths of various types, any of which can be a starting point for exploring synthesis and sampling methods. Hardware synths can, of course, also be used to explore these methods, though, because the interface is typically a small screen, the synth elements and their interconnection are less clear. In addition to softsynths that come with your sequencer/DAW, there are a number of freeware softsynths available. (You can find links to these freeware softsynths on the book's website.)

EXPLORE YOUR SOFTSYNTHS

Taking Stock

The first step is to take stock of what softsynths you have available. A few softsynths, such as Native Instruments' Reaktor, can be programmed for almost any synthesis type. However, most softsynths use a specific synthesis method. For those synths, the following are some questions you should consider for each:

- Plug-in format? Standalone? ReWire?
- Does it use sampling or synthesis?
- If synthesis, which method?
- If an analog-modeling synth, how many oscillators are available, and what waveforms/noise are available for each oscillator?
- If some other synthesis method, what controls over the sound generation are available?
- How many filters are available and what types of filters?
- What are its dedicated envelopes (e.g., amplitude and filter envelopes)?
- Any other envelopes that can be routed to various destinations?

- Number of LFOs?
- How is modulation routing handled?

Exploring Presets

Once you understand the basic features of a given softsynth, it is useful to explore how those features are used by various presets. Aside from a greater understanding of your softsynth's inner workings, this will also help you understand what the fundamental elements are for a given type of patch.

- Choose a category of patches, such as lead, bass, or pad.
- Choose two or three patches from that category.
- What are the common settings between those patches?
- What are the major differences?
- Change the patches to eliminate the differences and see if the patches are still clearly leads, basses, or pads.
- Repeat this for other categories.

Messing with Presets

Once you've explored commonalities among presets, it's useful to modify synthesis parameters systematically to determine their effect on the overall sound. For some complex patches, it can be difficult to hear the changes made by a single knob or slider. For this exercise, it is best to choose a patch that doesn't change wildly over time. If any of the changes below become too extreme, you may have to return them to approximately their original state so that you can hear the subsequent changes. Be sure to listen carefully to the timbre after each change to get a clear sense of the effect that a given parameter has on the timbre.

- Choose a lead or bass patch and play some notes to get a sense of the basic timbre.
- *Oscillators*: adjust the waveform and tuning of the oscillator(s) (or other "source" controls if it's not an analog-modeling synth).
- *Filter*: adjust the cutoff frequency, resonance, and filter type.
- *Filter envelope*: adjust the filter envelope segments and the envelope amount.
- *Amplitude envelope*: adjust the amplitude envelope segments.
- *Other envelopes*: adjust any other envelopes that are routed to synthesizer elements.
- *LFOs*: adjust the shape (waveform), rate, and amount of any LFO that's routed to a synthesizer element.
- *Modulation routing*: use the modulation routing to route the modulation wheel (or some other knob or slider on your controller) to an LFO amount and that LFO to the pitch of the oscillator to create vibrato control; to hear this, play notes on your controller and move the mod wheel.

- *Modulation routing*: use the modulation routing to route the modulation wheel (or some other knob or slider on your controller) to an LFO amount and that LFO to the cutoff frequency of a resonant low pass filter to create wah-wah control.
- *Modulation routing*: use the modulation routing to route the modulation wheel (or some other knob or slider on your controller) to an LFO amount and that LFO to the overall level to create a tremolo control.

Exploring Other Synths

Many software synthesizers can be downloaded, installed, and used in a "demo" mode. A synth in demo mode will be limited in some way in time (usable for only some number of days or minutes at a time), in functionality (can't save any changes or record any audio), or both. However, demo mode is still very useful for becoming acquainted with a particular synth or synth method. If you have only analog-modeling or sampling softsynths, this is an excellent way to explore some different synthesis techniques. (Links to some softsynths available as demos can be found on the book's website.)

MAKE SOME PATCHES FROM SCRATCH

In this part, you'll use an analog-modeling synth to construct patches from scratch. Most sequencer/DAWs come with a softsynth that fits the analog-modeling description, so these exercises should be widely accessible. If yours does not, several analog-modeling synths are available. (See the book's website for links.)

Initialize Your Synth Patch

If possible, you should first "initialize" your synth patch. This is often a drop-down menu item or a right-click (control-click) contextual menu item. This act sets up a simple, generic patch that is the best starting place for building your own patches. If this function is not available, you can manually initialize a patch as follows:

- *Oscillator*: turn off all but one oscillator; remove any detuning; remove any special effects in the oscillator like FM or ring modulation; set a basic waveform such as a sawtooth.
- *Filter*: set the filter to be a low pass filter with resonance; set the cutoff frequency at medium-to-high and the resonance at 0.
- *Amplitude envelope*: set the amplitude envelope to have no attack, no decay, 100 percent sustain, and no release.
- *Filter envelope*: set the filter envelope to have no attack, no decay, no sustain, and no release, and turn the filter "amount" to 0.
- *Other envelopes*: do the same for any other envelope (besides the amplitude envelope).
- *LFOs*: set the LFO(s) to have a rate of 0 and an amount of 0.

- *Modulation routing*: turn off any modulation routing not taken care of by the previous acts.
- *Effects*: turn off any built-in effects such as delay or chorus.
- When you play this patch, you should hear a fairly boring sound.

Bass Patch

The following steps are some suggestions for creating a usable bass patch. Once you've created the basic bass patch, you should experiment with the parameter settings to create a patch that is to your liking. You may want to sequence a short bass line for this instrument and set it to loop while you're experimenting.

- *Oscillators*: use two oscillators, both set to sawtooth waves.
- *Oscillators*: detune one oscillator up 5 to 10 cents and detune the other down 5 to 10 cents.
- *Filter*: set the filter to be a low pass filter with resonance.
- *Filter*: set the cutoff frequency to the midpoint and the resonance to mid-to-high.
- *Filter envelope*: short attack, short decay, low-to-mid sustain, and no release (release would also depend on the release value in the amplitude envelope); experiment with the envelope amount.
- *Amplitude envelope*: short attack, short decay, medium sustain, and no release (to get a plucked sound, set the sustain to 0 and control the duration with the decay control).

Lead Patch

The following steps are some suggestions for a usable lead patch. Once you've created the basic lead patch, you should experiment with the parameter settings to create a patch that is to your liking. You may want to sequence a short lead line for this instrument and set it to loop while you're experimenting.

- *Oscillators*: use two oscillators with a different waveform for each; the combination should be a penetrating sound.
- *Oscillators*: set the polyphony to 1 and add a small amount of portamento so the patch slides a little bit between pitches (these settings may not be in the oscillator section).
- *LFO/modulation routings*: route the mod wheel input to the LFO amount and the LFO to the oscillator(s) for vibrato; adjust the rate for a "natural" sounding vibrato—you'll use the mod wheel to add vibrato to sustained notes.
- *Filter*: set the filter to be a low pass filter with resonance.
- *Filter*: set the cutoff frequency to the midpoint and the resonance to mid-to-high.
- *Filter envelope*: short attack, short decay, low sustain, and no release (release would also depend on the release value in the amplitude envelope); experiment with the envelope amount.
- *Amplitude envelope*: short attack, short decay, mid-to-high sustain, and no release.

Pad Patch

The following steps are some suggestions for a usable pad. Once you've created the basic pad, you should experiment with the parameter settings to create a patch that is to your liking. Because pads are generally lingering and wavering, there's quite a bit of latitude here to create anything from a tasteful pad to a wild, demented one.

- *Oscillators*: use two or more oscillators with a different waveform for each; the combination should be an exotic "synthy" sound.
- *Oscillators*: detune the oscillators quite a bit from one another *or* set them to be a constant interval like a third or fifth apart.
- *LFO/modulation routing*: route the LFO to the oscillator(s) for vibrato; adjust the rate and amount/depth for a "natural" sounding vibrato—*or* use a slow rate with a modest amount/depth so that the pitch wavers slowly up and down during the note.
- *Filter*: set the filter to be a low pass filter with resonance.
- *Filter*: set the cutoff frequency to low-to-mid and the resonance to mid-to-high.
- *Filter envelope*: set all segments and the filter amount to zero—you'll control the filter with the mod wheel.
- *Modulation routing*: route the mod wheel to the cutoff frequency of the filter—this will allow you to control the evolution of the timbre over the length of the note.
- *Amplitude envelope*: medium-to-long attack, no decay, maximum sustain, and medium-to-long release—this note will slowly rise to maximum and then slowly release once you've released the key(s).

Some substitute pad patch instructions:

- *Modulation routing*: route the mod wheel to the amount of the LFO which is routed to the oscillators—the mod wheel will be used to control the addition of vibrato over the course of a long pad note/chord.
- *Filter*: if available, set the filter to be a notch filter with a medium cutoff frequency and medium resonance (which would control the width of the notch).
- *Filter envelope*: set all segments and the filter amount to zero—you'll control the filter with a second LFO.
- *LFO2/modulation routing*: route a second LFO to the cutoff frequency of the filter and adjust the rate to be slow and the amount/depth to be fairly large, so that the notch sweeps across the full spectrum slowly during the pad note/chord.

EXPLORE ALTERNATE SOFTWARE SYNTHESIS PROGRAMS

With the excellent softsynths that are available with today's sequencer/DAWs, it's tempting to stick with those softsynths. However, there are still some timbres and effects that can best be achieved using alternate software synthesis programs. The distinguishing characteristic of most of this software is that it is completely programmable from the ground up. Many of these programs are non-commercial and available as freeware.

There are a few programs like this that are commercial, such as Native Instruments' Reaktor, which can act as a standard softsynth plug-in, or Cycling74's Max/MSP. There is a version of Max/MSP called Max for Live that allows you to program instruments and effects in Max/MSP within Ableton's Live. If you have access to Reaktor or Max/MSP, they are excellent places to explore unusual synthesis techniques. However, you can explore alternate synthesis environments using freeware programs.

Programs such as PD (Pure Data), Csound, and Supercollider don't provide the preset sliders and knobs that other softsynths do. Instead, they allow you to build synthesis algorithms from the ground up and provide varying support for creating graphical interfaces. As a result, these programs can take some time to get used to and even more time to master. Their advantage is their ultimate flexibility and expandability. In addition, their from-the-ground-up nature provides you with a much deeper understanding of the synthesis techniques discussed in this section. (The book's website contains links to these alternate software synthesis programs and links to tutorials and examples.)

CREATE YOUR OWN SAMPLE SETS

If you have access to a sampler that will let you import your own samples, such as Logic's EXS24, Kontakt, or Reason's NN-XT, you can use your understanding of keymapping, multisampling, velocity switching, and looping to create your own sampled instruments.

Creating a Realistic Sampled Instrument

Recording Your Own Samples

One way of obtaining instrument samples is to record them following these steps:

- Decide how many samples you wish to record across the range of the instrument; this will determine the size of the key zones.
- Decide how many dynamic levels you wish to record for each key zone; about three velocity zones are enough for these purposes.
- Record the samples in a studio using a good performer, an appropriate high-quality microphone, a relatively noise-free signal path, and appropriate levels. It is best to use a non-reverberant, or dry, space so that you can later choose how much reverb to add in your sequencer/DAW.

Using Existing Recordings

There are some instrument samples suitable for this activity available on the Internet, most notably the University of Iowa Musical Instrument Samples (see the book's website for the link). This is excellent material for the purposes of understanding sampling.

Editing the Recordings

Whether you record your own samples or use downloaded samples, you'll then need to edit the samples into individual sample files, one note per file. You can perform this editing in your DAW and export each individual sample, or you can use an editor such as BIAS's Peak, which has special sample editing features, or use the freeware program Audacity. You'll want to take care at this stage to remove all extra space in front of the sample so that there is not a delay when it is triggered by a key.

Looping Considerations

Once you have the individual samples, you can load them into your sampler. At some point, you'll need to try to loop these samples to create an instrument that can sustain notes. Some samplers, such as Kontakt and EXS24, have built-in loop editors, but others may not have any special looping functions. In that case, you would want to use an audio file editor that does have those features, such as BIAS's Peak, and loop the samples before importing them into the sampler.

Import into Sampler and Play Back

As you load the samples into your sampler, you will set up a key zone and a velocity zone, and choose a root key for each sample. The actual commands for these tasks differ from sampler to sampler, but it is usually very graphically oriented. In addition, if you have not already looped the samples in an external editor, you'll use the capabilities of your sampler to set and refine the loop for each sampler.

At this point, you now have a sampled instrument that is keymapped, multisampled, velocity switched, and looped. Try sequencing some music playing this instrument and evaluate the strengths and weaknesses of your instrument.

Creating a Sound Effects Sample Set

Samplers are, of course, not limited to reproducing acoustic instrument sounds. Anything you can record, you can import into a sampler. This opens up the possibility of creating sampled instruments from any type of sound. Percussive sounds are a natural for this, making garden tools and children's toys available as the source for a drum part. In addition, samples can include vocal sounds or sounds processed in other software and imported into the sampler.

To explore this, choose a collection of sounds that are thematically related to each other, such as garden tools, noises you can make with your mouth, or words edited from political speeches. Record and edit these sounds as described above when instrument samples were discussed and import them into your sampler. The one step that is optional in this situation is looping, because many of these sounds are not designed to be sustained sounds.

SECTION V

Computer Notation and Computer-assisted Instruction

OVERVIEW

Computer notation software has changed dramatically the way that music notation is created. Unlike ink-and-paper notation, music notated on the computer is endlessly editable and can automatically generate individual parts from a large score—a task that is very time-consuming otherwise. In addition, computer notation has changed the way that composers and arrangers work. Notes entered into a computer can be played back regardless of the complexity, allowing us to not only "proof-hear" our work in the final editing stages, but to hear partial sketches from the very beginning. This makes computer notation software not just a tool for producing high-quality graphic output, but also a creative environment where ideas are tested, revised, and tested again. In recent years, there has been an increased focus on the quality of playback within notation programs, leading to the use of higher-quality samples for playback and more complete rendering of musical gestures such as trills and glissandi.

Computer-assisted instruction (CAI) programs cover a wide range of topics, including musicianship, theory, performance, and composition. Within each topic, these programs come in many forms, ranging from games for children to drill programs for high school and college students. For children, the game environment makes learning fun and for high school and college students the drill programs allow them to work at their own pace and repeat exercises as often as necessary to achieve mastery of the material. CAI can also encompass using many of the programs from the other sections of this book to allow students to create and modify music and sound.

WHAT'S IN THIS SECTION?

Previous sections have included a separate chapter on "What Do I Need?," and "Further Reading" and "Suggested Activities" covered the entire section. In this section, those topics are covered within each chapter.

Chapter 15: Computer Notation

This chapter covers:

- the process of computer notation;
- score setup, scanned input, and file import;
- note entry, including step-time MIDI, real-time MIDI, and audio;
- entry of other notation elements;
- layout;
- special features, including plug-ins, educational worksheets, and flexible performance playback;
- output as audio files and data files;
- notation data, including MusicXML;
- music fonts;
- computer notation: What do I need?;
- further reading;
- suggested activities.

Chapter 16: Computer-assisted Instruction

This chapter covers:

- CAI for musicianship and theory;
- CAI for musical form and analysis;
- CAI for history, terminology, and instruments;
- CAI for performance skills;
- CAI for creative skills;
- CAI: What do I need?;
- further reading.

CHAPTER 15

Computer Notation

The purpose of this chapter is to explore the various features common to notation programs and discuss issues related to the encoding of musical data for visual display, as opposed to the performance encoding of musical data as MIDI that we saw in Chapter 9, "Midi Messages." Notation software fulfills a very different function from that of the sequencer/DAWs discussed earlier in the book. While both types of programs allow you to organize music in time, sequencer/DAWs are oriented toward aural output and notation programs are primarily concerned with visual output. Even though the sound playback in notation programs has become quite sophisticated, with high-quality sample libraries and mappings between visual elements and playback parameters, notation programs are fundamentally specialized graphics programs.

There are a variety of programs available for music notation whose capabilities range from simple four-part writing for a harmony class to lead sheets and guitar tablature to full orchestra scores with almost any notation imaginable. For many purposes, a program with limited capabilities is sufficient. If all you want to do is write lead sheets, the ability of a full-featured program to do avant-garde classical notation is wasted along with the extra money such a program costs. On the other hand, for classical composers, film composers, and professional copyists, a full-featured notation program is essential and worth every penny.

The two notation programs that dominate the market at the time of this writing are MakeMusic's Finale and Sibelius. However, there are a number of other notation programs that are quite capable, such as Opus 1 Music's NoteAbility Pro, GenieSoft's Overture, and NOTION Music's NOTION3. In addition, there are a variety of programs with somewhat more limited capabilities designed for various markets that include MakeMusic's Finale Allegro, Finale PrintMusic, Finale Songwriter, Finale Notepad, Sibelius's Sibelius First, NOTION Music's PROGRESSION, NOTION Music's PROTÉGÉ, and GenieSoft's ScoreWriter. (Links to these programs are available on the book's website.)

The full-featured programs that will serve as the examples in this chapter are Finale, Sibelius, NoteAbility Pro, Overture, and NOTION3. There are undoubtedly other programs that could make this list, but these five will serve to illustrate the various features of notation programs. Though these programs will likely change by the time you read this, the examples presented will give you a sense of the various ways that a notation program might implement a common notation feature.

THE PROCESS OF COMPUTER NOTATION

Computer notation offers many advantages over traditional pen-and-ink hand notation, including the ability to "proof-hear" scores with playback, to edit and re-edit scores at will, to extract parts from a score, and to produce publisher quality output. The *process* of computer notation also differs substantially from that of hand notation. With hand notation, as soon as you've drawn the first notehead, you've already made a decision about the size of the music; with the second notehead, you've made a spacing decision; when you reach the end of a system, the number of measures per system are fixed; and so on. The process of entering notes and the process of laying out the page are fully intertwined in hand notation. On the other hand, computer notation is more like the musical equivalent of word processing: you can enter notational elements and change any and every aspect of them later, from the shape of the notes to the size of the page to the layout.

The process of computer notation can be thought of in three separate phases: setup, entry, and layout. The **setup** phase includes specifying the number of staves, the clefs, key signatures, time signatures, and staff groupings. The **entry** phase includes inputting such elements as notes, dynamics, articulations, slurs, lyrics, and chords. Proofreading and editing are typically included in this phase as well as just before printing in the layout phase. The **layout** phase includes spacing the music, sizing the page, choosing the number of measures per system, and choosing the number of systems per page. This is a crucial process and there is often a good deal of back and forth necessary to achieve the right layout. For example, you may have to resize the music after choosing the number of measures per system if the notes are too crowded, or you may have to reorganize the number of measures per system to accommodate page turns.

Naturally, these three phases are not mutually exclusive. You may well decide while entering notes that you want to make changes to the setup, such as adding or deleting an instrument or changing the key signature or time signature. During the layout phase, you might decide to make changes to the setup or changes to the entry items. You might choose to use notation software as a creative "sketchpad" and enter notes or rhythms without knowing their ultimate key or instrument. In such a circumstance, "entry" takes precedence and the "setup" will take place gradually as the music evolves. This is a perfectly valid and even common use of notation software.

Some care must be taken when using notation software as a creative environment rather than as a notation production environment. Notation programs typically impose a "difficulty penalty" for some kinds of notation. By hand, it is almost as easy to sketch a passage that changes meter every bar and mixes duplets, triplets, and quintuplets, as it is to sketch a passage of all quarter notes in a simple meter. In a notation program straight quarter notes are far easier than constantly changing groupings, which can encourage a simplification of musical ideas, thus allowing the process of notating the music to dictate the music's content. *As usual, you, as the user, are responsible for the final output of the program regardless of the limitations imposed by the software.*

With sequencer/DAWs, there is a great deal of similarity among the various pieces of software in terms of available functions and in terms of the interface to those functions (see Figure 15.1). Notation programs tend to vary more from program to program. For example, Finale has a tool-based interface where each task is prefaced by choosing the right tool from a palette of tools ("a tool for every task"). Editing notation elements often involves choosing the tool that was used to enter those elements, though there is a powerful "Selection Tool" that can be used to perform some editing on many different notational elements. Keyboard shortcuts are available for many of the functions.

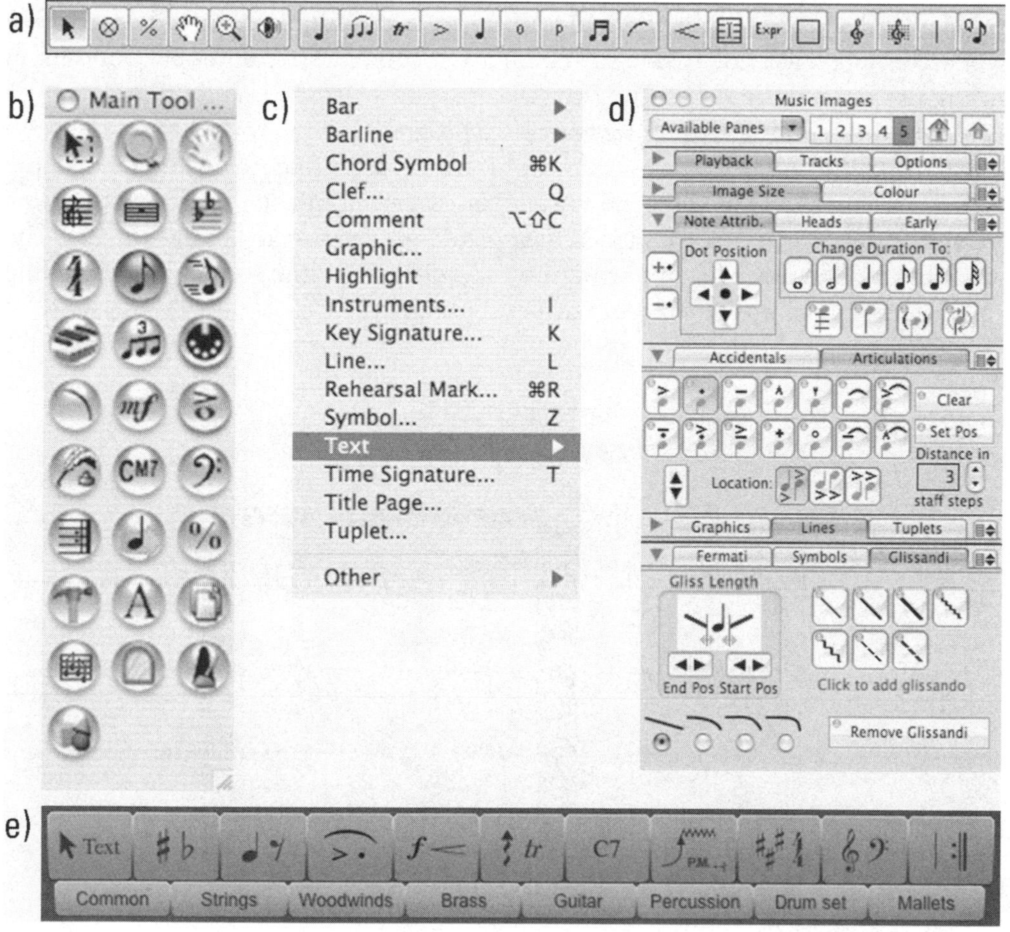

Figure 15.1 The tools interface in various programs: (a) Overture 4 (courtesy of GenieSoft); (b) Finale 2009 (courtesy of MakeMusic, Inc.); (c) Sibelius 6 (courtesy of Sibelius, Inc.); (d) NoteAbility Pro (courtesy of Opus 1 Music); and (e) NOTION3 (courtesy of NOTION Music, Inc.).

On the other hand, Sibelius generally houses its functions in menus, but its primary method of entry and editing is based on extensive keyboard shortcuts. The manual even suggests that you put the mouse out of reach when you're learning the program to see how long you can go without it. Both programs allow you to do similar things, but you have to go about it in a different way for each program.

We will examine general features of notation software by looking at the setup, entry, and layout phases of the computer notation process.

SETUP

Most notation programs provide an automated interface for the initial setup of a score and tools for customizing that setup further as needed. You could create a score one staff at a time, but the automated score setup feature is a great timesaver. Both Finale and Sibelius utilize an opening window with many action choices, including creating a new score, importing a document, or scanning a document. The other programs jump right to the score creation.

When creating a new score, most notation programs allow you to choose from a collection of preset templates or create your own custom score by specifying the instruments, the notation style ("handwritten" or classical font), the time signature, key signature, and tempo (see Figure 15.2). Templates are particularly useful since all the setup has been done for you. Importing files saved in other file formats and scanning documents are also common ways of starting a project.

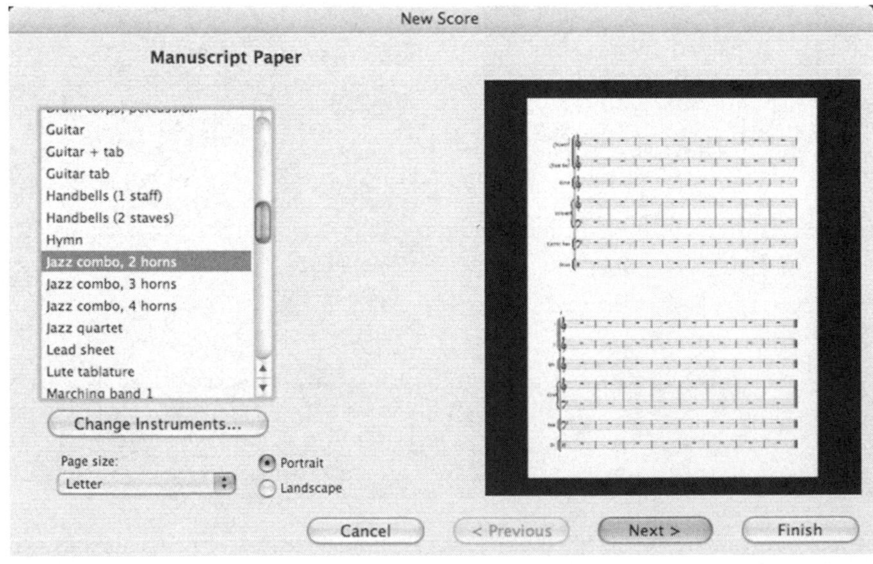

Figure 15.2 Score creation window in Sibelius 6.

Scanning

If you have an existing piece of printed music that you need to edit, transpose, or extract parts from, you can use a scanner in conjunction with software that performs Music Optical Character Recognition, or **Music OCR**. There are many regular OCR programs including freeware that allow you to scan a page of regular text and convert that scanned image into electronic text. However, music is much more complicated than lines of text because of the variety of horizontal and vertical configurations and the multiplicity of symbols, shapes, and text found in music. With Music OCR, you can convert an existing score into an editable form; hopefully with far less effort than would be required to enter each note and symbol from scratch.

Both Finale and Sibelius support scanning music using "lite" versions of specialty Music OCR software. Finale comes with Musitek's SmartScore Lite and Sibelius is bundled with Neuratron's PhotoScore Lite. Both scanning software packages can be upgraded to full standalone versions, SmartScore X Professional Edition and PhotoScore Ultimate, which include recognition of more staves, voices, and symbols.

Those programs and other dedicated Music OCR software, such as Visiv's SharpEye, allow output in common music file formats such as Standard MIDI Files (SMFs), MusicXML files, and NIFF files. The Standard MIDI file was discussed in Chapter 10, "MIDI Sequencing," and MusicXML and NIFF files will be discussed further below. Once saved in one of those formats, the file can be imported into a notation program (for SMF, MusicXML, NIFF files) or a sequencer/DAW (for SMF files).

Scanning allows for very quick entry of an entire body of notes and symbols from an existing sheet of music. However, given the complexity of music notation, Music OCR is more successful with some scores than with others. In most cases, at least some amount of correction within a notation program is to be expected, and some scores will require substantial editing.

Figure 15.3 shows Music OCR in PhotoScore Lite 5 with the scanned image at the top and the converted image at the bottom. Note that the lite version doesn't read

Figure 15.3 Music OCR in PhotoScore Lite 5. The scanned image is shown at the top and the converted score is shown at the bottom.

slurs or lyrics; the full version is required for that. In addition, the measure at the bottom right shows an error in the reading of the rhythm, perhaps due to a slur in the scanned image that cuts across the note stems. This kind of minor error is common in Music OCR software.

File Importing

If you have a music file that was created in another program such as a sequencer or another notation program, you can save it in an interchange file format and import it into the notation program that you're using. Most music applications won't read each other's exclusive file formats directly.

The most common interchange file format for music data (as opposed to audio) is the **Standard MIDI File**, or **SMF**, which uses the ".mid" filename extension. This file type was discussed in Chapter 10, "MIDI Sequencing." Because the standard MIDI file is based on the MIDI specification, which is a sound-related code, it lacks data that is essential for a notation program, such as clefs, the number of measures per system, the number of systems per page, music size, music font, slurs, accents, and dynamic markings. SMFs do include such information as tempo, time signature, and key signature.

Despite these deficiencies, SMFs have the advantage of being supported by most music programs, including all major notation programs and all major sequencer/DAWs. After importing an SMF, many notation elements, such as dynamics and articulations, must be added. In addition, if the SMF originated in a MIDI sequencer, the rhythms may need to be quantized. Quantization was discussed in Chapter 10, "MIDI Sequencing," and will be discussed more in this chapter under "MIDI Input."

Figure 15.4a shows the MIDI file import dialog box in Finale 2009. The "Quant Settings" button brings up the dialog box shown in Figure 15.4b that allows you to choose the smallest note value and whether to allow triplets.

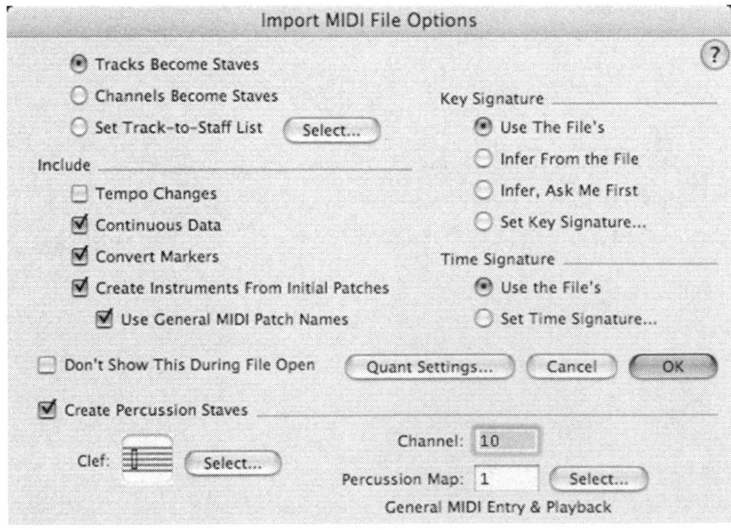

Figure 15.4a The MIDI file import dialog box in Finale 2009.

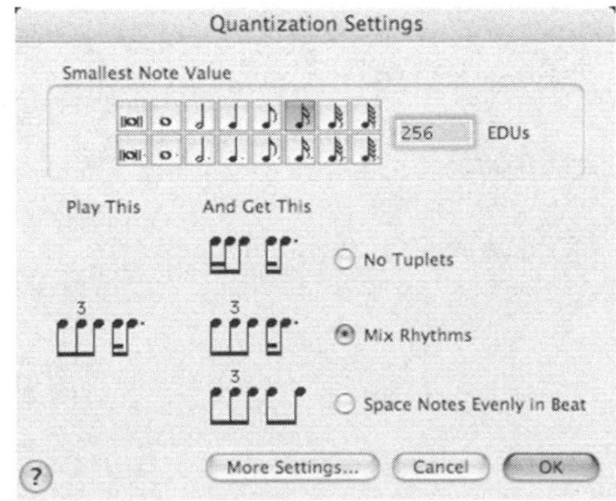

Figure 15.4b The Quant Settings dialog box for MIDI file importing in Finale 2009.

The deficiencies in the Standard MIDI File with regard to notation file transfer have long been recognized. As a result, there have been a number of attempts to develop an interchange file format that supports notation features. One such effort, **NIFF** (Notation Interchange File Format), was adopted by a number of programs, particularly Music OCR programs such as PhotoScore, SmartScore, and SharpEye. While support for NIFF is still present in these programs, it is essentially obsolete. The mostly widely supported interchange format for music is now **MusicXML** developed by Recordare. MusicXML and NIFF both encode important notation information that is unavailable in the Standard MIDI File. MusicXML will be discussed in a bit more detail later in the chapter.

NOTE ENTRY

If you start a notation project from scratch, rather than through scanning or file importing, you can use a variety of methods for entering notes. Depending on the capabilities of the program, it is possible to input notes with a mouse and computer keyboard, with a MIDI controller, or with a microphone.

Mouse/Keyboard

Note input using the mouse and computer keyboard is intuitive and instantly attractive, but it is usually less efficient than MIDI input. However, **mouse/keyboard input** has the advantage that it doesn't require any external hardware (see Figure 15.5).

Mouse/keyboard input can be executed in one or more of the following ways depending on the program:

- All mouse: duration selected from palette, note clicked into staff.
- Mouse/keyboard: duration selected with a keystroke (for example, "e" for eighth note), note clicked into staff (or selected from onscreen music keyboard).

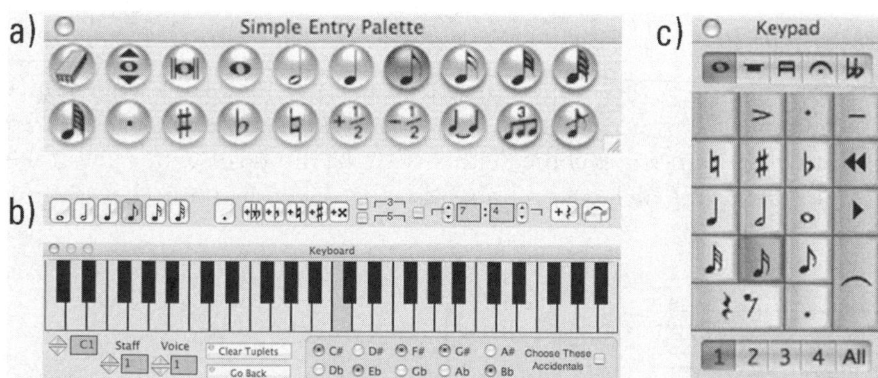

Figure 15.5 Note palettes from several programs: (a) Finale 2009, (b) NoteAbility Pro including onscreen keyboard, and (c) Sibelius 5.

- All computer keyboard: duration selected with a keystroke, note selected with a keystroke. This particular method can be quite fast.

MIDI Input

MIDI input is probably the most commonly used of the note entry methods. MIDI note-on messages provide a key number and velocity value, but no inherent duration or timing information. The computer can record the time that note-on and note-off events arrive, but it is up to the notation software to interpret these as notated durations. The duration can either be chosen in advance with the mouse or the computer keyboard (step time) or the software can use the time between note-on and note-off events combined with a metronome value in beats per minute to generate the appropriate duration (real time).

Notation software can determine the pitch from the key number of the note-on message, but the enharmonic spelling of that pitch is indeterminate. Each key on a keyboard controller is assigned a single key number in the note-on/note-off MIDI messages, but in notation, each key can have two or more legitimate spellings depending on the musical context. For example, the key that is three half-steps above middle C is key number 63 in a MIDI note message, but can be spelled as D♯, E♭, or F♭♭ (see Figure 15.6).

To partially resolve this issue, notation software can look to the key signature. In the key of C major, the pitch that is three semitones above C is usually spelled E♭ (a pitch borrowed from the parallel minor). In the key of E, that pitch will usually be spelled D♯ (the leading tone). The spelling of that note as F♭♭ would be a little unusual—perhaps as the diminished seventh interval in a G♭ fully diminished seventh chord.

However, there are often cases where using the key signature doesn't yield the proper enharmonic spelling and you have to change it manually. This difference in the way that sound-related data (MIDI) and musical notation data are represented will be discussed further below.

As mentioned above, there are two primary ways to enter notation data with MIDI: step time and real time.

Step Time

Step-time entry for notation is very similar to step-time entry for MIDI sequencing. This differs from the mouse/keyboard methods above only in that the pitch is entered with a MIDI keyboard—the duration is chosen either with the mouse or with a keystroke on the computer keyboard. Which you choose first is dependent on the specific program (see Figure 15.7).

Figure 15.6 Three enharmonic spellings of a note that could be indicated by the same MIDI key number.

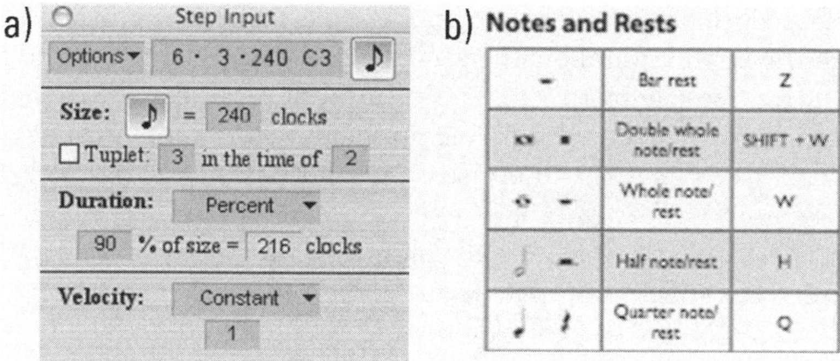

Figure 15.7 (a) The sequencer-like step-time dialog box from Overture 4, and (b) a small portion of the keyboard shortcut listing for durations from NOTION3.

Real time

Real-time entry for notation is similar to real-time entry for MIDI sequencing. The key numbers are provided by the note-on messages, but real-time MIDI input requires some form of metronome that allows the program to interpret the timing of the MIDI note-on/note-off messages as musical durations. The metronome is usually set to a predetermined value, but some programs can employ a form of **tempo following**. In Finale, real-time entry is accomplished using the Hyperscribe tool, in which you can set the metronome to follow your tempo, indicated by tapping on a footpedal or playing a selected note (see Figure 15.8a). In Sibelius, real-time entry is called "Flexi-time," which has a rubato setting that tells the program how much to follow your tempo. This setting ranges from "low" flexibility, or "non rubato," to "high" flexibility, or "molto rubato" (see Figure 15.8b).

In addition, durations must be **quantized** to be a multiple of some minimum duration value. Because it is unlikely that we will always play perfectly in time with a

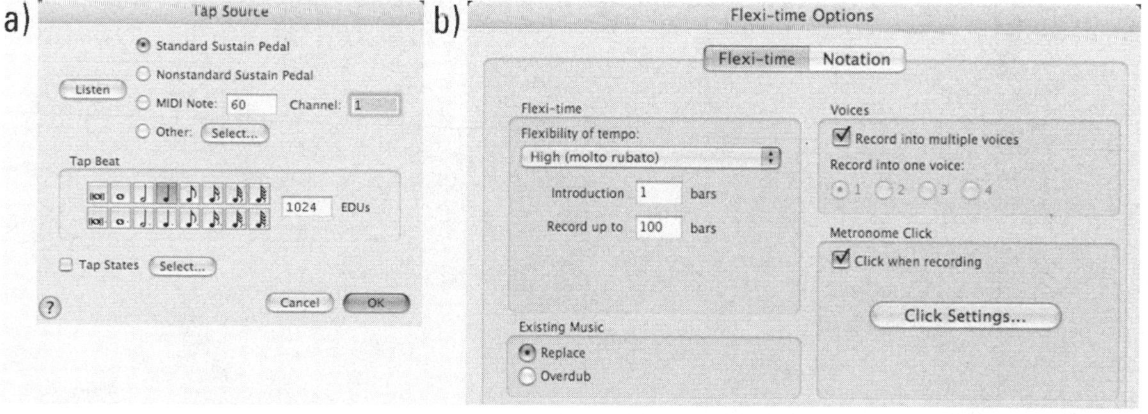

Figure 15.8 (a) The tap source dialog box within Finale 2009's Hyperscribe tool, and (b) Flexi-time options within Sibelius 5.

metronome, we will have to help the notation program decide whether we meant to have a 128th note rest on the downbeat followed by a doubly dotted 32nd note or just a 16th note on the downbeat (see Figure 15.9b). This quantization can happen during the real-time entry (input quantize) or after depending on the program. Input quantization is more "notation-like" (see Figure 15.4b on page 260 and Figure 15.9a) whereas quantizing after the fact is more "sequencing-like" (see Figure 10.18 on page 174).

Many notation programs allow you to record in real time on to more than one staff by using a MIDI key number as a **split point**; pitches above the key number are directed to the upper staff, while pitches below the key number are directed to the lower staff. Some programs use a flexible split point that depends on the program's analysis of where your hands are on the keyboard. Naturally, multi-staff recording is particularly useful for keyboard music.

Many notation programs can also record other MIDI information, such as patch change messages, control change messages, aftertouch, and pitch bend. This information is used for playback purposes and isn't usually translated into graphic elements.

Real-time MIDI entry will likely require some editing, if only to fix the occasional misspelled accidental, but its speed in the hands of a decent keyboard player can make this entry method quite efficient overall.

Audio Input

Audio can also be used for note input in Finale using its MicNotator feature (see Figure 15.10) and in Sibelius by using Neuratron's AudioScore Lite, which is bundled with it. MicNotator takes audio from a single-line instrument and analyzes the pitch as it's being

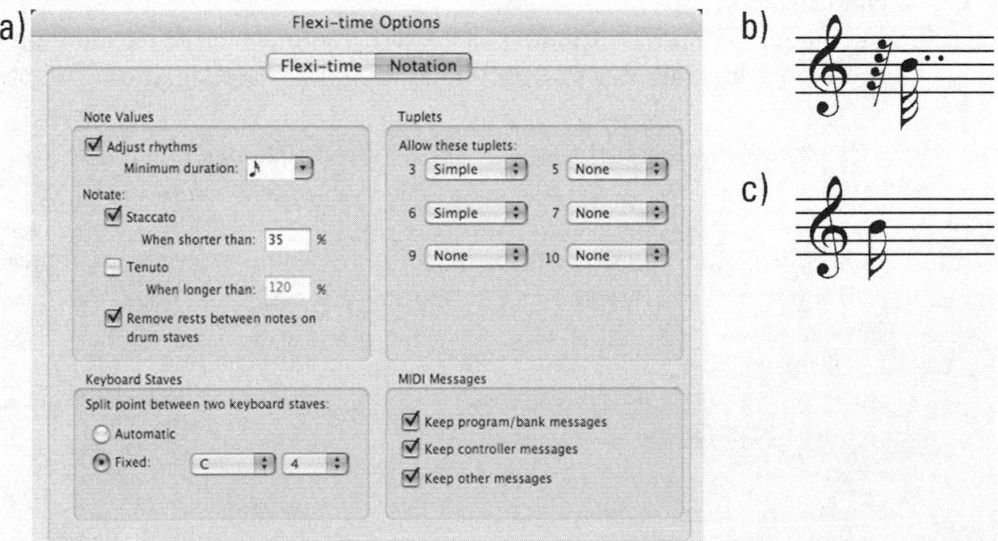

Figure 15.9 (a) Input quantize options for Flexi-time within Sibelius 5, (b) possible notation without proper quantization, and (c) possible notation with proper quantization.

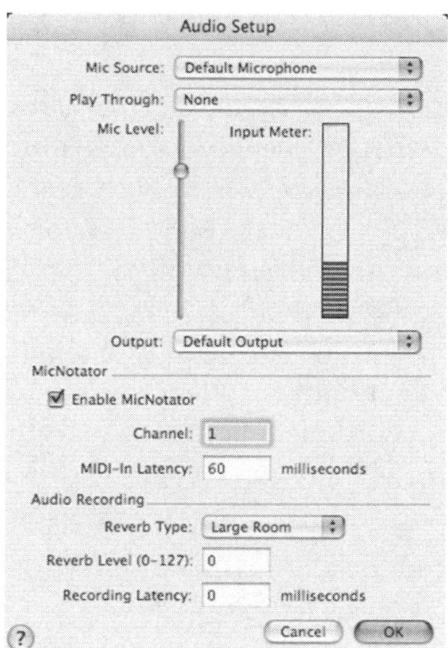

Figure 15.10 The audio setup dialog box in Finale 2009 showing the MicNotator feature.

played. AudioScore Lite records a single-line performance, transcribes it, and allows you to send it to Sibelius for further editing. The same issues with regard to enharmonic spelling and determining duration that were found in MIDI input are present here as well. As with real-time MIDI input, **audio input** will almost inevitably require some correction, but if the speed of audio entry is significantly faster for you than other methods, then it would worth the effort.

Audio can be used to input pitches in any program that accepts MIDI input by using a hardware pitch-to-MIDI converter. This device performs a similar function to Finale's MicNotator feature, but appears to the computer to be just another MIDI controller. An example of this is Sonuus's G2M guitar-to-MIDI converter. This kind of conversion is also available in some non-notation software, both in real time using microphone input or non-real time using an audio file. Examples of software pitch-to-MIDI converters include Widisoft's WIDI Audio to MIDI cross-platform plug-in and Neuratron's AudioScore Ultimate. Widisoft's Windows-only WIDI Recognition System analyzes audio files rather than real-time input. Features like this are available in some sequencer/DAWs as well. Most hardware and software pitch-to-MIDI converters operate best on monophonic (single-line) input, though some can extract pitch data from more complex audio.

Though notation programs do not typically feature extensive audio support, Finale and Sibelius do allow an audio track to be imported, or recorded in Finale's case, and played back along with the notation. NoteAbility allows for more than one audio file to be associated with the score. This allows a notation program to include a live element such as a vocal track or an instrumental solo to enhance the playback from notation. It can also be used as an aid in manual transcription.

ENTRY OF OTHER NOTATIONAL ELEMENTS

Music notation, of course, consists of far more than just notes. Notation programs allow you to enter all of the standard elements, including time signature changes, key signature changes, articulations, dynamics, expressions, slurs, crescendos/diminuendos, lyrics, and chords. These items are typically chosen using the mouse, keyboard shortcuts, or a combination of the two. In general, the less you use the mouse, the faster you can work. Each of these notational elements typically requires its own method of entry, leading most programs to separate these elements into their own tool, palette, mode, or menu items. Figure 15.11 shows how some of these elements are handled in a variety of programs.

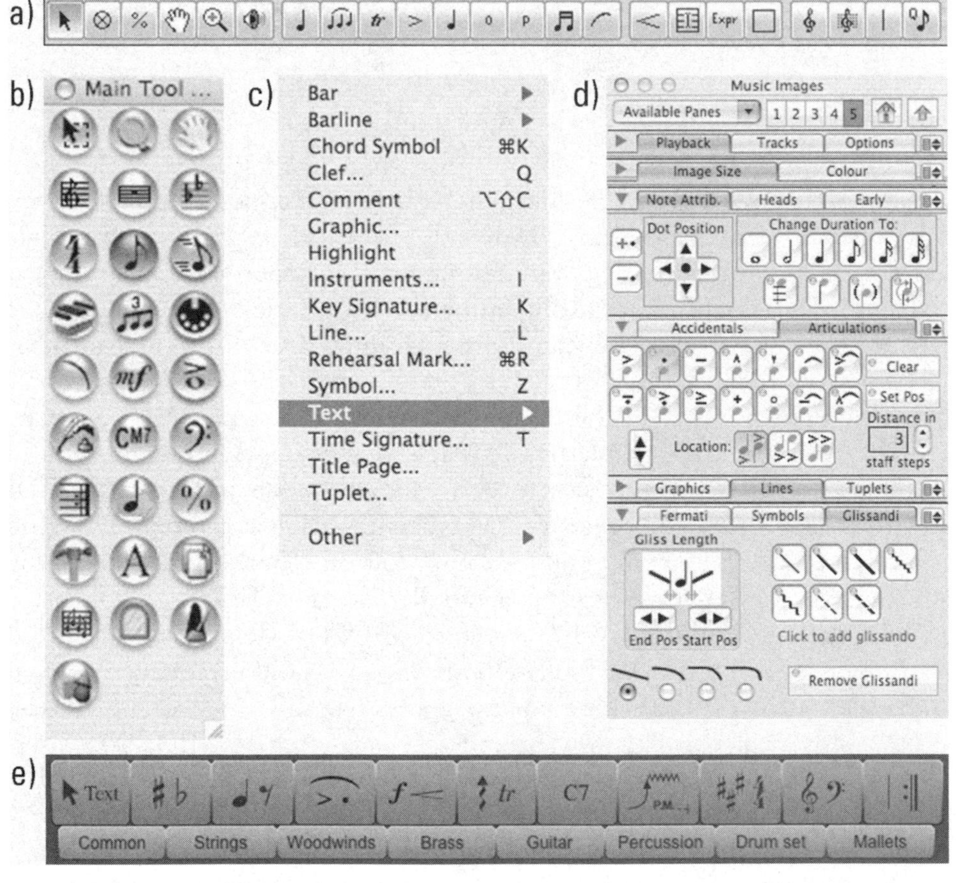

Figure 15.11 A variety of non-note musical elements in notation software: (a) the Time Signature dialog box in Sibelius 5, (b) the Key signature dialog box in NOTION3, (c) the Lyrics submenu in Sibelius 5, (d) the Dynamics pane and instrument-specific score markings pane in NOTION3, (e) the slur palette in Overture 4, (f) the Special tools palette in Finale 2009, (g) the Chord Definition dialog box in Finale 2009, and (h) the Articulations pane in NoteAbility Pro.

The following are brief comments on the ways in which notation programs handle a variety of **non-note notation elements**:

- *Time signatures* range from the everyday, such 3/4 and 4/4, to the more complex, such as 7/8 (grouped as 2+2+3 or 2+3+2 or 3+2+2), to the unusual, such as 1/128. A full-featured program can handle the entire range, whereas a more limited program may not allow you to get more complex than, say, 6/8.
- *Key signatures* range from the standard major/minor key signatures, to custom key signatures found, for example, in some works by Bartok, to the lack of a key signature (not to be confused with C major/A minor) found in many contemporary concert works. A full-featured program can handle the entire range, whereas a more limited program may be restricted to the major/minor key signatures.
- *Articulations* include accents, staccatos, and tenutos. These markings are typically attached to a particular note so that they move position if the note moves position.
- *Dynamics and text expressions* can be attached to individual notes, to measures in a score, or to a page of a score. Most programs have a "library" of commonly used dynamics and text expressions and provide a method for adding your own to the library.
- *Lyrics* are handled as a special kind of text. Lyric syllables are attached to notes, hyphens are used to indicate when words are distributed across two or more notes, lines are used to indicate melismas, and groups of lyrics may be positioned differently to allow for multiple verses in popular styles.
- *Chord symbols* are another form of specialized text. The chord "suffixes" are specially formatted and often require unique symbols not used in text expressions or lyrics. *Guitar fretboards* are specialized graphical symbols indicating guitar fingerings and are found in pop genres.
- *Slurs, crescendos/diminuendos, 8va/8vb indications, and other shapes* are typically attached to notes or positions in the measure and these shapes stretch to accommodate spacing changes in the music.
- *. . . and more.* There are many other possible entry items and editing techniques in addition to those mentioned above. Most full-featured notation programs provide minute control over visual elements, including alternate noteheads, specialized stems and beams, positioning defaults for elements, music fonts, and text fonts.

LAYOUT

Once the notation elements are entered in the score, the third phase of computer notation begins: layout. Layout involves spacing the music, choosing the size of the music on the page, the number of measures per system, and the number of systems per page, and hiding empty staves in a system for larger scores (see Figure 15.12). Fortunately music notation programs provide default settings for most of these layout elements. Often the default music spacing (the spacing between notes and alignment of notes in different

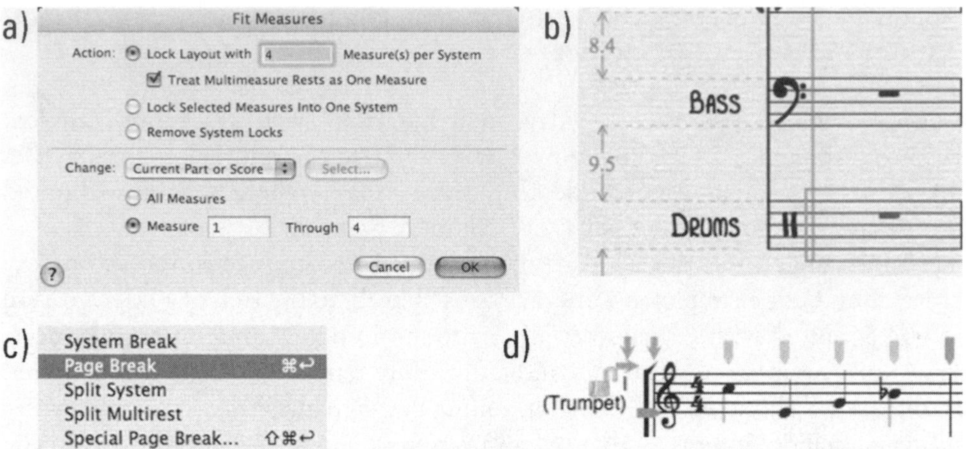

Figure 15.12 Some layout views: (a) the Fit Measures dialog box in Finale 2009, (b) the distance between staves shown in Sibelius 5, (c) the Break submenu in the Layout menu of Sibelius 5, and (d) some of the note spacing controls in NoteAbility Pro.

staves of a system) is acceptable, but the number of measures per system and systems per page may not provide logical system breaks or workable page turns in the case of performance parts.

SPECIAL FEATURES

In addition to the standard features mentioned above, several notation programs have unusual features that are worth noting. For example, both Finale and Sibelius support plug-ins that provide utilities to modify or generate music. Both programs ship with a variety of plug-ins and others are available from third parties, much like audio processing plug-ins or virtual instrument plug-ins for sequencer/DAWs. However, instead of acting on audio, these plug-ins act on notation data, such as notes, chords, and dynamics. These plug-ins range from utilities that add cautionary accidentals or check instrument ranges to plug-ins that aid in composing and arranging by automatically harmonizing an ensemble from a lead sheet or by generating 12-tone rows (see Figure 15.13).

Finale and Sibelius also provide special features for music education, including the automatic creation of worksheets for scales, arpeggios, and chord progressions, posters, and aids for improvisation (see Figure 15.14). In addition, Finale files can be saved in a format for use by MakeMusic's SmartMusic intelligent accompaniment software, which can be used by students at all levels as a practice aid. SmartMusic will be discussed further in the next chapter, "Computer-assisted Instruction."

The program NOTION3 promotes a flexible tempo performance using its "NTempo" feature, which allows you to control playback by tapping keys on the computer keyboard. To use this feature, you create a special NTempo track with rhythmic values that will be the values you tap, place NOTION3 into "performance" mode, and begin

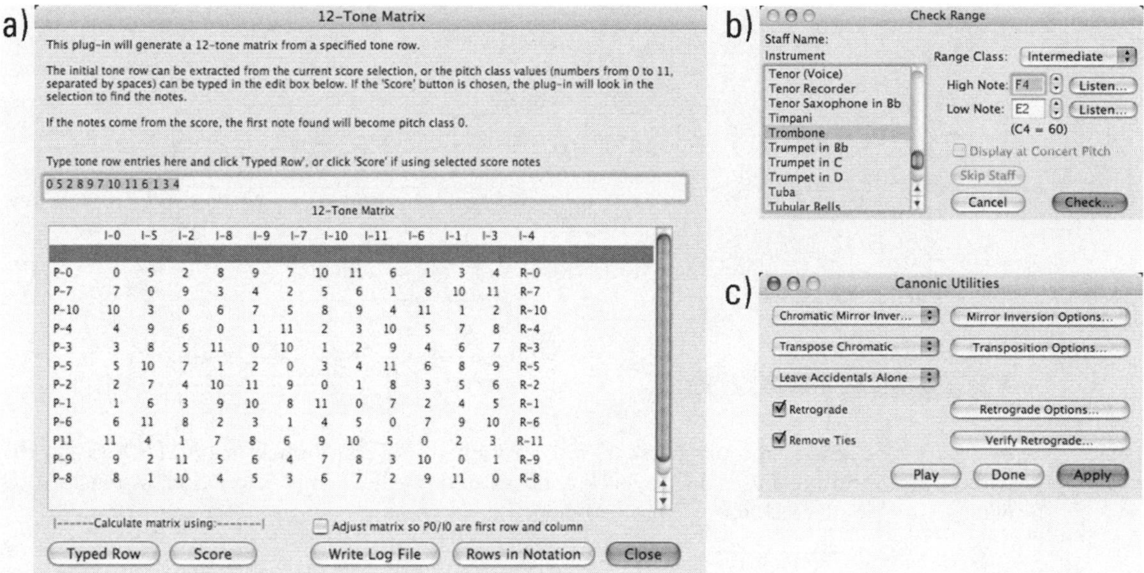

	I-0	I-5	I-2	I-8	I-9	I-7	I-10	I-11	I-6	I-1	I-3	I-4	
P-0	0	5	2	8	9	7	10	11	6	1	3	4	R-0
P-7	7	0	9	3	4	2	5	6	1	8	10	11	R-7
P-10	10	3	0	6	7	5	8	9	4	11	1	2	R-10
P-4	4	9	6	0	1	11	2	3	10	5	7	8	R-4
P-3	3	8	5	11	0	10	1	2	9	4	6	7	R-3
P-5	5	10	7	1	2	0	3	4	11	6	8	9	R-5
P-2	2	7	4	10	11	9	0	1	8	3	5	6	R-2
P-1	1	6	3	9	10	8	11	0	7	2	4	5	R-1
P-6	6	11	8	2	3	1	4	5	0	7	9	10	R-6
P11	11	4	1	7	8	6	9	10	5	0	2	3	R-11
P-9	9	2	11	5	6	4	7	8	3	10	0	1	R-9
P-8	8	1	10	4	5	3	6	7	2	9	11	0	R-8

Figure 15.13 Some plug-ins: (a) the 12-Tone Matrix plug-in from Sibelius 5, (b) the Check Range plug-in from Finale 2009, and (c) the Canonic Utilities plug-in from Finale 2009.

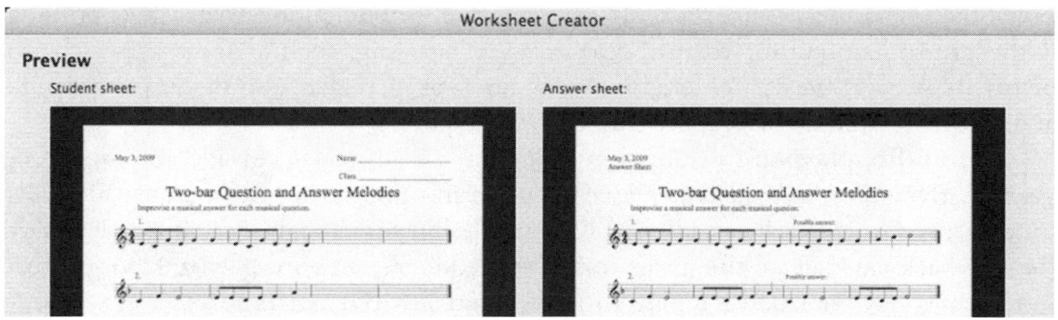

Figure 15.14 The Worksheet Creator in Sibelius 5 showing the first two two-bar question and answer melodies with a student worksheet and an answer sheet.

tapping (see Figure 15.15a and b). NOTION3 promotes this feature as a live performance tool where the tapping itself can serve as a "conducted" performance in situations where electronic instruments are needed to supplement real instruments. Your variable rate of tapping can also be saved as an NTempo session, which can be reloaded and played back. Finale offers a variable "tappable" tempo feature through the tempo track in its studio view (see Figure 15.15c), and Sibelius offers such a feature through its "Live Tempo" function. In each of these cases, the tempo alterations from the tapping playback can be stored and edited. Most notation programs will play back the tempo changes, accelerandos, and ritardandos that are indicated in the score, but the tappable tempo has the potential to provide more realistic performances from notation programs.

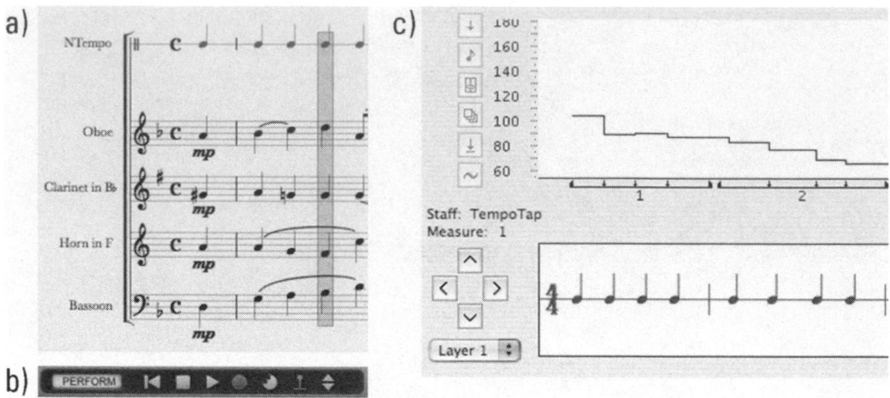

Figure 15.15 Flexible tempo playback: (a) a score with an NTempo track in NOTION3, (b) the "Perform" button in NOTION3's playback controls, and (c) the TempoTap editor in Finale 2009 showing a variable playback tempo that was tapped in by the user.

NOTATION SOFTWARE OUTPUT

Notation programs are primarily designed to produce printed music, so naturally printing is the primary output for them. Some facets of printing, such as fonts are discussed below. However, the data entered into a notation program can also be output through audio playback, audio file export, and data file export.

The **audio playback** in notation programs has advanced considerably in recent years. Early audio playback either used simple piano timbres or mediocre-quality GM instruments. Finale, Sibelius, and NOTION3 each ship with a sophisticated sample library for playback and all of the programs discussed here support playback via virtual instruments (AU and/or VST plug-ins) and external MIDI instruments.

In addition to the sounds used for playback, the programs discussed also support playing back the dynamic, expressive, and articulation markings along with any tempo alterations. Finale uses its "Human Playback" feature to interpret the rhythmic feel of the music in styles including straight, jazz, funk, and reggae (see Figure 15.16). Rubato tempo can be controlled by using any rubato entered through Hyperscribe or by recording tempo changes in the tempo track in the Studio view (see Figure 15.15c). Sibelius has variable degrees of rubato playback, from "Meccanico" to "Molto Rubato," and allows the feel to be controlled by a "Rhythmic Feel" setting, which includes such styles as straight, swing, waltz, shuffle, and samba. NOTION3 uses its NTempo function (see Figure 15.15a and b) and NoteAbility its Tempo Map for variable tempos.

Since notation programs can play back a score, they can also export that audio performance as an **audio file** in formats such as AIFF, WAVE, and MP3 (each program supports one or more audio file formats). Once exported as audio, these files can be burned to CD, loaded to a personal listening device, or put online.

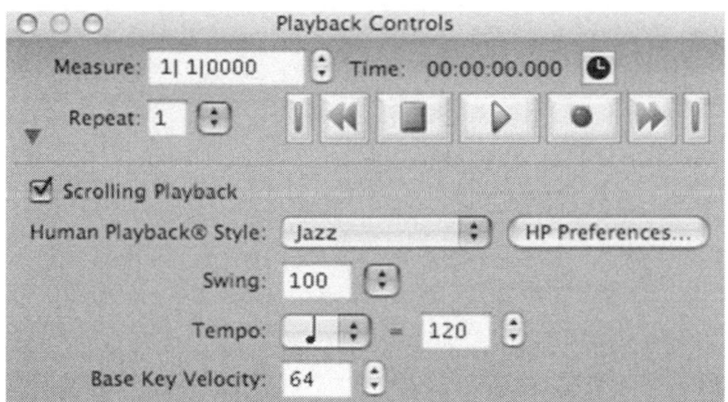

Figure 15.16 Playback options in Finale 2009, including its Human Playback Style.

Notation programs can also output their information as a **data file**. In addition to the exclusive file format that each program uses, you can also export your file as a Standard MIDI File (SMF) or a MusicXML file in some of the programs. SMFs preserve note, tempo, key signature, and time signature information, but no other layout details. MusicXML encodes much more notation-specific information and is thus more suited to transfer from one notation program to another. SMFs are useful for transfer from a notation program to a sequencer and vice versa. In addition to these standard formats, MakeMusic's Finale can also export files in a format suitable for use with its SmartMusic intelligent accompaniment software as mentioned above.

Sibelius can export its files along with a webpage for use with its free Scorch web browser plug-in. Once uploaded to a web server and viewed in a browser via Scorch, the file can be played back, transposed, printed, or saved by the viewer. MakeMusic offers a free Finale Reader that can open, play, and print Finale files as well as MusicXML files that are downloaded to your hard drive, though it's not a web browser plug-in like Scorch. Both Finale and Sibelius allow their files to be uploaded to their websites for distribution to others.

NOTATION DATA

There are a wide variety of ways to encode music data, each of which has its advantages and disadvantages for a given application. We've already looked at encoding music data as MIDI in Chapter 9, "MIDI Messages." However, as discussed above in the section on note entry, MIDI messages and SMFs have their drawbacks for music notation. When discussing note entry using a MIDI keyboard, we noted that a single key number in a MIDI message could be represented in several different ways in notation through enharmonic spellings (see Figure 15.6 on page 262). The differences between enharmonic spellings in notation are important structural and performance cues for musicians. MIDI can be described as a "sound-related" code, whereas notation programs require "musical notation" codes.

There are many coding schemes that have been developed for notation over the years, including DARMS, SCORE, GUIDO, MuseData, Humdrum, NIFF, and

MusicXML. In addition, each notation program typically uses its own proprietary, and usually private, code for its file format. The topic of music notation codes is involved and interesting, but for our purposes we'll focus on MusicXML, which is supported for import by most current notation programs and for export by several of them.

MusicXML is a specific instance of an **XML** (Extensible Markup Language). The "ML" part of XML is related to the "ML" of HTML, and an XML uses elements such as tags that are similar to the HTML code that underlies webpages. XML is a general specification for creating markup languages, so the creator of an XML develops a markup code (tags) and then creates a file (or files) to provide the definition for those tags, a DTD file (Document Type Definition) or an XSD file (XML Schema Definition).

As an example of MusicXML encoding, the notation shown in Figure 15.17a was created in Finale 2009 and then exported as a MusicXML file. Finale has built-in support for Music XML import and export and enhanced support is available through a purchasable plug-in from Recordare, the company that developed MusicXML. An excerpt of the MusicXML file that includes just the data associated with the notes themselves is shown in Figure 15.17b. The tags relating to clef, key signature, time signature, and barlines are not shown.

The two notes in Figure 15.17a are represented by the two <note> and </note> pairs in Figure 15.17b. Each note has pitch tags that specify it in terms of its note name,

a)

b)

```
<note default-x="122">
        <pitch>
                <step>C</step>
                <alter>1</alter>
                <octave>5</octave>
        </pitch>
        <duration>2</duration>
        <voice>1</voice>
        <type>half</type>
        <accidental>sharp</accidental>
        <stem default-y="-50.5">down</stem>
</note>
<note default-x="200">
        <pitch>
                <step>F</step>
                <octave>5</octave>
        </pitch>
        <duration>2</duration>
        <voice>1</voice>
        <type>half</type>
        <accidental>natural</accidental>
        <stem default-y="-36">down</stem>
</note>
```

c)

Parts per quarter note (PPQN) = 480				
Delta Time = 0	Note-on	ch. 1	73	64
Delta Time = 960	Note-off	ch. 1	73	64
Delta Time = 0	Note-on	ch. 1	77	64
Delta Time = 960	Note-off	ch. 1	77	64

Figure 15.17 A musical notation code versus a sound-related code: (a) a small notation example, (b) notes from that example in Music XML code, and (c) notes from that example as they might appear in a Standard MIDI File (SMF).

any chromatic alteration, and the octave, with 5 representing the octave above middle C. Also within the note tags are information related to duration, the voice (many notation programs allow for multiple independent voices on one staff), the type of note ("half" for half note), and any accidental. There is also a set of tags for stem direction. As you can see, essential data concerning the visual representation of the music is present in this code.

The code shown in Figure 15.17c presents the same data as it might be found in a SMF. This code is *not* an excerpt from an SMF itself; it is an approximation of such data presented in plain text and decimal digits to make it easier to read. First, the PPQN (parts per quarter note) is defined as the basis for time designations in the file. Each event in the file is preceded by a "delta time," which is the number of ticks elapsed since the last event. Familiar note-on and note-off messages specify the notes themselves. The C♯ is represented by MIDI key number 73 (which could also represent a D♭) and the F♮ is represented by MIDI key number 77 (which could also be E♯). No indication is given concerning accidentals or stem direction. As you can see from even this simple example, sound-related codes (MIDI) and musical notation codes (MusicXML) encode music data to satisfy very different sets of requirements.

The screenshots in Figure 15.18 show some original notation created in Finale 2009 (Figure 15.18a), that notation transferred to Sibelius 5 using an SMF (Figure 15.18b), and that notation transferred to Sibelius 5 using Finale's built-in MusicXML export (Figure 15.18c). The MusicXML transfer gets all of the note spellings and much of the layout right—a stray tempo marking and some improperly placed triplet brackets are the biggest "problems." Among the problems with the SMF transfer, on the other hand, are the missing triplets, dynamics, phrase markings, the mangled grace note, lack of transposition information for the clarinet, the lack of information about the correct number of measures per system, and the lack of separation between the two staves of the piano (they are combined because they were on the same MIDI channel in Finale).

MUSIC FONTS

Many of the musical images used by a notation program are drawn from one or more **music fonts**. Music fonts are collections of musical images, such as noteheads, stems, clefs, accidentals, and dynamics. In a music font, regular keystrokes plus modifiers (shift, option/alt, command/control) on a computer keyboard are mapped to the musical images. This allows the program to store the keystroke (a small amount of data) in the actual notation file and keep the image that is mapped to that keystroke (a larger amount of data) in a separate file—the font file. This also allows the music images to be changed quickly from one font to another. For example, for a jazz piece you may want to switch from a classical-looking font to a font that looks more "handwritten." This same mapping of keystroke to image is true with regular text fonts as well, but it seems more "normal" to us because when we type an "A" on the computer keyboard we see an image of an "A" on the screen and on the printed page.

Figure 15.18 SMF versus MusicXML file transfer: (a) original notation, (b) file transferred using an SMF, and (c) file transferred using MusicXML.

Most notation programs use their own specially designed fonts, though there are several common fonts, such as the Sonata font, that are available and can be used by various notation programs. The fonts that come with Finale 2009 include the Maestro font (its default font), the Engraver font, and the Jazz font ("handwritten look"). Sibelius 5 uses several fonts, including the Opus and Helsinki fonts for classical images and the Inkpen2 and Reprise fonts for jazz. NoteAbility comes with the Scriabin font, Overture with the Aloisen font, and NOTION3 with the Stava font. Most of these programs can use any font that is installed in the system, allowing you to use a different notation font from the default one if you find it more aesthetically pleasing. In addition to standard music fonts, there are a wide variety of other fonts available for notation programs that provide images suitable for medieval music, microtonal music, or contemporary concert music. Figure 15.19 shows a portion of the mapping between keystrokes and images in a jazz font and a classical font.

a)

Key	Alone	With Shift	With Option	Option-shift
A				
B				
C				
D				
E				
F				

b)

								(	)
	!	"	#	$	%	&	'	(	)
	+	,	-	.		0	1	2	3
*	+	,	-	.	/	0	1	2	3
4	5	6	7	8	9	–	–		
4	5	6	7	8	9	:	;	<	=
>						DC			
>	?	@	A	B	C	D	E	F	G
								mp	
H	I	J	K	L	M	N	O	P	Q
								fz	
R	S	T	U	V	W	X	Y	Z	[
							c	DS	
\	]	^	_	`	a	b	c	d	e

Figure 15.19 A portion of the mapping between keystrokes and music images in (a) the Jazz font in Finale 2009, and (b) the Scriabin font in NoteAbility.

Occasionally, there will be a problem with the music font and the system will substitute a generic text font instead. Figure 15.20 shows a musical example using a music font and that same example with a regular text font (Times) substituted for most of the musical images.

Most music fonts are outline, or vector, fonts that are stored as scalable descriptions of how to draw an image rather than as the actual pixels of the image itself; those fonts are called "bitmap" fonts. The advantage to outline fonts is that they look better when resized than bitmap fonts. Bitmap fonts are usually provided at a variety of sizes so that the images don't have to be resized, which would result in poorer image quality.

Figure 15.20 Font error: (a) a musical excerpt rendered with a music font, and (b) the same excerpt with the music font replaced by a standard text font.

In addition, outline fonts will result in better images when used with a printer that supports the particular outline font type. The various outline font types include TrueType fonts, Postscript fonts, and newer OpenType fonts.

COMPUTER NOTATION: WHAT DO I NEED?

In Section II, "Audio," and Section III, "MIDI," there were separate chapters to describe the hardware and software necessary to carry out activities at various levels. Computer notation requires MIDI input and audio output, so the systems described in Chapters 7 and 11 are relevant. As a result, the discussion of what is needed for computer notation can be presented briefly here.

Hardware

At the most basic level, computer notation requires only a standard computer; notes and other elements can be entered solely using the mouse and keyboard. This would be the same hardware system as Audio System 0 from Chapter 7. It is useful, however, to have a controller keyboard to enter notes as found in MIDI and Audio System 1 from Chapter 11 (see Figure 11.1 on page 184). A keyboard controller of any size can be used, though for extensive note entry a 61-key controller or larger may be desirable. The microphone in MIDI and Audio System 1 is optional, but it could be used for note entry using Finale's MicNotator feature or Neuratron's AudioScore Lite, which is bundled with Sibelius.

A scanner, of course, is necessary for input via scanning using SmartScore Lite in Finale, PhotoScore Lite with Sibelius, or the full versions of either of those scanning programs. If you do an extensive amount of scanning, a dedicated flatbed scanner would be desirable. If scanning is only occasionally needed, a scanner included in an all-in-one printer might be sufficient, though Musitek, which makes SmartScore, specifically advises against it. The companies that make the dedicated scanning programs (Musitek, Neuratron, Visiv) list system requirements and/or compatible scanners on their websites. (The website for this book has links to these system requirements.)

A high-quality printer is a necessary component of a computer notation system. For the occasional printout, any printer will do, but for any extensive amount of notation printing a quality laser printer of 600 dpi or higher resolution that supports PostScript and TrueType fonts is essential. In broad terms, you get what you pay for, and cheap inkjet printers are unlikely to be satisfactory for extensive notation printing.

Software

This chapter focused on the full versions of the various notation programs that have few or no limitations with regard to number of staves or available features. However, there are many notation programs available that impose some limitations but come at a lower cost and may sufficiently serve your needs. Fortunately, most companies that make more than one level of notation program provide feature comparisons of their various products. (The website for this book has links to these feature comparisons.)

FURTHER READING

In order to use computer notation software properly it is important to understand the fundamentals of music notation. Gardner Read's *Music notation: A manual of modern practice* (2nd ed., 1979) is a classic reference guide for music notation by hand, and Kurt Stone's *Music notation in the twentieth century* (1980) is an excellent guide for notating some of the more complex techniques found in the twentieth century. Though neither of these books so much as mentions computer notation, they provide a strong background for understanding and evaluating the notation created with computer programs. In addition, Samuel Adler's *The study of orchestration* (3rd ed., 2002) provides many guidelines for notating music for orchestral instruments.

In terms of specific programs, there are several books each for Finale and Sibelius, including Marc Schonbrun's *Mastering Sibelius 5* (2008) and Keith A. Bajura's *Finale for composers* (2004). These books are useful, but they become dated as new versions of the software are released. The tutorials provided by Sibelius and MakeMusic (Finale) can serve to fill the gaps or perhaps even take the place of separate program-specific books.

For a detailed exploration of sound-related and musical notation codes, Eleanor Selfridge-Field's *Beyond MIDI: A handbook of musical codes* (1997) is an excellent resource. Materials related to the current state of MusicXML, which was created after Selfridge-Field's book was published, can be found at Recordare's website (www.recordare.com/xml.html).

SUGGESTED ACTIVITIES

This section provides some suggested activities relating to computer notation. These activities can be carried out with any full-featured notation program as well as several of the more limited programs. If your notation program's documentation includes tutorials, it is valuable to go through those first before engaging in the activities listed here, so that you can translate the instructions here into your notation program's "language."

Re-creating existing notation is one of the better ways to learn to use a notation program. The more exacting you are with yourself in re-creating your chosen example, the more you will learn about manipulating notational elements with your software. It is important to remember that you are responsible for the results, not the program.

If you don't have the appropriate music on hand for any of these exercises, you may be able to find them in your school's library or in a public library. You can also find public domain music on the Internet, though due to the nature of current copyright laws, most of the public domain music available is from the early part of the twentieth century and before. (Links to some of the websites containing freely available public domain sheet music are on the book's website, though you must be careful that the works are actually in the public domain and are not being pirated.)

Re-create a Lead Sheet

A lead sheet consists of a single staff with melody, chord symbols, and lyrics and is usually associated with jazz and pop music. Lead sheets are particularly useful as an initial exercise because they are usually not too long and have a variety of entry elements (notes, chords, lyrics). Many lead sheets also contain repeats and first and second endings.

You can find suitable lead sheets in a variety of places, including jazz "fake" books and books of popular songs. If the music you have has both a piano part and a vocal line with lyrics and chord symbols, you can ignore the piano part and treat the voice part like a lead sheet.

The assignment should include the following:

- Desired assignment elements: single staff, first and second endings, notes, chord symbols with guitar fretboards, and lyrics (one or two verses).
- Note entry techniques: mouse and computer keyboard or step-time entry with MIDI keyboard

The precise steps for re-creating a lead sheet in your software will depend on the specific software you use, but the basic outline is as follows:

- *Setup*
  - Create the single staff with the appropriate clef and key signature.
  - Add or delete measures so that you have the correct number.
  - Add the repeat marks and first and second endings if applicable.
- *Entry*
  - Enter the notes with the appropriate accidentals and ties.
  - Enter the lyrics using a second verse where it is called for.
  - Enter the chords and show both the chord symbol and the guitar fretboards.
- *Layout*
  - Arrange the music on the page to appear like the example you are using, including the correct number of measures per system and systems per page.
  - Create any indents or shortened systems found in the original.

Re-create Piano-vocal Music

Piano-vocal music will have a vocal staff with lyrics and a two-stave piano part. It may also have chord symbols and guitar fretboards. If your lead sheet example from the previous exercise included a piano part, you can use that same example here and add the piano part to the lead sheet you just created. Public domain piano-vocal scores are also available on the Internet, particularly songs by such composers as Schubert and Schumann. If the song is particularly long, use just one or two pages so that you can concentrate on each element.

The assignment should include the following:

- Desired assignment elements (beyond the lead sheet): vocal staff and piano staff, two voices in the right hand of the piano part (one stem up, the other stem down), dynamics, and metronome marking.
- Note entry techniques: step-time entry with MIDI keyboard and real-time entry with MIDI keyboard.

The precise steps for re-creating a lead sheet in your software will depend on the specific software you use, but the basic outline is as follows:

- *Setup*
  - Create the vocal staff and piano staves with the appropriate clefs and key signature.
  - Add or delete measures so that you have the correct number.
  - Add the repeat marks and first and second endings if applicable.
- *Entry*
  - Enter the notes with the appropriate accidentals and ties. Try each different note entry method, including step-time entry and real-time entry. If more than one voice is present in one of the piano staves of your example, re-create that in your version.
  - Enter the lyrics using a second verse where it is called for.
  - Enter the chords, if applicable, and show both the chord symbol and the guitar fretboards.
  - Enter dynamics, if applicable.
- *Layout*
  - Arrange the music on the page to appear like the example you are using, including the correct number of measures per system and systems per page.
  - Create any indents or shortened systems found in the original.

Re-create or Arrange a Small Combo Score

A combo score in a jazz style will consist of two or three horns (drawn from trumpets, saxes, and trombones) plus a rhythm section of piano, bass, and drums. If you can't find such a score in your library, you can use the piano-vocal music from the previous exercise and arrange it for a combo. However, it is useful to use an existing piece as a guide so that you can see the special symbols used in jazz, such as slash notation and rhythmic slash notation for piano chords, one-bar or multiple-bar repeat symbols, and drum kit notation. A jazz combo score will likely be more difficult to find in the public domain.

The assignment should include the following:

- Desired assignment elements:
  - jazz "handwritten" style font;
  - two or three horn parts (one or more transposing parts), piano, bass, and drums;
  - chord symbols, chord slashes and rhythmic chord slashes in the piano part;
  - one- or two-bar repeats in one of the parts;
  - slurs, articulations, dynamics, crescendos/diminuendos, and text expressions;
  - extract at least one part.
- Note entry techniques: step-time entry with MIDI keyboard and real-time entry with MIDI keyboard.

The precise steps for re-creating a lead sheet in your software will depend on the specific software you use, but the basic outline is as follows:

- *Setup*
  - Create the horn and rhythm section staves.
  - Add or delete measures so that you have the correct number.
  - Add the repeat marks and first and second endings if applicable.
- *Entry*
  - Enter the notes with the appropriate accidentals and ties. Enter in concert pitch or transposed pitch depending on whether the original is transposed or in C. Try each different note entry method including step-time entry and real-time entry.
  - Enter the chord symbols (no fretboards this time).
  - Enter articulations, slurs, dynamics, crescendos/diminuendos, metronome marking, and text expressions.
  - Enter chord slashes, rhythmic chord slashes, and one-bar or multi-bar repeats.
- *Layout*
  - Arrange the music on the page to appear like the example you are using, including the correct number of measures per system and systems per page.
  - Create any indents or shortened systems found in the original.

Re-create a Larger Score

Once you've re-created a lead sheet, piano-vocal music, and a small combo score, you can expand to a larger score, such as an orchestral score or big band score. If you want to challenge yourself, you might choose a score with some complex elements, such as the different simultaneous time signatures found in Stravinsky's *The Rite of Spring*. The steps for this assignment are similar to those of the small combo score.

Exporting

In the previous few exercises, you saved your document in the native, exclusive file format for your notation program. In this exercise, you'll experiment with different output types (some might not be available in all programs):

- *Standard MIDI File*. You can now open it up in a sequencer/DAW and manipulate it further there or open it up in another notation program.
- *MusicXML* (if available). You can now open it up in another notation program. Try this with both the SMF and the MusicXML file and notice the different results.
- *Audio file*. You can now burn this to a CD (WAVE or AIFF) or upload it to a webpage (MP3/MP4).
- *Web-based file* (Sibelius's Scorch format). Export the file in a web-based format and open it up in your browser.
- *Graphics file* (if available). Export all or part of your file in a standard graphics format (JPEG or TIFF) suitable for use in PowerPoint or Keynote presentations or in webpages. The EPS file format is useful for exporting notation to be used in vector drawing programs such as Adobe Illustrator.
- *PDF* (if available). In Mac OS X, printing as a PDF is built into the print dialog box. Otherwise you would need Adobe Acrobat (not just the Acrobat Reader) to create PDF files. PDF files can be uploaded to websites, emailed, or burned to data CDs.

REVIEW OF KEY TERMS

CHAPTER 16

Computer-assisted Instruction

Computer-assisted instruction (CAI) software for music is designed to assist the student in the acquisition of musical knowledge and skills. The type of "student" at which CAI software is targeted ranges from pre-school and elementary school children who have no experience in music, to middle school and high school students who have started playing instruments and acquiring skills, to college music majors training for professional careers in music. In addition, CAI software is useful to hobbyists for whom the study of music is an exercise in personal enrichment.

This wide range of ages, experience, and goals is reflected in the diverse software that is available. Software that appeals to pre-school children and software that appeals to high school students will be necessarily quite different, even if similar skills are addressed. Similarly, software designed to assist a hobbyist in learning to play guitar and software designed to assist a budding professional in developing aural skills will take very different approaches.

In addition to software that is solely for CAI, any of the software discussed in this book so far can be used in an educational context. For example, audio recording and editing software can be used to teach the properties of sound, MIDI sequencing software can be used to teach arranging and form, software samplers can be used to teach the instruments of the orchestra, and notation programs can be used to teach composition and improvisation. These are only a few of the many ways that music software can be used in music instruction. Because those programs have already been discussed at some length, this chapter will focus on dedicated CAI software and discuss the educational application of other software only briefly.

There are many different types of CAI software that address such topics as musicianship, theory, analysis, history, repertoire, performance, and composition. Some pieces of software focus on just one category, while others encompass many. Software for children in particular seems to encompass a broad range of activities. Software for high school and college students often focuses more narrowly on a topic, such as musicianship and theory.

In addition to addressing varying topics, CAI software also comes in various forms. The most common form is the standalone application, purchased as a package or as a download, but there are also a few freeware programs available and a variety of websites, most of them free, that feature CAI activities. We don't often think of websites as being "software," but in addition to straight-ahead HTML (hypertext markup language), many websites make extensive use of JavaScript, Java, and Flash to generate their content. Browsers can be seen as self-contained platforms for this kind of software.

CAI FOR MUSICIANSHIP AND THEORY

Musicianship and theory are both broad topics. Musicianship includes ear training, sight singing, and rhythm reading, and theory includes note reading, intervals, chord types, scales, chord progressions, and perhaps larger musical units such as phrase, section, and form. Most CAI programs that deal with both musicianship and theory naturally connect these two areas so that, for example, a module in which the student is asked to identify the size and quality of a heard interval is complemented by a module in which the student is asked to notate an interval given by its size and quality. At the heart of these activities is the connection between the heard musical event and notation.

At the pre-school and elementary school level, the ear training component of a program might involve such activities as comparing two notes in terms of pitch, loudness, and timbre, identifying durations and rhythmic patterns, and identifying simple scales and melodic patterns. Rhythm reading might involve having the student read a simple rhythm or listen to a rhythm and then tap it on a key of the computer keyboard. The theory component of a program at this level might involve identifying notes on the staff, simple key signatures, simple scales, and basic rhythmic notation. Some software encourages larger-scale understanding of musical structures by playing a phrase, or several phrases, and then having the student reconstruct it from smaller logical units, such as a beginning, middle, and end.

The ear training component of a program for advanced middle school, high school, and college levels might involve identifying various features of a musical event, such as the interval between two notes, the quality and inversion of a chord, the type of scale, the functional identification of chords in a progression, the transcription of melody, and the transcription of rhythm. Some programs include exercises that require singing intervals, scales, and melodies into a microphone, though such activities pose problems in a computer lab setting. The theory component of a program at this level might include constructing intervals, scales, chords, and chord progressions. Some programs also include harmony, counterpoint, and composition.

Most of these programs naturally focus on pitch (intervals, chords, melodies, chord progressions) and rhythm (rhythmic units, rhythmic phrases). However, there are other dimensions of sound that are addressed by a few. These include timbre and instrumentation, intonation, musical style (popular and classical), frequency range, time intervals, spectral makeup, and dynamic range. Timbre and instrumentation are frequently covered in programs for children and less often in the programs for college students. Topics such as frequency range, time intervals, spectral makeup, and dynamic range fall into the realm of audio engineering, where identifying frequency bands that need boosting or cutting or problematic compressor settings becomes as important as traditional musicianship. There are a few websites and audio CD aids for these sorts of skills.

In addition to the content of the instruction itself, some CAI programs are designed to appeal to younger children through the use of animated figures and game-style drills. As a result, there is a complex interaction between the content of a CAI program and the way it is presented. A high school student who is just learning the basics may require similar content to an elementary student who is also learning the basics, but the high school student is less likely to be attracted to animated characters aimed at the elementary student.

There are many software titles and websites available for ear training and theory at all levels. Here I will outline the basic features of a few representative titles in various forms and at various levels, including software (downloadable or packaged), websites, software specifically for children, and websites specifically for children. Any of the software or websites that cover beginning material could be appropriate for children, but the software and websites in the "for children" categories are designed to appeal specifically to younger students.

Naturally, software changes over time, so some of the programs and websites may have changed to some degree since the time of this writing. It is also important to note that there are many fine programs that are not covered in detail below. (You can find links to some other software below and more links are available on the book's website.)

Theory/Ear Training Software

Alfred's Interactive Musician

Type: Ear training and theory
Level: All levels
Platform: Macintosh, Windows
URL: www.alfred.com/
Features:

- Modules:
  - Pitch Training: single note, interval, melody, scale, chord.
  - Sight-Reading: sight-reading involving one or two hands.
  - Rhythm: reading, reading two hands, dictation, custom, custom two hands.
- 50–150 levels in each ranging from first grade to twelfth and advanced.
- Intervals, scales, chords, range are all customizable (important for advanced user because they start at such an early grade level).
- Chords range from triads up to 7, 9, 11, 13.
- Exercises involve listening and playing the answer on an onscreen or external keyboard rather than by clicking in a staff.

Figure 16.1 The scale module in Alfred's Interactive Musician. (Courtesy of Alfred, Inc.)

- Custom rhythm reading allows you to create your own rhythmic exercises and then be tested on them.
- Record keeping (keeps track of student scores).
- Alfred publishes several other CAI products including Essentials of Music Theory.

EarMaster School by EarMaster

Type: Ear training
Level: Intermediate to advanced
Platform: Macintosh, Windows
URL: www.earmaster.com/
Features:

- Standard tutor and Jazz tutor.
- Standard tutor modules: interval comparison, interval identification, chord identification, chord inversions, chord progressions, scale identification, rhythm reading, rhythm imitation, rhythmic dictation, rhythmic correction, melodic dictation.
- Jazz tutor modules: chord identification, chord progression, rhythm reading, rhythm imitation, rhythm dictation, rhythm correction.
- Singing input.
- Keyboard, guitar fretboard, and notation interfaces as well as MIDI input.
- Web-based guide to content accessible through Help menu.
- Record keeping.

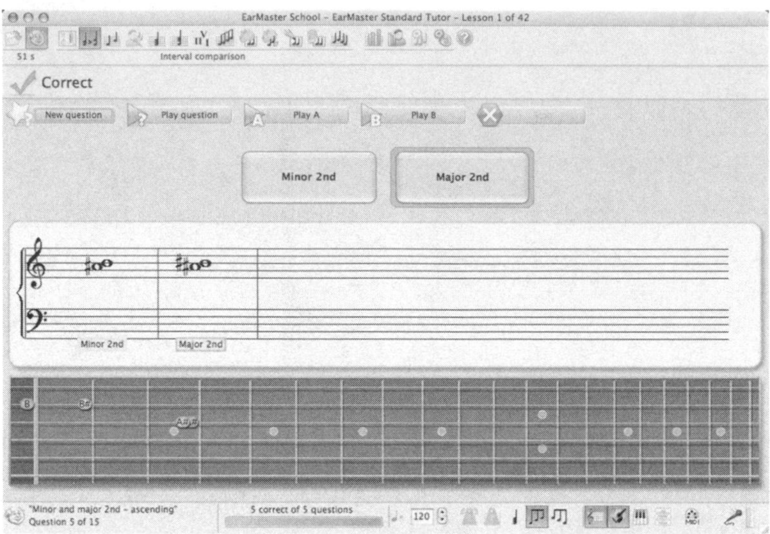

Figure 16.2 Interval ear training in EarMaster School. This view shows the staff and guitar fretboard views. (Courtesy of EarMaster)

MacGAMUT by MacGAMUT Music Software International

Type: Ear training and theory
Level: Intermediate to advanced
Platform: Macintosh, Windows
URL: www.macgamut.com/
Features:

- Modules: Intervals, Scales, Chords, Rhythmic Dictation, Harmonic Dictation, Melodic Dictation.
- Intervals, Scales, and Chords modules have four exercises: aural, written, keyboard, and "make my own drill."
- Each module/exercise has 10–20 levels.
- Two modes: regular and practice mode. Regular mode enforces a progression from one level to the next. Practice mode can be done at any level.
- Completing a level involves getting eight out of last ten correct.
- Record keeping.
- Includes MacGAMUT Music Theory Basics ebook, currently covering intervals and scales.

Practica Musica by Ars Nova Software

Type: Ear training and theory
Level: Intermediate to advanced
Platform: Macintosh, Windows
URL: www.ars-nova.com/

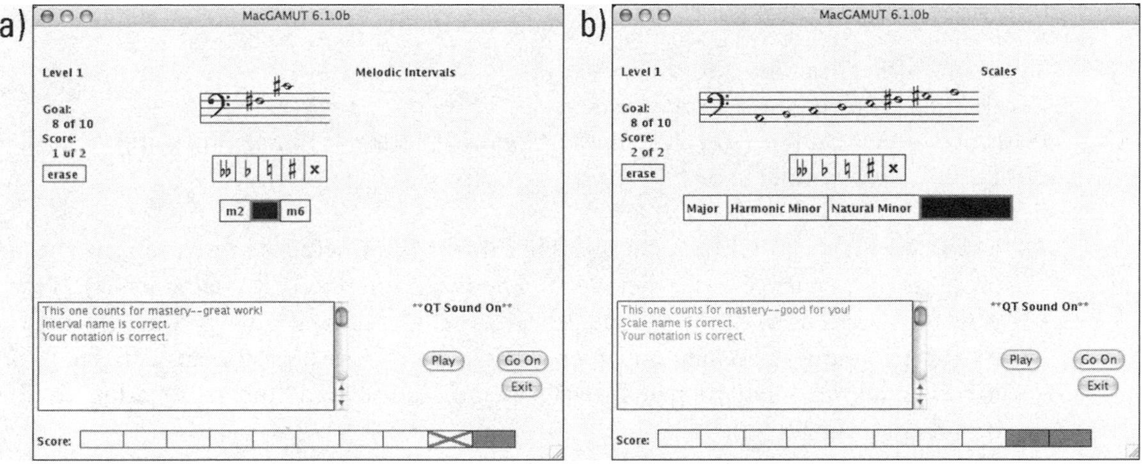

Figure 16.3 Screens in MacGAMUT 6: (a) the Intervals module showing aural training, and (b) the Scales module showing aural training. (Courtesy of MacGAMUT Software International)

Features:

- Modules: Course 1 (The Basics), Exploring Theory Course (linked to included text), Original 17 Activities, Activities by Topic, Write Your Own Music, AP Theory Prep.
- Over 100 activities, including interval size identification, interval quality discrimination, scale writing, rhythm tapping, and melody playing.
- Activities are a mix of notation- or keyboard-based exercises (e.g., notate the scale or play a scale on the keyboard) and listening exercises (e.g., distinguish between intervals of the same size but differing quality).
- Activities in Course 1 (The Basics) pop up a short explanation/tutorial in the web browser.
- Level order is enforced.
- Completing a level involves obtaining a certain number of points.
- Record keeping.
- Includes "Exploring Theory with Practica Musica" web-based ebook, accessible through a menu.

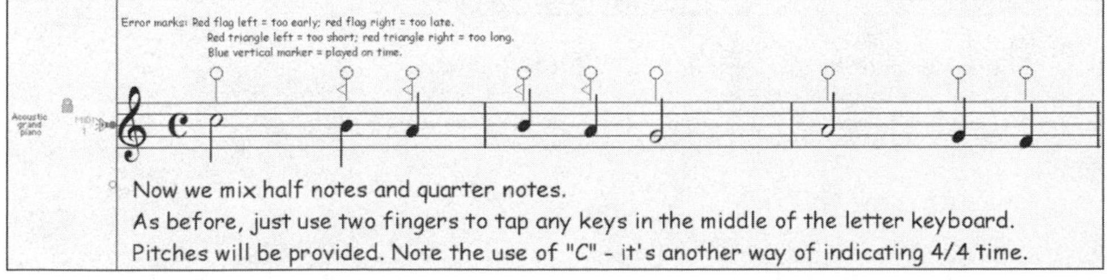

Figure 16.4 The rhythm reading screen in Practica Musica. (Courtesy of Ars Nova Software)

GNU Solfege (freeware)

Type: Ear training and theory
Level: Intermediate to advanced
Platform: Macintosh (uses X11 and XCode), Windows, Linux (freeware)
URL: www.solfege.org/
Features:

- Modules: Intervals, Chords, Scales, Rhythms, Misc (includes intonation, harmonic progressions, cadences, and dictation), Theory (name intervals, name scales), Tests.
- Not fully interactive: intervals and chords include singing but with no evaluation by the program—you sing and then press a button to hear the answer; dictation involves taking standard pencil-and-paper dictation and then comparing to the onscreen answer.
- Intonation exercises require Csound to be installed.
- Tests include intervals, chords, cadences, solfege syllables.
- Free, but not as easy to set up as the commercial programs.
- No record keeping.

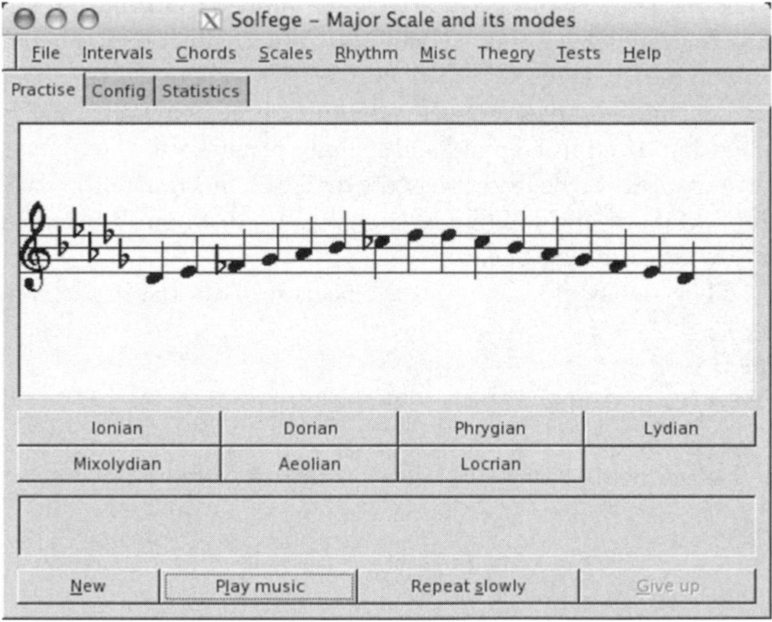

Figure 16.5 The scale identification window in GNU Solfege.

Counterpointer by Ars Nova Software

Type: Theory (harmony and counterpoint)
Level: Intermediate to advanced
Platform: Macintosh, Windows
URL: www.ars-nova.com/
Features:

- First through fifth species in duple time, second to fifth species in triple time.
- Four-part harmony from Roman numerals or from figured bass.
- Cantus firmus can be generated by the program or drawn from Fux.
- Students creates counterpoint for a given cantus firmus on screen in a manner similar to a notation program and Counterpointer evaluates it and notes errors.
- Includes web-based instructions in using Counterpointer and in counterpoint in general accessed through a menu item.
- Record keeping.

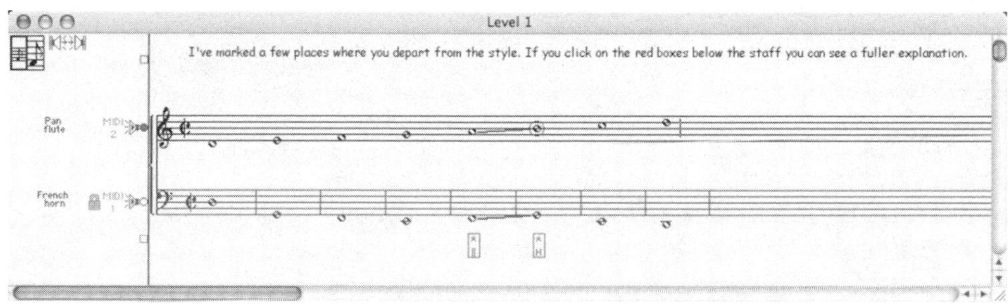

Figure 16.6 Evaluation of a first species exercise in Counterpointer, showing parallel thirds that create a tritone cross-relation error. (Courtesy of Ars Nova Software)

Other Ear Training/Theory Software

- *MiBAC Music Lessons I* and *II* (www.mibac.com/)
- *Musition* and *Auralia* (risingsoftware.com/)
- Several programs from *ECSMedia* (www.ecsmedia.com/)

Theory/Ear Training Websites

MusicTheory.net by Ricci Adams

Type: Ear training and theory
Level: Beginning to intermediate
Platform: Website
URL: www.musictheory.net/

Figure 16.7 The scale ear trainer at MusicTheory.net. (Courtesy of Ricci Adams)

Features:

- Modules: Lessons, Trainers, Utilities.
- Lessons cover basic information about the staff, note durations, scales, key signatures, and intervals.
- Trainers include note, key, interval, and triad written drills and interval, scale, and chord ear training drills.
- Utilities include a chord calculator, a 12-tone matrix generator, and a staff paper generator.
- No record keeping.

Teoría by José Rodríguez Alvira

Type: Ear training and theory
Level: Beginning to advanced
Platform: Website
URL: www.teoria.com/
Features:

- Modules: Tutorials, Exercises, Reference.
- Tutorial topics include: reading music, intervals, scales, chords, harmonic functions, and musical forms.
- Exercises include: rhythm, notes, intervals, scales, key signatures, chords, harmonic functions, and jazz chords and scales.
- Reference section is an alphabetized list of terms, some of which link back to the tutorials.
- No record keeping.

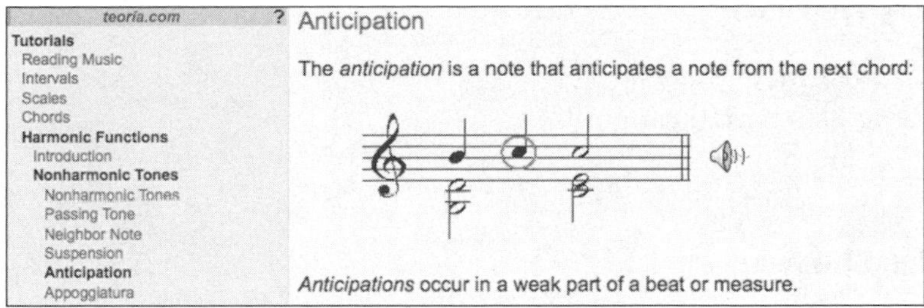

Figure 16.8 A short definition and demonstration of anticipation at Teoria.com. (Courtesy of José Rodríguez Alvira)

Post-Ut by Christopher Ariza

Type: "Sonic measure" ear training
Level: Intermediate to advanced
Platform: Website
URL: www.flexatone.net/post-ut/
Features:

- Modules: Training Sessions and Exams
- Approximately 40 Exams, including frequency identification, time interval identification, spectral density identification, dynamic range identification, acoustic audio analysis, and pitch interval.
- Training Sessions include such topics as single band-filtered noise, single sine, low pass-filtered noise, pulse noise, multiple sine harmonic, multiple sine inharmonic, dynamic noise burst, acoustic band pass filter, acoustic low pass filter, quartertone melodic pitch intervals, quartertone harmonic pitch intervals, semitone melodic pitch intervals, and semitone harmonic pitch intervals.
- Record keeping.

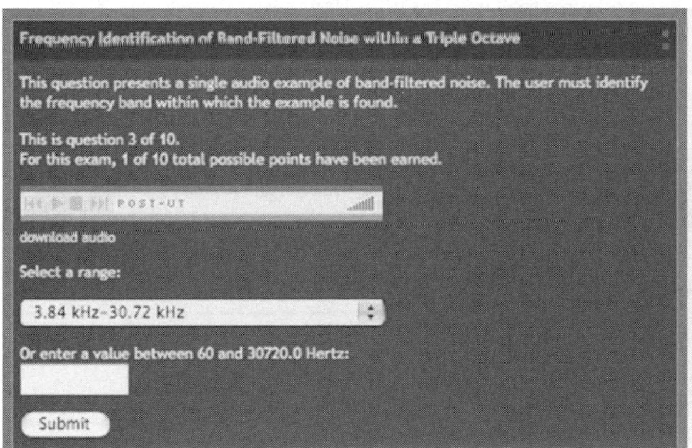

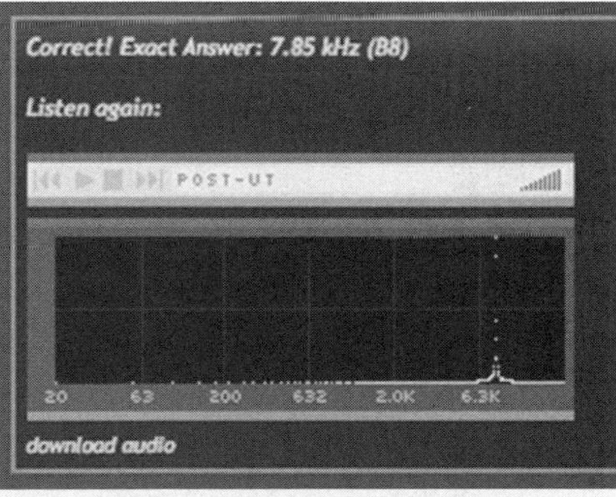

Figure 16.9 Frequency band identification of band-filtered noise question and answer at Post-Ut. (Courtesy of Christopher Ariza)

Other Ear Training/Theory Websites

- *Big Ears* (www.ossmann.com/bigears/)
- *Free Online Ear Training* (www.trainear.com/)
- *Good Ear* (www.good-ear.com/)

Theory/Ear Training for Children

ECSMedia Software—Various Programs

Type: Ear training and theory
Level: Beginning, intermediate
Platform: Most Macintosh and Windows, some Windows only, some not compatible with newer Macintosh systems
URL: www.ecsmedia.com/
Features:

- Many programs specifically designed for children. Over 30 programs overall in ear training, music theory, and note reading that cover all levels.
- Examples of ECSMedia programs suitable for children:
  - *Adventures in Musicland* (game-based ear training and note reading): MusicMatch, Melody Mixup, Picture Perfect, Sound Concentration.
  - *Early Keyboard Skills* (drill-based note reading) (see Figure 16.11): show note letter for pressed key, show staff position for pressed key, drill key-to-lettername, drill lettername-to-key, drill staff position-to-key.
  - *Early Music Skills* (drill-based note reading): line and space notes, line and space numbers, up and down, stepping and skipping.

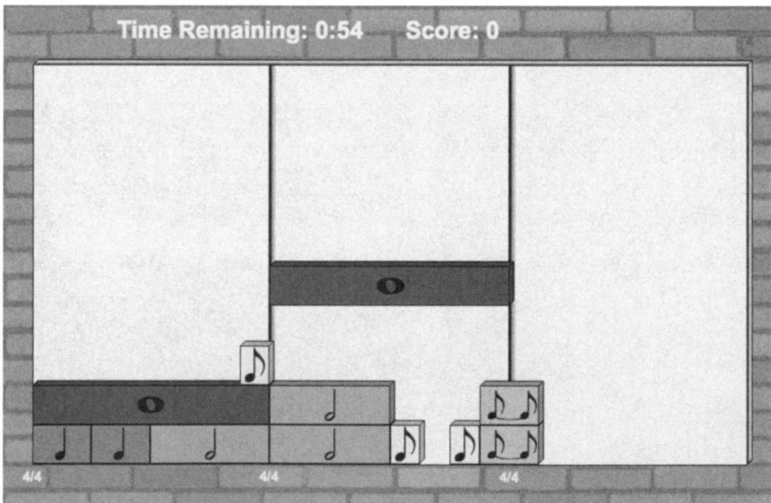

Figure 16.10 The game Musicus with time signiture at 4/4. (Courtesy of FreeHand Music)

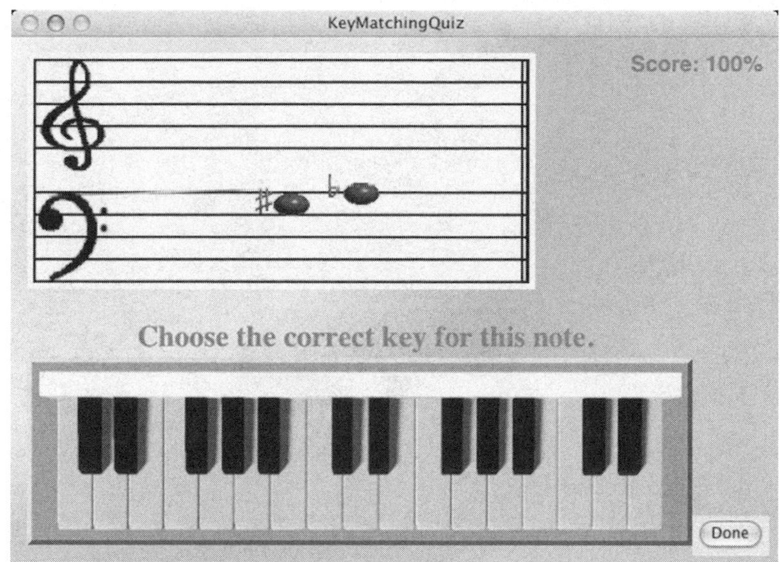

Figure 16.11 Note-matching drill in Early Keyboard Skills. (Courtesy of FreeHand Music)

  - *Musicus* (game-based rhythm drill) (see Figure 16.10): Tetris-like game played with rhythm blocks fitting into meters. Various speeds and meters.
- Most include record keeping.

Music Ace I and II

Type: Ear training and theory
Level: Beginning, intermediate
Platform: Macintosh, Windows
URL: www.harmonicvision.com/
Features:

- Music Ace I (see Figure 16.12): 24 sessions including pitch comparison, loudness comparison, notes of the staff (treble, bass, grand, ledger lines), notes on a keyboard, key signature, and introduction to scales.
- Music Ace II (see Figure 16.13): 24 sessions including beat and tempo, rhythms, key signatures and scales, intervals, time signatures, and introduction to harmony.
- Each session has a lesson in several levels guided by an animated character and a game in several levels.
- A doodle pad in each allows the student to compose music in the staff using various pitches, instruments, and note lengths.
- Record keeping.

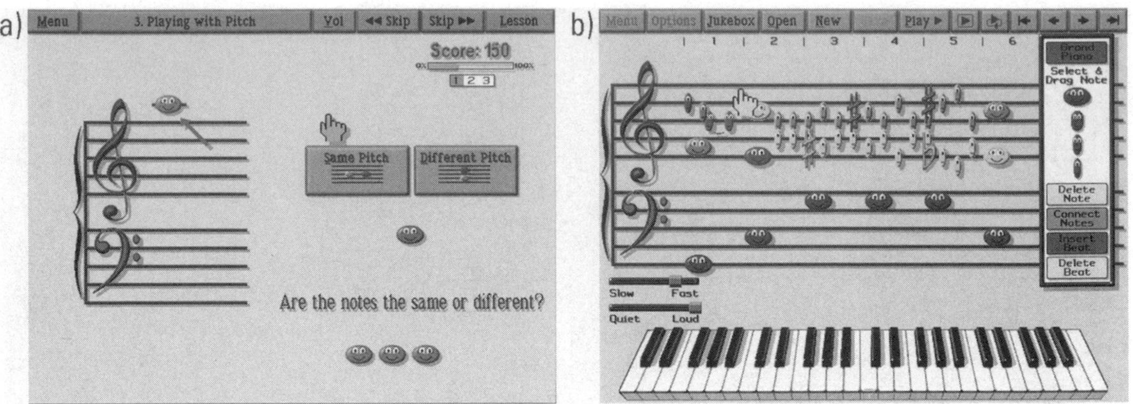

Figure 16.12 From Music Ace I: (a) a pitch comparison game, and (b) a doodle pad. (Courtesy of Harmonic Vision, Inc. Copyright © Harmonic Vision, Inc.)

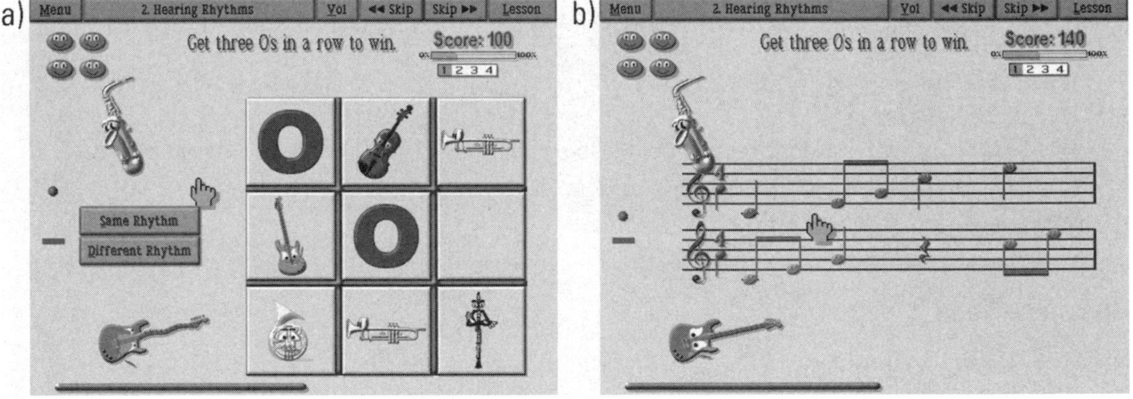

Figure 16.13 Rhythm comparison game from Music Ace II: (a) main screen, and (b) notated rhythms that were compared. (Courtesy of Harmonic Vision, Inc. Copyright © Harmonic Vision, Inc.)

Music Games International—Three Games

Type: Ear training and theory
Level: Beginning, intermediate
Platform: Windows only (CD-ROM, download), website (selected excerpts)
URL: www.musicgames.net/
Features:

- Three games (CD-ROM): Nutcracker Music, Magic Flute Game (see Figure 16.14), Alice in Vivaldi's Four Seasons.
- Some excerpts from these games can be played online, including "Flying Instruments," "12 Steps Game," and "Orchestra Game."

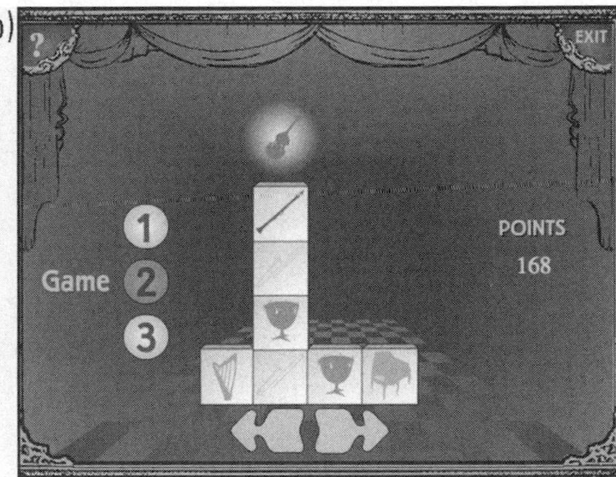

Figure 16.14 (a) "Orchestra Game" from the Magic Flute Game, and (b) "Flying Instruments" from Nutcracker Music. (Courtesy of Music Games International)

- Some excerpts from these games can be downloaded and played on a PC, including the online excerpts plus "Music Riddles" and "3 Stages Game."

Other Ear Training/Theory Programs/Websites for Children

- *Carnegie Hall Online Listening Adventures* (www.carnegiehall.org/article/explore_and_learn/art_online_resources_listening_adventures.html).
- *DSOKids* (Dallas Symphony Orchestra) (www.dsokids.com/).
- *Groovy Music* (www.sibelius.com/products/groovy/index.html).
- *KidZone* (New York Philharmonic) (www.nyphilkids.org/).
- *MiDisaurus Music* (www.town4kids.com/us_music_school.htm).

CAI FOR MUSICAL FORM AND ANALYSIS

The theory components of the software and websites in the previous section were largely concerned with identification of musical entities such as notes, intervals, chords, chord progressions, and cadences. Musical analysis involves recognizing the way that those entities are combined to form larger musical units of phrases, sections, movements, and entire works. Some of the previously mentioned programs delve into that area a bit in the form of melodic and rhythmic phrases for dictation, though the phrase and form implications are seldom explicit. Practica Musica, for example, has a chapter on the elements of form in its web-based "Exploring Theory," but it is not significantly addressed in the exercises. It is more common to find exercises related to themes and phrases in children's software than in the standard theory/ear training software aimed at high school and college students.

There are a number of multimedia guides available for various pieces of music, often associated with music appreciation or music history. Most of these are available only after purchasing a textbook or otherwise purchasing access to those materials. ECSMedia publishes several "TimeSketches" in its **TimeSketch Series** for particular recordings of well-known pieces of music, such as Mozart's Symphony No. 40 (see Figure 16.15), Dvorak's "New World" Symphony, and music from the Miles Davis album *Kind of Blue*. The TimeSketch series analyzes music as a succession of "bubbles" that are in turn nested within larger bubbles (see Figure 16.15). For example, a piece in sonata form would have the first theme and second theme represented by their own bubbles. Those bubbles would then be nested within a larger bubble representing the exposition or the recapitulation. Clicking on a bubble would cause the CD playback to jump to that location, allowing the user to quickly grasp the materials that make up the form. In addition, context-sensitive text during playback provides a kind of play-by-play of the piece. Pre-made guides such as these are helpful for studying particular works and modeling this particular analytic approach.

ECSMedia also publishes the **TimeSketch Editor** and **Editor Pro**, which allow the instructor or student to create such "bubble charts" for music from a CD or a soundfile, create explanatory introductory text, and add running text commentary. The results will be similar to the charts sold in ECSMedia's TimeSketch Series. Such software is useful in educational settings because students can create their own analyses and instructors can create custom charts for materials in their courses.

There are also some freeware resources for creating such guides. One example is Scott Lipscomb and Marc Jacoby's **Bubble Machine** (www.lipscomb.umn.edu/

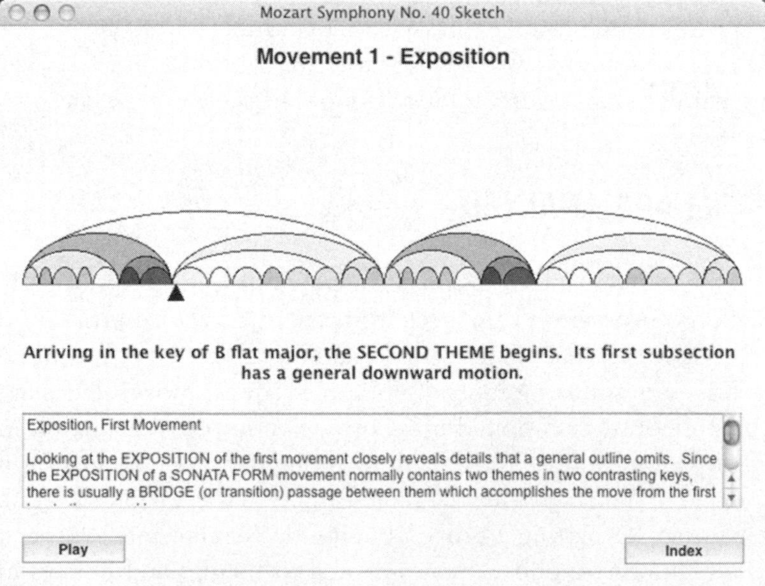

Figure 16.15 Thematic analysis for Mozart's Symphony No. 40 by Anne Silverberg, showing the exposition in the first movement, from ECSMedia's TimeSketch Series. (Courtesy of FreeHand Music)

bubblemachine/), which allows you to create very simple bubble charts (see Figure 16.16). Bubble Machine lacks the running text and other features of the TimeSketch Editor, but it is has the advantage of being free and straightforward to use. Scott Lipscomb has also created a variety of **Form Templates** (www.lipscomb.umn.edu/form_templates.htm) for creating interactive listening guides in such forms as AABA and Sonata Form (see Figure 16.17). The resultant guide has more information concerning form

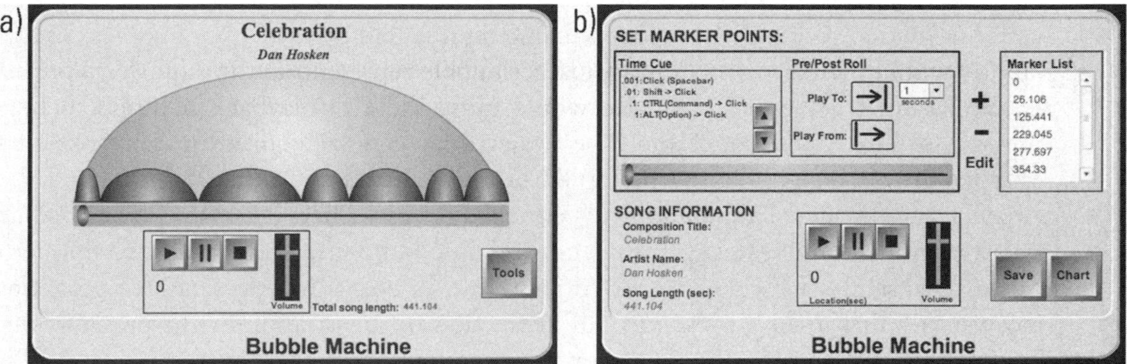

Figure 16.16 Bubble Machine: (a) custom bubble chart for this piece, and (b) the tools for creating the chart. (Courtesy of Scott Lipscomb and Marc Jacoby)

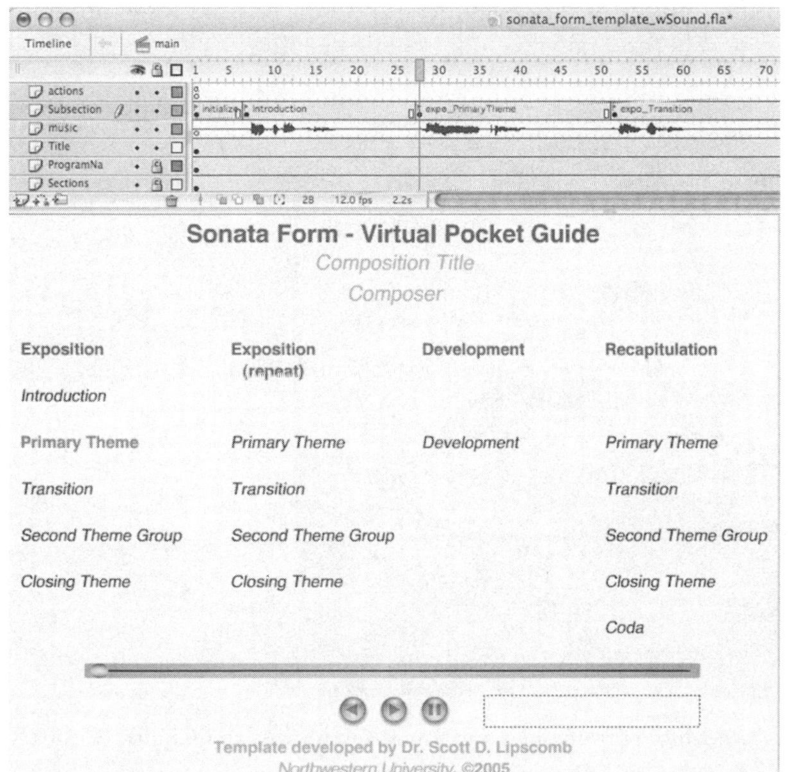

Figure 16.17 Sonata Form Virtual Pocket Guide from Form Templates shown in the Flash editor. (Courtesy of Scott Lipscomb)

than is available with Bubble Machine, but the templates are Flash files and require the use of Adobe's **Flash** multimedia authoring software to customize the guides for different pieces. Naturally, it is possible to use a program like Flash to create such guides from scratch without the templates. However, that is a significant leap in difficulty above using such tools as TimeSketch Editor or Bubble Machine.

CAI FOR HISTORY, TERMINOLOGY, AND INSTRUMENTS

This category involves information acquisition rather than the skill acquisition represented by the previous categories, though this is a fairly loose distinction, as topics such as interval spelling could conceivably be called information acquisition. Software and websites in this category allow for drilling on definitions and historical facts and the presentation of material in a multimedia enriched format. There are many informational websites available concerning music history or composers, including such modern information staples as Wikipedia, so I'll focus instead on a few representative programs and websites that involve some form of interaction or special multimedia presentation. (Links to more resources like this are available on the book's website.)

ECSMedia publishes several programs for presenting and drilling history, composers, and terminology, such as Music Composer Quiz, Music History Review: Composers, and Music Terminology for Bands, Orchestras, and Choirs (see Figure 16.18). These programs are based around multiple-choice quizzes and the terminology program includes a glossary of terms. The programs include record keeping.

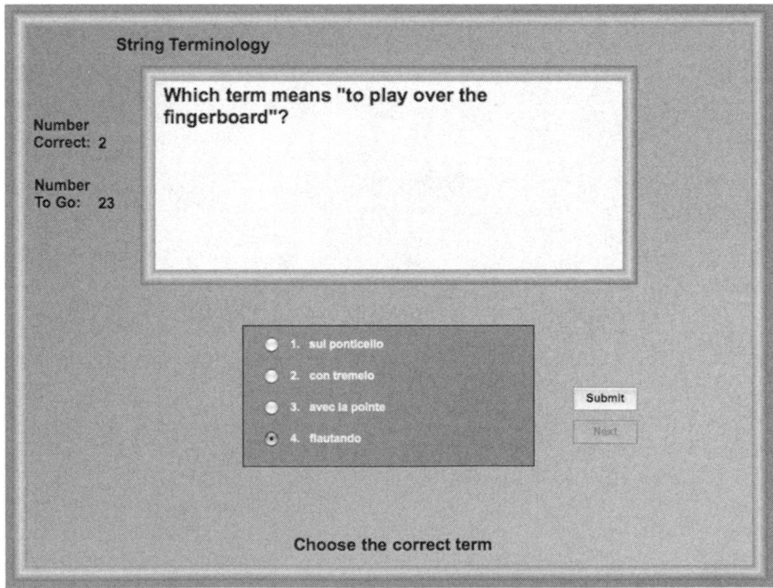

Figure 16.18 Quiz screen from Music Terminology for Bands, Orchestras, and Choirs. (Courtesy of FreeHand Music)

Sibelius Instruments is a multimedia compendium of instruments and ensembles (www.sibelius.com/products/instruments/). The ensemble pages include orchestras, bands, and chamber ensembles of various sizes and eras. An individual ensemble page presents information about the makeup of the ensemble, its origins, and a recommended listening list, and is accompanied by a relevant excerpt. Figure 16.19 shows the ensemble page for the Late Romantic Orchestra. Clicking on an instrument on the ensemble page brings up that instrument's page, which includes its history, playing techniques, notated range for various levels of performers, and sound and notation excerpts of characteristic music (see Figure 16.20). There are many resources concerning musical instruments in print and on the web, but a multimedia presentation such as this one brings the topic to life in a special way.

There are a number of websites that present musical information, but most are not especially multimedia enriched. Some arts education and advocacy organizations, such as ArtsEdge, which is an educational program of the John F. Kennedy Center for the Performing Arts, bring special resources and expertise to bear on their subjects. In addition to educational materials and lesson plans for various topics in the arts, ArtsEdge provides multimedia resources such as **Jazz In Time** (http://artsedge.kennedy-center.org/jazzintime/). This is a multimedia jazz timeline from pre-1900 to the present. Each decade is represented by one to three jazz styles, each of which is briefly described and illustrated with a substantial excerpt from a characteristic performance (see Figure 16.21). This is an example of a tightly focused web resource that presents material economically and elegantly.

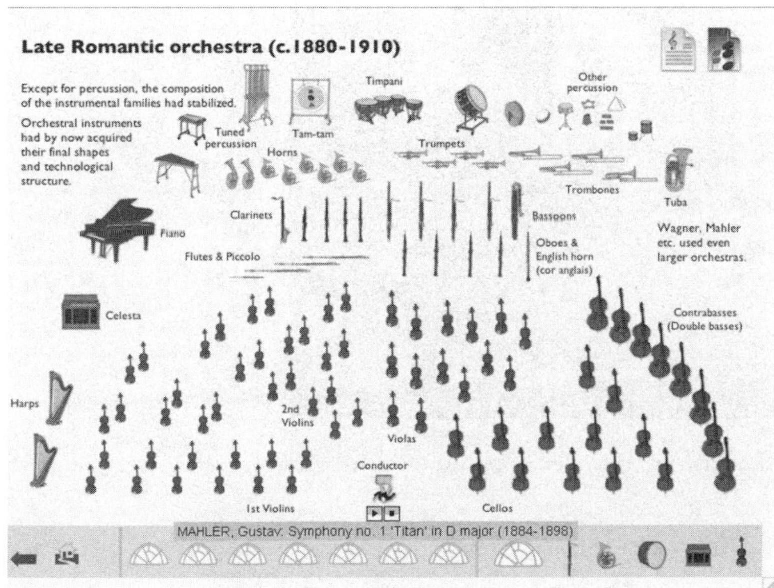

Figure 16.19 Late Romantic Orchestra page from Sibelius Instruments. (Courtesy of Sibelius)

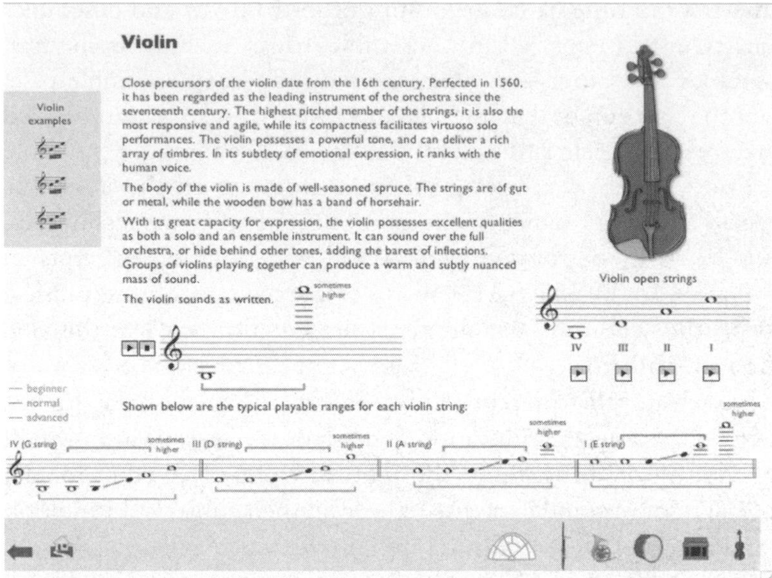

Figure 16.20 Violin page from Sibelius Instruments. (Courtesy of Sibelius)

Figure 16.21 1960s' page showing Free Jazz description and excerpt from Jazz In Time. (Courtesy of ArtsEdge)

Other History, Terminology, and Instruments Programs

- *The Bach Chorales: Multimedia Performance Series* (www.pgmusic.com/bachchorales.htm).
- *Oscar Peterson Multimedia CD-ROM* (www.pgmusic.com/oscarpetersoncd.htm).

CAI FOR PERFORMANCE SKILLS

While theory and ear training are certainly essential performance skills, there are a number of programs that allow students at all levels to improve their performance on their specific instrument.

Practicing along with accompaniment is a vital exercise in the development of performance technique. Because it is rare to get an extensive amount of time with a live accompanist, there is a need for software that can provide this accompaniment. A live accompanist is always listening to the performer for tempo variations and for errors in order to maintain synchronization. Accompaniment programs range from interaction with the performer through audio, as with MakeMusic's SmartMusic, to interaction with the performer through MIDI, as with TimeWarp Technologies' Home Concert Xtreme, to fixed tempo accompaniment, as with PGMusic's Band-in-a-Box.

SmartMusic (www.smartmusic.com/) allows the user to choose from a wide range of standard repertoire, scale exercises, and methods books, import files created in MakeMusic's Finale notation software, and import MP3 files. Once the particular piece for practice is chosen, SmartMusic plays back the accompaniment using sampled/synthesized sounds, or audio in the case of MP3s, and the performer plays the solo part into a microphone. SmartMusic has several different accompaniment modes depending on the chosen material, including "Intelligent Accompaniment" (see Figure 16.22), where the program can follow the tempo and location of the performer, "Strict Tempo Accompaniment," where the program plays at a settable tempo but does not follow the performer, and "Strict Tempo with Assessment," where the program plays at a settable tempo and then marks the performer's errors onscreen (see Figure 16.23). The tempo and key of a piece can be changed even when using MP3 files.

Home Concert Xtreme (www.timewarptech.com/) is also a flexible accompaniment system, but the performer interacts with the program solely through MIDI and the repertoire is in the form of SMFs that you create, download from a free site, or purchase from a publisher. Once a MIDI file is loaded, the user designates tracks to show as notation and the program follows the performer's location and tempo while playing back the accompaniment tracks (see Figure 16.24). Because the input is solely MIDI, this program is more suitable to keyboard instruments, though there are a number of MIDI controllers for other instrumentalists (see Chapter 8, "MIDI Hardware").

Band-in-a-Box (www.pgmusic.com/) automatically generates an accompaniment based on a user-created chord progression and a style chosen from a wide variety of jazz, blues, rock, and country styles. Band-in-a-box does not employ the tempo

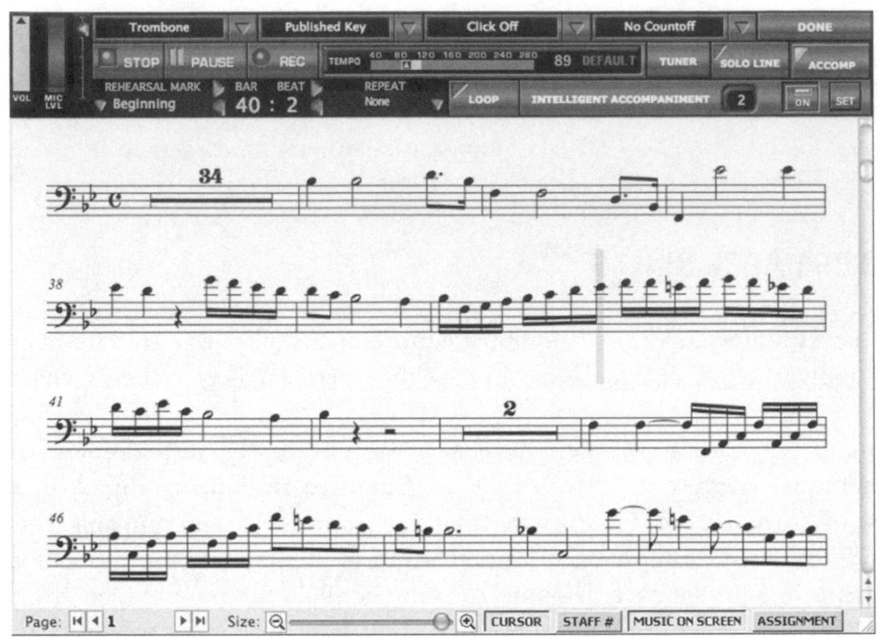

Figure 16.22 SmartMusic in Intelligent Accompaniment mode. The value of "2" for Intelligent Accompaniment indicates that the program will change its tempo only a small amount in response to the performance. A larger number indicates more tempo following. (Courtesy of MakeMusic, Inc.)

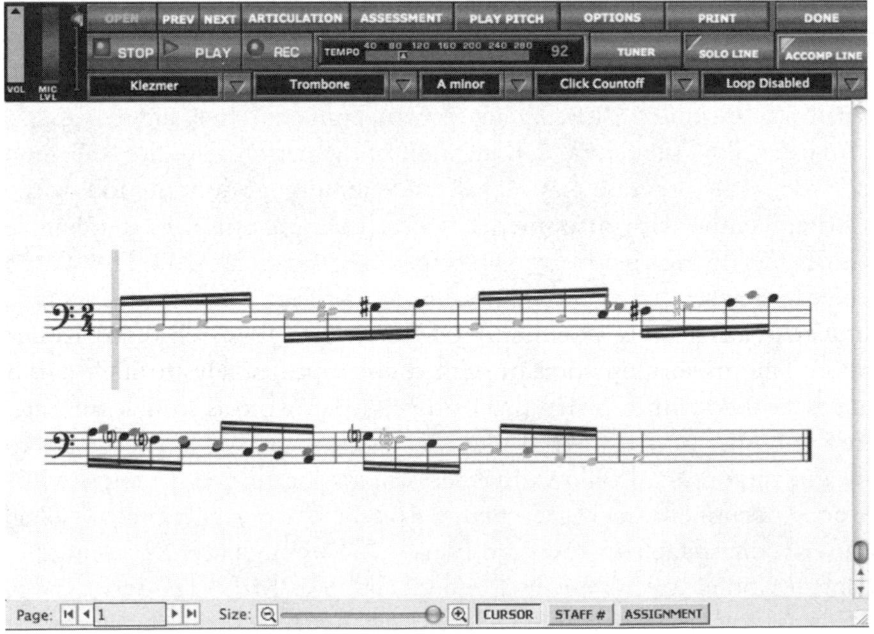

Figure 16.23 SmartMusic showing assessment of a scale performance. Highlighted notes were performed correctly, normal-looking notes were not played, and "double" notes indicate incorrect performance. (Courtesy of MakeMusic, Inc.)

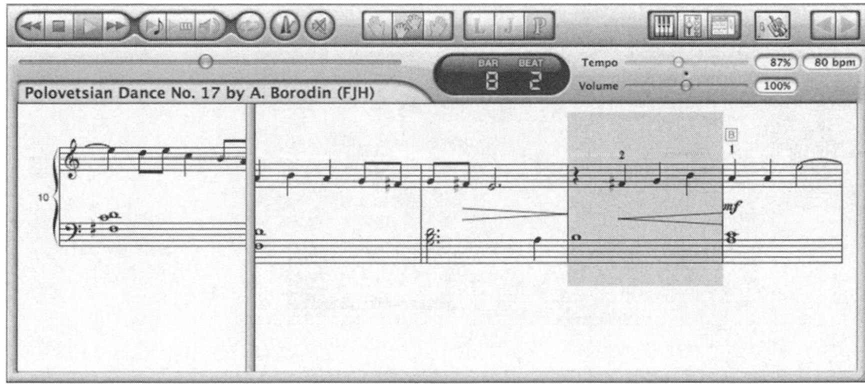

Figure 16.24 Home Concert Xtreme showing tempo following. The shaded box indicates the current position and the separator in the middle of the music allows the performer to look ahead in the music. (Courtesy of TimeWarp Technologies)

following of SmartMusic or Home Concert Xtreme, but given its focus on groove-based popular styles, that is not a particularly desired feature. Band-in-a-Box originally featured only MIDI-based accompaniment but has now made available a wide variety of audio tracks called RealTracks and RealDrums. When a user chooses a style that utilizes these audio performances, Band-in-a-Box extracts chunks of music from the audio files and stitches them together to create a new performance that follows the user's chord progression. These accompaniments can also include audio-based solo instrument lines as well.

Finale and the aforementioned Sibelius also have features that can aid performance skills through their worksheets. These worksheets include scales, intervals, and arpeggios as well as aids to improvisation for various instruments and entire ensembles (see Figure 15.14 on page 269). In addition, even without a specialized accompaniment program such as those discussed above, you can still create custom accompaniments in notation programs or sequencer/DAWs.

Another form of performance assistance comes in the form of a **transcription aid**, such as Ronimusic's Amazing Slow Downer, PGMusic's SlowBlast, or Reed Kotler Music's Transkriber. The primary function of each of these programs is to slow down a recording during playback with a minimum of quality degradation so that you can more easily transcribe the music (see Figure 16.25).

CAI FOR CREATIVE SKILLS

Composition, improvisation, and other creative activities are fundamental musical skills and need to be nurtured in students at all levels, regardless of whether they would consider themselves "composers." Most of the programs that were discussed earlier in the book can be used to encourage creative approaches to music. Recorded audio or audio loops

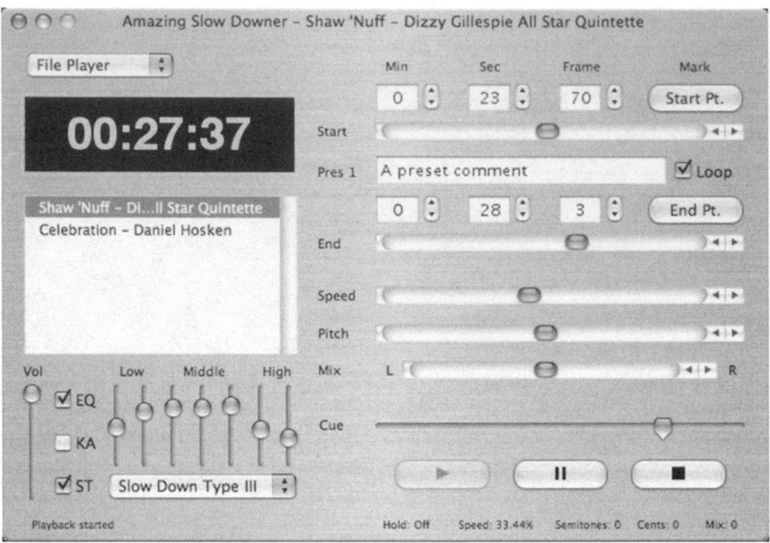

Figure 16.25 The Amazing Slow Downer shown looping a small section of a be-bop jazz recording with the speed at about 33 percent. (Courtesy of Ronimusic)

can be edited, processed, and organized in a DAW to create everything from straightforward percussive grooves to strange sonic landscapes. MIDI recorded into a sequencer can be reorganized, arranged, and re-orchestrated to create complex pieces. Software synthesizers can be used to design functional or unusual sounds to be controlled by sequencers. And, finally, notation programs can be used for composition and arranging. In addition to these open-ended creative environments, there are a number of programs that are either primarily concerned with musical creation or have creative activities embedded within them.

Sibelius's **Compass** (www.sibelius.com/) is an educational composition package that includes teaching guides, lessons, worksheets, and quizzes along with the relatively sophisticated Tracker program that allows the student to carry out various creative activities. Tracker is essentially a sequencer that contains prefabricated materials, such as scales, pitch shapes, rhythms, and chords, along with tools for transforming this material using such processes as augmentation and retrograde. In addition, rhythms can be applied to existing chord progressions to create rhythmic harmonic parts.

Many theory and ear training programs for children contain creative components. For example, **Music Ace I and II**, which were discussed above as theory and ear training programs for children, both contain a "Doodle Pad" that allows children to freely create their own small pieces using the concepts covered in the sessions (see Figure 16.12b on page 294). In addition, there are several programs for children that focus solely on creativity.

Morton Subotnick's **Making Music** and **Making More Music** (www.creatingmusic.com/) both have several activities that involve creating music by drawing, by manipulating blocks of melody, and by manipulating onscreen images that represent rhythmic elements. The Creating Music website itself contains several creative activities designed for children (see Figure 16.26). ECSMedia publishes **Cloud 9**, which also provides several different creative activities for children, including the "Freeform Flyer" in which the child uses the keyboard to manipulate an onscreen airplane that leaves clouds behind (see Figure 16.27). When the child presses play, the heights of the various clouds are interpreted as pitch and their left-to-right positions are interpreted as time/rhythm.

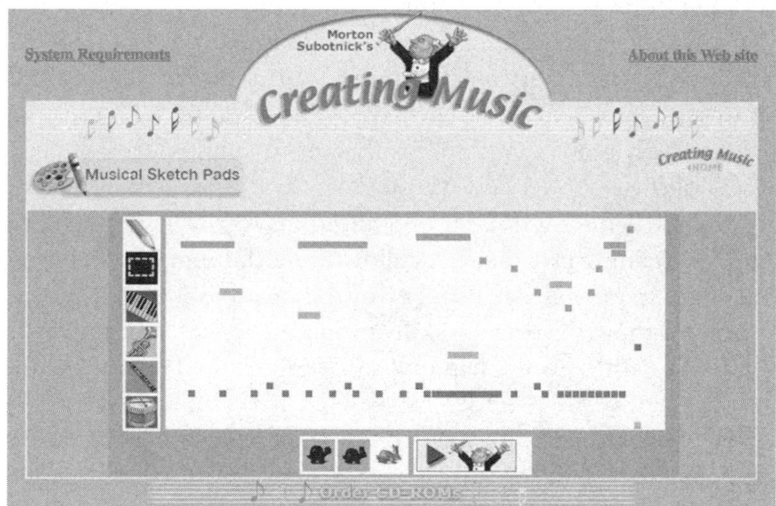

Figure 16.26 Musical Sketch Pad from the creatingmusic.com website. (Courtesy of Creating Music)

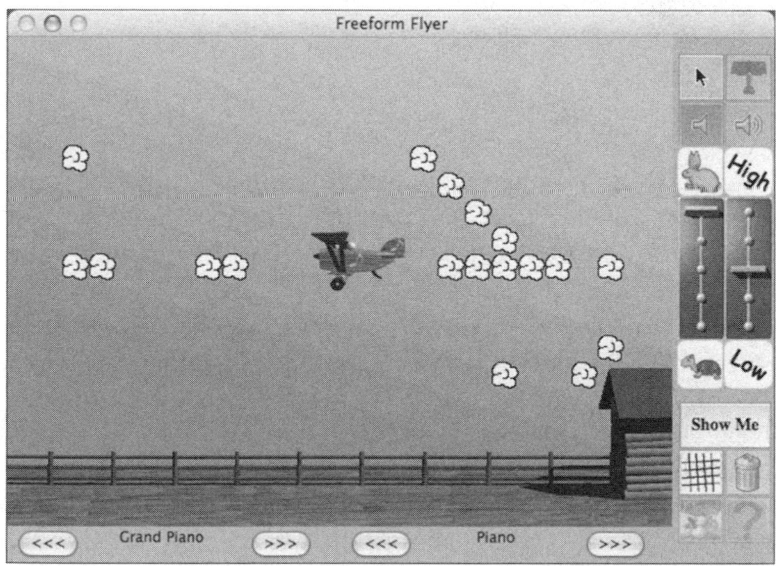

Figure 16.27 "Freeform Flyer" from Cloud 9. (Courtesy of FreeHand Music)

COMPUTER-ASSISTED INSTRUCTION: WHAT DO I NEED?

In Section II, "Audio," and Section III, "MIDI," there were separate chapters to describe the hardware and software necessary to carry out activities at various levels. CAI involves MIDI input and output and/or audio input and output, so the systems described in Chapters 7 and 11 are sufficient and any modifications can be briefly covered here. In terms of software, your choices would be dictated by your goals in using CAI and your preferences from among the various competing products.

Many CAI programs require only a standard computer with input from the mouse and computer keyboard and output in the form of audio and onscreen display. This is true for most of the programs in theory/ear training, form and analysis, and history/terminology/instruments, as well as some of the programs dealing with creative activities. Audio System 0 from Chapter 7 would be sufficient for these needs.

Many CAI programs also allow optional MIDI input and/or optional audio input, making a controller keyboard and a microphone useful additions to the system. These programs include the theory/ear training programs that allow for MIDI input for entering answers and those that test singing, as well as a number of the creative skills programs. Other programs such as some of the performance skills programs *require* MIDI and/or audio input. MIDI and Audio System 1 from Chapter 11 (see Figure 11.1) would fulfill these needs.

A keyboard controller of any size can be used, though a 61-note controller or larger would be important for performance skills programs involving a keyboard. The USB microphone that is part of MIDI and Audio System 1 is sufficient for these purposes, but for a program like SmartMusic it would be useful to have a microphone that clipped on to your instrument or mounted on a microphone stand. Naturally, any of the more complex MIDI and Audio Systems from Chapter 11 would also work.

FURTHER READING

Using CAI software in your teaching naturally requires a strong understanding of the pedagogy for the subject matter, whether it be ear training, theory, performance, or composition. Choosing CAI software then becomes a matter of determining what software aligns best with your pedagogical approach and complements it.

In K-12 education, using CAI software effectively in your teaching requires that these technologies be integrated into a standards-based approach. Thomas Rudolph et al.'s *Technology strategies for music education* (2nd ed., 2005) defines areas of technology competency and then relates them to the music standards created by the National Association for Music Education (www.menc.org/) and set out in the *National standards for arts education* (http://artsedge.kennedy-center.org/teach/standards/). Scott Watson's *Technology guide for music educators* (2006) provides an overview of a variety of hardware and software organized by the areas of technology competency defined in *Technology strategies for music education* (see above).

In addition to those materials, there are two organizations dedicated to technology and music education. Both of the books mentioned in the previous paragraph originated with the Technology Institute for Music Educators (TI:ME, www.ti-me.org/), whose mission is to help K-12 educators apply technology in music teaching and learning. The Association for Technology in Music Instruction (ATMI, http://atmionline.org/) has a similar goal but is focused more on the dissemination of research and pedagogical strategies developed in colleges and universities. Both of these organizations have useful resources and opportunities for professional development.

REVIEW OF KEY TERMS

TimeSketch Series 296
TimeSketch Editor 296
Editor Pro 296
Bubble Machine 296
Form Templates 297
Flash 298
ECSMedia 298
Sibelius Instruments 299
Jazz In Time 299
SmartMusic 301
Home Concert Xtreme 301
Band-in-a-Box 301
Finale 303
transcription aids 303
Compass 304
Music Ace I and II 304
Making Music/Making More Music 304
Cloud 9 305

APPENDIX

The Music Computer

OVERVIEW

This appendix provides an introduction to computer hardware, software, and networks with an emphasis on aspects of computing that are particularly relevant to music. Computer engineering and computer science are fields unto themselves, and, while we should understand underlying principles wherever we can, the hardcore nuts and bolts of computing are not as important as the environment that modern computing provides for music technology. Accordingly, this appendix will be concerned with the important concepts that we encounter when using a computer for musical purposes.

Though music technology is not solely computer-based, the computer is central to many of the things we do every day in music tech. For example, while microphones and preamps don't require a computer, any discussion of recording would be incomplete if it did not also cover the computer audio interface. Hardware synthesizers also don't require a computer, but the very fact that "hardware" must be specified in their description highlights the increasing migration of sound generation from special purpose devices (hardware synthesizers) to general-purpose computers. Even in live settings, computers have made their way on stage and into orchestra pits.

As with many of the topics in this text, computing is split up into hardware and software. These are, of course, not mutually exclusive, so software will make an appearance in the hardware chapter and vice versa. Though often considered separately from computer hardware and software, networking hardware and software will be integrated into their respective chapters, as modern networking is really an extension of the computer rather than something completely different.

WHAT'S IN THIS APPENDIX?

Part 1: Computer Hardware

This chapter covers:

- standard input/output hardware, such as the keyboard and mouse;
- musical input/output hardware, including MIDI and audio interfaces along with MIDI controllers and MIDI-controllable devices;
- computer processing components, including the CPU and RAM with a focus on what is needed for various musical tasks;
- computer storage, including hard disks, removable drives, file systems, and storage in the "cloud"; the sizes of these storage devices will be considered in the context of the size of the information that we need to store for various musical purposes;
- network connections, including Internet service providers and LANs, with the speed of these connections considered in the context of what information we need to transfer over them.

Part 2: Computer Software

This chapter covers:

- the function of operating system software, including device drivers and graphical and command-line interfaces;
- types of application software, including freeware and open source software;
- types of malicious software (malware), such as viruses and worms, and strategies for avoiding them;
- software licenses and the rights that they grant and restrictions they impose;
- types of copy protection schemes used by music software;
- important aspects of file saving and information about file formats;
- Internet addresses and the relationship between IP numbers and URLs;
- types of computer relationships, including client-server and peer-to-peer (P2P), along with examples of each using various Internet technologies;
- Internet 2 and the ways in which it is being used for music.

At the end of the Appendix, there are suggestions for "Further Reading" and a list of "Suggested Activities" related to the material.

APPENDIX PART 1

Computer Hardware

Music technology encompasses a wide variety of hardware, but much of today's music technology centers on the computer. At a number of points in this text non-computer-based hardware such as microphones and speakers has been discussed, but it is nevertheless important to have an understanding of the hardware features of a computer that are especially relevant to musical activity.

INPUTS AND OUTPUTS

The most basic human interactions with computers concern providing information to the computer and receiving information back.

Standard Input and Output Hardware

Standard input/output hardware is well known. On the input side, the most common devices are the computer keyboard and the mouse. In addition, touchscreen technology is becoming more and more common, particularly in cell phone computing. Cell phones, of course, are just specialized computers, and many of the smartphones have taken on attributes once associated solely with computers, such as running software, sending and receiving email, and linking up to the Internet.

We regularly input information to computers using cameras when video chatting, scanning UPC codes when checking out at the grocery score, or inadvertently providing our moving image to security cameras or stoplight cameras when driving. A microphone is another common input, even in non-musical circumstances such as the aforementioned video chatting (not much of a chat without audio), or speaking a selection into an automated voice-answering system when calling any sufficiently bureaucratic organization. We also input information physically through controls other than computer keyboards or mice, such as game controllers.

On the output side, the most common devices are the monitor and the printer. Computers also regularly output information through speakers, including our favorite (legal!) music downloads, current viral videos, or annoying error sounds. Computers can also provide physical output to game controllers, such as force feedback joysticks or the Wii remote when it vibrates.

For both input and output, an argument could be made for hard disks, flash drives, network cables, and Wi-Fi. However, those devices will be placed in their own categories as storage devices and network hardware.

Music Input and Output Hardware

Most, if not all, computers come out of the box with the ability to take audio input through a built-in microphone and stereo mini-jack input (which is the same as a small headphone jack), and to produce audio output through a stereo mini-jack. However, these built-in inputs and outputs are usually of mediocre quality.

For semiprofessional and professional projects, an **audio interface** is needed. An audio interface is typically a small box equipped with the necessary audio inputs that connects to your computer through a standard USB or FireWire cable. Audio interfaces may also take the form of a card installed in a desktop computer, connected by a cable to a "breakout box" with the controls and connections. The connectors on a basic audio interface allow you to connect a microphone, guitar, and/or keyboard as inputs, and powered speakers and headphones as outputs. More complex interfaces have more input and output connections and a variety of other features (see Figures A1.1 and A1.2).

In addition to audio, many musicians need MIDI input and output. MIDI (Musical Instrument Digital Interface) is a standard format for music data (notes, not audio) used by synthesizers and computers. MIDI devices include keyboard **controllers** that send MIDI notes to the computer (see Figure A1.3a), **modules** that receive MIDI data from the computer and produce sound, and **synthesizers** that consist of both a keyboard and a sound generator—essentially a controller and module combined in the same plastic case.

Many controllers, modules, and synthesizers connect directly to a computer through a standard USB cable. Others use special MIDI cables to connect to a **MIDI interface** that in turn connects to the computer via USB (see Figure A1.3b). To simplify matters, many audio interfaces also have MIDI input and output jacks, allowing one box to serve as both a MIDI and audio interface. There is much more on audio and MIDI in Sections II and III.

Aside from standard MIDI and audio devices, there are many other input and output devices that can be used for music (see Table A1.1). On the input side these include standard button-and-joystick game controllers, motion-based game controllers such as the Wii remote, touchscreen devices, cell phones with appropriate software and Bluetooth or wireless connectivity, cameras used in conjunction with motion sensing or facial recognition software, and non-keyboard musical controllers such as MIDI guitars, MIDI violins, MIDI Mallet controllers, and MIDI horns. On the output side, many

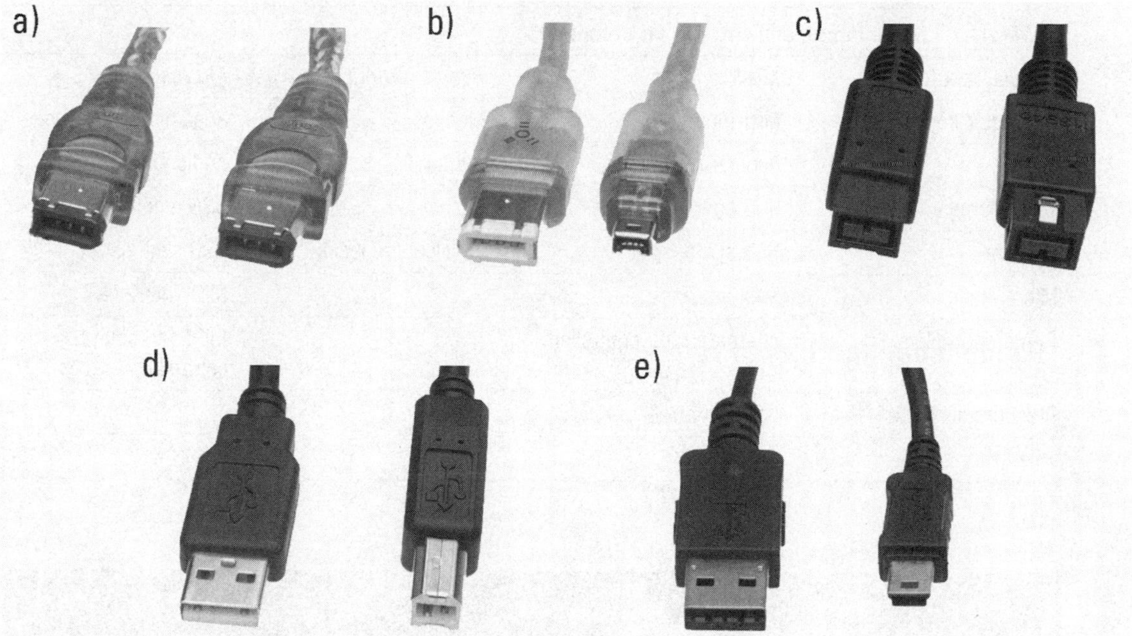

Figure A1.1 Various connector cables: (a) FireWire 400 6-pin to 6-pin, typical for FireWire audio interfaces; (b) FireWire 400 6-pin to 4-pin, typical for FireWire video cameras; (c) FireWire 800, typical for high-speed FireWire devices such as external hard drives; (d) USB A-connector (computer) to B-connector (device), typical for USB audio and MIDI interfaces; and (e) USB A-connector (computer) to mini-B-connector (device), found on portable recorders and cameras. (Not shown) Micro-A and Micro-B connectors found on cell phones and cameras.

Figure A1.2 FireWire audio interface: M-Audio FireWire Solo. (Courtesy of M-Audio)

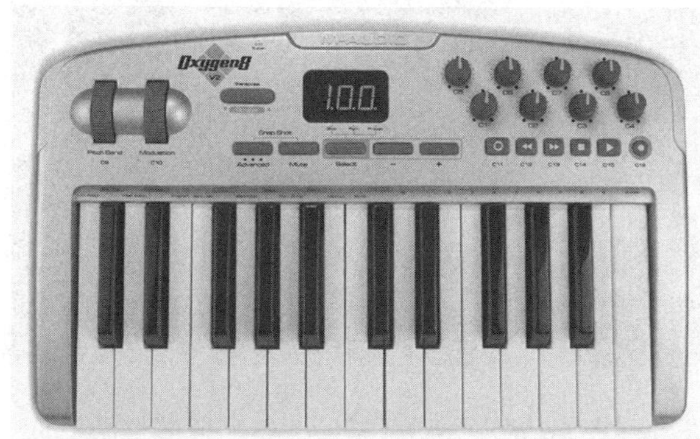

Figure A1.3a USB MIDI controller: M-Audio Oxygen8 V2. (Courtesy of M-Audio)

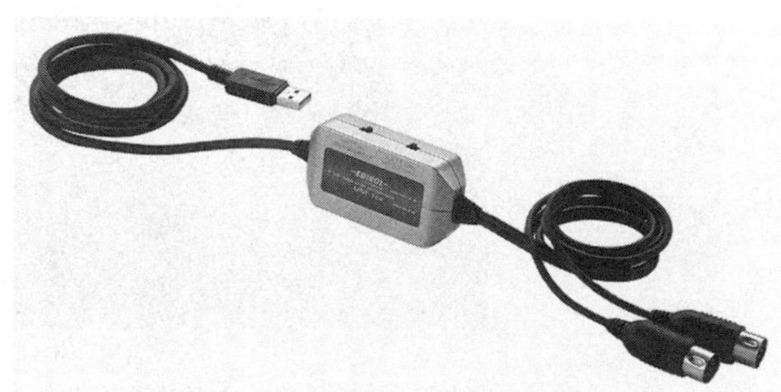

Figure A1.3b USB MIDI interface: Edirol UM-1EX. (Special thanks to Roland Corporation)

Table A1.1 Some inputs and outputs for computers

Regular input	*Musical input*	*Regular output*	*Musical output*
Computer keyboard	Microphone	Monitor	Speakers/headphones
Mouse	Audio interface	Printer	Audio interface
Touchscreen	USB controller	Speakers	USB module
Camera	USB synthesizer	Physical feedback	USB synthesizer
Microphone	MIDI interface		MIDI interface
Game controllers	Alternate MIDI controllers		MIDI and sound controlled devices
Pressure sensors	Game controllers		
	Cell phones		

Figure A1.4a A MIDI-controllable water fountain. (Courtesy of Erich Altvater, Atlantic Fountains)

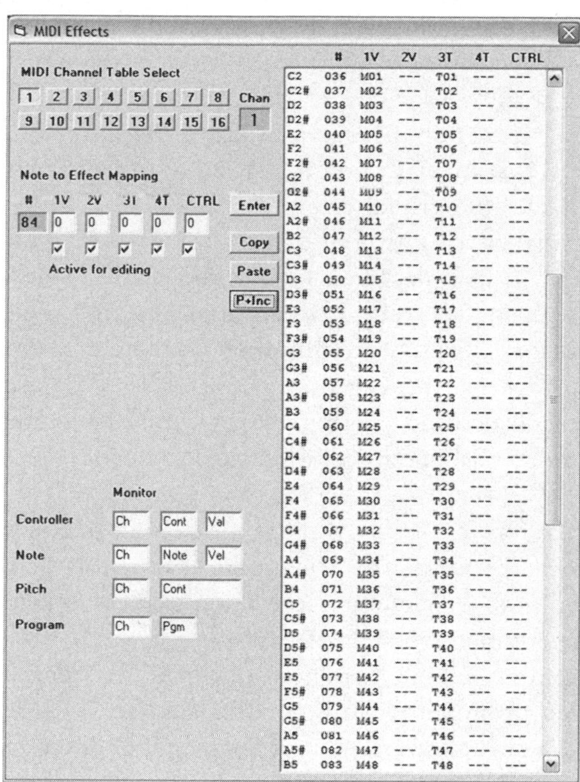

Figure A1.4b MIDI effects screen of Access 3.0 musical fountain show control software. (Courtesy of Erich Altvater, Atlantic Fountains)

different devices have been outfitted for MIDI and sound control, such as theatre lights, video decks, and water fountains.

PROCESSING

The processing system in a computer is responsible for receiving data input, acting on that input according to stored instructions, and then storing the result or sending it out. There are many technical details that go into a processing system, but the main concerns for a music computer can be boiled down to two things: speed and size. How fast is the CPU (central processing unit) and how much RAM (random access memory) does it have?

The CPU

For relatively simple music tasks like running ear training or notation programs, a relatively up-to-date laptop or desktop will have a fast enough **CPU**. More complex tasks such as audio recording, live sound processing, and software sound generation, require a faster CPU, such as those found in higher-end laptops and desktops. For very complex tasks in professional settings, such as recording and processing dozens of audio tracks in a professional recording studio, you may need the fastest CPU you can find/afford, which means using a high-end desktop computer. The next question is just what "fast" means when applied to a CPU and a processing system in general.

The CPU is responsible for fetching program instructions from memory and executing them. There are many elements that impact upon the speed of that process, including its architecture, its clock speed, and the processor bus speed.

The **architecture** of a CPU is the actual physical structure of the integrated circuit chip. Each architecture is given a name by its manufacturer, such as the AMD Athlon or the Intel Core i7, and microprocessor manufacturers are constantly updating their product lines. Most CPUs have two or more **cores**, which means that there are two or more copies of the core elements of a processor packaged into one chip (see Figure A1.5a). In addition, some of the higher-end desktop computers have more than one multi-core processor. Both of these facets of CPU architecture have a dramatic effect on the overall speed.

CPUs differ quite a bit in the way that they are constructed. One significant result of these differences is that one chip may take longer to execute an instruction than another. The actual time that a CPU takes to execute an instruction is measured in clock cycles, the duration of which is determined by the clock speed.

The **clock speed** is measured in gigahertz (GHz), or billions of cycles per second. CPU clock speed and architecture figure prominently in computer ads ("2.66 GHz Quad-core Intel Xeon Processor"), though direct comparisons of the speeds of different processors are actually quite tricky due to differences in architecture. Another speed factor for the processing system is the speed of the processor bus.

The speed of the **processor bus**, also called the **front-side bus** or **FSB**, determines how fast information is transferred from various processing components, such as RAM,

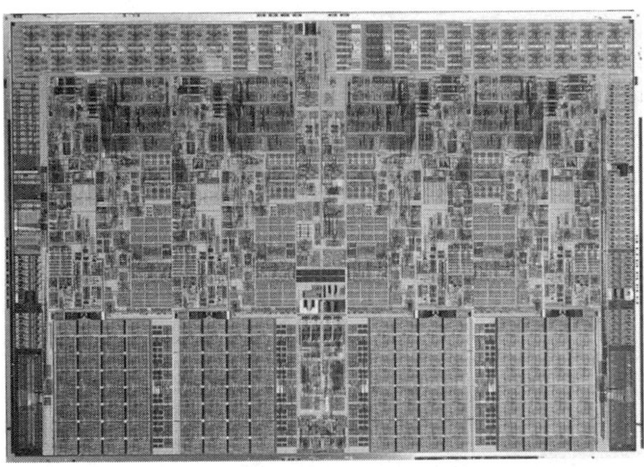

Figure A1.5a Intel Core i7 "Nehalem" Multi-core Central Processing Unit. (Courtesy of Nick Knupffer, Intel Corporation)

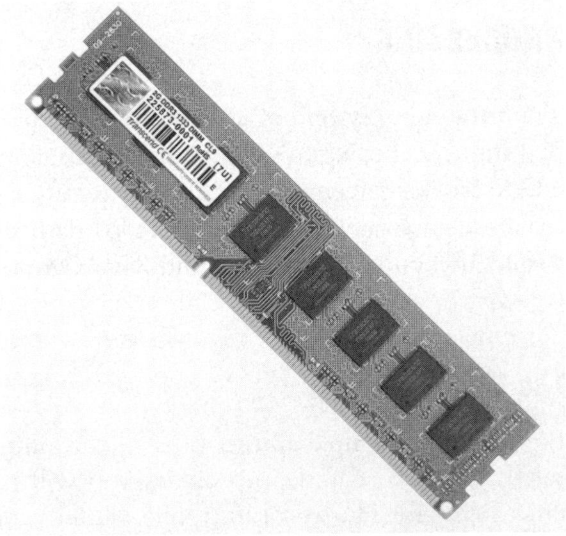

Figure A1.5b 2 GB DDR3 RAM. (Courtesy of Transcend Information, Inc.)

to the CPU (see Figure A1.5b). Program instructions can only get from memory to the processor as fast as the processor bus can carry them, so this can be a limiting factor on processor speed. The processor bus speed isn't as common a specification in computer ads, but, because the speed of main memory (RAM) is typically the same as the speed of the processor bus, it is reflected in the stated memory speed. The processor bus speeds in desktops and faster laptops have recently risen into the GHz range.

The CPU architecture, the clock speed, and the processor bus speed all impact the overall processing speed of the computer. It is possible to determine a theoretical maximum speed for such a processing system by using these specifications along with some other details such as the chipset and motherboard, but it is more valuable to test the system in action.

One common way to measure practical performance is to use **benchmarking**. Benchmarking involves running a practical test on a given computer and comparing its performance to that of other computers. This process allows the actual performance of various components of a computer system to be tested and compared to those of other systems. This is a common practice in the technology media (e.g., *PCWorld* or *MacWorld* magazines) when new computer systems or other technologies have been released. Manufacturers often list the ideal specifications, such as those discussed above, in their marketing campaigns when the actual performance as measured by benchmarking may tell a different story.

RAM

RAM, also referred to as main memory, is the changeable memory in a computer that stores program instructions and temporary data while the computer is running. When the computer is turned off, the RAM is cleared.

When you're working on a document, whether a word processing document or a notation document, the information that you enter is stored in RAM. This information is, in turn, copied to the hard drive or other storage medium when you execute a "save" command, or when the program auto-saves if it has that feature. Any information entered after the last save is lost if power to the RAM is interrupted. Operating systems do their best to rescue unsaved data, but that is no substitute for regularly saving the data to a storage device such as a hard drive or flash drive. The mantra of the computer user should always be "Save Early and Save Often."

With regard to RAM, we are most concerned with how much there is. The speed and type are important to the overall functioning of the computer, but that decision is already made for us when we choose a computer with a particular processor and FSB speed.

The amount of RAM in a given computer system is typically configurable by the user and expandable up to a given limit. At the time of this writing, typical computer systems ship with 2 to 4 GB (gigabytes) of RAM, with high-end systems expanding to as much as 32 GB. For standard applications such as word processing, spreadsheeting, web surfing, and less-intensive musical applications such as notation and computer-assisted instruction (CAI), you don't need an extraordinary amount of RAM. However, for many audio recording and synthesis applications and other media-intensive functions such as video editing, it is important to have a substantial amount of RAM—more than is in the computer's basic configuration. It is a common experience of computer users in the music field to find the amount of RAM in their computer limiting after only one or two years.

When the amount of RAM is too small for an application, computers can use **virtual memory**. Virtual memory involves the computer system using a portion of the hard drive for instructions or data that don't fit in RAM. The CPU can call up data or instructions stored in RAM very quickly. However, it takes a relatively long time to call up data or instructions from the hard drive. If a computer system has to use virtual memory—sometimes referred to as "paging" or "swapping"—then the overall processing system inevitably becomes slower. This slowness can range from annoying to debilitating when you're using the computer in a professional musical setting. For music computer systems, it is a good idea to have enough RAM to prevent the system ever having to utilize virtual memory.

STORAGE

When you first enter information (text, MIDI, audio) into a computer, the data is stored temporarily in RAM. When the computer shuts down, the information in RAM is lost, so it is necessary to save this data as a file on some sort of storage device. As with processing, we are most concerned about speed and size when it comes to storage: can I access the data fast enough and is the disk large enough for my data needs?

Hard Disk Drives and Solid State Drives

Hard disk drives (**HDDs**) and **solid state drives** (**SSDs**) are the primary non-volatile storage media in a computer. At the time of this writing, most computers have HDDs, but SSDs are options in some systems. HDDs consist of rigid spinning platters whose surface is covered in a magnetic material (see Figure A1.6a). Data is written to, and read from, this surface by a head on a little arm that floats over the surface, a bit like the stylus on the arm of a record player. SSDs are related to the common removable USB flash drive and have no moving parts (see Figures A1.6b and A1.6c). As a result, they can be more robust and shock resistant than the spinning-platter HDD, and much quieter. At the time of this writing, SSDs are somewhat new to the computer market, though they've long been used in portable recorders, smartphones and iPods.

Speed is an important factor for storage media used by audio-intensive music applications. The hard drive must be able to read and write data fast enough to play back or record many tracks of audio simultaneously. For MIDI sequencing, notation, and CAI, this kind of speed is less important.

Figure A1.6a Hard disk drive (HDD) with cover removed, showing platter and actuator arm with read/write head.

Figure A1.6b Solid state drive (SSD). (Courtesy of Samsung Electronics Co., Ltd)

Figure A1.6c 8 GB high-speed USB flash drive. (Courtesy of Transcend Information, Inc.)

The speed of an HDD is related to its rotation speed in RPM (revolutions per minute). Slower drives, associated with laptops and less expensive desktop computers, spin at 4,200 RPM, 5,400 RPM, or 7,200 RPM. Faster drives in high-performance machines designed for such applications as digital audio, digital video, and gaming spin at 10,000 RPM or more. HDD and SSD manufacturers sometimes list their speeds in terms of their media transfer rates in megabytes per second (MBps). However, as with processing speeds, benchmarks provide better real-world results.

In general, SSDs are faster than HDDs, but are currently smaller in capacity and higher in price per GB. For the moment, HDDs are used in high-performance systems and SSDs are options on some laptops and netbooks, where they allow the computer to boot more quickly and extend battery life. Because SSDs are so new to the market, this situation is likely to change rapidly as the technology improves.

In addition to the raw RPM and media transfer rate specifications, the speed of an HDD can be impacted by **fragmentation**. This occurs when parts of various files on a disk are spread out over many different regions of the physical disk. Computers are able to reconstruct the continuous files, but moving the read head to different parts of the disk to read the different chunks takes more time than if the parts of the files were physically next to each other on the disk (unfragmented). If the drive becomes fragmented enough, this delay can cause performance problems for data-intensive applications such as multi-track audio recording. SSDs don't suffer from fragmentation in the same way.

Modern operating systems attempt to keep fragmentation to a minimum, but that's not always possible. It's common, therefore, for music computer systems designed for high performance to have one hard drive for the operating system and applications and a separate hard drive for data (recorded audio, samples). This way the data drive, which sees the most read/write activity, can be **defragmented** using a utility program while the other drive is left alone.

Portable Storage Media

One of the more common types of portable storage media is the USB **flash drive**, which goes by various, often proprietary, names, such as "ThumbDrive," "TravelDrive," and "JumpDrive." These flash drives use the same sort of memory as the SSDs mentioned above. With USB flash drives so convenient, it would be nice to use them for various kinds of musical work. They are fine for activities such as notation, CAI, and MIDI sequencing, but reading and writing multiple tracks of audio is highly dependent on the specific USB flash drive used.

There are a number of USB flash drives that describe themselves as "high-speed"; these are more suitable for a light amount of audio recording than their normal-speed counterparts. In addition, there are a number of portable audio recorders that use flash memory as their storage medium. The performance of a particular high-speed flash drive is best determined using benchmarks that test the transfer rate for reading data and the transfer rate for writing data (writing is slower than reading on flash drives).

Recordable DVDs and CDs are **optical storage media**, meaning that the information stored there is read by a laser, and information is stored by using a laser to burn parts of a dye layer on the disc, thereby preventing reflection from the surface beneath it. Recordable DVDs and CDs come in rewritable forms (RW), so in theory they could be used as regular working storage. In practice, optical media are typically used to back up data or as a way of distributing files (so-called "write once, read many," or WORM media), rather than as media that are written and rewritten to many times in a single computing session. In addition, there are devices that use CD-Rs as a direct two-channel (stereo) recording medium.

The standard DVD has been joined by the **Blu-ray** format, which has become the dominant high-definition DVD distribution standard. Blu-ray has been most closely associated with commercial movie releases, but optical drives that write Blu-ray data discs (BD-R for write-once and BD-RE for rewritable) are becoming available in some computer systems.

Storage Capacity

The **storage capacity** of a device is measured in bytes with a metric prefix in front of it, such as kilo-, mega-, or giga-, representing a thousand bytes, a million bytes, and a billion bytes respectively. A byte itself consists of eight binary digits, or bits. In many instances in computing, a metric prefix is actually 1,024 times the next smaller prefix. So, a kilobyte is really 1,024 bytes, and a megabyte is 1,024 kilobytes. This value is used because it is a power of two, and thus is more sensible in a binary numbering system such as that used by computers. For our purposes, the difference is small enough that this discrepancy can be ignored, and we can simply think of a kilobyte as being 1,000 bytes.

Table A1.2 Metric prefixes

Name	*Symbol*	*Approximate number of bytes*
Kilobyte	KB	1,000 bytes
Megabyte	MB	1,000 KB ≈ 1,000,000 bytes
Gigabyte	GB	1,000 MB ≈ 1,000,000,000 bytes
Terabyte	TB	1,000 GB ≈ 1,000,000,000,000 bytes
Petabyte	PB	1,000 TB ≈ 1,000,000,000,000,000 bytes

Table A1.3 Current storage media sizes/size ranges

Storage device	*Current size (or Current size range)*
Hard disk drive	160 GB to 1 TB (more if disks are in an RAID array)*
Solid state drive	128 GB to 256 GB (smaller sizes in "netbooks")*
USB flash drive	1 GB to 8 GB
Blu-ray DVD (BD-R/RE)	25 GB (single layer) or 50 GB (double layer)
DVD±R/RW	4.7 GB (single layer) or 8.5 GB (double layer)
CD-R/RW	700 MB (also measured as 80 minutes)

* Based on a representative sample of systems from various U.S. manufacturers.

Table A1.4 Approximate sizes of common file types

File type	*File size*
Word processing file (.doc, moderate formatting and few images)	~15 KB/page
Picture file (.jpg, scanned color image, 8.5 × 11″, 96 dpi)*	~250 KB
Picture file (.tif, scanned image, grayscale, 8.5 × 11″, 300 dpi)	~8 MB
MIDI file (.mid, type 1, 16 tracks, many controllers)	~150 KB/min
Audio file (.mp3, .mp4/.m4a, 256 kbps)	~2 MB/min
Audio file (.aif, .wav, CD-quality)	~10 MB/min
Audio file (96 KHz/24 bit—"high def" audio, 5.1 surround)	~100 MB/min
Video file (iTunes standard TV/movie download)**	~13 MB/min
Video file (iTunes HD TV/movie download)**	~33 MB/min
Video on standard DVD**	~50 MB/min
Video on Blu-ray**	~250 MB/min

* ~10:1 compression ratio using a compression level of about 15 percent in the scanning software. JPEG compression ratios vary widely depending on the actual image being compressed and the compression settings.
** Based on an average of representative titles.

Table A1.2 gives these approximate definitions for the metric storage sizes. The symbol "≈" means "is approximately equal to."

Table A1.3 shows the common sizes or size ranges for various storage media. Both smaller and larger sizes are available for HDDs, SSDs, and flash drives, but the table shows just the range for common base configurations of computer systems at the time of this writing. You should note that this changes *very* quickly so you'll need to do a bit of research to find out what the current sizes are.

The media sizes in Table A1.3 are all well and good, but they don't really tell us how many term papers or digital music files can be stored on a given medium. Table A1.4 shows some approximate sizes for a variety of file types. Naturally, the sizes are approximate and will vary from file to file. For example, a file containing a term paper would vary greatly in size depending on whether or not images have been embedded into the file. Compressed sound, picture, and video files change depending on the nature of the content and/or the settings of the particular compression method used. More details relating to the size of audio files are found in Chapter 5, "Digital Audio Data."

File Systems and Volumes

Your computer's operating system interacts with a disk through the disk's **file system**, in which information is organized hierarchically in folders, or directories. There are many different file systems in use, but a given operating system will tend to have a preferred format. Windows computers currently use the NTFS file system for the hard drive, Mac OS X computers use the HFS+ file system (also called Mac OS Extended), Linux (or GNU/Linux) systems use the ext3 or ext4 file systems, and many systems running UNIX use the Unix File System (UFS). Removable flash drives are usually formatted with the FAT16 or FAT32 file systems, which are Windows file systems used for smaller drives, though some are formatted with the NTFS file system.

The primary reason why you need to know this information is that it explains some incompatibilities between the format of a drive (HDDs, SSDs, and removable disks) and the operating system that you're using. At the time of this writing, computers running Mac OS X can read and write to FAT16 and FAT32 formatted disks without any special software and can read from, but not write to, NTFS formatted disks. Special software is available that can enable this functionality.

Windows computers, however, are unable to read HFS+ formatted disks without special software. This suggests FAT16 or FAT32 as the logical choice for a removable flash disk that needs to be used with both Macs and PCs. Many external hard drives are formatted with the NTFS or FAT32 file systems, which can be read by Macs and PCs, but can also easily be reformatted to the HFS+ file system, the native Mac format.

A disk can have more than one file system on it through a process known as **partitioning**. A disk, or partition of a disk, with a file system is seen by the operating system as a **volume**. Windows systems also refer to volumes as **logical drives**. In the normal course of computing, you may write files to a volume on the hard disk drive, a volume on a flash drive, and a volume on a network-connected drive.

Storage in the "Cloud"

To this point, we've been discussing storage in terms of drives and media that are directly attached to the computer you're using. Remote storage has long been common in commercial settings, but in recent years remote storage and remote applications have become popular with home computer users as well. Storing data remotely and using Internet-based applications to access that data is referred to as **cloud computing**, with the diffuse structure of the Internet being the "cloud."

Storage in the cloud takes on many forms, such as remote storage of files through Apple's MobileMe, email in Gmail accounts, word processing and spreadsheet documents in Google Docs, pictures in Flickr, videos on YouTube, and calendars in Google Calendar. Several Internet resources, such as Google and MobileMe, include multiple cloud computing functions. In cloud computing, information that was once stored on a local hard drive or flash drive is now stored on remote servers and accessed through web-based applications. This trend has sparked the development of **netbooks**, which are small, inexpensive laptop computers designed primarily to access the Internet and interact with web-based services. They typically have limited storage and less powerful processors, and run operating systems that are less resource intensive, such as Windows XP or Linux.

Storing files in the cloud is an attractive option because your files are available from any computer hooked up to the Internet, and you can share these files with others, as with your vacation photos in Flickr, or not share them, as with your home budget stored in Google Docs. Concerns about cloud computing focus on the possibility of losing access to your files due to a failure of a company's servers or due to the possibility of a company's bankruptcy or other business-related meltdown. These possibilities could make your files unobtainable for a period of time or, in the worst case, unrecoverable.

Naturally, the loss of control of your files or just plain loss of your files is the worst-case scenario and your files could just as well be lost due to a failure of your own hard disk or flash drive. As with most computing situations, a solid backup strategy for your files is essential and would take much of the risk out of cloud computing.

NETWORK CONNECTIONS

There are many types of computer networks that encompass everything from a room full of computers, to a campus full of computers, to a world full of computers. Computers on these networks can share data and other types of resources. The most prominent network is, of course, the Internet.

The Internet

The Internet is a network of networks made up of academic, governmental, business, and private networks that are physically connected to one another through copper wires, fiber-optic cable, and wireless. These networks communicate with one another through a shared set of protocols called the **Internet Protocol Suite**, or **TCP/IP**. It is the TCP/IP that allows networks that are quite different from one another to communicate reliably—there's even a (humorous) specification for connecting a network of message-carrying homing pigeons to the Internet. There are many types of networks that connect to the Internet, but here we'll focus on two of the most common: ISPs and LANs.

Internet Service Providers

Internet service providers (**ISPs**) are private networks that sell access to their networks to individual users, groups, and companies. Through their networks, they also provide access to the Internet, meaning that they provide connections between their networks and other networks and so on, until the data you send can reach all of the networks that comprise the Internet. In addition to Internet access, ISPs also provide email accounts and may provide other services such as webpage hosting.

There are a variety of ways to connect to an ISP, though many ISPs support just one method. These methods include:

- *Dial-up*, which uses a **modem** that connects your computer to your phone line. Other devices connected to your phone line such as phones and fax machines cannot be used while connected through dial-up.
- *High-speed dial-up*, which is a variant on dial-up in which the data being transmitted, particularly pictures, is compressed—made smaller by the loss of some quality—on the fly by your modem (going out) or your ISP's modem (coming in).
- *Digital Subscriber Line (DSL)*, which is another method of connecting to the Internet via a modem connected to a phone line. This is a higher-speed method than either dial-up or high-speed dial-up and allows you to use your phone and fax at the same time you are connected to your ISP.
- *Cable Internet*, which uses a modem that connects your computer to your cable TV wire. **Cable** can transmit cable TV and Internet data at the same time.
- *Fiber to the home (FTTH)*, which uses a modem to connect your computer to **fiber-optic cable**. This offers the possibility of much faster connection speeds, though at the time of this writing it is still somewhat rare.
- *Wireless broadband (WiBB, also WiMax)*, which is a wireless method of connecting to an ISP, called a WISP in this case for Wireless ISP. Standard Wi-Fi (see below) connects devices in a home to a cable, DSL, or FTTH connection. Wireless **broadband** allows you to connect directly to your ISP via fixed line-of-sight antennas. WiMax is one of the technologies being used to provide Internet service to entire municipalities.
- *Mobile broadband*, which uses cell phone networks to allow your computer, through a special PC card, or your cell phone to connect to the Internet. These are currently called "3G" networks for "third generation," though 4G networks are beginning to emerge.

There are a number of differences in the way each of these technologies works, but apart from general reliability, the measurement of most interest to you is usually speed, also called **bandwidth**, which is measured in kilo- or megabits per second. The actual experienced speed would be determined by a test of the network in action, such as using an automated bandwidth test that measures the speeds of a file downloaded from a server and another file uploaded to a server, and comparing them to other types of connection. This is a form of benchmarking.

Table A1.5 lists the current common ideal speeds of these various connection types as measured in kilobits per second (kbps) or megabits per second (mbps). There will be differences between ideal speeds and experienced speeds depending on a variety of factors, such as Internet traffic and the specific route that data takes through the various networks. These ideal speeds will likely change quickly, but this table will give you a starting point for comparing the technologies. The most volatile parameter of these connection types is price, which will not be considered here because it is likely to change *too* quickly. You should note that the "downstream" speed (downloading) is faster than the "upstream" speed (uploading) for many of these technologies.

In addition to Internet connectivity, these methods of connection are also often used for television (digital TV, analog/digital cable) and telephone services, including **Voice over Internet Protocol (VoIP)**, which delivers phone audio using the same TCP/IP methods that are used to send data on the Internet. With VoIP, the telephone signals become just another Internet data stream, albeit one that requires some special handling to avoid having data packets drop out. There are also other commercial methods for connecting to the Internet, including dedicated, rather than shared, lines such as T1 and T3 lines, but these are typically used by businesses rather than individual users.

Local Area Networks

Local area networks (LANs) are another common way of gaining access to the Internet. These networks are typically run by universities and corporations to provide

Table A1.5 **ISP types and current range of connection speeds**

ISP connection type	*Typical range of speeds**
Dial-up	56 kbps
High-speed dial-up	56–320 kbps (with compression)
DSL	768 kbps–6 mbps (down)/384 kbps–768 kbps (up)
Cable Internet	6 mbps–15 mbps (down)/512 kbps–1 mbps (up)
Fiber to the home (FTTM)	10–50 mbps (down)/2–20 mbps (up)
Wireless broadband (WiMax)	1–4 mbps
Mobile broadband ("3G" network)	600 kbps–1.4 mbps (down)/350–800 kbps (up)

*Based on public claims by a representative group of U.S. providers.

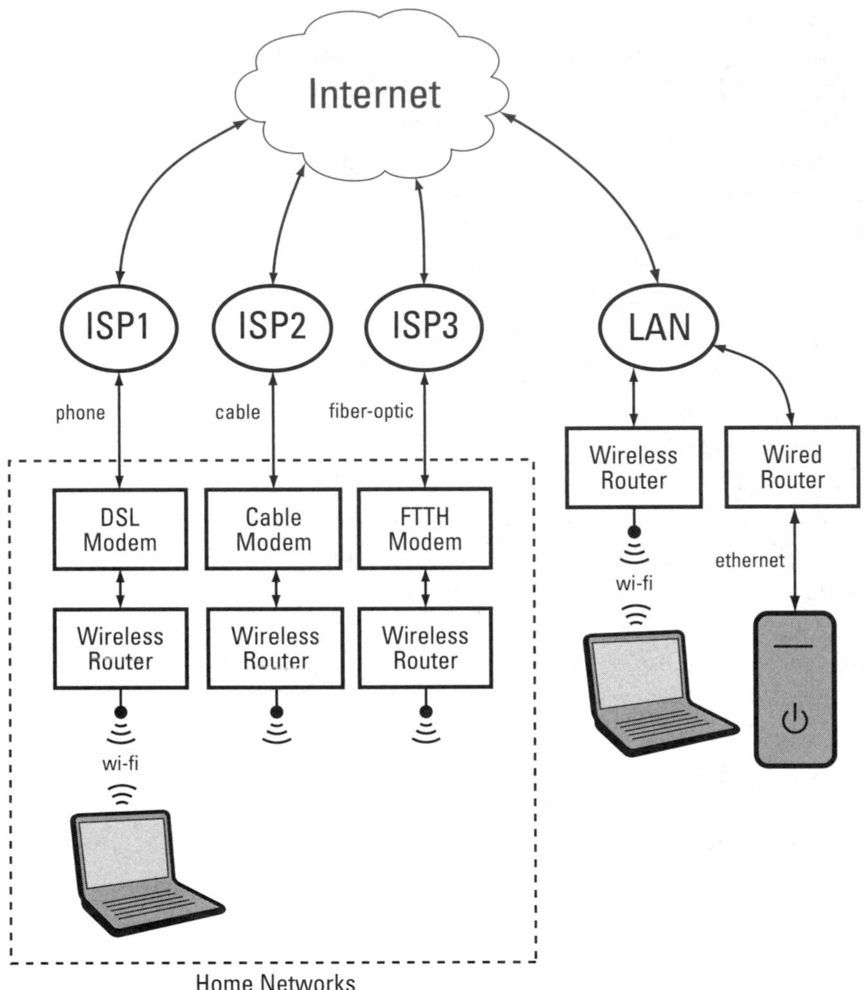

Figure A1.7 Various types of Internet connections.

high-bandwidth connectivity for computers within the network and connectivity between computers in the LAN and the Internet. Devices in a LAN are connected through Ethernet (wired) or Wi-Fi (wireless). A corporation or university will often provide various services over a LAN, including file sharing, network printing, and various applications. For example, a university LAN may provide access to online registration for students, online access to student records, access to a Learning Management System, such as Moodle or Blackboard, and services typically offered by ISPs, such as email and website hosting.

There are various speeds offered by **Ethernet** connections depending on the type of cabling and the type of network devices (routers). Older "10 base-T" Ethernet has largely given way to 100 base-T and 1000 base-T ("gigabit Ethernet"). The speed of Wi-Fi connections will be discussed below.

It is also possible to consider as a LAN a home network connected to a **Wi-Fi** (wireless) router, which is in turn connected to a cable modem or DSL modem. The home LAN often provides only Internet connectivity, but some people include network printers and network data backup devices in their home LANs. Increasingly, home LANs include not just computers, but game consoles such as Wii and Xbox, TV set-top boxes such as Apple TV and Netflix's Roku, and Wi-Fi-enabled smartphones and other handheld devices such as Apple's iPod touch and Nintendo DSi.

There are currently three Wi-Fi standards in use in home LANs: 802.11b, 802.11g, and 802.11n, which are usually referred to by the letters that conclude their standard designations: B, G, and N. These three Wi-Fi standards differ in speed, carrying distance, and frequency range (for N). The frequency range may seem to be a bit of an obscure parameter, but Wi-Fi B and G both operate in the same frequency range as many wireless phones, which can cause interference. Wi-Fi N can operate at that frequency or another that doesn't run the risk of interference with wireless phones. At the time of this writing, 802.11n was recently finalized, so some details about its performance may change.

Table A1.6 provides ideal top speeds for the various Wi-Fi standards and Ethernet connections. When compared to the ISP connection speeds listed in the previous table, you may notice that the limiting factor in Internet access speed in a home LAN is the connection speed to the ISP. These internal LAN connection speeds are most relevant to transfers that take place within the network.

Connection Speeds in Perspective

To get an idea of just what these connection speeds mean, Table A1.7 lists the download times for various file types and various connection types. For the file types, the sizes listed in Table A1.4 (page 321) are used. For connection types, such as DSL, that have a range of connection speeds, a reasonable speed within the range was chosen. As discussed above, these connection speeds are ideal and will vary from place to place, from provider to provider, and even from day to day. The goal of this table is to give you a general sense of the impact of file sizes and connection speeds on download times.

Table A1.6 **Wi-Fi and Ethernet ideal top connectivity speeds**

Connection type	*Speed*
Wi-Fi "B"	11 mbps
Wi-Fi "G"	54 mbps
Wi-Fi "N"	150 to 600 mbps
Ethernet 10 base-T	10 mbps
Ethernet 100 base-T	100 mbps
Ethernet 1000 base-T	1,000 mbps (1 gbps)

Table A1.7 Approximate download times at various connection speeds

		Approximate download times			
File type	*File size*	*Dial-up*	*DSL (3 mbps)*	*Cable (10 mbps)*	*FTTH (20 mbps)*
20-page .doc	300 KB	44 sec	0.82 sec	0.25 sec	0.12 sec
.jpg file	250 KB	37 sec	0.68 sec	0.2 sec	0.1 sec
.tiff file	8 MB	20 min	22 sec	6.7 sec	3.4 sec
3-min MP3	6 MB	14 min	16 sec	4.8 sec	2.4 sec
3-min CD-quality song	30 MB	70 min	80 sec	24 sec	12 sec
3-min hi-def surround sound	300 MB	12 hrs	13 min	4 min	2 min
21-min TV show (iTunes)	273 MB	11 hrs	13 min	4 min	2 min
2-hour HD movie (iTunes)	3.9 GB	7 days	3 hours	56 min	28 min

REVIEW OF KEY TERMS

audio interface 312
controllers 312
modules 312
synthesizers 312
MIDI interface 312
CPU 315
architecture 316
cores 316
clock speed 316
processor bus/front-side bus (FSB) 316
benchmarking 317
RAM 317
virtual memory 318
hard disk drives (HDDs) 318
solid state drives (SSDs) 318
fragmentation/defragmentation 319
flash drive 320
optical storage media 320
Blu-ray 320
storage capacity 320
file system 322
partitioning 322
volumes/logical drives 322
cloud computing 323
netbooks 323
Internet Protocol Suite (TCP/IP) 324
Internet service providers (ISPs) 324
modem 324
cable 324
fiber-optic cable 324
broadband 324
bandwidth 325
Voice over Internet Protocol (VoIP) 325
local area networks (LANs) 325
Ethernet 326
Wi-Fi 327

APPENDIX PART 2

Computer Software

The hardware discussed in Appendix Part 1 provides the necessary basic infrastructure for computing. However, it is software that makes a computer useful. It is software that lets us type a paper, calculate a budget, notate music, record audio, and sequence MIDI. The software that allows us to perform these tasks is called **application software**, also referred to as just applications or programs. In between the application software (discussed later) and the computer hardware is another important type of software called the **operating system**, or **OS**.

THE OPERATING SYSTEM

When we click a mouse or play on a MIDI keyboard, the OS passes that input to the application software. When the application software responds to that input by italicizing a word or synthesizing a sound, the OS passes that output to the monitor screen or speakers. In this way, the OS connects your gestures to the application software, and the output of that software back to you. The OS also allows the application software to communicate with the processing system, storage devices, and network connections (see Figure A2.1)

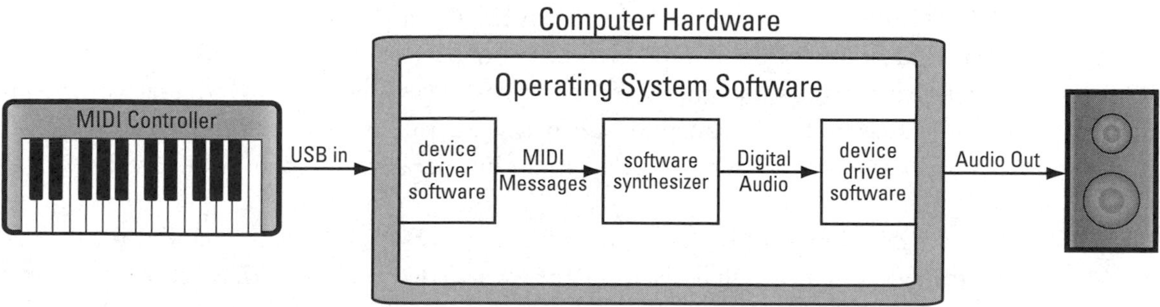

Figure A2.1 The flow of data between hardware inputs and outputs, device drivers, the OS, and application software.

Common Operating Systems

The two most common operating systems for personal computers are Microsoft's **Windows** and Apple's **Mac OS**. Marketing campaigns often pit "PCs" against "Macs," but what they're really doing is pitting Windows against the Mac OS. In terms of the actual hardware, PCs and Macs use similar components, though the way those components are configured within a computer has an important effect on the computer's performance. In the general computer market, PCs have a dominant market share, with Macs having a strong presence in several niche markets, including graphic design and music.

Despite the high profile of Windows and Mac OS, there are several other operating systems in use, including **Linux** (also called GNU/Linux) and all of its variations, UNIX and all of its variations, and Solaris. Scientists and information technology professionals are the primary users of these operating systems, though there is currently a small but growing use of Linux-derived operating systems in consumer computers, particularly the small netbooks.

Though the Mac versus PC rhetoric can get heated and irrational, both Windows and the Mac OS are suitable for music, and many applications are written to work with either. It is worth noting that, at the time of this writing, there are some prominent music applications that are Mac-only or PC-only, such as the sequencer/DAWs Logic Pro and Digital Performer (Mac-only), and Sonar (PC-only). There are relatively few pieces of commercial software available for Linux or UNIX, though there is a great deal of freeware available for them, some of it created at top university computer music laboratories at places such as Stanford and Princeton.

Device Drivers

One of the primary functions of an operating system is to facilitate communication between application software, such as notation or recording programs, and input/output hardware, such as MIDI keyboards and audio interfaces. A **device driver** is a chunk of software that works with the OS to allow the latter to communicate with a specific piece of hardware.

An OS already has the necessary drivers to communicate with the hardware that was sold as part of the computer system, such as the keyboard and the mouse, and will likely have drivers for other standard pieces of peripheral hardware that you might buy, such as a printer. If you purchase hardware that is not standard for a computer system, such as a MIDI keyboard or an audio interface, you may need to install a driver for it.

Most hardware you purchase comes with a CD or DVD that includes the device driver, though you may well find a more up-to-date driver on the manufacturer's website. Devices that describe themselves as "class compliant," such as some simple MIDI interfaces and controller keyboards, don't require a separate driver to be installed.

The User Experience—the GUI

When you use a computer, you see graphical images on a screen and use a mouse to manipulate those images or select items from a menu. When you perform these actions, you are interacting with the operating system's **graphical user interface**, or **GUI** (pronounced "gooey"). Technically, a GUI is not required for an OS, but it is the dominant way for users to interact with computers (see Figure A2.2a).

Some computer users, mostly scientists and computer professionals, prefer to interact with an OS using a **command-line interface**, or **CLI**, instead of a GUI. In UNIX-based operating systems, the CLI is also referred to as the **shell**. In a CLI, all of the actions you wish the operating system to execute are typed in as text. For example, to move a file called "myfile.pdf" from the current directory, or folder, to a sub-directory called "MyFiles," you would type "mv myfile.pdf MyFiles" and then hit return (see Figure A2.2b). CLIs can be very efficient, particularly when working with large numbers of files.

CLIs are closely associated with Linux and UNIX operating systems. However, there are a number of GUIs available for Linux, and CLIs are built into both Windows and Mac OS (see Figures A2.2b and A2.2c).

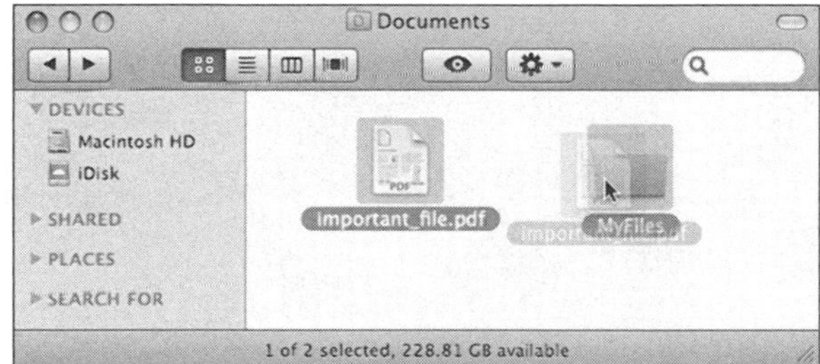

Figure A2.2a A file being moved into a folder/directory using the Mac OS X Leopard GUI. (Screenshot reprinted with permission from Apple Inc.)

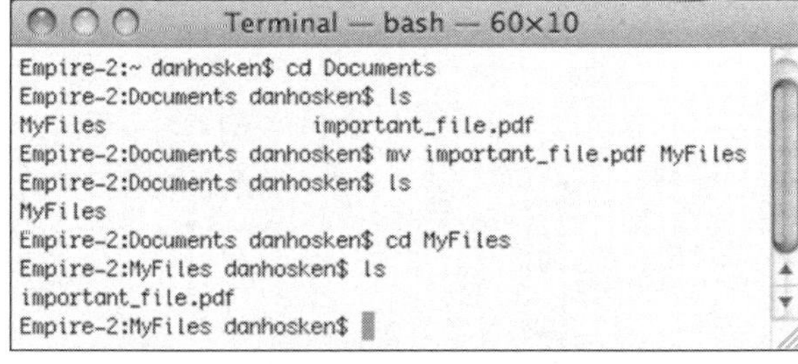

Figure A2.2b The same operation accomplished using the Terminal application in Mac OS X Leopard.

```
Command Prompt
C:\Users\Dan Hosken>cd Documents

C:\Users\Dan Hosken\Documents>dir
 Volume in drive C is Vista
 Volume Serial Number is

 Directory of C:\Users\Dan Hosken\Documents

06/10/2009  11:59 PM    <DIR>          .
06/10/2009  11:59 PM    <DIR>          ..
06/23/2006  10:31 AM           153,208 ImportantFile.pdf
06/10/2009  11:56 PM    <DIR>          MyFiles
               1 File(s)        153,208 bytes
               3 Dir(s)  18,570,678,272 bytes free

C:\Users\Dan Hosken\Documents>move ImportantFile.pdf MyFiles
        1 file(s) moved.

C:\Users\Dan Hosken\Documents>cd MyFiles

C:\Users\Dan Hosken\Documents\MyFiles>dir
 Volume in drive C is Vista
 Volume Serial Number is C0F9-DCBB

 Directory of C:\Users\Dan Hosken\Documents\MyFiles

06/11/2009  12:02 AM    <DIR>          .
06/11/2009  12:02 AM    <DIR>          ..
06/23/2006  10:31 AM           153,208 ImportantFile.pdf
               1 File(s)        153,208 bytes
               2 Dir(s)  18,570,407,936 bytes free

C:\Users\Dan Hosken\Documents\MyFiles>
```

Figure A2.2c A file being moved into a folder/directory in the Windows Vista CLI. (Courtesy of Microsoft)

File System Access

In addition to facilitating interactions between you, the computer hardware, and the application software, the OS also provides you access to the computer's file system.

File systems are organized hierarchically on each volume (HDD, flash drive, CD-R) starting with a **root directory**, or **root folder**, which can contain files, applications, and other folders. Each of these folders can in turn contain files, applications, and other folders, and so on. The file system thus "grows" out of the root directory and can contain numerous branches and sub-branches. Figure A2.3 shows a typical directory structure in which the OS, application software, and user files are stored in distinct locations.

The OS provides access to this file structure so that the files, applications, and folders can be renamed, copied, backed up, deleted, and opened. In Mac OS X, these functions are carried out through the **Finder**; in Microsoft Windows, these functions are carried out using **Windows Explorer**, which is different from the Internet Explorer web browser.

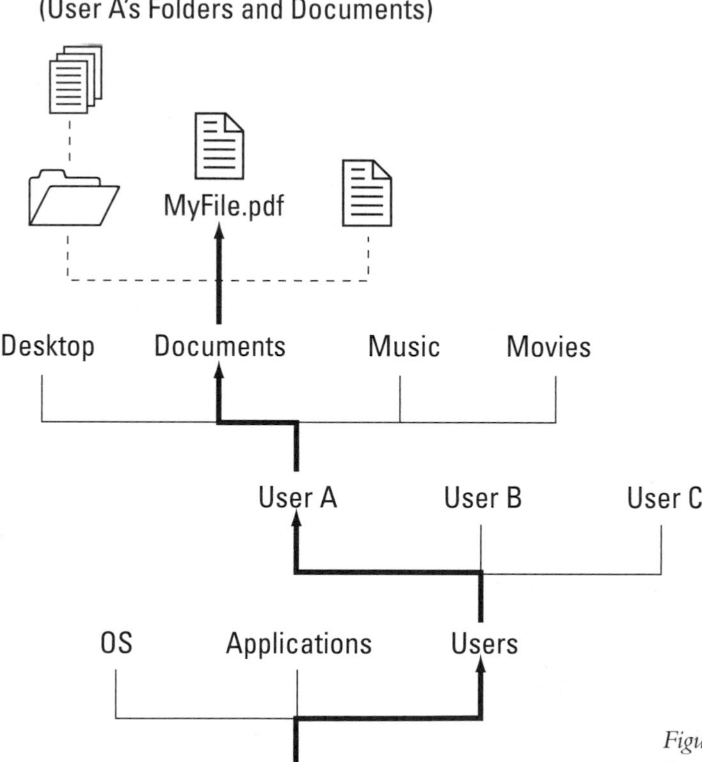

Figure A2.3 A typical directory structure showing the path /Users/User A/Documents/MyFile.pdf.

APPLICATION SOFTWARE

Application software is all of the software that you run on the computer to accomplish tasks, and includes word processing software, web browsers, computer notation software, and recording software. Application software is often software that you buy, but there are other legal ways of obtaining it through shareware, freeware, open source software, and web-based applications.

The first basic category of application software is **commercial software**, which is sold in a package or as downloadable software. Either way, the transaction is not, on the surface, any different from buying any other merchandise. As we'll discuss later in the chapter, software purchases are legally quite different from purchasing a TV, as software belongs to a class of property called **intellectual property**. Most of the software used on a daily basis by musicians is commercial software, developed by for-profit companies and sold to you. However, there are quite a few pieces of music software that are sophisticated and powerful and that can be downloaded for a small donation or for free.

Shareware is software that is free to download and free to try out, *without* any major limitations, such as the inability to save or the inability to print. However, some define it more simply as "try before you buy" software and there is the possibility of major functional limitations or a time limitation. If you use a piece of shareware regularly, you are morally obligated to pay a small fee (often less than $50) to the developer—an obligation that is enforced through the honor system. Some companies and programmers provide **demo** versions of their software and call them "shareware." These demos are functionally limited in some important way, such as lacking the ability to save or print, or they are fully functional, but only for a limited period of time.

Freeware is just what it sounds like: free software. Some freeware is made by the same for-profit companies that sell other pieces of software. For example, Apple makes and sells the Mac OS and the Logic Pro sequencer, but they also make iTunes and give that away for free. Some for-profit companies give away "lite" versions of the software they sell. These versions are fully functional but have limited features compared to the full versions, with the expectation that some percentage of the lite version users will want to upgrade to the full versions.

Some companies give away software that can be used in a limited way for free and then sell access to more advanced services. For example, the popular text, audio and video chatting software, Skype, is free to download and free to use for computer-to-computer calls, but requires you to upgrade the service for a fee in order to call out to regular phones and cell phones. In all of these cases, freeware provided by a for-profit corporation is part of a larger business plan.

Some freeware, however, is created by independent programmers, academic researchers, or organizations that provide free software either as a hobby, or as a service to the community, or out of a conviction that some software should be free. Some of this freeware is simple and limited, but there are many pieces of freeware that are powerful and sophisticated, and can compete with the products of for-profit companies. One example of this is the popular Firefox web browser, distributed by the Mozilla project. (See the book's website for links to prominent freeware music programs.)

Many pieces of freeware are also **open source**, meaning that not only is the application itself free to download, but the programming source code is also free to download. The source code is only of interest to programmers, but the fact that the source code is open means that it can be examined and improved upon by programmers around the world. This generally means better software for everyone. The most famous example of open source software is the Linux operating system, but there are many other prominent examples, including the Firefox web browser and the Apache web server software. In the music world, there are many open source projects, including Csound, a powerful software synthesizer, and Audacity, a multi-track audio editor and processor.

All of the applications discussed above are traditional pieces of software that are installed on your local hard drive and allow you to save files to your hard drive and other media. However, there is a growing class of software that is delivered through a web browser in which the data is stored on remote servers. This type of web-based, software-as-service computing is known as **cloud computing**. This was discussed in Appendix Part 1, "Computer Hardware," in terms of storing data "in the cloud." The best-known examples of web-based applications are Google Docs, which give you access to web-based email, a calendar, a word processor, a spreadsheet, and a presentation tool. This paradigm may become more common as users become more comfortable storing their data, pictures, and videos away from their computers.

MALWARE—BAD SOFTWARE

Malware stands for "malicious software" and includes viruses, worms, Trojan horses, and spyware. Each of these types of malware operates in a different way, but they all cause problems and you must take steps to avoid them. **Viruses** generally require your active participation, through opening an infected document or launching an infected program. Once activated, viruses can replicate themselves by infecting other programs or documents. Aside from the general rule that you shouldn't open any email attachment from someone you don't know, you should also have anti-virus software running on your computer. Anti-virus software actively scans documents and applications for known viruses by comparing them to a set of virus definitions. These definitions must be updated on a regular basis to allow the software to keep up with new viruses.

Unlike viruses, **worms** don't need your active intervention to spread. They worm their way into your system and then worm their way to other computers on the same network or other networks connected to yours. Both viruses and worms are often designed to take advantage of security flaws in your operating system. Keeping your OS up-to-date by installing regular "patches," or updates, can help to keep these at bay. Both Windows and Mac OS have features that automatically search for new patches at some regular interval. Many worm outbreaks occur because some users and system administrators fail to keep their systems patched.

Trojan horses are malicious programs that disguise themselves as useful programs or install along with useful programs. Their apparent usefulness tricks you into actively installing them. The effects of a Trojan horse vary from annoying, such as changing your icons, to destructive, such as deleting files from your hard drive. Again, anti-virus software with up-to-date definitions and a properly patched OS are the best ways to avoid this problem, along with careful attention to what you're installing at any given time.

Spyware is malware delivered in any of the above ways that sends information about your computer, or the information that is stored or transmitted from your computer, to someone else. Some spyware merely tracks your web browsing history, while some attempts to steal more critical information, such as passwords or credit card numbers. Some anti-virus software can search for spyware, or you may need a separate anti-spyware sweeping program.

Some malicious activities take the form of **phishing** (sounds like "fishing") scams, in which an email is sent to you with a dire warning, such as that your bank account is going to be frozen or your email shut off unless you click on a link and provide your username and password. These links take you to fake websites with login and password fields that may look very much like your bank's real website, complete with appropriate logos.

The way to avoid a phishing scam is first to recognize that your bank or university wouldn't send such an email asking for that information, and then to never click on the link in an email like that. Most web browsers and email programs have a function that lets you view the actual source code of an email encoded in HTML (hypertext markup language). This function allows you to see the actual web address underlying the link, which is usually not your bank's website (see Figure A2.4).

Though malware is a serious concern—the last thing you need is a virus when you're trying to complete a project—many warnings about malware are **hoaxes**. It's difficult to tell which emailed warnings are truly hoaxes and which aren't. Sometimes the language of the hoax is overly dramatic, overly vague, or lacks concrete sources. There are several websites that collect these warnings and evaluate whether they are hoaxes or not, such as snopes.com and websites by Symantec and McAfee, which both sell antivirus programs. Some people consider hoaxes themselves to be a form of malware.

Here is a brief summary of the techniques discussed above for avoiding malware. These won't work in all cases and malware is a fact of life, but these techniques can help you be safer:

- Keep your operating system patched.
- Use anti-virus software and keep definitions up to date.
- Use spyware sweeping software and keep it up to date.
- Don't open email attachments from someone you don't know.
- Don't provide your login and password through email.
- Don't click on a link in an email and provide your login and password.
- Check malware hoax sites when you receive warnings.

a)

Dear YourBank Customer,

This is an official notification from YourBank that your account will be deactivated if not renewed immediately. Renew your account by clicking here:

https://www.YourBank.com/index.jsp

Thank you, sincerely,
YourBank Customer Support

© 2009 YourBank Team. All rights reserved.

b)

```
Renew your account by clicking here:
<a href="http://someotherURL/login/user/update/index.htm">
        https://www.YourBank.com/index.jsp
</a>
```

Figure A2.4 (a) An excerpt from a phishing scam email that the author received. "YourBank" replaces the name of a well-known bank. Note that the link appears to point to YourBank's website. (b) The HTML code that creates the link. Clicking on that link will take you to the URL that appears just after the "<a". This is not the URL for YourBank and the login screen there would be designed to steal your login name and password.

SOFTWARE LICENSES

When you purchase commercial software in a package or as a download, what you are buying is not the software itself, but a **license** to use the software. If you have purchased packaged software, you *do* own the physical disks themselves, but the content of the disks is controlled by holder of the **copyright** to that software. The same is true when you purchase a CD or DVD.

You own the physical CD or DVD and are welcome to play Frisbee with it or use it to prop up a table leg, but with regard to the songs or movies contained on it, you are only purchasing the right to use them in a limited way. For example, you have the right to view a DVD you have purchased in your home, but not the right to rent out a theater and charge admission—that would require purchasing another, more expensive, set of rights from the copyright holder. Even shareware, freeware, and open source software are subject to copyright and licensing.

Copyright law determines the rights that the publisher has to the software. The rights that you are then granted by the publisher flow from this copyright law and are typically stated in the **end-user license agreement**, or **EULA** (pronounced "you-la") (see Figure A2.5). Copyright law is a complicated topic and is important for musicians to understand, but even partial coverage of it is beyond the scope of this text. However, it is useful in this context to understand a little bit about what's contained in a typical EULA. (See the book's website for links to more information concerning copyright law.)

The EULA for a piece of software is either a document that is included with packaged software, or onscreen text that you must "agree" to in order to install software. The EULA for an operating system or other software that is preinstalled on a computer that you purchase is typically either physically packaged with the computer or agreed to via a mouse click during the setup process. Sometimes the very act of unpacking the computer is claimed by the manufacturer to constitute agreement with the EULA.

Every EULA is different and reflects differing intentions by the software's creators. A typical EULA may include:

- the number of computers on which you are allowed to install the software;
- whether you can make backup copies;
- whether you have the right to create commercial products with the software (for example, can you sell the music you make with the software?);
- whether you can modify the software (usually you can't);
- whether you can transfer (sell) the software (often you can, but then you can no longer use it yourself);
- any warranty (usually minimal or none);
- limitations on the liability of the software publisher (usually very limited liability).

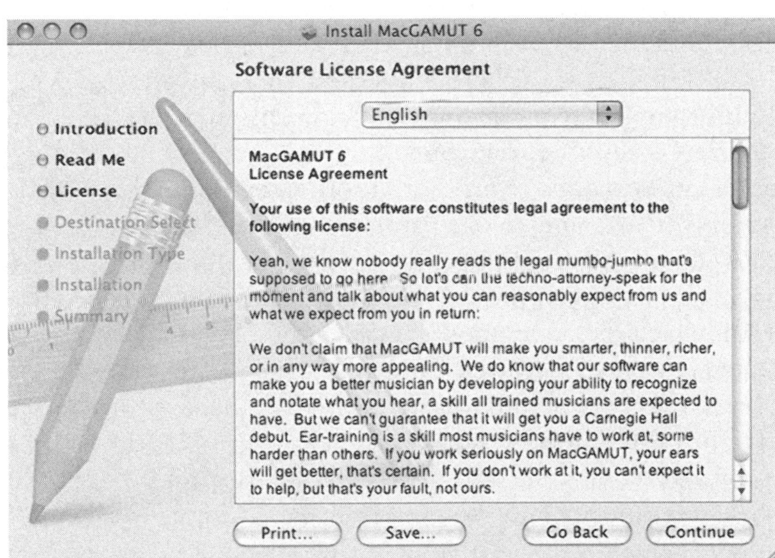

Figure A2.5 EULA screen during installation of MacGAMUT ear training software. This is a very unusual EULA, which begins: "Yeah, we know nobody really reads the legal mumbo-jumbo that's supposed to go here." (Courtesy of MacGAMUT Software International)

A EULA is typically very long and can be very "lawyer-ly" in its language, which encourages you *not* to read it and simply click "agree" during the software install process. This practice isn't a good idea, since the EULA determines what you're allowed to do with "your" software, but it is entirely in keeping with human nature.

There is a similar concept to the EULA that is important to understand: **terms of service** (**TOS**). TOS are agreements that you enter into when you wish to use an online service. This is somewhat different from a EULA because you aren't actually purchasing or downloading software that's covered under copyright, but instead are utilizing an Internet-based service such as Facebook, Twitter, PayPal, Flickr, YouTube, or the iTunes store. TOS may include age requirements, statements of responsibility for account security, etiquette, and rights to uploaded content.

Just as it is important to understand the basic outlines of a EULA, it is also important to understand the terms under which you are using a service. For example, if you are using a site to upload and share your photos, what rights does the website proprietor have to your pictures? Can they be used in promotions or advertisements? Can they be deleted if they don't conform to rules of content? Most TOS are reasonable and you may agree readily to their restrictions, but there's no common standard that all services must meet. If you're uploading your own music to one of these services, it is certainly very important for you to understand what rights to your work you are granting to the service.

COPY PROTECTION

While the EULA you agree to when you install a piece of commercial software usually legally restricts you from copying the software and giving it to a friend or 20,000 friends, it does not by itself actually prevent you from doing so any more than a speed limit physically restricts you from breaking it. To protect against software **piracy**, many software companies, and a large number of music software companies in particular, equip their software with some form of **copy protection**.

One of the more common forms of copy protection is the **key code**. A key code is a string of letters and numbers that is unique to a particular software license. This key code must typically be entered during software installation or the first time the software is run, and authorizes that computer to run the software. Frequently, the original CD-ROM or DVD-ROM from which the program was installed must be in the computer when the key code is entered. Some key codes must be verified with the software company over the Internet at the time of authorization, allowing the company to see how many computers have been authorized with a given key code.

A second common copy protection scheme is the **challenge/response** system. In this system, when you first run the software, you are presented with a "challenge," which is a series of letters and numbers that is unique to the computer on which you have installed the software (see Figure A2.6). This is different from a key code, which is unique to the software license. This challenge is typically entered, along with the serial number, on a web-based form or emailed to the company.

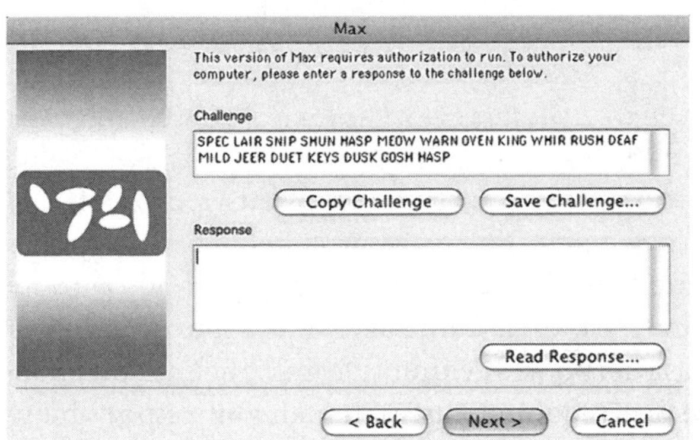

Figure A2.6 The challenge-response screen used to authorize Max/MSP software. (Courtesy of Cycling74, Inc.)

Once the company has verified that you have a valid serial number, they send back a "response," which is also a series of letters and numbers. The software can then be launched and the response pasted in a dialogue box beneath the challenge to authorize the computer. Because the challenge code and the corresponding response are specific to your computer, they are useless to anyone who wishes to pirate the software. One of the drawbacks to challenge/responses is that a hard drive failure will also delete the authorization, forcing the user to request another "response" after reinstalling the software.

A third common copy protection scheme is the **dongle**, which is a small USB device that contains an electronic serial number. In order to run the software, the dongle must be attached to the computer. Because this dongle is a physical device, it makes it very difficult to pirate the software.

A variation on the dongle is the iLok, which is a USB device that can be authorized for many different pieces of software. One advantage to the dongle or iLok is that you can install your software on many different machines, and only the machine with the dongle attached can actually run the software at a given time. One disadvantage is that the authorization for your software is entirely contained on a very small device that is eminently lose-able and steal-able. Once lost or stolen, your investment in the software can be lost.

It is common to hear people talk about **cracked software**—software for which the copy protection scheme has been defeated. Cracked software is, of course, illegal software. It is illegal to distribute cracked software and it is illegal to download and use it. There are many different rationales that people use to justify pirating software, including the "I'm just a student and software's expensive" argument and the "I'm stickin' it to the man" argument. Naturally, none of these arguments makes piracy legal, but neither do they make piracy moral. The state of U.S. copyright law is the subject of much debate, but few would argue that pirating something of value should be legalized. It's important to note that defeating a copy protection scheme is usually a violation of the EULA, even if you own the software and don't give the cracked copy to anyone else.

FILE SAVING AND FILE FORMATS

Most of this chapter has been given over to a discussion of software issues, but most software is of limited value unless you enter data into it, and this data is of little value unless is can be saved to some storage medium. When working with software you should remember to *save early, save often, and make backups*. The early and often edicts are pretty clear, but it's very important to make sure that you have your data backed up on more than one medium, such as hard drive and flash disk, hard drive and external drive, or flash disk and online storage. Drives and disks fail, and without proper backup you could lose everything from your stored email to your tax records to your latest grand composition or funky track. There's an old saying, or at least old by computer standards: there are two kinds of people in this world, people who *have* lost data and people who *will* lose data.

When saving a file, you typically have to supply three pieces of information: the name, the location, and the format (see Figures A2.7a and A2.7b). A **filename** is limited in terms of length and in terms of the characters that it can contain. While it is tempting to put a complete description of the file in the filename ("Term paper for important class due in October.doc"), it is better to keep filenames relatively short so that they can be seen easily in one of the standard GUI window views. In situations where you share a computer, such as a computer lab environment, including your name in the filename is a good idea.

The second critical piece of information used when saving the file is the **file location**. While there are standard places in both the Mac OS and Windows to store documents, both operating systems will let you save documents in a variety of places. Being disciplined about your file system by having carefully named folders, sub-folders, and documents can save you a great deal of time. The location of a file is usually shown in the "Save" window of an OS in a graphical format. Another representation of the location of a file is the **pathname**, which shows explicitly the directories and sub-directories that lead to the file (hence the term "path") (see Figure A2.8).

The **file format** determines the kind of information that is encoded in the file and the organization of that data within the file itself. Whenever you save a document, you are saving it in some format. If you're unaware of the format, you've either accepted the default (usually not a bad option) or the program only saves documents in one format (see Figure A2.7c). There are two general types of file formats: exclusive and interchange.

An **exclusive file format** is one that is specific to a particular application or group of applications. Most other applications don't save or read documents in that format. Table A2.1 contains a sampling of exclusive file formats for music and their associated applications.

An **interchange file format** is one that can be created and read by applications from a variety of software publishers. Interchange formats are quite common for media files, such as audio and video files. Many pieces of music software that allow you to record and process digital audio store data concerning the *organization* of the audio files in exclusive file formats and the digital audio files themselves in interchange file formats. For example, the recording software Pro Tools saves its session file in an exclusive .ptf

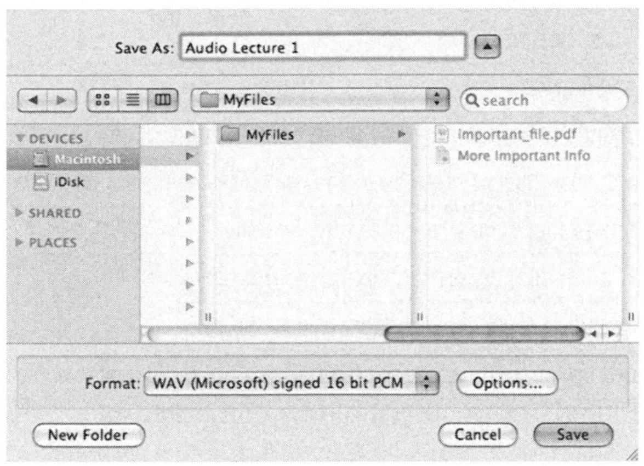

Figure A2.7a The Mac OS X Leopard save dialog box. Note the text box for the filename, the graphical method for choosing location, and the pop-up menu for the file format.

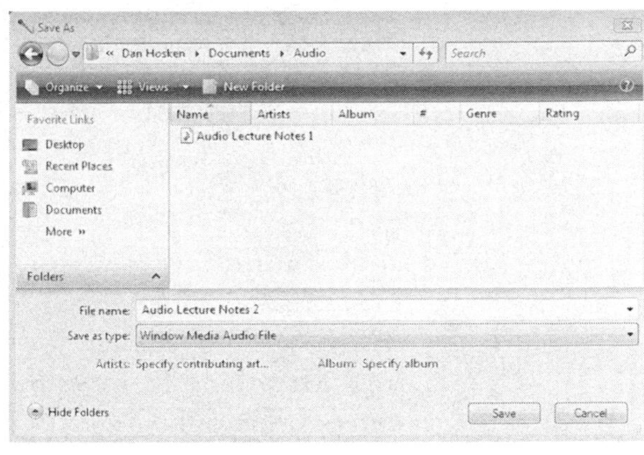

Figure A2.7b The Windows Vista save dialog box showing a similar interface for choosing the filename, location, and file format.

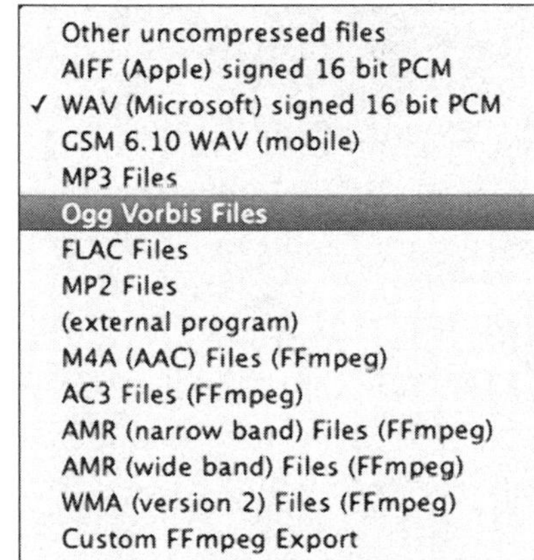

Figure A2.7c File format export options in Audacity.

Figure A2.8 Mac OS X Leopard info dialog box showing the file's pathname. Same path as Figure A2.7a.

***Table A2.1* Some exclusive file formats and their associated applications**

Exclusive file format (extension)	*Associated application*
.rns	Reason rack file
.ens	Reaktor ensemble file
.mus	Finale notation software
.sib	Sibelius music software
.ptf	Pro Tools session file
.cpr	Cubase Sequencer file

Table A2.2 Interchange file formats and short descriptions

Interchange file format (extension)	*File description and use*
.txt	Plain text file; readable/writable by any word processing application
.rtf	Rich text format; readable/writable by most word processing applications
.jpg	Compressed image file; widely readable and writable
.wav	Uncompressed audio file; widely readable and writable
.aif	Uncompressed audio file; widely readable and writable
.mp3	MPEG-1, layer 3 compressed audio file; widely readable and writable

format, but the actual audio is saved as broadcast wave files, .wav, which is an interchange format. Table A2.2 contains a sampling of interchange file formats and the types of applications that can open them.

When working with files, we are most concerned with whether the file is in an exclusive format or an interchange format, because that determines whether we have the software necessary to make use of the file. However, there is another important distinction to be made between open file formats and proprietary file formats. **Open file formats** are standardized either by a standards body, such as the ISO (International Standards Organization), or by a non-commercial group or company. These formats change only relatively slowly using an open deliberation process. **Proprietary formats**, on the other hand, are usually in the hands of a commercial entity and can be changed by them at any time.

Examples of open audio file formats include AAC/MP4, Ogg, AIFF, and Broadcast Wave. Examples of proprietary file formats include WMA (Windows Media Audio) owned by Microsoft and Real Audio owned by Real Media. WMA can be considered an interchange file format because many pieces of software can read it and write it, but it is not open, so Microsoft could, in theory, change it at any time.

Another distinction between file formats is those that are copy protected and those that aren't. Copy protection for files, as opposed to applications, is referred to as **digital rights management** (**DRM**). Files that are protected by DRM can only be used in ways prescribed by the copyright holder or distributor, so audio files that are protected by DRM cannot be endlessly copied and given away. For years, iTunes, one of the most popular online music stores, used a form of DRM for its files. Their AAC/MP4 files had the extension .m4p, indicating that they were protected by DRM. iTunes has since abandoned DRM, but it lives on in other media such as DVD with its Content Scramble System (CSS) and Blu-ray with its BD+.

INTERNET ADDRESSES

We now turn to Internet software and data. IP addresses and their associated domain names serve as the basic location information for computers on the Internet.

IP Addresses

Every computer connected directly to the Internet has a unique address called an **IP (Internet Protocol) address**. An IP address is represented by a group of four numbers separated by a dot, such as 130.166.238.195. There are two basic kinds of IP addresses: static and dynamic. **Static IP addresses** are typically used by computers that provide some service to other computers, such as web servers or file servers. A static IP requires a special arrangement with an ISP or manager of a LAN so that the particular IP address is reserved only for that computer.

Most computers that do not act as servers will use a **dynamic IP address** in which a new IP number is assigned periodically. An ISP, LAN, or other network is assigned a range of IP numbers to assign in turn to computers on their networks. While this IP address is dynamic or changeable, the IP address doesn't change very often when "always on" connections such as fiber, DSL, and cable are used.

A home LAN will typically have one IP address acquired from the ISP by the modem upon connection. A **wireless router** attached to the modem (or built into it) allows multiple computers to share the single IP address. Each computer accessing the router is assigned a private IP number that is not seen by any Internet devices outside of the home LAN. This allows an ISP to issue only one IP address to a home network, thereby preserving its pool of available IP addresses. The number of available IP addresses is rapidly dwindling under the current IP version (IPv4). The next IP version, IPv6, which has a much larger address space, is slowly being adopted.

Domain Names and URLs

While an IP address is the primary identity of a computer or other device connected to the Internet, a group of four numbers is not very "people friendly." When attempting to access a particular web server or other computer over a network it is extremely useful to be able to type in a logical, readable name rather than a sequence of numbers. This logical, readable name is referred to as a **domain name** or a **hostname** (they are technically somewhat different, but similar enough for our purposes).

A domain name is an important part of a **Uniform Resource Locator** (**URL**). A URL consists of a protocol, such as http or ftp, followed by a domain name (or hostname) and optionally a path within that domain and specific file in that path. Consider the following URL:

http://www.csun.edu/music/index.html

It starts out with http (for **Hypertext Transfer Protocol**), which is the standard protocol for transferring webpages over the network. The domain name is www.csun.edu, which represents the computer acting as the web server at that institution, the pathname is music, which is a sub-directory of the main webpage, and the file being displayed is named index.html.

When you type such a URL into your web browser, or click on a link, your computer contacts a **domain name server** that translates that domain name into an IP address. Once the translation is made, your request to have a webpage transferred to your computer is passed to the computer with that IP address. Your IP address, or the IP address assigned to your wireless router, is attached to that request so that the server knows where to deliver the requested webpage. This is a typical example of a client-server computer relationship.

NETWORK COMPUTER RELATIONSHIPS

Client-Server

The dominant relationship between computers on the Internet is a **client-server** relationship (see Figure A2.9). Client-server simply means that one computer (the client) uses software (client software) to make a request for a service from another computer (the server) that is running specialized software to deliver that service (server software). There are many different types of servers on the Internet providing a variety of services, such as email, webpages, forums, and mailing lists.

To get an idea of how the client-server computer relationship works, recall the URL discussed above. When you click on a link or type that URL into your browser's address bar, your computer sends a message to the server computer represented by

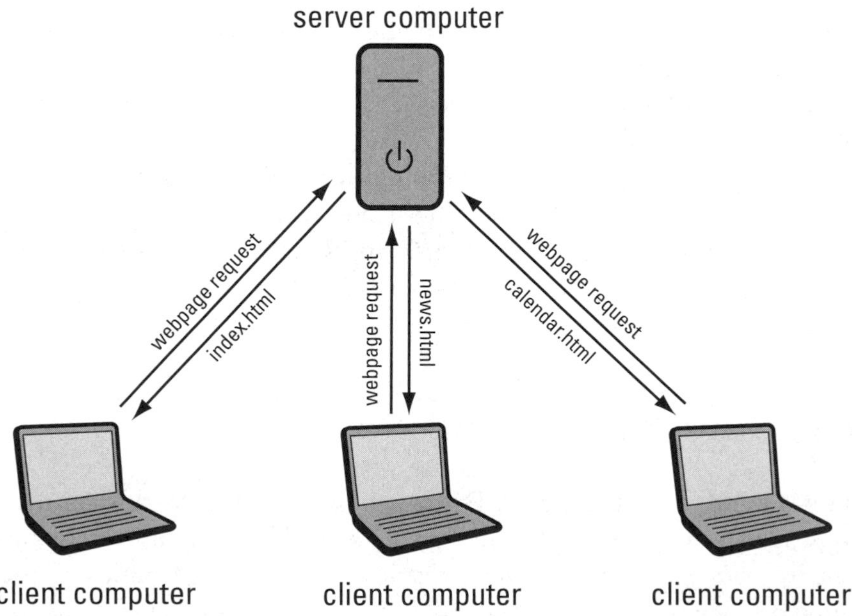

Figure A2.9 Three client computers making various webpage requests of one server.

www.csun.edu requesting that the webpage index.html be copied to your computer over the network. In this case, your browser is the client software and your computer is the client computer. The server computer is www.csun.edu and the server software, such as the open source Apache web server software, processes the webpage request. The service itself is the transfer of the webpage. Upon receipt of the HTML-encoded webpage, the client software, a browser such as Firefox, renders it into readable form.

This is a fundamentally hierarchical, one-way relationship where your computer is making a request of the server for information. A different type of computer-to-computer relationship is found in peer-to-peer.

Peer-to-Peer

Peer-to-peer, or **P2P**, is the computer relationship that has received the most attention from the popular press and in legal circles. When two computers communicate P2P, each acts as both a server *and* a client at the same time. This is very different from the strictly hierarchical relationship that exists in client-server computing (see Figure A2.10).

P2P was made famous by the Napster application, which allowed computer users to make media files on their hard drives, particularly MP3s, available to other computer users on the Internet, who in turn would make their media files available. Thus, while you download files from a particular computer, that computer's owner could be downloading files from yours or anyone else's who is running the software. In this situation, your computer is acting as both a client and a server at the same time. Even following Napster's demise, as a result of music industry lawsuits, and rebirth as a digital music store, file sharing is still a prominent P2P activity through software such as Shareaza and BitTorrent.

Another popular P2P application is Skype, which allows you to place "phone calls," plus video and text chat, to other users over the Internet. Because no central server is involved in routing these calls, it is a P2P application. Skype sends its information using Voice over Internet Protocol (VoIP), just as most commercial digital phone services do.

Internet addresses and network computer relationships provide the infrastructure for the actual activities that take place over the Internet.

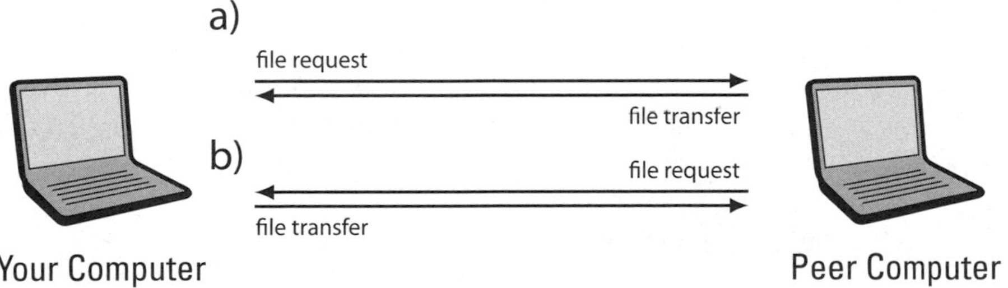

Figure A2.10 Two computers in a peer-to-peer relationship: (a) your computer acting as a "client," and (b) your computer acting as a "server".

INTERNET ACTIVITIES AND WEB 2.0

The various activities that you can engage in on the Internet can be divided into three broad and sometimes intersecting categories: information, communication, and collaboration.

Internet Information

In the information category are webpages, interactive webpages, streaming audio and video, podcasting, client-server file transfers, and search. Each of these is based generally on one-way communication from the content creator to you. Of course, *you* could be the content creator, in which case the one-way flow is from you to your readers, listeners, or viewers. Even though file transfers are not an obvious fit for the "information" category, when they are executed using the client-server model, they are similarly one-way.

Webpages are probably the best-known information resources on the Internet. Traditional webpages that simply present information are encoded using **HTML** (Hypertext Markup Language) or **XHTML** (Extensible Hypertext Markup Language), which is a somewhat stricter form of HTML. In HTML, sections of text are "marked up" by enclosing them in bracketed instructions called tags. For example, to display this:

> To hear my *awesome* new track, click <u>here</u>.

you would type the following into an HTML document:

```
To hear my <em>awesome</em> new track,
click <a href="newtrack.mp3"> here </a>
```

The <em> and </em> tags indicate that the enclosed text should be displayed as emphasized, which usually means in italics. The <a> and </a> tags indicate that the enclosed text is a hyperlink and is usually displayed with an underline or some other distinguishing characteristic. The href attribute within the <a> tag indicates the page or file that will be called up when you click on the link. The fact that it is not a full URL indicates that the file newtrack.mp3 is in the same directory on the server as the webpage that references it.

Though this is used here as an example of HTML, a direct link to an audio file like this is a simple way of making audio available on the Internet, though the results vary by platform and browser. To give the user a bit of control over the audio, you can use the <embed> tag:

```
<embed src="newtrack.mp3"></embed>
```

These tags are not really proper HTML, though for the moment they still work. The <object> tag is the officially sanctioned tag for purposes like this. There are a number of other details regarding the <embed> and <object> tags that allow you to give the user various kinds of control over the media. These details are beyond the scope of this chapter, but see the book's website for links to explanations and examples of embedding media in webpages.

HTML is relatively simple to learn and it is valuable to know at least the basics. The phishing example earlier in the chapter is ample evidence of this (see Figure A2.4 on page 336). There are many tools available that allow you to create webpages in a WYSIWYG (What You See Is What You Get) environment so that you don't have to code the HTML by hand. To get an idea of the codes that generate a webpage, you can view the underlying HTML code for a page in most browsers by choosing a menu command similar to "View Page Source" (the command is in different places in different browsers). However, you should be aware that most commercial webpages are quite complicated and use additional codes beyond HTML: it can take a bit of time to decipher what codes are associated with which display elements.

Interactive webpages take HTML a step further by incorporating **JavaScript**, which can cause the page to change based on a user's actions. JavaScript is a bit like a small programming language created to allow webpage designers to quickly and easily incorporate interactivity into a webpage. For example, the JavaScript event "onmouseover" (on mouse over) can be used to change an image or execute some other action when you move your mouse over a particular element on the page. This is used regularly to create sophisticated links that show an additional submenu when you move your mouse over that link.

In addition to JavaScript, Flash and Java applets are often used to enhance interactivity. An **applet** is a small application that runs within a browser. **Java applets** are created using the Java programming language, which was created by Sun Microsystems, and **Flash applets** are created using the Adobe Flash multimedia programming environment. The Flash programming environment has a graphical interface as well as deep scripting capabilities, and is popular for multimedia. Both Java and Flash have been used to create powerful programs, such as videogames, that run directly in the browser. Java and Flash applets depend on browser plug-ins in order to run.

Flash is frequently used for **audio** and **video streaming**. There are a number of pre-made Flash audio players available for adding sophisticated audio control to a website, such as XSPF Web Music Player, Google Reader MP3 Player, and Yahoo! Media Player (see Figures A2.11a and A2.11b). These are embedded into websites using the <object> tag, which references a Flash applet. Yahoo! has a clever technique for calling up its Yahoo! Media Player: a bit of JavaScript embedded into the HTML page causes any audio linked using simple <a> and </a> tags to automatically call up its Flash-based Media Player. (See the book's website for links to Flash- and Java-based music players.)

Many video sites on the web, including YouTube and Hulu, use JavaScript in combination with Flash to play video. In addition, there are video players similar to the audio players discussed above available for non-commercial websites.

Podcasting is another method for distributing audio and video information. A podcast consists of two items: the media and the feed. The media for a podcast is generally

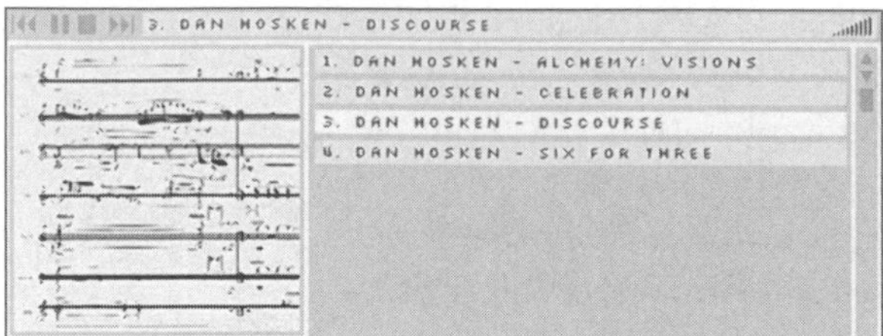

Figure A2.11a Flash-based XSPF Web Music Player playing XSPF formatted playlist.

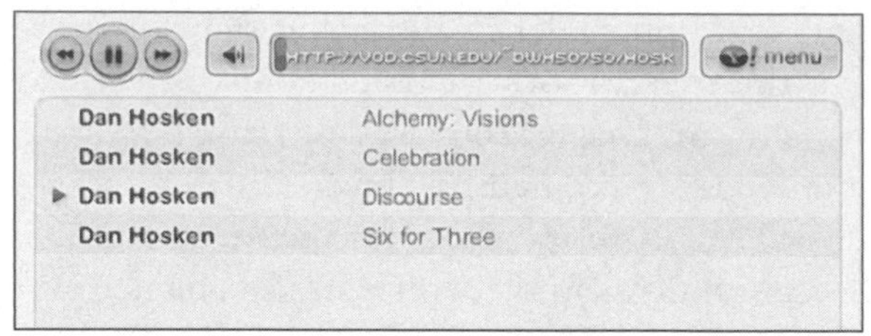

Figure A2.11b Flash-based Yahoo! Media Player playing XSPF formatted playlist.

nothing more than a compressed audio or a video file stored on a web server. What makes podcasting different from downloading and streaming is that the file is made available through an **RSS feed (**Really Simple Syndication feed). An RSS feed is a document encoded in **XML** (Extensible Markup Language) and stored on a web server that defines a channel and items within that channel.

An example of a channel might be a series of audio news stories about music called "Music Here Today." The items then would be the individual news stories stored as separate audio files. A story one day about a prominent performer coming to town would be one item, a story on another day about a world première of a composition would be another item, and so on. Each time the podcast creator uploads a new audio file of a story to the web server, he or she adds a new item to the RSS feed. Now with the media and feed both available on the Internet, someone needs to subscribe to the feed.

Client software known as an **aggregator** or **podcatcher** is required in order to subscribe to a podcast. This is simply a matter of pasting the URL for the RSS feed into a field in the aggregator or clicking on a webpage link that subscribes automatically. The aggregator then checks the RSS feed periodically and downloads items that have been added since the last time it was checked. The best-known aggregator is Apple's iTunes. As the "syndication" part of RSS indicates, podcasting uses a news metaphor for distributing media, and many radio and TV networks make their material available as podcasts.

Downloading files from a server is another type of one-way information flow on the Internet. Common downloads include applications, application updates, drivers, video, audio, and documents. Though there are several protocols used to download files, including HTTP, one of the standards is the **File Transfer Protocol**, or **FTP**. To transfer files using FTP, you can use dedicated client software, a web browser that supports FTP downloading, or a web browser with a plug-in that provides fuller FTP support. Usually, an FTP client is only necessary when you're uploading to a server; your web browser typically handles FTP downloads.

The final Internet activity in the information category is **search**. The other activities in this category were largely based on a one-way flow of information from the content creator to the user. Search is a more complex activity, because, while you have little control over a search engine's index of websites, the search terms that you enter determine what is retrieved from that index. The index itself is constructed by automated web "crawling" software that visits webpages and takes note of what is there.

The most common search method is the keyword search in which you type a series of words into a field and submit them to the search engine. The search engine then retrieves links to relevant pages from its index and displays them in your browser. All of the popular search engines also have "advanced search" features that allow you to specify an exact string of words, exclude pages that have some words, and restrict the search to a particular domain, such as intel.com. Search is not necessarily a neutral and objective act, as the book *Blown to bits* (Abelson, Ledeen, and Lewis, 2008: 109–160) carefully illustrates, so a search has to be seen as a starting point rather than a final destination.

Internet Communication

The second category of Internet activity, communication, includes email, message boards, mailing lists, and live text, audio, and video chat. Each of these activities represents communication between you and one or more people. One division to make in this category is between synchronous, or real-time, communications and asynchronous communications. Email, message boards, and mailing lists are asynchronous and text, audio, and video chat are synchronous.

Email, the "smash hit" of the early Internet (Abbate, 1999: 106), requires little explanation, but the value of message boards and mailing lists to music technology deserves some recognition. **Message boards**, also referred to as forums or bulletin boards, operate in an asynchronous post-and-reply format in which posts are organized into topics, or threads. This format has been widely adopted by hardware and software user groups. Threading allows contributors and interested readers to home in on discussions of interest, and the asynchronous nature allows members to post when a problem arises and then wait for other community members with the appropriate knowledge to check the board and reply. When you begin using a particular piece of hardware or software, you should search for the appropriate message boards. Some are sponsored by the company itself and may feature knowledgeable employees or even programmers as contributors.

Mailing lists, also referred to as LISTSERVs, serve a similar purpose to message boards. The chief difference is that mailing lists utilize your email, which you presumably check frequently, as opposed to a website that you must remember to visit. The downside to mailing lists is that it is more difficult to follow a thread that takes place over several days or weeks because it is split among different emails, whereas threads in message boards remain coherent. Though they are categorized under communication here, message boards and mailing lists could just as well be discussed under collaboration, as they represent community-generated information sources.

Text, **audio**, and **video chat** is synchronous, or real time, as opposed to the asynchronous activities just mentioned. Transferring text over a network naturally requires much less bandwidth (connection speed) than audio or video, so there are more text-based chat, or instant messaging, clients than audio or video. However, there are several clients, such as iChat on the Macintosh and the cross-platform Skype, that allow everything from text (instant messaging) to video communication. Of course, if clients like Skype and iChat can carry voice, then they can carry other audio as well, making musical performance and rehearsal using them conceivable.

Low latency (delay) and predictable timing are among the most important features for remote music performance. This is difficult to achieve over the Internet because variations in traffic and local network speeds can cause variations in the timing of transmitted data. Performances involving high-quality, low-latency video and audio are taking place over Internet2, which will be discussed later in this appendix.

Internet Collaboration

The third category of Internet activity involves collaboration. Collaborative activities include wiki editing, media sharing, blogging, microblogging, and social networking. In addition, several of the topics discussed previously are relevant here as well, including message boards and audio/video remote performance.

Wikis are websites that allow users to create and edit the content. The most famous example, of course, is Wikipedia, the user-generated encyclopedia. However, wikis are used in a variety of contexts to allow users to collaborate in creating information. A wiki-based website is very different from the websites discussed earlier, and the very idea of wikis upends the notion of singular authorship inherent in informational websites.

Media sharing sites include YouTube and Vimeo for video and Flickr and Snapfish for pictures. What distinguishes these sites from the video streaming sites of traditional content creators is that much of the content is user-generated. Despite the user-created aspect of these sites, they still follow the traditional client-server model, unlike peer-to-peer filesharing using Shareaza or BitTorrent discussed above.

Blogging can be distinguished from traditional informational websites by the speed and ease with which a blogger can post and the ability of readers to comment on those posts, which is a form of user-generated content. Sites that host blogs, such as Blogger.com, provide a simple interface for creating blog posts and host the resultant blog. This eliminates the need for bloggers to create their content in a web authoring application such as Dreamweaver and upload it to their own website hosting space.

The best-known form of **microblogging** is Twitter, which limits your posts to 140 characters. The small size of these posts encourages microblogging from mobile phones rather than computers, enhancing the spontaneity and immediacy of it. Though microblogging is associated by name with blogging, it more resembles a form of broadcast text messaging. Due to the nature of Twitter, in which you "follow" people—receive their tweets—and are perhaps followed by others, it has aspects of a social networking site as well.

Social networking sites, such as Facebook, foster the explicit creation of communities around common interests or common social relationships. By definition their content is user-created, though the users may also include businesses, universities, and other institutions. The idea of user-generated content and its inherent questioning of traditional authorship is one of the most important principles of Web 2.0.

Web 2.0 and YOU

Web 2.0 is a term that is used to distinguish the traditional information-based authority-driven web (Web 1.0) from the dynamic, interactive, user-focused web of today. Many of the activities above, particularly in the "collaboration" category, utilize user-generated content and user collaboration as their primary information sources. Even activities such as podcasting, which is fundamentally a one-way communication, contribute to the Web 2.0 concept, because podcasting is highly democratic. Anyone can create and syndicate a series of audio lectures or interviews, just as blogging allows anyone to generate what amount to their own interactive webpages quickly and easily.

Wikis, and Wikipedia in particular, provide an excellent example of the Web 2.0 concept. The way that information is created in Wikipedia is sometimes referred to as "crowd-sourcing," in which a problem—in this case the gathering of information about a wide variety of topics—is given to the crowd to solve. Anyone can participate regardless of whether they bear a stamp of authority, such as a particular college degree, a relevant job title, or experience. The end result is a live, dynamic source for information about almost any topic. The information is uneven and can be controversial, but it is convenient and plentiful even as it challenges the information literacy skills of the reader.

Search is another emblematic Web 2.0 idea. The traditional hierarchical presentation of a Web 1.0 directory with its categorized list of hyperlinks has given way to a keyword-indexed database drawn from diverse sources. In this, the democratic nature of Web 2.0 becomes paramount: a search on a current topic is just as likely to pull up a blog post as an Associated Press story.

In 2006, *Time Magazine* named its person of the year as "You," and featured a computer screen as a mirror on the cover in recognition of the Web 2.0 phenomenon. Naturally, discussion has turned to Web 3.0, but opinion is not clearly settled on just what that will be.

INTERNET2

Just as there is Web 2.0 in contrast to Web 1.0, there is also **Internet2** in contrast to the original Internet "1." The Internet that we all know and use every day has its roots in the ARPAnet network of the 1970s, which was a research project involving members of government agencies, educational institutions, and corporations. Using ARPAnet, those researchers developed the core technologies that underlie the Internet and fundamental applications such as email.

Those technologies and applications carried over to the development of the Internet in the 1980s and helped make the Internet the essential tool for education, research, and commerce that it is today. As wonderful as the Internet is, demands on it increase every day, and users expect audio, video, and interactivity to work quickly and flawlessly. To accommodate these increasing demands, the Internet will continually have to change and adapt.

The Internet2 consortium was formed in the mid-1990s to allow researchers from academia, business, and the government to explore new networking technologies that will improve speed and reliability, and develop new applications for this faster more robust future Internet. Internet2 projects route data over a high-speed network "backbone" that allows for far higher bandwidth than typical Internet connections. There are many interesting applications of Internet2, but most of the prominent musical experiments involve the concept of telepresence.

Telepresence involves two or more parties interacting over a remote connection, such as Internet2, as if they were physically in each other's presence. This typically involves high-resolution video and audio with very little lag time, or latency. Video and audio applications such as videoconferencing are possible today, of course, over the regular Internet. However, the experience is often plagued by low-resolution video, low frame rates, and frequent dropouts. It's possible to interact this way, but you don't have a strong sense of being in the other's presence, and the timing is seldom tight enough for musical purposes.

Many of the Internet2 research projects in music involve education and performance. Remote education holds the promise of delivering masterclasses with world-renowned performers to students at multiple remote locations and enabling remote rehearsal (see Figure A2.12). The interactions in a masterclass or rehearsal setting require the low-latency, high-resolution connection that Internet2 promises. Another educational application concerns distance learning. Full-resolution audio and video lectures and interaction with remote students again require low-latency connections.

Remote performance, referred to as **telematic performance**, brings performers from multiple locations together. Aside from the convenience of not having to travel and the inherent technological interest, telematic performance holds the possibility of bringing the unique sense of place of one location to another and vice versa. (See the book's website for links to remote teaching and telematic performance projects.)

Figure A2.12 New World Symphony cello masterclass via Internet2. (Courtesy of New World Symphony)

REVIEW OF KEY TERMS

application software 329
operating system (OS) 329
Windows 330
Mac OS 330
Linux 330
device driver 330
graphical user interface (GUI) 331
command-line interface (CLI)/shell 331
root directory/folder 332
Finder 332
Windows Explorer 332
commercial software 333
intellectual property 333
shareware 333
demos 333
freeware 333
open source 334
cloud computing 334
malware 334
viruses 334
worms 334
Trojan horses 335
spyware 335
phishing 335
hoaxes 335
licenses 336
copyright 336
end-user license agreement (EULA) 337
terms of service (TOS) 338
piracy 338
copy protection 338
key code 338
challenge/response 338
dongle 339
cracked software 339
filename 340
file location 340
pathname 340
file format 340
exclusive file format 340
interchange file format 340
open file format 342
proprietary file format 342
digital rights management (DRM) 342
IP (Internet Protocol) address 343
static IP address 343
dynamic IP address 343
wireless router 343
domain name/hostname 343
Uniform Resource Locator (URL) 343
HTTP (Hypertext Transfer Protocol) 343
domain name server 344
client-server 344
peer-to-peer (P2P) 345
webpages 346
HTML/XHTML 346
interactive webpages 347
JavaScript 347
applets 347
Java/Flash applets 347
audio/video streaming 347
podcasting 347
RSS feed 348
XML 348
aggregator/podcatcher 348
downloading 348
FTP (File Transfer Protocol) 348
search 348
message boards 349
mailing lists 349
text/audio/video chat 349
wikis 350
media sharing 350
blogging/microblogging 350
social networking 350
Web 2.0 351
Internet2 351
telepresence 352
telematic performance 352

Appendix
Further Reading

For a general history of computing, Paul Ceruzzi's *A history of modern computing* (2nd ed., 2003) is both in-depth and very readable. For a history specifically of the personal computer, Paul Freiberger and Michael Swaine's *Fire in the valley: The making of the personal computer* (2000) provides a blow-by-blow account of this fascinating process with interesting technical, social, and personal details. Many of the main players in that book are still making news today. Janet Abbate's *Inventing the Internet* (1999) chronicles the developments in networking hardware, data transmission, and software that influenced the ARPAnet project and eventually shaped the early Internet. For a real nuts and bolts look at computing hardware, Scott Mueller's *Upgrading and repairing PCs* (18th ed., 2008) is an excellent resource.

An essential book for understanding the nature of modern computing and the Internet is the wonderfully written *Blown to bits: Your life, liberty, and happiness after the digital explosion* by Hal Abelson, Ken Ledeen, and Harry Lewis (2008). This book takes us behind the basic technologies that we use every day, such as search and secure network communications, and helps us understand why we must grasp these details in order to understand how these technologies affect our lives. Equally important are Lawrence Lessig's *Free Culture* (2004) and *Remix* (2008), which take a critical look at the state of modern copyright law and how it impacts the way we interact with our digital culture.

Appendix
Suggested Activities

The following are some suggested activities relating to computer hardware and software.

UP-TO-DATE SPECIFICATIONS

Some of the specific information concerning computer hardware and software in this section will be out of date by the time you read this text. Given the pace of development in computing, this is inevitable.

- To learn the details of computer systems now, search common computer sales websites (dell.com and apple.com are good starting places) and fill in the following table for a desktop computer and a laptop computer. Look at both "average" systems and higher-end systems that might be suitable for data-intensive tasks such as audio recording.

Current computer system specifications

Components	*Desktop system*	*Laptop system*
Operating system (specific)		
CPU (include number of cores)		
Clock speed (in GHz)		
RAM (in GB)		
RAM expandable to . . .		
Hard drive type/size		
Optical drive (DVD-R, BD-R)		
Special features?		
Price		

- What are the specifications for the computer you're currently working on?
- Look up benchmarks for some current systems. Some links are available at the text's website or you can search for them. Do some systems appear to perform particularly well? Do others perform particularly poorly?
- Search for USB flash drives on various retailers' websites, such as amazon.com, walmart.com, or bestbuy.com. In particular, look for "high-speed" flash drives. What are the current sizes and costs for these drives?
- Look up a couple of different ISPs that serve your local area, such as cable, DSL, and FTTH (fiber to the home) ISPs. What are the current connection speeds and costs? What other services are provided by these ISPs?
- Choose one of the standard Internet connection bandwidth tests (some links are available at the book's website) and run it from your home computer and in a computer lab. What is your connection speed? Try some others: do they match?

SOFTWARE INFORMATION

- What are the current versions of Windows and Mac OS? What other operating systems are available from retailers?
- Search for some music shareware and freeware. What free software looks most exciting to you?
- Look up news about current malware. Sites such as snopes.com and the websites for Symantec and McAffee are good places to start. Are there any malware hoaxes going around?
- Look up and read the EULA for a piece of software that you use. Some of these can be hard to find after you've installed the software. (There are some links to EULAs on the book's website.) Are there any surprising items in them?
- Find out what copy protection is being used by your favorite music software.
- Search for music performance or education projects that utilize live interaction over the Internet or Internet2. (There are some links to such projects on the book's website.) What are some of the positive aspects of such projects? What are the negative aspects, if any? How would you like to use the Internet for live performance or education?

EXPLORE YOUR COMPUTER

- How do you copy files from the hard drive to a flash drive using the Finder in Mac OS or Windows Explorer in Windows? Try to do it *without* opening the file and choosing "Save As . . ."
- How do you properly eject a flash drive on your computer?
- Open up any program and choose "Save." Where are files stored by default on your computer? What is the default file format for this program? Are any other formats available? How do you change locations and save on a flash drive?

- How does your computer find patches for your operating system? How often is it set to look for them?
- Look at the system programs on your computer for configuring audio and MIDI input and output. In Windows, they are in the Control Panel accessible from the Start menu, and on Mac OS they are in the System Preferences and in the AudioMIDI setup application, which is in the Utilities folder inside the Applications folder. Some controls may only be available within music programs. What options are available for your MIDI and audio hardware?

Selected Bibliography

INTRODUCTION

Prensky, Marc. 2001. Digital natives, digital immigrants part I. *On The Horizon* 9(5): 1–6. www.marcprensky.com/writing/.

SECTION I: SOUND

American Speech-Language-Hearing Association (ASHA). Noise and hearing loss. www.asha.org/public/hearing/disorders/noise.htm.

Amos, Jonathan. 2003. Organ music "instils religious feelings." *BBC News Online*, September 8. http://news.bbc.co.uk/2/hi/science/nature/3087674.stm.

Angliss, Sarah, Richard Lord, Dan Simmons, Ciarán O'Keeffe, and Richard Wiseman. 2003. Infrasonic: summary of results. May 31. www.spacedog.biz/extras/Infrasonic/infrasonicResults.htm.

Chittka, L. and A. Brockmann. 2005. *Perception space—the final frontier.* PL.S. Biol 3(4): e137. doi: 10.1371/journal.pbio.0030137 [available under the Creative Commons Attribution License: http://creativecommons.org/licenses/by/3.0/legalcode].

Cook, Perry R. 1999. *Music, cognition, and computerized sound: An introduction to psychoacoustics.* Cambridge, MA: MIT Press.

Doctorow, Cory. 2008. Teen-repellent ultrasonic device violates kids' rights. February 22. www.boingboing.net/2008/02/22/teenrepellent-ultras.html.

Dodge, Charles and Thomas A. Jerse. 1997. *Computer music: Synthesis, composition, and performance.* 2nd ed. New York: Schirmer Books.

Fletcher, Neville H. and Thomas D. Rossing. 1998. *The physics of musical instruments.* 2nd ed. New York: Springer.

Helmholtz, Hermann von. 1954. *On the sensations of tone as a physiological basis for the theory of music.* 2nd English ed., trans. Alexander John Ellis. New York: Dover Publications.

Holmes, Thom. 2008. *Electronic and experimental music: Technology, music, and culture.* 3rd ed. New York: Routledge.

Isacoff, Stuart. 2001. *Temperament: The idea that solved music's greatest riddle.* 1st ed. New York: Alfred A. Knopf.

Johnston, Ian D. 2009. *Measured tones: The interplay of physics and music.* 3rd ed. Boca Raton, FL: CRC Press.

Levitin, Daniel J. 2006. *This is your brain on music: The science of a human obsession.* New York: Dutton.

Loy, D. Gareth. 2006. *Musimathics: The mathematical foundations of music*, Vol. 1. Cambridge, MA: MIT Press.

Moore, Brian C.J. 2003. *An introduction to the psychology of hearing.* 5th ed. San Diego, CA: Academic Press.

MosquitoUSA. 2009. The Mosquito ultrasonic crime deterrent. www.mosquitousa.com/.

Occupational Safety and Health Administration (US Department of Labor). 1999. Noise and hearing conservation. *OSHA Technical Manual.* www.osha.gov/dts/osta/otm/noise/.

Olson, Harry Ferdinand. 1967. *Music, physics and engineering.* 2nd ed. New York: Dover Publications.

Payne, Katharine. 1998. *Silent thunder: In the presence of elephants.* New York: Simon & Schuster.

Pierce, John Robinson. 1992. *The science of musical sound.* Rev. ed. New York: W.H. Freeman.

Portnuff, Cory and Brian Fligor. 2006. Output levels of portable digital music players. Paper presented at the *Noise-induced Hearing Loss in Children at Work and Play* conference, October 19–20 in Cincinnati, Ohio. http://nhca.affiniscape.com/associations/10915/files/Portnuff_Fligor_OutputLevelsofPortableDigitalMusicPl.swf.

Roederer, Juan. 2008. *The physics and psychophysics of music: An introduction*. 4th ed. New York: Springer.

Safety and Health in Arts Production and Entertainment (SHAPE). 2005. *Noise and hearing loss in musicians*. Vancouver: SHAPE. http://shape.bc.ca/resources/pdf/noisehearinglossmusicians.pdf.

Sallows, Kevin. 2001. *Listen while you work: hearing conservation for the arts*. Vancouver: SHAPE (Safety and Health in Arts Production and Entertainment). http://shape.bc.ca/resources/pdf/listen.pdf.

Sundberg, Johan. 1987. *The science of the singing voice*. DeKalb, IL: Northern Illinois University Press.

SECTION II: AUDIO

Apple, Inc. 2006. Apple core audio file format specification 1.0. http://developer.apple.com/mac/library/documentation/MusicAudio/Reference/CAFSpec/CAF_intro/CAF_intro.html.

Ballou, Glen. 2008. *Handbook for sound engineers*. 4th ed. Oxford: Focal Press.

Collins, Nicolas. 2009. *Handmade electronic music: The art of hardware hacking*. 2nd ed. New York: Routledge.

Dodge, Charles and Thomas A. Jerse. 1997. *Computer music: Synthesis, composition, and performance*. 2nd ed. New York: Schirmer Books.

Hall, Gary S. 2002. Cramped quarters. *Electronic Musician* 18(4) (April). http://emusician.com/tutorials/emusic_cramped_quarters/.

Holman, Tomlinson. 2002. *Sound for film and television*. 2nd ed. Boston, MA: Focal Press.

Huber, David Miles and Robert E. Runstein. 2005. *Modern recording techniques*. 6th ed. Boston, MA: Focal Press/Elsevier.

Katz, Mark. 2004. *Capturing sound: How technology has changed music*. Berkeley, CA: University of California Press.

Loy, D. Gareth. 2006. *Musimathics: The mathematical foundations of music*, Vol. 2. Cambridge, MA: MIT Press.

Microsoft Corporation. Windows media audio codecs. www.microsoft.com/windows/windowsmedia/forpros/codecs/audio.aspx.

Millard, A.J. 2005. *America on record: A history of recorded sound*. 2nd ed. New York: Cambridge University Press.

Myer, E. Brad and David R. Moran. 2007. Audibility of a CD-standard A/D/A loop inserted into high-resolution audio playback. *Journal of the Audio Engineering Society* 55(9): 775–779.

Pohlmann, Ken C. 2005. *Principles of digital audio*. 5th ed. New York: McGraw-Hill.

Rumsey, Francis and Tim McCormick. 2006. *Sound and recording: An introduction*. 5th ed. Boston, MA: Elsevier/Focal Press.

Steiglitz, Kenneth. 1996. *A DSP primer: With applications to digital audio and computer music*. Menlo Park, CA: Addison-Wesley.

Strawn, John and James F. McGill. 1985. *Digital audio engineering: An anthology*, The Computer Music and Digital Audio Series. Los Altos, CA: W. Kaufmann.

Thompson, Daniel M. 2005. *Understanding audio: Getting the most out of your project or professional recording studio*. Boston, MA: Berklee Press.

Watkinson, John. 2001. *The art of digital audio*. 3rd ed. Boston, MA: Focal Press.

SECTION III: MIDI

Chadabe, Joel. 1997. *Electric sound: The past and promise of electronic music*. Upper Saddle River, NJ: Prentice Hall.

Gordon, Reid. 2004. The history of Roland. Part 2: 1979–1985. *Sound On Sound* 20(2) (December). www.soundonsound.com/sos/dec04/articles/roland.htm.

Guérin, Robert. 2006. *MIDI power! The comprehensive guide*. 2nd ed. Boston, MA: Thomson Course Technology.

Holmes, Thom. 2008. *Electronic and experimental music: Technology, music, and culture.* 3rd ed. New York: Routledge.

Lehrman, Paul D. and Tim Tully. 1993. *MIDI for the professional.* New York: Amsco Publications.

Loy, Gareth. 1985. Musicians make a standard: the MIDI phenomenon. *Computer Music Journal* 9(4) (winter): 8–26.

Manning, Peter. 2004. *Electronic and computer music.* Rev. and expanded ed. New York: Oxford University Press.

MIDI Manufacturer's Association. 2003. *General MIDI 2.* Version 1.1. Los Angeles, CA: MIDI Manufacturer's Association.

———. 2006. *The complete MIDI 1.0 detailed specification: incorporating all recommended practices.* Los Angeles, CA: MIDI Manufacturer's Association.

Moog, Robert A. 1965. Voltage-controlled electronic music modules. *Journal of the Audio Engineering Society* 13(3) (July): 200–206.

———. 1986. Musical Instrument Digital Interface. *Journal of the Audio Engineering Society* 34(5) (May): 394–404.

Moore, F. Richard. 1998. The dysfunctions of MIDI. *The Computer Music Journal* 12(1) (Spring): 19–28.

Pejrolo, Andrea and Richard DeRosa. 2007. *Acoustic and MIDI orchestration for the contemporary composer.* 1st ed. Boston, MA: Focal Press.

Rona, Jeffrey C. 1990. *Synchronization, from reel to reel: A complete guide for the synchronization of audio, film & video.* Milwaukee, WI: H. Leonard Pub. Corp.

———. 1994. *The MIDI companion.* Rev. ed. Milwaukee, WI: Hal Leonard.

Théberge, Paul. 1997. *Any sound you can imagine: Making music/consuming technology.* Hanover, NH: Wesleyan University Press.

Vail, Mark. 2000. *Vintage synthesizers.* 2nd ed. San Francisco, CA: Miller Freeman Books.

———. 2004. Vintage gear: Oberheim DS-2 digital pre-MIDI sequencer. *Keyboard* 30(4) (April): 100.

Young, Robert W. 1939. Terminology for logarithmic frequency units. *Journal of the Acoustical Society of America* 11(1) (July): 134–139.

SECTION IV: SYNTHESIS AND SAMPLING

Aikin, Jim. 2004. *Power tools for synthesizer programming: The ultimate reference for sound design.* San Francisco, CA: Backbeat Books.

Boulanger, Richard Charles. 2000. *The Csound book: Perspectives in software synthesis, sound design, signal processing, and programming.* Cambridge, MA: MIT Press.

Chadabe, Joel. 1997. *Electric sound: The past and promise of electronic music.* Upper Saddle River, NJ: Prentice Hall.

Chowning, John and David Bristow. 1986. *FM theory and applications.* Tokyo: Yamaha Music Foundation.

Cook, Perry R. 2002. *Real sound synthesis for interactive applications.* Natick, MA: A.K. Peters.

Dodge, Charles and Thomas A. Jerse. 1997. *Computer music: Synthesis, composition, and performance.* 2nd ed. New York: Schirmer Books.

Holmes, Thom. 2008. *Electronic and experimental music: Technology, music, and culture.* 3rd ed. New York: Routledge.

Manning, Peter. 2004. *Electronic and computer music.* Rev. and expanded ed. New York: Oxford University Press.

McIntyre, M., R. Schumacher, and J. Woodhouse. 1983. On the oscillations of musical instruments. *Journal of the Acoustical Society of America* 74(5) (November): 1325–1345.

Moore, F. Richard. 1990. *Elements of computer music.* Englewood Cliffs, NJ: Prentice Hall.

Pellman, Samuel. 1994. *An introduction to the creation of electroacoustic music.* Belmont, CA: Wadsworth.

Roads, Curtis. 1996. *The computer music tutorial.* Cambridge, MA: MIT Press.

———. 2001. *Microsound.* Cambridge, MA: MIT Press.

SECTION V: COMPUTER NOTATION AND CAI

Adler, Samuel. 2002. *The study of orchestration.* 3rd ed. New York: W.W. Norton.

Bajura, K.V.A. and Amy Stabenow. 2004. *Finale for composers: An illustrated guide to Finale.* Pittsburgh, PA: Phoebus Apollo Music.

Consortium of National Arts Education Associations. 1994. *Dance, music, theatre, visual arts: What every young American should know and be able to do in the arts: National standards for arts education.* Reston, VA: Music Educators National Conference.

Read, Gardner. 1979. *Music notation: A manual of modern practice.* 2d ed. A Crescendo book. New York: Taplinger.

Recordare. MusicXML Definition. www.recordare.com/xml.html.

Rudolph, Thomas E., Floyd Richmond, David Mash, Peter Webster, William Bauer, and Kim Walls. 2005. *Technology strategies for music education.* 2nd ed. Wyncote, PA: TI:ME Publications.

Schonbrun, Marc. 2009. *Mastering Sibelius 5.* Boston, MA: Course Technology.

Selfridge-Field, Eleanor. 1997. *Beyond MIDI: The handbook of musical codes.* Cambridge, MA: MIT Press.

Stone, Kurt. 1980. *Music notation in the twentieth century: A practical guidebook.* 1st ed. New York: W.W. Norton.

Watson, Scott (ed.) 2006. *Technology guide for music educators.* Boston, MA: Thomson Course Technology PTR.

APPENDIX: COMPUTER HARDWARE AND SOFTWARE

Abbate, Janet. 1999. *Inventing the Internet.* Cambridge, MA: MIT Press.

Abelson, Harold, Ken Ledeen, and Harry R. Lewis. 2008. *Blown to bits: Your life, liberty, and happiness after the digital explosion.* Upper Saddle River, NJ: Addison-Wesley.

Ceruzzi, Paul E. 2003. *A history of modern computing.* 2nd ed. Cambridge, MA: MIT Press.

Freiberger, Paul and Michael Swaine. 2000. *Fire in the valley: The making of the personal computer.* New York: McGraw-Hill.

Grossman, Lev. 2006. Time's Person of the Year: You. *Time*, December 13. www.time.com/time/magazine/article/0,9171,1569514,00.html.

Internet2 Consortium. Internet2 arts and humanities initiative. www.internet2.edu/arts/.

Lessig, Lawrence. 2004. *Free culture: How big media uses technology and the law to lock down culture and control creativity.* New York: Penguin Press.

——. 2006. *Remix: Making art and commerce thrive in the hybrid economy.* New York: Penguin Press.

Mueller, Scott. 2008. *Upgrading and repairing PCs.* 18th ed. Indianapolis, IN: Que.

Null, Linda and Julia Lobur. 2006. *The essentials of computer organization and architecture.* 2nd ed. Sudbury, MA: Jones and Bartlett Publishers.

O'Reilly, Tim. 2005. What is Web 2.0: design patterns and business models for the next generation of software. O'Reilly Media, September 30. http://oreilly.com/web2/archive/what-is-web-20.html.

Silberschatz, Abraham, Peter B. Galvin, and Greg Gagne. 2009. *Operating system concepts.* 8th ed. Hoboken, NJ: John Wiley.

Index